MW01016250

Roadmap to mySAP®.com

José Antonio Hernandez

Roadmap to mySAP®.com

ISBN: 1-931841-15-2

Library of Congress Catalog Card Number: 200100110471

Printed in the United States of America

01 02 03 04 05 RI 10 9 8 7 6 5 4 3 2 1

Publisher:
Stacy L. Hiquet

Associate Marketing Manager:
Heather Buzzingham

Managing Editor:
Sandy Doell

Book Production Editorial:
Argosy

Developmental Editor:
Robert Lyfareff

Technical Reviewer:
Raj Krishnan

Cover Design:
Mike Tanamachi

To all the good-hearted people
who seek peace and justice in the world

Acknowledgments

I want to take this opportunity to give my sincere thanks to the many people who helped me and supported me through the sometimes painful process of making this book project a reality.

In the first place, I want to thank my main contributor and collaborator, José Pablo de Pedro, managing director of realTech Spain, who demonstrated not only his impressive technical knowledge, but also his friendship and support.

I want to thank all my friends and colleagues at realTech and SAP for providing me with insights, documentation, suggestions, and material: Fernando López, Felipe Cabeza, César Martín, Guido Schneider, Alex Brietz, Alex Kerwien, José Manuel Nieto, Javier Millares, and Ángel Fernández.

I also want to thank my editors at Premier Press, and Eve Minkoff, for her patience, understanding, help, and support.

Finally, to my family and friends: Ricardo, Sergio, Celia, Africa, Esther, Willy, Enric, Olga, and Fernando Moreno. Thank you very much for your caring support. I love you all.

José A. Hernandez

Madrid, September, 2001

Contributions

This is my fifth book on SAP and, without any doubt, the most challenging one, considering the ever-changing strategies and technologies around this amazing and impressive e-business platform. It took me much longer than expected and would never have seen the shelves of bookstores if it wasn't for the tremendous help of the many contributions and aid I received from so many organizations, friends, and colleagues around the globe (Australia, England, Germany, Italy, United States, and Spain).

I thank you all sincerely, even if was just a letter of support, a hint, or a full chapter.

- José Pablo de Pedro, managing director of realTech Spain and one of the most brilliant SAP consultants around, was the main contributor for Chapters 2, 4, and 6.
- César Martín, author of books about Linux and Web editing and programming and consultant at realTech Spain, contributed to the full Chapter 8.
- Guido Schneider, the long-time head of the IT Integration and Security department at realTech and now managing director of his own company dedicated to security consulting, SecurIntegration, contributed to several sections and reviews in Chapters 4, 5, 7, and 9.
- Alexander Brietz, head of the IT department at realTech AG for a long time, specializing as a security consultant in firewalls, networks, and other security-related issues, contributed to sections of Chapter 7 and reviewed Chapters 4, 5, and 7.
- Alexander Kerwien, consultant at realTech AG, specializing in ITS and Enterprise Portals, contributed with sections and reviews of Chapters 4 and 5.
- Fernando López, consulting manager at realTech Spain, contributed to the CRM sections of Chapter 3.
- Felipe Cabeza, with more than 10 years of experience in the SAP world, is one of the best SAP consultants around, working as senior consultant and project leader for realTech in complex SAP projects. He contributed with the sections about Enterprise Buyer in Chapter 3.
- Ángel Fernández, head of the Learning and Education department at SAP and now in GEDAS group, contributed to some sections about Knowledge Management in Chapter 3.

- José Manuel Nieto, from SAP Spain, helped out with the chapter about Marketplaces and offered other useful suggestions.

Additional contributions in form of mail, suggestions, and other material came from the following great people: Tim Steuer, Sven Degenhardt, Giampaolo Lupi, Warwich Chai, Peter Stier, Angela Pellegrino, Fabrizio Grisoni, Simon Greaves, Harald Sussek, Rafael Cano, Pedro Ley, Isabel Lamas, Javier Millares, and Eladio Valencia.

About the Author

José Antonio Hernandez is Co-Managing Director of realTech in Spain. Working for many years as a software engineer in companies such as Ericsson, Digital Equipment, and Telefónica, he has been an SAP consultant since 1994 and has completed numerous SAP implementation projects. His duties as a technical leader in large R/3 implementations in Europe have given him a broad understanding of the intricacies of SAP R/3. He is the author of previous best-selling titles such as *The SAP R/3 Handbook*, *SAP R/3 Implementation Guide*, and *Así es SAP R/3.* Hernandez has also published several articles about SAP Security and taught several SAP Basis System training courses as well as other custom courses on security, archiving, technical implementation, and mySAP.com.

Contents at a Glance

Contents

Introduction

Introduction: E-business According to SAP

At the speed of the Internet, SAP is again making a hit with its solid roadmap to e-business, including the set of solutions represented by the mySAP.com collaborative platform, and its building on the success of the worldwide-acclaimed R/3 applications.

Although SAP R/3 systems were commonly defined as the standard and integrated application ERP (Enterprise Resource Planner) software, covering the critical business information of companies, the mySAP.com platform, along with its strategy, takes a step forward over the solid functionality of its predecessors. The mySAP.com platform embraces an aggressive position on e-commerce and e-procurement and provides a full offering of Web-enabled software products, ready for the challenges and possibilities in a new world of e-business collaboration through the Internet.

At the same speed at which dot-com companies emerge, an overwhelming amount of information, acronyms, and everyday new standards around the mySAP.com world appear, making it hard for companies to keep pace with the technology and causing consultants to tremble at the unknown. This exponentially increasing amount of information is becoming hard to digest for most of the people who want to get a clear understanding of the big picture or of the technical details of the mySAP.com platform.

This book, *Roadmap to mySAP.com*, tries to depict the big picture of this new Web computing and e-business philosophy. The goal of this book is to provide an extremely useful reference to every professional, consultant, or IT employee involved with SAP technology. The book explains the main concepts of SAP's Internet strategy: the solutions, applications, and supporting systems; the components and architectures; and the administration and development duties. It includes practical examples of the technology being explained so that readers can more easily approach the technology and start real hands-on work.

The book covers the latest SAP technology as of the FCS release of the SAP Web Application Server, including common functionality of R/3 releases 4.6C and upward, as well as the new releases of the mySAP.com components.

I have tried not only to expose my own limited experience of mySAP.com, but to gather as much collaboration as possible from consultants, customers, and the general SAP community.

Intended Audience

The language and the approach of the author to the issues described make the reading of this book appropriate for most people, both those already familiar with SAP systems as well as those first approaching this technology. There are chapters with a more advanced technical content, however, so for a more thorough understanding, some technical background in Web technology will be of help.

This book is intended for mySAP functional and technical consultants, mySAP end users, IT professionals, project managers, and project team members. It will be useful for those in the process of implementing, evaluating, or migrating to mySAP.

For those readers with little or no familiarity with the world of SAP, the initial chapters, Chapters 1, 2, and 3, as well as Chapter 9, should be easy to read and understand, as those are meant to be introductory reference chapters to the world of SAP and mySAP, mySAP technology, mySAP Cross-Industry Solutions, and mySAP projects.

In summary, *Roadmap to mySAP.com* is intended both for those interested in an introduction to the mySAP.com world, as well as those who already have a good technical background in R/3 systems but lack the knowledge of the new SAP Internet strategy.

Features at a Glance

The following list summarizes the features and benefits intended for the readers of this book.

- Serves as an easy-to-use and easy-to-understand guide to the world of mySAP.com and SAP R/3
- Includes practical examples of the technology
- Covers functionality of mySAP technology
- Introduces the main aspects of the main mySAP Cross-Industry Solutions
- Provides a complete explanation of common concepts in Web technology
- Includes a very good overview of mySAP Workplace and mySAP Marketplace
- Compiles the most frequently asked questions of SAP professionals about mySAP.com
- Acts as an excellent source for training
- Includes great background information on new standards, such as XML and DCOM

- Covers development topics about SAP and the Internet with a full chapter about the SAP Web Application Server
- Includes some programming examples using Business Objects
- Helps to protect mySAP systems with a good explanation of the security services
- Acts as a great source for finding additional information and references
- Provides many configuration considerations and tips
- Introduces the most advanced topics and implementation aids for starting mySAP projects

Book Structure

This book is made up of nine chapters, which can be read independently of each other by people with certain knowledge and experience of the SAP and mySAP environments. Following is a summary of the aim and contents of each of the chapters.

The first chapter, "E-business, the Net Economy, and SAP," is a general introductory chapter to the world of e-business and the Net economy and how SAP and SAP solutions approach this recent economic paradigm. The chapter goes on to present SAP's history and strategic evolution from the R/3 product to mySAP.com and contains an initial description of the Internet Business Framework. It then introduces the mySAP.com collaborative platform, its initial strategy and elements, and the new definition and classification of mySAP solutions. This chapter sets the framework of mySAP's solutions, whose technological insights will be explained in the rest of the book.

The second chapter, "mySAP Technology," is meant to explain the technological foundation of the mySAP.com strategy. It first deals with the SAP's Business Framework architecture, present in previous SAP releases (up to R/3 4.5), such as ALE (*Application Link Enabled*), BAPIs (*business application programming interfaces*), and ITS (*Internet Transaction Server*). It then discusses how from the concepts of "componentization" and "openness" SAP has built on to a new generation of Web technology and Web standards, including HTML/HTTP, LDAP (*Light Directory Access Protocol*), XML (*Extensible Markup Language*), and others. The SAP's Internet Business Framework also provides the collaboration technology for building a solid Web application infrastructure at all levels (presentation, application, data). It explains the DCOM connector and the Business Connector, including some examples of their use and deployment in the mySAP world.

This chapter goes on to explain the available user interfaces (SAPGUI for Windows, Java, and HTML) and finally introduces some of the common topics and the technical foundation from R/3, such as the CCMS (*Computing Center Management System*), the System Administration Assistant, the printing system and the transport system.

Chapter 3, "mySAP Cross-Industry Solutions: CRM, E-Procurement, Business Intelligence," contains an introduction to some of the main software solutions within the mySAP platform, such as the mySAP CRM (*Customer Relationship Management*), with a description of its components and architecture, including Internet Sales, Mobile Sales, or the Customer Interaction Center. It also explains the e-procurement solution known as Enterprise Buyer, formerly known as SAP BBP (*Business-to-Business Procurement*). Finally, the chapter explains some of the applications grouped under the mySAP Business Intelligence umbrella, such as the SAP Knowledge Management, the SAP Business Information Warehouse, and the SAP Strategic Enterprise Management, which are key to many other mySAP components.

Chapter 4, "SAP Internet Transaction Server," deals with the ITS. With this chapter, the book starts a more practical approach, because ITS is typically required for almost every configuration of the mySAP.com solutions. The ITS architecture and components are introduced and explained: W-Gate, A-Gate, SAP@Web Studio, and so on, as well as the IACs (*Internet Application Components*). It then provides an overview of the installation procedure and how to configure and manage ITS. The chapter then describes HTML templates, WebReporting, and WebRFC and provides some easy and practical examples that teach users and consultants how to work with these components.

The objective of Chapter 5, "mySAP Workplace," is to provide an overview of the initial SAP solution for designing and building an Enterprise Portal. This includes explaining the technical background and architecture, an overview of the Workplace configuration process, and a description of how can it be connected to other SAP or external components and applications. The chapter deals with the user management within the mySAP.com platform, so it begins with the classical foundation of the R/3 authorization system to the role-based scenarios within the mySAP Workplace. It also explains how to build MiniApps for the Workplace and discusses the Drag&Relate functions. Finally, Chapter 5 introduces the main options for integrating non-SAP systems and applications and how to handle CUA (*Central User Administration*).

The aim of Chapter 6, "mySAP Marketplace," is to explain the SAP and CommerceOne initiative for building and deploying virtual marketplaces, known also as e-marketplaces. This chapter includes a great deal of information and features of the main components available from SAPMarkets, mainly the MarketSet platform and services for collaborative e-business. The information included in this chapter has been compiled and summarized from a large amount of documents and white papers from SAP and SAPMarkets, which have been reprinted with permission.

Chapter 7, "Dealing with Security within mySAP Environments," deals with one of the hottest topics in Web-enabled applications: security. It includes an introduction to SAP's general security concepts, relating back to issues dealt with in previous chapters, such as the authorization concept, roles, and the CUA. It then takes a deep approach into Single Sign-On solutions, the SNC (*Secure Network Communications*) interface, digital signatures, data encryption, and privacy protection for user data. There are additional sections explaining available security options for user authentication, such as cookies, X.509 certificates for Internet connections, and standards such as HTTPS (*HTTP over Secure Sockets Layer*) or the PKI (*Public Key Infrastructure*) technologies.

Chapter 8, "SAP Web Application Server," contains a clear and practical overview of the new naming and new technology for the basic and future technical background of all mySAP solutions, such as the SAP WAS (*SAP Web Application Server*). The SAP WAS is the new name for the SAP Basis system, which was at the technical core of every SAP solution. In the mySAP age, the SAP Basis system became both the core and the development platform of choice for creating dynamic, scalable, and collaborative Web applications for the mySAP.com infrastructure, as well as for non-SAP Web applications. The chapter introduces the reader to the Web world and how it works; then it goes into explaining what a Web application server is and introduces the SAP WAS architecture, the development model, the Business Server Pages, and the utilities included in the system. Some simple and clear examples are included to familiarize readers with this new environment.

Finally, the aim of Chapter 9, "mySAP.com Projects," is to depict the big picture of mySAP.com implementation projects: what can be considered a mySAP.com project, what implementation tools are available, and what tools are coming up. ASAP (*AcceleratedSAP*) is introduced, with its main phases explained. The chapter includes what is known as migrating to mySAP.com and the main reasons and benefits for doing so. It also introduces the SAP initiative known as SAP Best Practices, which are preconfigured mySAP systems, and how they are built and designed. As a practical section, a guide on implementing an Enterprise Portal based on the mySAP Workplace is introduced, with a step-bystep approach and hints on solving every issue. Several sections in this chapter introduce a topic that is not showing up on project managers' radars but that has changed drastically from classical R/3 projects: the technology issues, which are now more important than ever, because the system's complexity has grown exponentially. Finally, there is an overview of what is coming with the release of SAP R/3 Enterprise, the new wave of classical R/3 solutions perfectly embedded within the mySAP.com strategy, platform, and solutions.

Chapter 1

E-business, the Net Economy, and SAP

This first chapter's objective is to explain SAP's strategy for providing electronic commerce solutions in the age of the Net economy. In other words, this chapter discusses how SAP tries to help its customers in their e-business strategies by providing a full set of software and service solutions that completely embrace the Internet strategy with a solid, standard-based, and advanced technological foundation.

The fact that SAP is also becoming quite successful in e-business solutions is not a question of luck or being there at the right moment. In fact, many analysts questioned the initial SAP Internet strategy. SAP did not get here from a lucky and successful start-up, but from the solid strategy it built around its leading ERP (*Enterprise Resource Planner*) product, R/3. Like most software companies that need to grow and add value for their shareholders, employees, and customers, mySAP.com is only the start of the e-business (r)evolution; from here, SAP goes forward and is ready to surprise us all.

The following sections introduce the basic concepts of electronic commerce, e-business, and the Net economy. The chapter then gives an overview of the strategic evolution of SAP's software solutions, and finally it introduces the mySAP.com strategy.

For SAP, mySAP.com is defined as the collaborative e-business platform that includes *all* of the SAP solutions, technologies, and services. The following sections introduce all of the solutions, and the main objective of this book is to clearly describe each of the solutions.

The Age of Electronic Commerce

The Internet has revolutionized the way people communicate (compare the number of letters we write by hand today with several years ago), relate, shop, do their garage sales, find weather information, take training courses, make a hotel booking, order pizza, read the news, and so on. This is just a tiny example of what people can do, but there are other entities out there that have been changed by the Internet—the main one being business companies.

These changes are only the tip of the iceberg compared with the vast marketplace that the Internet has uncovered for business. For companies, the electronic way of conducting business has also shown a great potential for opportunities, for collaboration, for growing market potential, and for saving costs. At the same time, the Internet has also forced them to adapt to these new ways, which present even more challenges than traditional commerce.

Software, hardware, and consulting companies have also seen how the electronic commerce created a large marketplace for their new products and services. The SAP answer is the mySAP.com strategy, or in other words, as introduced above, we can already say that mySAP.com is SAP's e-business solution.

In the next sections, I will introduce where SAP comes from and how it got here.

Enterprise Resource Planner Software

The Enterprise Resource Planner (commonly know as ERP) software also revolutionized the way companies conduct their traditional business. ERP provided integrated business processes so that companies could see a cost reduction and better efficiency in the way they operated with their business partners (customers, providers, banks, authorities, and so on) and internal users. The clear leader in this area has been SAP R/3.

SAP had two main products on the business software market: mainframe system R/2 and client/server R/3. Both still are, in 2001, business application solutions that include a great level of complexity and business and organizational experience. But above all, they are business solutions providing a high degree of integration of *business processes.*

For SAP, a business process is the complete functional chain involved in business practices, whatever module or application software had to deal with it. That means that the process chain might run across different modules. SAP sometimes referred to this kind of feature as an *internal data highway*. For instance, what travel expenses, sales orders, inventory, materials management, and almost all types of functions have in common is that most of them finally link with the finance modules. SAP understands that business practices and organizations change often and quickly, so it left the systems flexible enough to be able to adapt efficiently.

SAP R/3, which provided functionality for several of the mySAP Cross-Industry Solutions such as mySAP Financials (traditional SAP R/3 financial modules), includes a large amount of predefined business processes across all functional modules, which customers can freely select and use for their own way of doing business.

ERP systems such as R/3 were often implemented as a result of a business process reengineering, which was based on an analysis of current business processes and how to improve them. Many companies could radically improve their efficiency, but this change process could not (and can never) stop in a global and vast marketplace where the competition is in every corner (or one click away).

From internal integrated ERP systems, companies look further to improve their supply chain and therefore to extend the reach of their processes to other partner companies. This step forward is known as *interenterprise collaboration* and the goal is to integrate and make the supply chain more efficient. That was the origin of the SAP SCOPE (*Supply Chain Optimization Planning and Execution*) initiative, and later of the mySAP SCM (*Supply Change Management*) solution.

One step further ahead in the Web age is known as *e-community collaboration*, where companies reach to create value for their businesses through collaboration with business communities in the vast Internet marketplaces.

Figure 1-1 shows this evolution of business processes in and among companies.

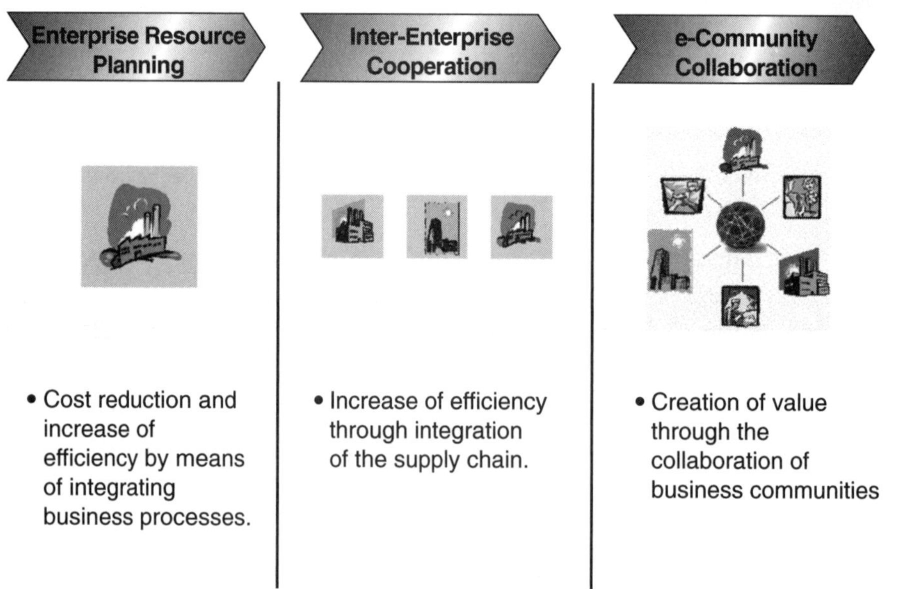

FIGURE 1-1 *Evolution of business processes*

Electronic Commerce

The simplest way to define electronic commerce is as the capacity for buying and selling goods or services using electronic media such as the Internet, EDI (*Electronic Data Interchange*), and so on. Some ways of conducting electronic commerce have already existed for many years, even before the expansion and revolution of the Internet. The possibilities of such previous methods of electronic commerce, such as EDI, direct modem communications, and so on, had many limitations in terms of efficiency, cost, and implementation and usually required establishing a one-to-one communication among business partners.

The Internet has provided the possibility of an increase in efficiency and reduced cost for the communication among business partners (no need for one-to-one communication channels) and, additionally, is seen as a huge market with endless opportunities.

According to analysts' definitions, electronic commerce is a superset of technologies, applications, and business processes that link companies, consumers, and communities.

Electronic commerce comprises the full chain of the business processes, and therefore includes the full commerce cycle, which can range from marketing awareness to post-sales support. Because the full chain of the business process includes many different roles, an electronic way of conducting business must also take these roles into account; it's not just a *seller* and a *buyer*, but there are also resellers, banks, logistic brokers, transport agencies, security providers, and so on.

The reason that electronic commerce is being firmly adopted is the potential savings. It is well known and demonstrated how the new methods of business enabled by electronic commerce can create many opportunities for lowering costs, for example, optimizing the purchasing process. Some companies have realized the following benefits:

- A reduction in the cost of purchasing from $45.00 down to $1.50 for each purchase order
- 50 percent less time in the procurement process

If the new global economy has firmly adopted electronic ways to conduct business, SAP, as a major software player and provider of technological solutions, is at the forefront of the industry. Its mySAP.com is the solid bet and the foundation for conducting and supporting these new methods of business.

Forms of Electronic Commerce

Because of the methods and the roles taking place in the different business processes that are conducted electronically through the Internet, there are several forms of electronic commerce. The most important or better known ones are the following:

- **B2B, Business to Business.** This form is when two or more business partners (normally companies) perform business transactions using the Internet. The most typical example is the procurement (purchasing, provisioning, and so on) of services or products by a requester company to a provider or vendor. In this area, mySAP.com provides the mySAP e-procurement solutions for handling the procurement scenarios through the Web. Part of the mySAP e-procurement, the mySAP BBP (Business to Business Procurement), is introduced with greater detail in Chapter 4. Other B2B scenarios might include when a company makes a request to a transport company for the shipping of goods ordered or sold. Another example might be companies that offer training services through the Web to other companies (e-learning).
- **B2C, Business to Consumer.** This is the best-known type of electronic commerce by end users who perform their shopping through the Internet. There are thousands of Internet shops around for any good or service that one could imagine (CDs, books, perfumes, meat, pizza, translations, software, hardware, and so on). In this type of electronic commerce, the main and active role is played by the consumers.
- **B2R, Business to Reseller.** This can be considered a subtype of B2B, where production companies use and perform their business processes not directly with their consumers, but with distributors and resellers that are then in charge of using their channels for selling.
- **C2C, Consumer to Consumer.** This special form of electronic commerce is established among end consumers who interchange goods or services using other agents, such as auction providers. An analogy to C2C could be a garage sale, but on the Web.

There are many other forms of electronic commerce; sometimes there is a combination of previous forms. Electronic commerce does not always have a commerce or selling objective; it might have the purpose of providing public services to citizens. Some of these other ways are as follows:

- **B2B2C, Business to Business to Consumer.** This is a combination of B2B and B2C. An example is the business processes that could be established between automotive car parts providers, car makers, car dealers, and consumers.
- **P2C, Public to Citizens.** An example of this is a process that could be provided so that citizens could perform and fulfill their tax obligations with the government.
- **X2Y.** This stands for any other form of electronic commerce that you or, normally, those guru analysts can think of.

Challenges of Electronic Commerce

Electronic commerce provides lots of opportunities for increasing the efficiency of business processes, thus creating potential savings, as well as for opening new ways of conducting business, opening new channels, enlarging the market, or creating new business models. But there are also many challenges in order to be successful.

As it has been for the last 30 years or more, the technology plays the role of enabler, the means for automated support to businesses, and as such, it is extremely important to search for the best technological foundation and to enable it. However, the critical key to success is to always have a clear picture of the business models and the business processes. Without a business model, technology is no more than a useless commodity.

So, as stated, there are enormous opportunities—but also big challenges—to confront to be successful. Because the businesses are potentially open to the whole world, likewise with the competition. Therefore, some of the challenges that must be taken into consideration are the following:

- Transparency
- Competition and competitiveness
- Price
- Customer information
- Logistics

In summary, customers (either businesses or end consumers) will have a much better chance to compare features, prices, service, post-sales support, efficiency of the process, and so on.

The Net Economy

The new business models that are derived from the opportunities provided by the electronic commerce have created some type of economic revolution in the Web age. The term *Net economy* has been the result of this revolution, and it can be defined as the new economic models that arise from the electronic commerce using the Web, which mean new ways of conducting business within a global, worldwide economy.

Out of these forms of electronic commerce, it seems that market analysts agree that the biggest business potential is among businesses, that is, the B2B market. Figure 1-2 shows a forecast by reputed analysts for the B2B market.

In the age of electronic commerce and the Net economy, the Internet is the greatest platform for communication, because it has simplified that communication and the exchange of information among all business partners or roles taking place in the commercial business processes.

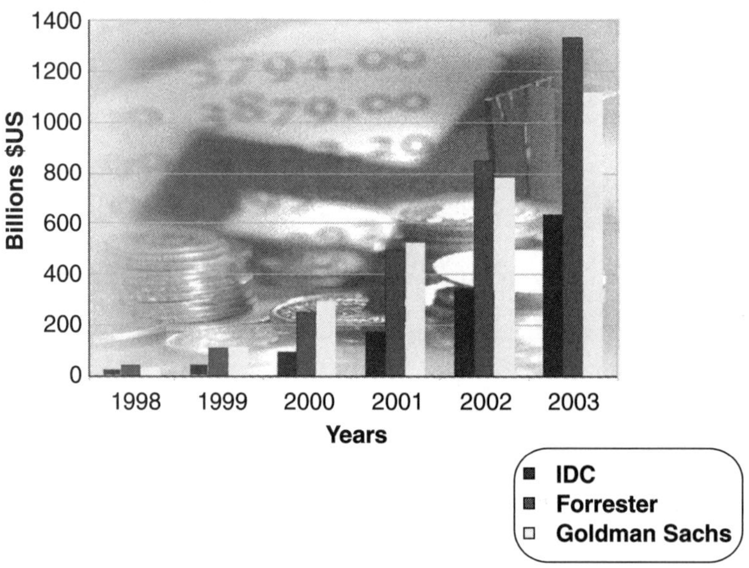

FIGURE 1-2 *B2B market forecast*

The Strategic Evolution of SAP Solutions

The following sections are meant to provide an overview of SAP's recent history and its evolution: how SAP AG changed from a traditional software vendor to a global provider of e-business solutions. In this sense, the following topics introduce the evolution of SAP software solutions: R/2 and R/3 enterprise applications, the emergence of the New Dimension products, the mySAP Industry Solutions, and so on, up to mySAP. In order to fully understand this evolution, some important topics are also discussed, such as the EnjoySAP initiative and the technological framework architecture represented by the Business Framework and the Internet Business Framework. Many of the topics introduced in the following sections are discussed with greater detail in the following chapters.

SAP's Brief History

SAP AG started operations in 1972 and became successful in the '80s with its SAP R/2 solution. SAP R/3, introduced in 1992, was the business solution that really placed SAP in its leadership position, making it extremely successful in the '90s. The year 1996, with the introduction of release 3.1 of R/3, saw the first SAP Internet-enabled solutions. 1998 was a crucial year in which SAP transformed from a single product company to a global business solutions company with the introduction of the New Dimension products and the first releases of Industry Solutions. The "first draft" of mySAP.com was introduced in 1999. The first years of the new millennium (2001–2003) will be the new crucial years for the massive deployment and benefits offered by the mySAP.com strategy. Figure 1-3 shows the recent SAP history and how it evolved from a traditional, integrated, and solid ERP software company to offer a full set of e-business solutions in the open and global world of the Net economy.

In the earlier days of computing and information technology, the need for automating certain processes usually started with the hardware platforms. Beyond the hardware, companies then used to select basic development software, usually programming languages, and with those elements they developed and created their own in-house applications. They usually began with financial applications, such as accounting, general ledger, accounts payable and receivables, and also with human resources, such as basic payroll. The normal evolution was also to develop other

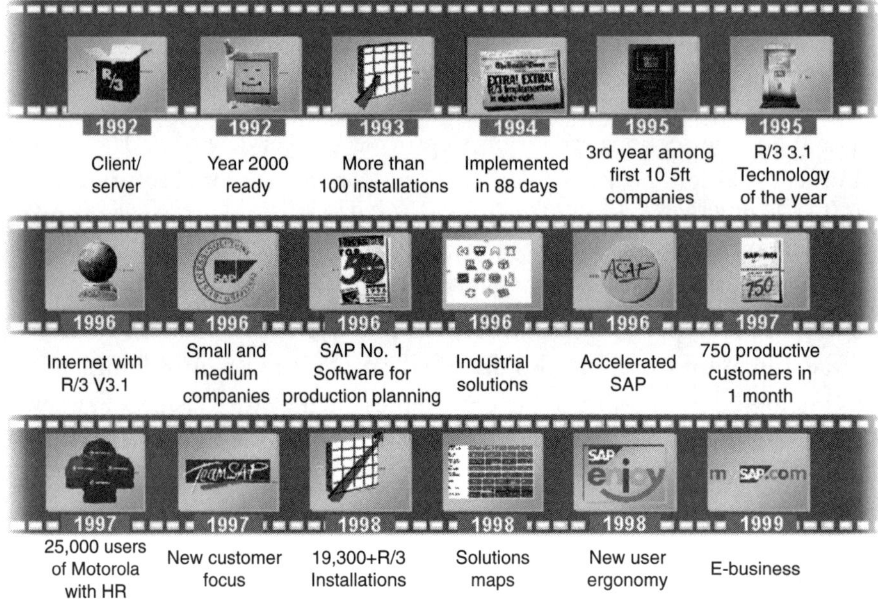

FIGURE 1-3 *SAP brief history* Copyright by SAP AG

more complex applications, such as those for materials management, warehouse, distribution, and sales.

In the '70s, SAP AG, just like other software companies, saw the possibility of developing software that could be deployed not by a single company, but by many. This software could be developed once and sold to several companies. This was the birth of standard business applications. But this "standard" software could be better deployed in business areas or processes that were common among similar companies, for instance, the accounting processes.

The adoption of standard software systems was neither quick nor easy. On one hand were technical reasons, such as the dependency on hardware and software platforms in which these applications were developed. But more complicated to handle was the fact that even similar companies from the same industries did not behave as uniformly as one might think. Additionally, there were many dependencies on the way companies behaved according to their country or region, for instance, differences in the way a payroll is calculated, or differences in taxes, currencies, and so on.

The first problem started to be solved with the emergence of *open systems architectures*. The second problem was dealt with by having a configuration and customization process that was much more complex and detailed and, at the same time, flexible enough so that it could provide similar but different functional possibilities according to the type of company or its geographical location.

With the emergence of networks, PCs, databases, and the massive deployment of information technology systems during the '80s, there was also the wave of developing applications, coming mainly from software companies, that could run on, and be portable among, different hardware and operating systems. As stated above, this was the start of the open systems architecture, whose main representative was the UNIX operating system. Later, Windows NT, even coming from a single vendor, was so spread out that it was also considered a de facto open system.

SAP introduced flexible configuration in their R/2 mainframe system to address the issue of diverse business practices. SAP R/2 included great functionality for several business areas such as accounting, warehousing, distribution, materials management, human resources, and so on. SAP reached approximately 3,000 R/2 installations all over the world.

The emergence of open systems, global networks, downsizing, and reengineering were some of the reasons to evolve the R/2 solutions to an open client/server software system such as SAP R/3, which made its debut in 1992.

SAP R/3 quickly became a worldwide success. It initially had less functionality than R/2, but it caught up quickly, and by 1996, it had surpassed the functions covered by R/2. The number of R/3 customers and installations grew exponentially, from approximately 900 installations at the end of 1993 to more than 20,000 by the year 2000, becoming the worldwide leader of ERP software, the first larger European software company, and among the five largest worldwide.

SAP R/3 demonstrated that a standard off the shelf application package can be adopted successfully by companies diverse in their business practices. This enabled companies to migrate to standard application packages to manage their "back office" operations.

Around 1996, SAP added industry specific functionality that allowed it to be deployed in specialized industry areas such as petroleum, the software industry, etc. This addressed issues specific to industries such as products of an oil company or pharmaceutical or automotive industries. This was the starting point of the SAP Vertical Industry Solutions, which is currently a very important piece of the mySAP strategy, now known as the mySAP Industry Solutions. At the same time, this approach led to the beginning of moving from traditional back office applications (accounting, materials management, payroll, and so on) into front office applications and areas that are needed in a large number of businesses, such as data warehousing, customer relationship management, and others. Before getting into this story, and for a better understanding of the foundation of mySAP, let's briefly review these previous SAP solutions.

SAP R/2

SAP R/2 was introduced in the late '70s as SAP AG standard business software that ran on mainframe equipment by IBM, Siemens, and compatible companies. With this software, SAP got more than 3,000 customer systems installed. Although most customers have since migrated to SAP R/3, at the beginning of the new millennium, there were still more than 1,000 customers running R/2. SAP has committed support for these systems up to the year 2004.

The SAP R/2 system was mainly targeted at enterprises with data intensive and centralized industries, and because of the cost of the mainframe hardware and maintenance, it was usually acquired by large corporations.

R/2 was the predecessor of the client/server R/3 system and included comprehensive fully functional business applications, including financials, logistics, and human resources. The SAP R/2 applications were first developed using a macro assembler programming language. The ABAP (*Advanced Business Application Programming*) language was introduced in later releases.

R/2 included approximately 2,000 tables, of which 800 were for customizing. One of the big differences was that the access was made using terminals in character mode. Figure 1-4 is the traditional representation of the R/2 system.

SAP R/3

As introduced earlier, SAP R/3 was a technical evolution of R/2. Whether the initial thoughts for the design of R/3 were to have a product for small and medium business is not completely clear; however, it was soon adopted by many large and midsize businesses around the world. It became the strategic business application for those companies that were migrating their legacy applications and were also on their way to downsizing their systems to client/server computing, which was cheaper and more scalable.

FIGURE 1-4 *SAP R/2* Copyright by SAP AG

As a standard business application solution, R/3 covered a large deal of functionality, from finances to production planning, from payroll to sales and distribution, all of which was based on the business process concept. The integration of the SAP's application module became one of the best features of the R/3 system.

SAP added a lot of value to its R/3 flagship product by providing a good set of services together with its partners and also by including efficient implementation tools and a full-featured development environment to enhance the system in those areas not covered by the standard.

Because SAP R/3 is so important as the foundation of mySAP.com, the next sections review in greater detail some of the main components, features, and technology that are found in R/3.

Releases 3.0 and 3.1

The initial release 1.0 of R/3 was in 1992, by 1994 release 2.2 was out, and it was 1995 that saw the appearance of release 3.0, which was a major change. In 1996, R/3 release 3.1, also known as the Internet release, was out.

The main features of the initial releases that remained and were further enhanced in each release included the following:

- Open, portable, scalable, and client/server systems
- The concept of integrated business processes with a built-in reference model and data model
- The ABAP/4 development environment
- Customizing tools
- Simple Windows-based GUI (*graphical user interface*)

Releases 3.0 and 3.1 were a definitive step forward for SAP in building a solid technological and functional foundation for what was to come. With these releases, R/3 was improved in the following areas:

- The Business Framework Architecture was introduced, which was designed for a better and easier introduction of new functionality and new applications into existing R/3 systems, as such providing a broader openness for connecting other R/3 and external systems.
- Introduction of new APIs (*application programming interfaces*) and standard calls for add-ons such as GIS (*Geographical Information Systems*), CAD (*computer-aided design*), archiving, electronic banking, Electronic Data Interchange (EDI), ArchiveLink, and others.
- ALE (*Application Link Enabled*) technology, which initially was meant for larger and distributed systems that maintained their semantic integration, is now widely used in mySAP scenarios as well. ALE is based on interfaces that can link several R/3 systems or R/3 systems with external systems. Chapter 6, "mySAP Workplace," about Enterprise Portals, has some practical examples of how ALE is used to integrated component systems into mySAP.
- The possibility for integrating standard PC (normally Microsoft Windows) applications such as the Microsoft Office tools was introduced.
- Better and easier GUI (classical SAPGUI) with new personalization capabilities and better ergonomic options was added.
- Improvements to the technical architecture, including new tools for installing or upgrading R/3 systems and for tuning its memory and configuration parameters, were added.

- Improved transport system for moving customizing and development objects from one system (normally development) to others (normally productive systems) was included.
- The introduction of the first ITS (*Internet Transaction Server*), making R/3 intranet and Internet ready. This feature made it possible for the first time for system users to run transactions from an Internet browser. ITS is still very important in the overall mySAP technical foundation, and Chapter 5 is completely dedicated to explaining this system.
- An enhanced Workflow system, with many object-oriented features, was introduced. SAP calls it business workflow. SAP followed it up with Web flow (workflow over the web across SAP systems or even from non-SAP systems).
- The introduction of object-oriented BAPIs (*business application programming interfaces*), which will definitively enable in an easy way the communication of R/3 systems with external web-based applications.

SAP R/3, with the release of 3.1, was first to broaden the typical three-tier client server architecture to a multitier one by introducing a new layer, known as the Internet layer, located between the presentation and application layers. With this approach, SAP increased the potential access to the system for thousands of users or "business partners." The following new components and features were introduced:

- **IACs (*Internet Application Components*).** These were the new components on R/3 application servers that allow the use of software modules to support business transactions through an Internet layer. Initially, SAP provided a short number of IACs, around 40, including components for human resources applications.
- **Web Browser.** An Internet browser including Java-enabled components becomes a new user interface (a new presentation). Most typical browsers, such as Netscape Navigator and Microsoft Internet Explorer, are fully supported.
- **Web Server.** This is the typical Internet server that, in the case of R/3 applications, allows the Internet or intranet world to communicate with the SAP business processes.
- **ITS (*Internet Transaction Server*).** This is the component located at the Internet level in the architecture and connects the Web server with the SAP IACs.

- **SAP Automation.** This is the programming interface that allows Internet components and other applications to interact with R/3.

Besides total support for the Internet layer, within the business engineering tools, release 3.1 incorporated a new process configuration based on models. This feature allowed for a quicker and more dynamic configuration of the business processes that was oriented to the processes. The system included several "industry" models, which could be used directly by customers, thus reducing the time needed for configuring and customizing the system.

With the introduction of the R/3 solutions for supporting business processes through the Internet, it was possible for companies to widen their business by providing a new communication channel between companies and between customers and companies.

With release 3.1 of SAP R/3, the possibility of using three different types of Internet and intranet scenarios for supporting electronic commerce was standard. The types were as follows:

- Intranet corporate applications
- Intercompany applications, extending the possibilities of the supply chain management.
- Applications from consumer to companies enables final customers with a simple Internet browser to communicate with and trigger transactions with an R/3 system

These technical advances were possible within the architecture enabled by the Business Framework.

Business Framework Architecture

The Business Framework is the architecture established by SAP for the componentization, that is, it's an architecture that is based on integrated and open products, which are grouped around the R/3 applications. This architecture is perfectly aligned with SAP strategy to make R/3 a family of integrated products that can be installed, managed, and upgraded independently, without affecting other system's components.

Technologically, Business Framework is supported and based on the arrival of new integration technologies, based on standard object-oriented interfaces.

The componentization of business applications software has the objective of solving some of the biggest problems of companies regarding the lifecycle of applications, such as the software maintenance, as well as making use of new functionality, versions, and technology, whose pace of release and development is not the same as changes required in businesses. Figure 1-5 shows an example of what could be considered componentization enabled by the Business Framework architecture.

The Business Framework architecture has greatly opened the business door to the Internet world and electronic commerce by using the interface mechanisms.

The following is a list of the main features and advantages provided by this type of architecture:

- Fast implementation of new functionality by easily incorporating new application components, from SAP or from other partners
- Allows the enhancement of functionality using standard interface technology

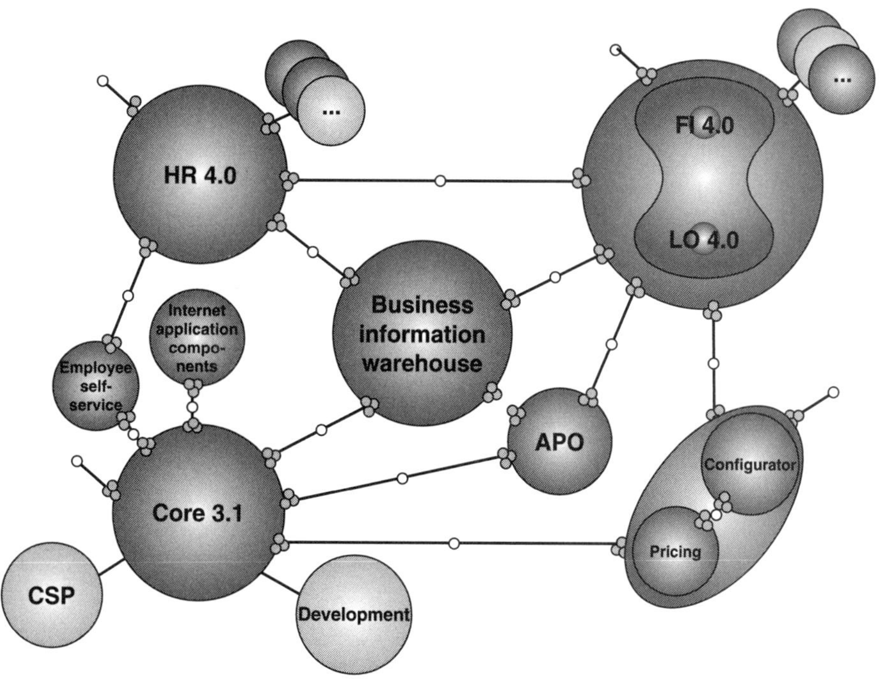

FIGURE 1-5 *Componentization with Business Framework* Copyright by SAP AG

- Application of new technologies without interfering and affecting other parts of the system
- Independence of versions between components
- Components can be changed or upgraded independently
- Can integrate SAP and non-SAP applications
- High availability and scalability
- Based on object-oriented technologies

Business Framework architecture is based on the following technologies:

- **Components (or Business Components).** Provide specific business functionality that can be perfectly integrated with the rest of the R/3 system using standard interfaces. Components have their own development and maintenance cycle.
- **Interfaces.** Provided by means of BAPIs, the SAP communication technology uses interfaces based on BOs, which are used for connecting and communicating different components.
- **Integration.** Provided by SAP using the ALE technology and also the SAP Business Workflow. With this technology, the system guarantees a total integration of components at the business process level, so it is independent of the system in charge of the particular business process.

There are parts of the SAP system that make up the logical core of the Business Framework, such as the Reference Model and the BOR (*Business Object Repository*), which are the components that guarantee the semantic integration of the business processes.

BAPIs

BAPIs are the access methods to the BOs (*Business Objects*) available in the SAP systems and are managed from the BOR within the ABAP Workbench.

BAPIs can be used as a mechanism to communicate R/3 with external applications using the Internet. BAPIs are object-oriented definitions of business entities. The concept behind BAPI is the key in the Business Framework architecture, as well as in the overall SAP R/3 Internet and electronic commerce strategy, as the object-oriented interface to integrate external applications. Based on BOs, such as company, vendor, employee, material, and so on, a BAPI defines the methods that can be used to interact and communicate with those objects. Release 3.1 already included more than 100 predefined BAPIs ready to integrate R/3 with third-party solutions and applications.

The external access to the data and processes of BOs is performed using BAPIs. For example, the BO "Material" includes a process for checking the availability of materials. This process, "CheckAvailability," can be performed by invoking the "Material.CheckAvailability" method of the BAPI.

Currently, BAPIs are implemented using function modules based on RFC *(Remote Function Call)*. Some of the advantages of this type of implementation are as follows:

- Better integration between standard business applications
- BOs can be accessed using object-oriented technology, such as COM/DCOM
- CORBA compliant
- Definition of BAPI interfaces are stable and commit the compatibility with future SAP R/3 releases
- Can be called from any development platform supporting RFC

Figure 1-6 shows some example of BAPIs.

R/3 Release 4.0

With the introduction of release 4.0 and in the context of the Business Framework, SAP's strategy for enterprise computing was to develop R/3 into a family of integrated components that can be upgraded independently.

Following a well-known study by the Gartner Group, SAP closely watched the strategy depicted for the survival of the enterprise software vendors and put the corresponding actions in place well before 1997. The four tips indicated were the following:

- **Trend to componentization.** This applies both in products and in sales force. This move can be clearly seen with the emergence of R/3 release 4.0.
- **Add consulting content.** This is another step that SAP has added to its overall business, although in a more silent way in order not to provoke the legion of consulting partners. If looking at SAP figures, 1997 and 1998 have seen a percentage growth both in revenue and in people from services and consulting.

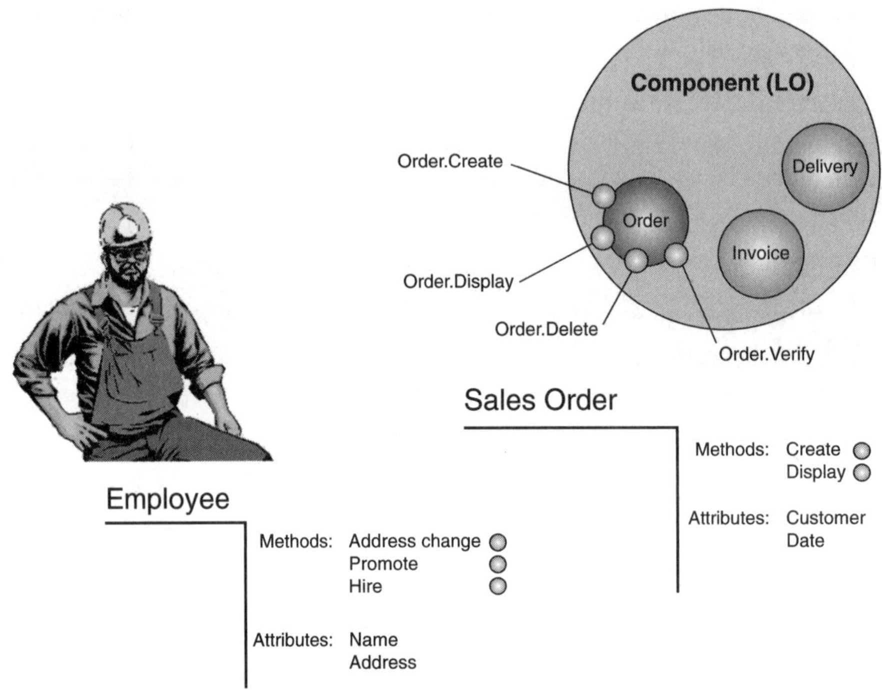

FIGURE 1-6 *Examples of BAPIs*

- **Develop industry-specific components or templates.** This is no new strategic direction for SAP, although it is true that for years there has been more marketing than real products. With release 4.0, some industries, such as retailers, and the public sector can find additional and specific business processes. However, Telecom companies have been waiting since 1995 for their piece of the cake.
- **Focus on fast implementation: methodologies and solutions.** ASAP (*AcceleratedSAP*) and TeamSAP are excellent examples of SAP reaction to the continuous criticism on implementation times and over-budgeted projects.

Besides the logical evolution of technological aspects and the incremental functionality of release 4.0, there are two features that should be particularly highlighted: componentization and inclusion of industry solutions. From a strategic and pragmatic point of view, we should also add to these features an increased accent on the use of solution sets for rapid implementation, such as ASAP.

Componentization is a practical consequence of possibility enabled by the Business Framework architecture. When SAP introduced release 4.0, it explained that R/3 had evolved into a family of distributed business components.

Among the new components and functional add-ons to the kernel R/3 application modules are the following:

- **Introduction of new distributed scenarios.** The new distributed scenarios use ALE and its integration using BAPIs.
- **Enhancements for the management of global supply chain.** These enhancements go from the provider of the provider to the customer of the customer and work together with the New Dimension products within the SCOPE and APO (*SAP Advanced Planner and Optimizer*) initiatives.
- **Introduction of new specific functionality.** The new specific functionality is for particular industry solutions, starting with retail and the public sector.
- **New Business Framework architecture components.** With these new components, customers can add new enhancement to the system independently of other R/3 functionality. For instance, there are a whole bunch of new Internet scenarios that can be used for business processes.
- **New business components.** Some of the new business components within New Dimension that were introduced at the time of the release of R/3 4.0 were: PDM (*Product Data Management*), ATP Server (*Available-to-Promise*), and the Business Information Warehouse, or the system of catalog and purchase requisitions using the Internet. These products could be installed separately and were also release-independent.

It was SAP's goal to include substantial improvement for implementing R/3 quicker, making it a business solution that's easy to use and easy to upgrade. With new R/3 Business Engineer components, the system includes an advanced mechanism for model-based configuration (business blueprints) and for continuous change management.

Technologically, the programming language ABAP/4 has evolved toward a completely object-oriented language based on the so-called ABAP Objects, which are called just ABAP since release 4.0. These new objects allow interoperability with other types of external and standard object architectures.

There are also enhancements in security and data integrity by means of using authentication and electronic signature techniques.

The extension of the SAP Business Workflow was also extended with the addition of new wizards for rapid Workflow scenarios configuration and deployments, as well as the possibility to launch Workflows from the Internet using forms with HTML formats.

R/3 Release 4.5

In 1998, release 4.5 was announced, and with it, SAP continued its process of introducing new functional components for logistics, financials, and human resources modules, many of which were based in a new open standard provided by the Business Framework architecture.

Release 4.5 was, at the time of its release, the strongest SAP yet to introduce and enhance industry solutions. This version included specific solutions for automotive, distribution, and consumer products.

Among new and enhanced technological features of this release, several must be highlighted: the new extensions for centralized systems management; new GUI components for integration with PC applications, including new ActiveX controls; more BAPIs; more enhancement and ease of use and configuration of the Business Workflow; enhanced features for object-oriented ABAP; archived documents accessible from the Internet using an enhanced Web ArchiveLink Interface (based on the standard HTTP protocol). There were also some major changes in the programs and utilities used for systems installations and for upgrading.

By using the architecture provided by the Business Framework, release 4.5 introduced new possibilities of extending the system using third-party solutions by means of BAPIs in lots of R/3 areas: enhanced system administration and control with CCMS, human resources management, enhanced global supply chain, report generation, and so on.

From a functional point of view, release 4.5 was equivalent to initial 4.6 releases, but a major change with a lot of importance in the mySAP strategy was about to take place: the EnjoySAP interface.

EnjoySAP

EnjoySAP was an SAP initiative with a *user-centric vision* mainly on the R/3 usability, that is, on enhancing the system from an end user point of view. The results from customers' and users' feedback, together with new strategic and marketing campaigns such as the New Dimension Solutions, established the cornerstone for release 4.6. It was initially known as the "EnjoySAP release" because it was the first R/3 release where the *enjoy* interface was tightly integrated into the system.

Previous R/3 releases included lots of new components, functionality, add-ons, industry solutions, technology progress, and new but not revolutionary user features. EnjoySAP completely changed the user interface, going beyond just designing appealing and colorful features by also fundamentally distinguishing between different types of users, delivering what is known as a role-based user interface. One of the features included in EnjoySAP that was demanded by users is the ability for tailoring the interface so that users can add their own icons of their most used functions to the application toolbar.

Figures 1-7 and 1-8 show the traditional graphical user interface (SAPGUI) and the new EnjoySAP interface.

In summary, EnjoySAP makes the software easier to use, to learn, and to customize. And with release 4.6, EnjoySAP is the key to getting a role-based interface, which is highly customizable with a redesign of applications with easier and more efficient interaction.

Role-based scenarios, which is a key concept in the mySAP world, is the capacity of customizing different options and applications for different types of users—professionals, occasionals, and so on—who have different needs and even with different fields in the same transaction.

It must be noted that release 4.6 was based on release 4.5 functionality and the EnjoySAP interface (the first 4.6 release gave more importance to usability than functionality).

Later EnjoySAP became the mySAP.com user interface.

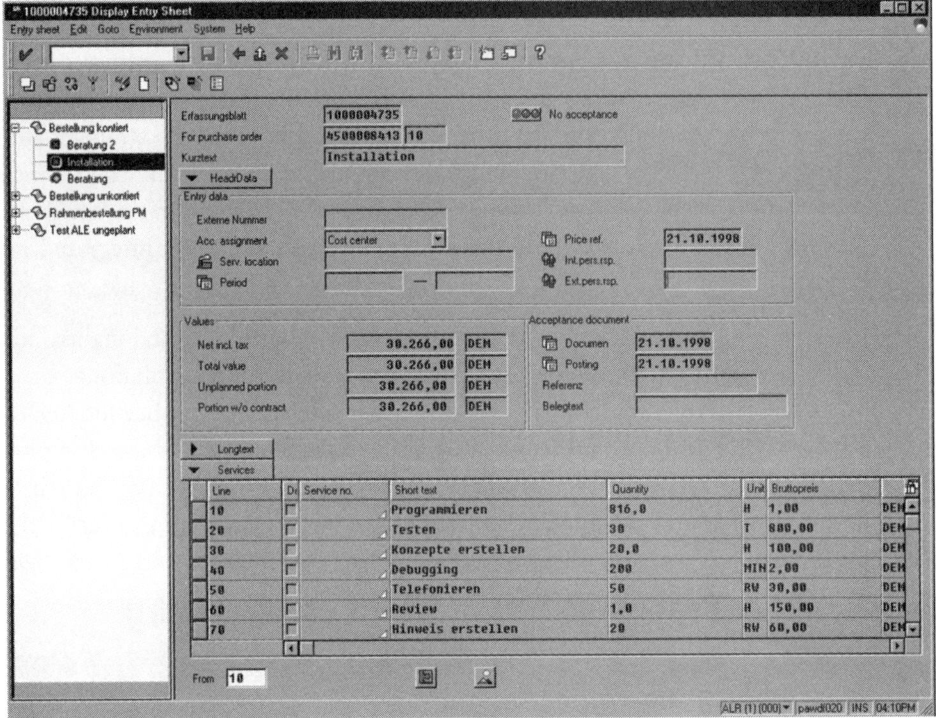

FIGURE 1-7 *Traditional SAPGUI*

Internet Business Framework

The next architectural step by SAP into the Internet world would be called the *Internet Business Framework* and was based on the Business Framework, to which all of the latest Web technologies were added.

The Internet Business Framework acts as the technological foundation of the mySAP.com e-business platform by providing Web-based technology infrastructure, like standard Web languages and protocols such as HTML, XML, LDAP, HTTP, Java, and so on.

By means of the Web technology, mySAP.com can provide the technological means for easy access, communication, and collaboration among the business communities in the Web.

The most representative achievement of the Internet Business Framework is the SAP Web Application Server, which completely overcomes and substitutes the traditional SAP Basis Middleware.

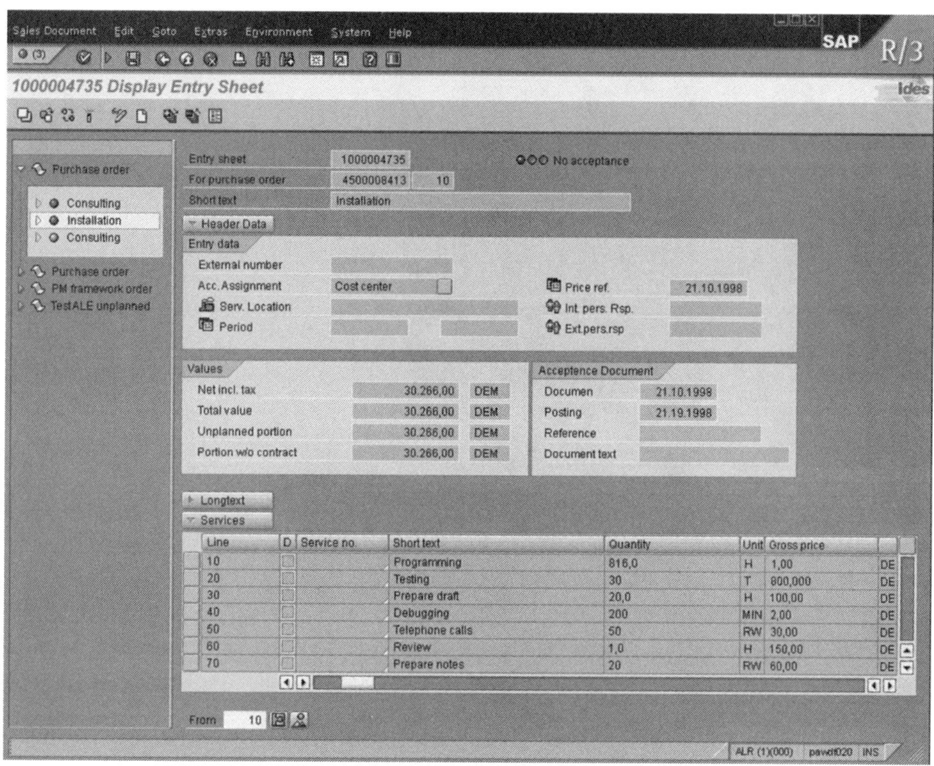

FIGURE 1-8 *EnjoySAP user interface*

Chapter 2, "mySAP Technology," explains the Internet Business Framework with greater detail, and Chapter 9 is completely dedicated to the SAP Web Application Server.

SAP's Vertical Industry Solutions

SAP R/3 was traditionally presented using the classic diamond figure as shown in Figure 1-9. There was a red area representing the financial applications, a green area for the logistics, and a yellow one for the human resources; the central blue color represented the SAP Basis Middleware and the development environment.

It was 1996 when SAP's industry solutions started to appear. As a base for many of them, SAP used previously developed solutions on R/2 or R/3, either developed by partners or by customers in different business areas.

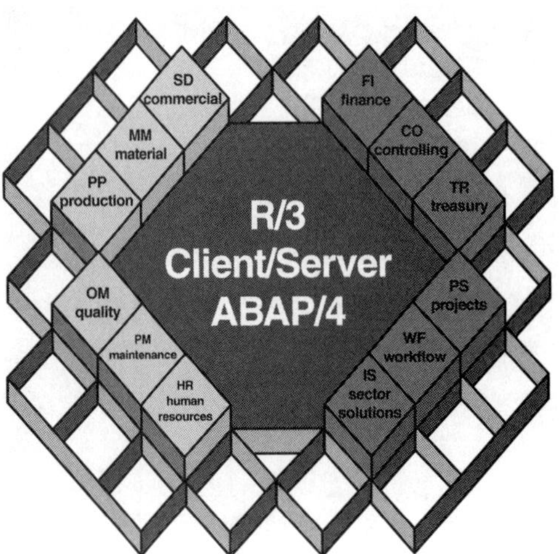

FIGURE 1-9 *Classical representation of SAP R/3* Copyright by SAP AG

The development of these industry solutions is first coordinated through the ICOEs (*Industry Centers of Expertise*), where the SAP experience in the development of standard software is joined by the business knowledge and requirements of its customers, as well as the experience of big consulting firms, for the inclusion of Best Business Practices for each industry sector.

The initial step in developing industry solutions is steadily consolidating and requiring the specialization of SAP's teams into different industries, which are then translated into the industry IBUs (*Industry Business Units*) that included and substituted previous ICOEs. These IBUs are responsible for gathering the market and industry knowledge and for developing specific solutions and applications for each of the industry sectors in which SAP is committed to provide. By the middle of 2001, there were 20 different industry solutions, already known as mySAP Industry Solutions. Figure 1-10 includes the list of the mySAP Industry Solutions.

New Dimension Products

By 1998, SAP was developing additional modules that initially were included within an IBU, but when looking closer at these new developments, SAP was aware that some of the requested functionality for these modules were common to

- mySAP Aerospace & Defense
- mySAP Automotive
- mySAP Banking
- mySAP Chemicals
- mySAP Consumer Products
- mySAP Engineering & Construction
- mySAP Healthcare
- mySAP Higher Education & Research
- mySAP High Tech
- mySAP Insurance
- mySAP Media
- mySAP Mill Products
- mySAP Mining
- mySAP Oil & Gas
- mySAP Pharmaceuticals
- mySAP Public Sector
- mySAP Retail
- mySAP Service Provider
- mySAP Telecommunications
- mySAP Utilities

FIGURE 1-10 *mySAP Industry Solutions*

different industry sectors. Examples of such common applications are the CIC (*Customer Interaction Center* or *Call Center*) and the SFA (*Sales Force Automation*), which match those systems that have the objective of automating sales and can be deployed in industries as different as consumer products, media, pharmaceutical, and others.

Because these modules could not be grouped under a specific industry solution, they were positioned by SAP as an equivalent to IBUs into the so-called SBUs (*Strategic Business Units*). Initially, SAP created the following three SBUs:

- **SAP SCM (*Supply Chain Management*).** This includes products such as SAP APO (*Advanced Planner and Optimizer*), SAP B2B (*Business to Business*), and SAP PDM (*Product Data Management*).
- **SAP CRM (*Customer Relationship Management*).** This includes SAP Sales, SAP Marketing, and SAP Services.
- **SAP BI (*Business Intelligence*).** This includes the SAP Business Information Warehouse and the SAP Knowledge Warehouse.

As we will see in Chapters 3 and 4, these New Dimension products were the predecessors for the mySAP Cross-Industry Solutions.

As can be seen from SAP products and solutions initiatives, from the initial R/3 application modules, SAP increased the number of solutions that could be sold separately from R/3 and that could also be deployed together with non-R/3 applications.

Solution Maps

The year was also 1998 when SAP was ready for completing its strategic move from being a single product (R/3) company to a company offering complete business solutions to its customers. That was the appropriate launch for the SAP Solution Maps for the different industry sectors in which it offers its solutions.

The Solution Maps gather not only the R/3 product vision, but also a full and structured view of the customer business. This is achieved by the firm's decision to complete their catalog of products and services so that they can offer their customer a complete solution, either directly with SAP products and services or with third-party products developed by complementary software partners.

In the Solution Maps, the customer business processes are collected in horizontal colored boxes. Different colors include different processes within the company.

To build a complete solution for the customer's business, it is necessary to deploy different products. As an example, Figure 1-11 shows the SAP Solution Map for the media industry.

In this case, SAP solution for the media industry included several modules of R/3, like FI for the financial accounting and asset management, CO for the economic and strategic management of business, TR for treasury, MM for procurement, HR for human resources, and so on. It would then include SBU applications, like the Business Warehouse, SAP Sales, and SAP Marketing. Finally, the IS-Media with its two modules—MAM (*Media Advertising Management*) and MSD (*Media Sales and Distribution*)—includes the management of selling advertising for papers, journals, magazines, television, radio, Internet, and others, as well as the management of subscriptions and paper and magazine sales and distribution.

Additionally, SAP considers it a must to provide its customers with a complete solution by developing required connections with those systems that must coexist with SAP. In SAP Media this is the case of production systems, like interface with content servers or with systems for the design and pagination of publications. This is achieved by the Business Framework architecture based on open interfaces that can be used by products of complementary software partners. This structure guarantees SAP customers a complete integration of products, providing a full Solution Map for the integrated management of their business.

Currently in the mySAP age, there are different types of Solution Maps. For instance, the Industry Solution Maps are a set of comprehensive tools that are used for fulfilling the requirements and providing the business solutions for a particu-

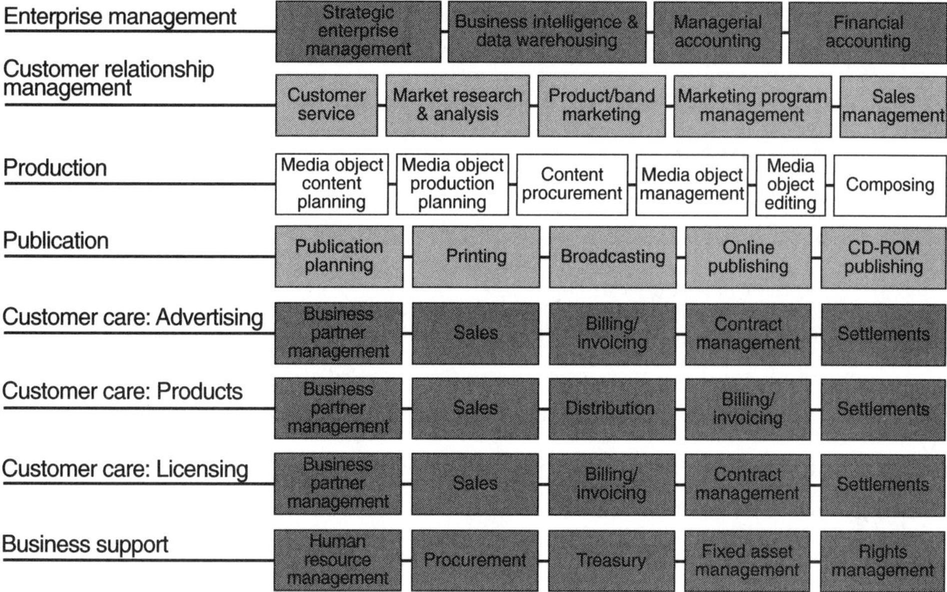

FIGURE 1-11 *SAP Solution Map for the media industry* Copyright by SAP AG

lar industry. Additionally, SAP provides Cross-Industry Solution Maps in the areas of Marketplace and the Corporate Function Solution Map.

Toward mySAP.com: From R/3 to e-business

The previous sections provided a brief overview of SAP's technical and functional foundations and the SAP product strategy, which all together have more or less provided the outcome of mySAP.com.

As already introduced, SAP defines mySAP.com as its e-business platform that includes all of the SAP solutions, technologies, and services.

The mySAP concept, and specifically the Enterprise Portal (mySAP Workplace), is designed to support itself in the broad knowledge and experience of the different industries and offers information that is better directed to the employees through the role concept.

Using the mySAP components, there are solutions that can cover the specific requirements of companies and their users, such as:

- Access to business solution applications
- Access to internal corporate information, reports, press releases
- Access to services available on the Internet
- Access to any user applications
- Access to marketplaces

mySAP.com can also be considered as an open, flexible, and comprehensive e-business solution environment, and as such, it can integrate not only all of the SAP software solutions, but also other non-SAP applications.

Within mySAP.com, companies can design their corporate portals and integrate specific Internet and Web-based applications.

One of the main design principles of mySAP is to facilitate the integration of business processes not only internally, but also among different companies (collaboration), which can be grouped by communities, with the purpose of increasing the effectiveness and productivity by potentially reducing the cost that collaboration can offer within a vast marketplace.

This complex and ambitious goal of mySAP.com is supported by the technological foundation of the Internet Business Framework, so that there is an easy exchange of data and communication among Internet applications using XML, security systems based on standard certificates by certification authorities, content standards, and so on.

With this initiative, SAP has made a considerable effort to meet the new demands and requirements of the companies that want to embrace (because there is no other way) the new economic models of the Net economy.

SAP achieves this by providing users with better integrated applications, a larger capacity, and with a standard way of accessing those applications.

Extending Business to the Internet

Previous sections in this chapter introduced the most important strategic movements of SAP, from the classical ERP to the e-business world represented by mySAP.com. Briefly, we can summarize SAP's Internet strategy:

- **1996: Release R/3 3.1.** Known as the Internet release; includes first release of ITS; introduction of the Business Framework, BAPI, IACs
- **1997: Release 4.0.** More IACs, first scenarios of Business to Business Procurement (BBP)
- **1998: Release 4.5.** EnjoySAP initiative, New Dimension products
- **1999: Release 4.6.** Internet Business Framework, (BBP) mySAP.com
- **2000.** One Step Business Transactions, SAPmarkets, CommerceOne
- **2001.** SAP Web Application Server, SAPPortals

When the mySAP.com strategy was announced, the concepts and components behind it were a bit confusing and quite different from what finally became a clear picture of mySAP.com in 2001. In order to fully understand it, we will briefly review what was proposed in 1999.

mySAP.com was proposed both as a strategy and as a set of solutions to provide *One Step Business Transactions* to those companies that wanted to embrace e-business by expanding traditional business using the Web or becoming part or using virtual marketplaces.

SAP explained why they chose the mySAP.com name as their biggest strategy and initiative for e-business solutions as follows:

- *my* is a well-known and much-used prefix that focuses on the capacity of users to personalize their working environment, so it indicates how its job position within the company, that is, its role, will be directly linked to their application environment. This is the part of the strategy directly linked with the mySAP Workplace.
- *SAP* was meant to represent the solid enterprise software for business processes, which SAP has been providing to thousands of customers with their traditional R/2 and R/3 systems. That foundation and the enormous number of customers as an installed base, together with the goal of smooth integration among the different components of the mySAP solutions, made a good starting point for the overall strategy.
- *.com* means the commitment of SAP to the new Net economy represented by the Internet, with its vast marketplaces and communication opportunities.

Figure 1-12 represents how mySAP.com was introduced back in 1999.

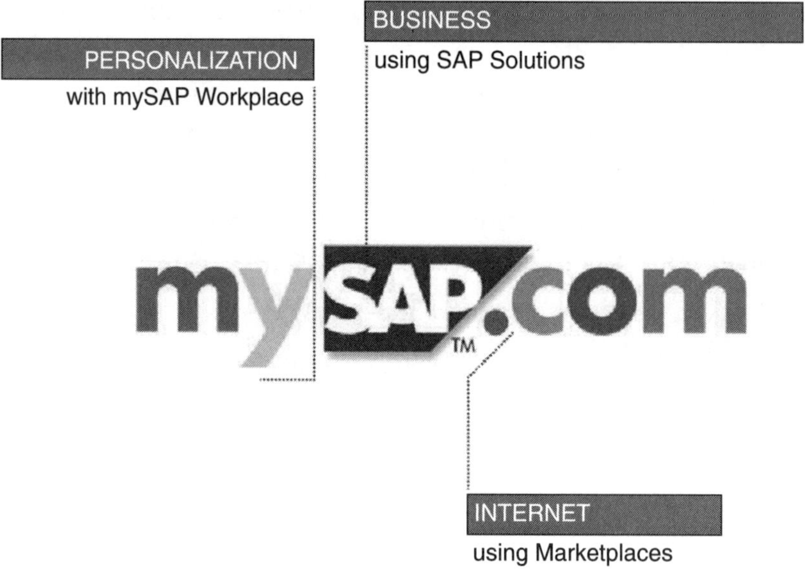

FIGURE 1-12 *mySAP.com as of 1999* Copyright by SAP AG

mySAP.com was introduced as SAP's strategy and environment of solutions for managing business processes in the Internet (the e-business strategy). mySAP.com includes solutions for designing corporate business portals, access to business and Internet applications, and marketplaces using Web technology such as XML.

With a simple approach, we could say that mySAP.com is the technical result of R/3 + EnjoySAP + Internet Business Framework including ITS and other Web technology. Figure 1-13 shows this.

As SAP described at the time, mySAP.com was the result that followed the same evolution of business, from integration to collaboration. The initial mySAP.com strategy included four main components or business-line solutions:

- **mySAP.com Workplace.** The role-based corporate portal, providing users with access to the applications or business processes they need, as well as to marketplaces or Single-Sign-on, all with browser access.
- **mySAP.com Marketplace.** The place for the collaborative communities. Provided the technology and services for enabling the collaboration among business partners in their business processes.

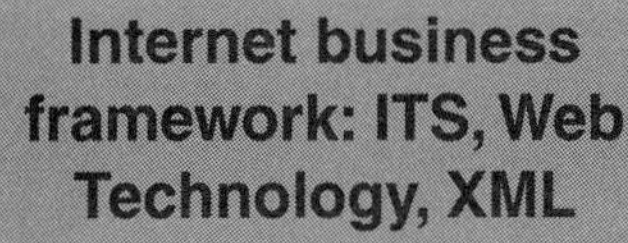

FIGURE 1-13 *Roadmap to mySAP.com*

- **mySAP.com Business Scenarios.** The new ways of accessing and using business applications. The fulfillment of role-based business processes, from beginning to end, application independent. They could include SAP R/3 applications, New Dimension products, and their extension to the Web.
- **MySAP.com Application Hosting.** SAP solution for providing Web based e-business hosted solutions.

This initial strategy was a little confusing: the role of previous R/3 technology and how it seamlessly integrated processes through the Web was not very clear; there were missing products; ASP (*Application Service Provider*) was not clear; and so on. Even the classification of the SAP solutions was confusing. This was resolved in 2001 by the One-Voice initiative, as well as by having more mature products in several areas, such as in CRM. The next section provides an overview of the SAP naming conventions as of summer of 2001. This initiative and the new classification of solutions have finally cleared up the strategy. The next section introduces the SAP One-Voice initiative.

mySAP.com Solutions

First, SAP wanted to make the definition of mySAP.com clear: It is the collaborative e-business platform that encompasses all SAP solutions, technologies, and services.

These solutions are classified in three different areas:

- Cross-Industry Solutions
- Infrastructure and Services
- Industry Solutions

The Cross-Industry Solutions include the following components:

- mySAP Workplace
- mySAP Customer Relationship Management
- mySAP Supply Chain Management
- mySAP Marketplace
- mySAP E-Procurement
- mySAP Business Intelligence
- mySAP Product Lifecycle Management
- mySAP Human Resources
- mySAP Financials
- mySAP Mobile Business

The Infrastructure and Services include:

- mySAP Technology
- mySAP Services
- mySAP Hosted Solutions

The mySAP Industry Solutions are the evolution of the industry solutions previously mentioned and integrate with the rest of the mySAP solutions. Figure 1-10 earlier in this chapter includes the list of the mySAP Industry Solutions.

In the rest of this book, chapters are dedicated to the most important components of the mySAP platform, especially the technology part, which is explained in Chapter 2, "mySAP Technology," as well as in Chapter 4, "SAP Internet Transaction Server," Chapter 7, "Dealing with Security within mySAP Environments," and Chapter 8, "The SAP Web Application Server."

Cross-Industry Solutions are explained in Chapters 3, 5, and 6, with special attention given to the Enterprise Portal solutions (mySAP Workplace) and the MarketSet (mySAP Marketplace).

The following sections make a brief introduction to the mySAP Hosted Solutions.

mySAP Hosted Solutions

Within the mySAP e-business platform, SAP has incorporated a full set of Hosted Solutions to provide the customer with an efficient way of implementing and outsourcing e-business solutions. This is the SAP offering for providing its customers a more cost-effective solution to approach e-business.

Some questions that arise include: Does this mean ASP? Why Hosted solutions within mySAP.com platform? Will SAP itself provide outsourcing infrastructure and services? How are systems implemented and configured?

The reason to include Hosted Solutions within the mySAP platform has to do with an additional and more efficient way of selling, acquiring, and renting software. Better yet, it is able to provide e-business solutions through the Web, without the need for customers to acquire and maintain costly equipment and to deal with long implementations with support, maintenance, and upgrades. According to most analysts, ASP will soon become the choice of many companies, especially of small and medium-sized ones. End users do not need any software installed on their desktop apart from a Web browser to be able to access the full set of applications and Web services provided by the mySAP platform.

According to SAP, mySAP Hosted Solutions would include evaluation and implementation of any of the mySAP.com applications; however, SAP itself will not offer the actual operation of the productive mySAP.com solution. This will continue to be provided by outsourcing and application-hosting partners.

SAP proposes several hosting models within the mySAP Hosted Solutions. These are:

- **Application Service Provider (ASP).** ASP is based on preconfigured solutions, meaning little or no customization of business processes. This is basically aimed to small and medium-sized companies.
- **Application Hosting.** This includes complete hosting packages of any mySAP application and a full set of implementation, operation, and support services. It additionally provides all of the required infrastructure.

- **Marketplace Hosting.** This provides companies with an efficient way of joining and operating within online marketplaces, allowing business partners to collaborate easily.

An example of an ASP can be accessed by any user visiting the SAP IDES systems at **www.sap.com/ides**.

It must be noted that ASP also presents several challenges for those providing this type of services. Some of these are application-related and others are quite technical.

As application challenges, at least the following must be considered:

- Easy and fast application configuration based on standard models per industry
- Fast training
- Initial data load and/or interfaces
- Upgrades
- Support and help desk

As for technical challenges, the providers of the services must consider the following points:

- Fast and efficient backups
- Selective restoration and recovery of data
- Monitoring multiple systems
- Transports among multiple systems
- Upgrades
- Patches
- Technical training
- Security
- Initial data load and/or interfaces
- Service levels
- Network throughput
- Response times

The good thing for customers is that all of these types of problems are handled and solved by the SAP implementation and hosting partners. The CD attached to this book includes some tools that can be used for easing the management of these types of complex environments.

Chapter 2

mySAP Technology

mySAP Technology is the naming standard that SAP uses for all the technologies produced by SAP. In this second chapter, we will be a bit more specific in explaining this important part of the mySAP infrastructure and service known as mySAP Technology, or what previously was better known as the SAP Basis Middleware.

As part of the new SAP naming convention (One-Voice initiative) as of April 2001, the mySAP technology components are named as SAP <*component name*> [*release identifier*]. What was formerly known as SAP Basis has been expanded in the last few years to support multiple SAP solutions and components. After SAP Basis release 4.6C, the new name became SAP Web Application Server, and at the time this book was published, the release was 6.10.

This second chapter is meant to explain the technological foundation of the mySAP.com strategy. It first deals with the SAP's Business Framework architecture, present in previous SAP releases, like ALE (*Application Link Enabled*), BAPIs (*Business Application Programming Interfaces*), and ITS (*Internet Transaction Server*). The chapter also discusses how from the concepts of "componentization" and "openness" SAP has built a new generation of openness and integration by means of Web technology and Web standards, including HTML/HTTP, LDAP (*Light Directory Access Protocol*), XML (*Extensible Markup Language*), and others. The SAP's Internet Business Framework provides the collaboration technology for building a solid Web application infrastructure at all levels (presentation, application, and data).

The second part of this chapter is meant to describe and introduce some of the features that users and system managers will find within mySAP.com components. It will briefly discuss the user interface and some of its options. For system managers, the chapter includes a basic explanation of classic technology and system administration topics, such as the transport system, the printing system, CCMS (*Computing Center Management System*), administration topics in the mySAP.com age, and others.

SAP Business Framework

As has been introduced in the first chapter, the SAP Business Framework is the architecture that SAP put in place for supporting seamless integration of components. This makes it perfectly suited to making a set of integrated products from SAP products that can be installed, managed, and upgraded independently without affecting other systems' components.

Business Framework was technically supported on integration technologies such as BAPIs and ALE, plus the underlying technology of the solid R/3 multitier client/server architecture, the standard communication protocol such as CPI-C (*Common Programming Interface-Communication*) and RFC (*Remote Function Calls*), the openness and independence of a hardware platform, or the portability of the applications based on the ABAP (*Advanced Business Application Programming*) language.

Business Framework architecture was based on the technological concepts of *components, interfaces,* and *integration.*

- The components would provide the business functionality. So for instance, the logistic applications, the Business Information Warehouse, the Business to Business Procurement, and many other applications could be considered components, which would integrate among themselves by using standard interfaces.
- The interfaces, mainly based on BAPIs, provided the communication technology, based on business objects, that would be used for connection and data exchange among the business components.
- Integration technologies were provided by means of ALE and others, like the SAP Business Workflow. The goal of these technologies was to guarantee the integration of the business processes among different components.

The evolution of the Business Framework toward Web standards and Web-based applications introduced the Internet Business Framework, which, as has been said several times, can be considered the technological foundation of the mySAP.com platform.

However, the fact that the client/server technology of the classical R/3 systems is still in place must be highlighted; the dispatcher and work processes are still behaving with the same technical advantages and solid architecture that made R/3 such a good software system. It has been quite evolved and enhanced, with new process architecture, new memory management, and support for protocols such as HTTP or the ability to interpret JavaScript directly. The following sections provide an overview of the classic features and technical characteristics of R/3 systems, many of which are present in the mySAP e-business platforms.

Client/Server Foundation

Client/server is a software concept that first appeared in the late '80s, but was deployed seriously and with a solid technical foundation in the early and mid '90s. As a software concept, it included *service providers* (servers) and *service requesters* (clients). A specific program could act as provider and requester at the same time. So for instance, the SAP R/3 typical application server was a service provider for the users (SAPGUI) but was a service requester of the database server.

The main point of this type of computing was the separation of the user-oriented tasks, and the execution of application tasks and the data management tasks. These three types of tasks are normally matched with the terms presentation, application, and data levels.

With client/server computing, it was possible and easier to distribute the workload of computer applications among different and cooperating computer programs or processes. From the very beginning, SAP R/3 systems were designed this way so that there was a presentation level (user interface or presentation server), an application level (application server), and a database level (database server). The software services provided by client/server computing would communicate among them using predefined interfaces over standard communication protocols, for instance, remote SQL calls from the application server to the database server over TCP/IP.

With the emergence of the Web, the ability to have a simple Internet browser as the user interface, and the development of ITS back in 1996, the classic three-tiered client/server architecture became a multitier system, just as can be seen in the diagram shown in Figure 2-1.

The classic three-level or multilevel client/server configurations offered a series of advantages that are still available in mySAP system environments, such as:

- **Efficient distribution of workload.** Because application servers work in parallel and communicate with the database, application tasks can be easily distributed. With R/3 systems, it was also common to find installations where one or more application servers were dedicated to specific tasks, such as background or printing.
- **Flexible configurations.** Client/server architectures offer many different ways of installing, distributing, or upgrading a system landscape. In the mySAP.com age, this flexibility has even been increased, with the ability

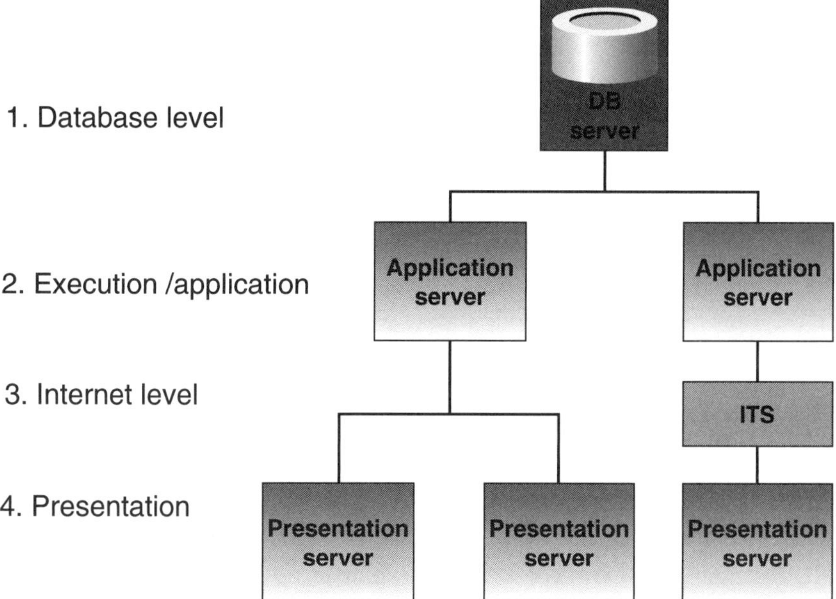

FIGURE 2-1 *SAP R/3 multitier client/server architecture*

to have several different mySAP components with several databases in a single server.

- **High scalability.** With client/server architectures, it is quite easy to increase or adapt the power capacity of the systems according to the changing needs of the business. So for instance, when the number of users or the load of the applications increases, it is quite simple to install additional application servers without the need to stop the systems.

RFC: A Key Communication Middleware

RFC, Remote Function Calls, is the standard programming interface long used by SAP for making remote calls among programs located on the same or on different systems. This means that a function that is developed in one system could be remotely called by another program.

R/3 has a function library where programmers can find useful subroutines to reuse in their ABAP programs. This library has the function modules organized in groups like arithmetic functions, character string manipulation functions, controlling functions, and so on. You can access this function library from the function builder transaction SE37. These functions, as well as each of the interface parameters, can be documented, helping the programmer to understand how to call these functions from ABAP.

Since release 2.0, SAP R/3 supports RFC in order to be able to call a function module from another R/3 system, from an R/2 system, or from external systems. This was a key factor in the current Business Framework strategy. The first types of RFC were synchronous RFC, allowing a program to call a function in another R/3 system and get the results online.

SAP provided libraries for non-SAP environments in order to call these function modules, like C and C++ libraries, in the supported SAP operating systems, including Windows, UNIX, Linux, OS/390, or OS/400. There has also been support for DLL (*Dynamic Link Library*) and ActiveX in Windows or Java RFC.

For transactional environments, SAP developed the tRFC (*transactional RFC*) in release 3.0. In this case, the program calls the remote function, and the system guarantees the delivery of the call, recalls in the case the partner system is not available, and assures that the function is executed only once. tRFC is asynchronous, but if the partner system is available, it is executed as soon as possible.

With release 4.6B, a new extension of tRFC was made, and it was called qRFC (*queued RFC*) in order to define an order and "queue" the calls that are executed one after the other. The queue can be in the source or in the target system. This qRFC can be downloaded to versions 3.1I of R/3.

BAPI

With release 3.0, SAP started the object-oriented approach. From that release, there is a Business Object Repository containing the SAP Business Objects, like a purchase order or a customer. These Business Objects have attributes or properties and methods like *Create*, *Release*, and others, depending on the object type. The methods of the Business Objects are implemented mainly as function modules, so they can be called in an object-oriented view or directly like function modules. Some of these methods were flagged by SAP as *stable methods*. This means that SAP guarantees that the method interface (export – import – Tables parameters) will not change in two major SAP releases. These stable methods are called BAPIs. BAPIs were announced for general availability in release 3.1G.

There are more than 1,100 BAPIs in release 4.6. SAP has published the BAPI catalog on the Internet (**www.sap.com/bapi**), allowing the developer community to develop external programs with a guarantee in the developing investment, because the program will work even if the customer changes the SAP release. These BAPIs were also used by SAP internally to develop initial load programs faster than the old batch input method and to integrate the different SAP applications with these BAPI calls.

IDOCs

IDOC (*intermediate documents*) history is related to the EDI (*Electronic Data Interchange*) interface. EDI was one of the first efforts to define a flat text format for business documents, like invoices or sales orders, so that they could be exchanged between systems and applications. SAP supported EDI from the very beginning, since release 2.0. The major problem in supporting EDI was that actually there are several substandards in EDI, like EDIFACT, ANSI X-12, ODETTE, and others (Europe, America, Automobile Industries), and there is the need for translating your internal documents to the substandard your partner speaks. In order to support this, SAP defined its own standard representation of the document, known as IDOCs. Then the customer can choose certified software that understands the IDOC format and translates it to the chosen EDI substandard, which is also in charge of sending and receiving the IDOCs. You can see a list of certified software third parties at **www.sap.com/csp**.

At the beginning, SAP defined IDOCs mainly for the type of documents used in EDI. Then SAP realized that these IDOCs could be used directly if the partner system was another SAP system. It started to use IDOCs to send and receive documents between SAP systems as well. IDOCs from older releases can be interpreted by newer SAP releases, and new releases can adapt the IDOC release, depending on the target system. This was the foundation of ALE.

ALE

The idea behind ALE was to be able to integrate applications in different SAP or non-SAP systems in a loosely coupled way. Imagine the scenario shown in Figure 2-2.

We want to have a central R/3 system with all the financial management and control in our headquarters and sales office in Houston, a second R/3 system in our

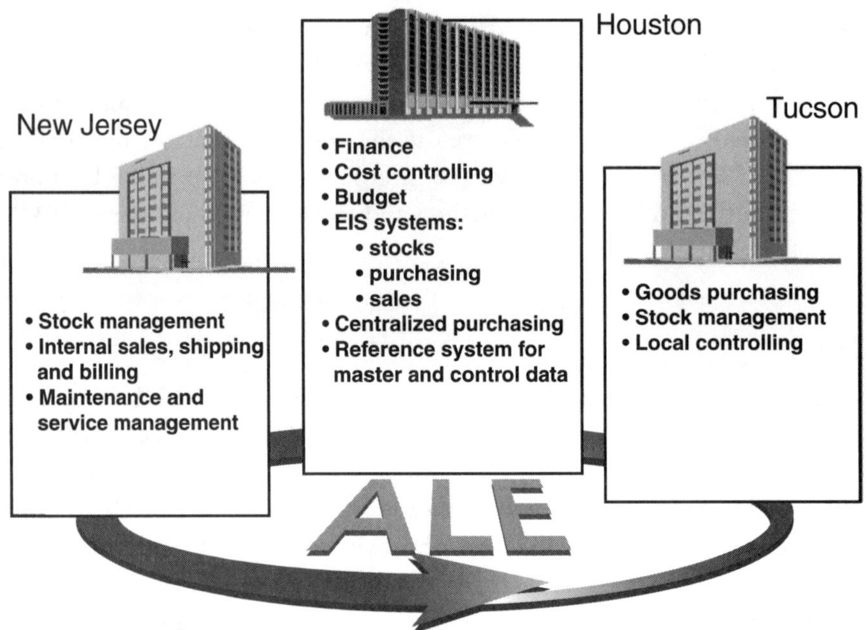

FIGURE 2-2 *ALE scenario*

factory in New Jersey, and a third in the Tucson office. It is possible to have different R/3 systems, each autonomous but integrated. When, for example, a relevant financial document is created in our sales office, it is sent to our central financial system automatically.

This could be useful for different reasons. Some large organizations have subsidiaries on different continents, and perhaps it makes little sense for support reasons to have the R/3 system for the plant in Singapore in the U.S. headquarters. It could be useful from the network point of view; the users connected inexpensively to their system in Singapore rather than by expensive lines to the central system with the bandwidth required for an online user. Other reasons are organizational reasons (in some cases the offices are nearly autonomous business units) or even performance reasons in order to distribute the load.

This is why SAP developed the ALE inside R/3. With ALE, you can define which systems participate in your ALE network (in the ALE world, a system is an external system or a *client* of an R/3 system) and which data should be sent from one system to the others. In ALE, it is possible to distribute master data (customers, materials), document data (purchase orders, financial documents, invoices), and also customizing data (entries in selected customizing tables).

In the case of distributing master data, you can, for example, define one system where you centrally maintain the materials and then distribute the creation or changes to the other systems. But the data distribution also can be defined with ranges and filters, for example, to define centrally some materials but allow the plants to have their own range for internal use, or even define a bidirectional maintenance (changes in any system are replicated to the other). This is defined in the ALE model.

ALE started using IDOCs in order to send and receive documents between systems (SAP or non-SAP). In the case of SAP systems, the IDOCs are sent usually by tRFC to the other system. If the partner is a non-SAP system, an IDOC translator that understands IDOCs and speaks with the other system can be used, as can file or CPIC interfaces.

When the BAPIs appeared, the ALE also included BAPIs for the new scenarios. For example, the Central User Administration scenario uses only BAPIs to exchange the user definition and roles between R/3 systems. Now this is used between mySAP components.

ALE is the foundation for what SAP calls the Business Framework. At the beginning, the ALE scenarios allowed integration between the different logical systems in the ALE network, but not the whole integration if all the components were in one central system. You have to look at each scenario's documentation to know which restrictions apply compared to a central system. The first complete application that was decoupled was the HR (*Human Resources*) module. With HR, all the possible interfaces between HR and the different applications were supported in ALE. In this way, it's possible to have a system with the HR module integrated with other SAP systems. One of the advantages of this approach is that you can change the release of one of the components of the Business Framework without changing the release of the others. Perhaps the customer needs the new release for the HR module because of legal reasons, but can maintain the financial system in the same release without involving the FI (*Financials*) people in the upgrade project. In the case of HR, this has other advantages, like improved security in a isolated system.

ALE uses workflow for error resolution and has tools for supporting multiple restore situations and systems synchronization. With mySAP, the Business Framework and its Internet evolution is used even more than before. With mySAP CRM, e-procurement (BBP), APO (*Advanced Planner and Optimizer*), Strategic Enterprise Management (SEM), and other systems integrated between them and the R/3 back ends, it is possible to change the release of one of them without disturbing the others.

ITS (*Internet Transaction Server*)

SAP soon joined its applications with the Internet world in release 3.1 (1996) by means of the ITS. ITS allows access to SAP R/3 scenarios from a Web browser and call function modules by means of a URL. It also allows for HTML access with the SAPGUI with the EnjoySAP interface to nearly all standard SAP transactions from a browser. ITS is also the portal service for the Workplace portal. ITS is one of the key pieces in the SAP Internet strategy and it is present in almost every mySAP system landscape. Chapter 4, "SAP Internet Transaction Server," discusses ITS in detail.

Internet Business Framework

One of the success factors for SAP was the seamless integration between applications. In SAP you can see the whole business process, no matter whether it has interaction with Finances (FI), Controlling (CO), Asset Management (AM), Sales and Distribution (SD), or Human Resource (HR) modules.

The next step we saw was the ALE that allows integration between applications in distributed systems. The Internet will increase the integration between processes not only inside one company, but also between companies as the common media to exchange data and information. SAP evolution is the integration between systems through the Internet, which is mainly what mySAP is for. SAP supports all of the Internet standards, as you will see, and participates actively in all Internet initiatives. mySAP allows Internet process integration with new scenarios that will revolutionize the way of doing business today.

As has been mentioned, the Internet Business Framework is the technological foundation of mySAP.com, based on the previous SAP Business Framework architecture and adding Web technology and standards. The following sections introduce some of these Web technologies, the protocols used, and the business standards. For instance:

- **HTML and HTTP.** HTTP is the protocol used between a Web browser and a Web server to exchange documents. These documents are called HTML pages. We will see that mySAP supports complete access through a Web browser with HTTP or HTTPS (HTTP over Secure Sockets Layer) in Chapter 4. You can find these and other Internet standards on the www.w3c.org Web site.

- **LDAP.** LDAP (Light Directory Access Protocol) is an open protocol to define directory services and how to access them. These directories can be user directories or file directories. These services are already included in operating systems like Windows 2000. SAP supports LDAP integration with the LDAP Connector in order to define the R/3 users or the HR employees centrally with LDAP support. More information about the LDAP integration will be explained in Chapter 7, "Dealing with Security within mySAP Environments."

XML

The HTML language was so successful for exchanging information between users (browsers) and machines (Web servers) that a similar method was created for exchanging information between machines or systems. XML is a tag (meta) language, similar to HTML, used to describe documents in a predefined way, understandable for machines. XML and HTML are based on SGML (*Standard Generalized Markup Language*), a formal definition on how to describe languages based on tags.

Here you can find an example of the data part of an XML document:

```
<order>
  <orderNo>4711</orderNo>
  <items>
    <item>
      <description>coca cola tins</description>
            <units>144</units>
      <price currency="USD">1.25</price>
    </item>
    <item> ...  </item>
    ...
  </items>
    <delDate format="mm/dd/yyyy">08/15/2005</delDate>
</order>
```

XML defines how you can define document standards based on tags, but it does not define the documents themselves. The door is open in order for third parties to define their own substandards for specific industries. XML is not only used for ERP (*Enterprise Resource Planner*) systems; there are XML specifications for patients at hospitals, for exchanging information between libraries, and so on. You can have a list of the XML initiatives in different sectors at **www.xml.org**.

Every XML document should have a DTD (*Data Type Definition*) at the beginning of the document. The DTD specifies which tags are allowed in the document data section and which parameters or values are allowed in the tags. The DTD could be in the sent document, could be just a URL to a Web site where the DTD is stored, or in practice could be an agreement between both parties and is not sent.

DTD definition is based on the SGML definition and is not based on tags but on a formal language. In order to facilitate this, a new standard has arrived known as XML Schema. XML Schema is like the DTD in the definition of the allowed tags and parameters, but it looks like XML as well. In the next example, you can see an example of a DTD and an XML schema.

```
DTD
<!DOCTYPE order [
  <!ELEMENT  order (orderNo,
                         items*,
                         delDate)>
  <!ELEMENT  orderNo      #PCDATA>
  <!ELEMENT  items        (item+)>
  <!ELEMENT  item         (description,
                         units,
                         price)>
  ...
  <!ATTLIST  price
              currency     (USD¦DEM) "USD">
]>
```

```
XML Schema
<elementType name="area">
     <sequence>
       <elementTypeRef name="city" minOccur="0" maxOccur="2"/>
```

```
    <elementTypeRef name="country" minOccur="1" maxOccur="1"/>
  </sequence>
```

SAP has participated in the XML world since the begining. The SAP Business Connector (see the later section "XML and the Business Connector") allows SAP to send and receive documents with XML and standard communication protocols like HTTP, HTTPS, FTP, or e-mail. SAP has defined a SAP XML for documents based on the IDOC definition, and an XML BAPI in order to define how to call BAPIs with XML and get the result in XML. (A similar initiative was done by Microsoft in order to call a COM object method by the Internet with SOAP [*Simple Object Access Protocol*].) SAP has participation in xml.org, RosettaNet XML definition initiative, BizTalk Microsoft initiative, and also supports EDI ports of type XML in release 4.6.

DCOM Connector

mySAP.com is also characterized as an open system e-business platform. One of the most important interfaces to the external world is the COM (*Common Object Model*) interface, the most useful interface in the Microsoft world. COM is the object-oriented model implementation from Microsoft. It's widely used in nearly all Windows applications nowadays.

In the COM world, applications expose their "objects" to other applications through the Windows registry. For example, a GIS (*Geographic Information System Application*) can expose its maps as objects, and the external application can show a map setting the object properties, like coordinates and scale and invoking the object methods, like SHOW or ZOOM, that are executed in the code of the GIS application. In the COM world, the external applications need to know these properties and methods, but the real work is encapsulated in the application that exports the object.

With this programming model, a VB (*Visual Basic*) programmer, ASP (*Active Server Pages*) pages in a Web server (nearly any programming language in Windows environment now can use COM) can easily access the objects exported from other applications, invoke them, and access their functions in the program. Almost all Windows commercial programs export their functionality in the form of COM objects.

As you can suppose, mySAP.com also does it. SAP R/3 has its own Business Object Repository from release 3.0. You can access it with transactions SWO1 and SWO2. Figure 2-3 shows an example of the Business Object Repository.

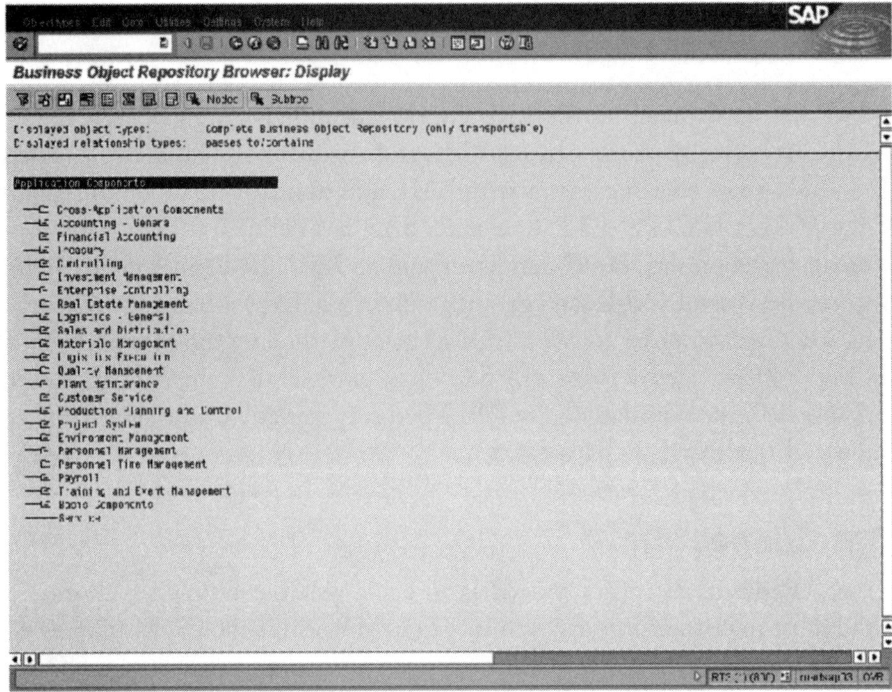

FIGURE 2-3 *The Business Object Repository*

The SAP Business Objects are classified in applications (like financial, logistics, and so on) and include the most typical objects used in the SAP system, like CUSTOMER, BANK, FI-DOCUMENT, and so on. These objects have methods like CREATE, UPDATE, or RELEASE. Some of these methods are set as "stable" from SAP and are called BAPIs. They appear with a green semaphore in the SAP object repository. Figure 2-4 shows an example of BAPIs within the object repository.

You can access all the BAPIs directly with the transaction BAPI from release 4.0 on. Stable means that SAP guarantees that the BAPI interface (import/export and table parameters) will not change in at least two big SAP releases. For example, if SAP delivered a BAPI in release 4.0B, its interface would be the same in 4.5 and 4.6. With the BAPIs approach, your investment in development is guaranteed for at least around two years, and your external program will work even if the release of your SAP system is upgraded in the meantime. SAP has created different ways to access these BAPIs from the external SAP world (Java, ActiveX, C++ libraries)

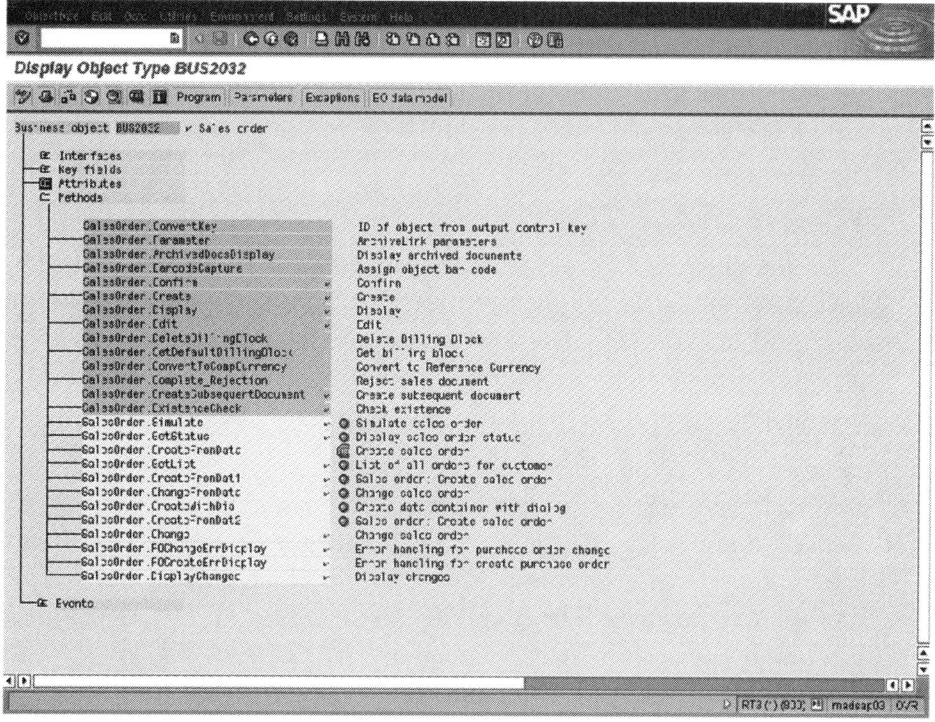

FIGURE 2-4 *Sales order BAPIs*

and one of the most popular, in performance and scalability, is the DCOM (*Distributed COM*) connector interface.

DCOM connector is a SAP development with support from Microsoft that enables the Windows COM world to access any BAPI or RFC module in a SAP system. DCOM means you can also access objects remotely defined in another server. Since release 3.0, ABAP can also access COM objects from SAP. In this way, ABAP has implemented instructions like CREATE OBJECT, SET/GET PROPERTY, and CALL METHOD and the programmer can access Windows objects and invoke the methods with it. These instructions are executed through the SAPGUI, which means that the ABAP sends an RFC to the SAPGUI and the SAPGUI executes the COM method. The biggest problem with this method is that it needs a user interface to be executed; for example, it will not work in a batch program.

From release 4.6D, the DCOM suite has a bidirectional interface. You can access COM objects from ABAP through a new component called COM4ABAP (*COM for ABAP*) that allows you to invoke COM objects without SAPGUI. In the last section of this chapter, bidirectional DCOM will be presented.

What Is COM/DCOM?

There are different ways to access a BAPI from the external SAP world. In the lower level you could, for example, use all of the RFC available platforms, like RFC API in DLL (*Dynamic Link Library*), C library in all the SAP supported platforms including Windows, different UNIX, and Linux, OS400, and OS/390, C++ library, or Java RFC. In this level, you can directly call the function module that implements the BAPI.

But SAP also supports object-oriented programming and has implemented ActiveX controls, Java BAPI, and CORBA support in order to call BAPIs. You can use the ActiveX controls in VB or ASP or in any Windows object-oriented programming language. The ActiveX controls are also called SAP Automation; it is a simple approach to start programming BAPIs from VB, for example. SAP Automation is included in the Desktop Development Kit option from SAPGUI installation and is also available for download from **saplabs.com**.

If your preferred programming language is Java, you have available a Java-BAPI (with the SAPGUI installation) and there are also CORBA implementations for BAPI programming, like Actional Control Broker (formerly VisualEdge). In the Windows world, you should choose between ActiveX and DCOM connector programming. ActiveX is a simple starting point, but if you need hundreds of connections to SAP, DCOM connector allows you the MTS (*Microsoft Transaction Server*) that defines pools of connections instead of a connection for a single user like the SAP Automation controls.

DCOM Connector Architecture

DCOM connector allows you to access the SAP objects, like local objects, in your programming environment. All the facilities in object-oriented programming languages—like the Intellisense editor in VB where you can see objects, select one and see the methods, select one and see the properties—are available with the DCOM connector. With the optional use of MTS, DCOM connector enables you to define and use the dispatching and queue possibilities of MTS.

The first thing that should be clear for you is that DCOM connector is a development environment, from which you can decide which SAP objects you want to use, and it creates C code and compiles it for your later development use. In the case of MTS, DCOM connector also creates MTS classes for you.

Basic Management

You can decide which R/3 systems you want to use with the DCOM connector. In the initial page of the DCOM connector, click on DESTINATIONS. Figure 2-5 shows an example.

From this screen, you can see all the R/3 systems you have defined. After the installation, the screen should be empty. A destination is how you address an R/3 system. You need to know the application server or the message server (if you want to log on with load balancing), and you need to supply a user, a client, and a password. This user is used just for the development process (accessing the object repository in R/3 and creating the resulting DLLs).

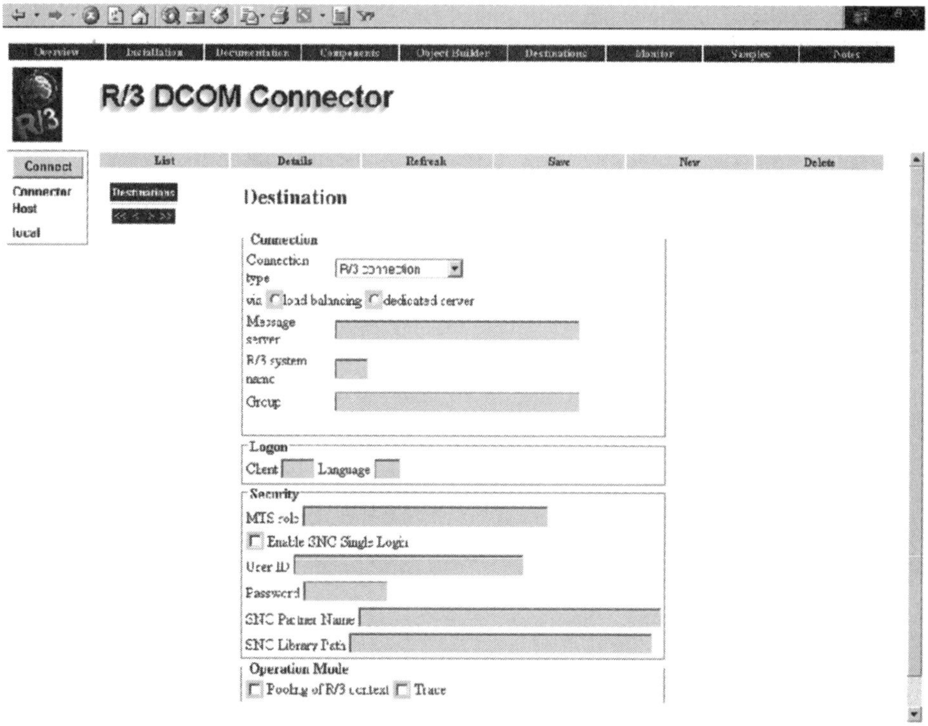

FIGURE 2-5 *Destinations in DCOM connector*

If you enter a group of users you have defined in MTS (for MTS security), enter the group here. All the packages are assigned to this group in MTS (so that only Windows users of this group can access these packages). Of course you can leave it blank if you are not using MTS. Pooling of R/3 context means you can reuse the open connection to R/3 for several RFC calls instead of closing the connection to R/3 each time.

Now you can save your destination. You normally need just one destination. If you access different R/3 release levels, perhaps you want to set up a different destination for each of them, because in each release you can find more objects as the release number increases.

Now if you click on the Object Builder at the bottom, you get the following screen, as shown next in Figure 2-6.

When you press logon, the DCOM CC (Component Connector) connects to R/3 and scans the Object Browser Repository (with RFC) to get a grouped view of all SAP objects. You can navigate in this screen, look for objects, and select them. The objects you want to include in your projects should be added with the ADD button. Figure 2-7 shows an example of the Object Builder after logon.

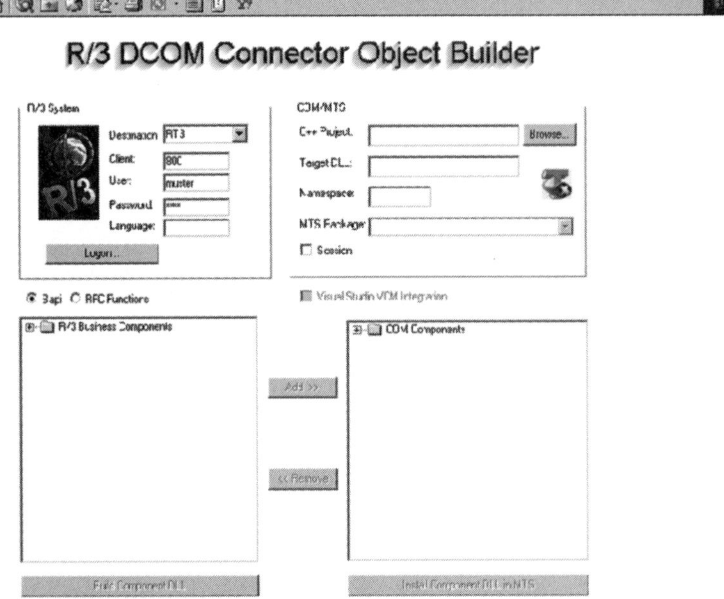

FIGURE 2-6 *Object Builder*

You can also select RFC functions if you click on the RFC radio button. In this way you can include RFC direct calls to any RFC module in R/3.

NOTE

Please observe that not all the function modules in R/3 are RFC enabled. You should check the RFC attribute in transaction SE37 in order for the function module to be called from outside.

Now after selecting some objects, we can generate our DLLs. You can select a namespace prefix you like. It will be the prefix for internal name in DLLs and MTS. Then you should select a directory and a name for your C++ project. As we stated before, DCOM connector creates a C program for you and compiles it. This is where you say where to store the source files for the program. You should create a directory for it beforehand. You also select a name for the MTS package (if you use MTS) and you can select the session attribute. You should know that if you want to establish all communication parameters or use transactional BAPI, you should set up the session flag.

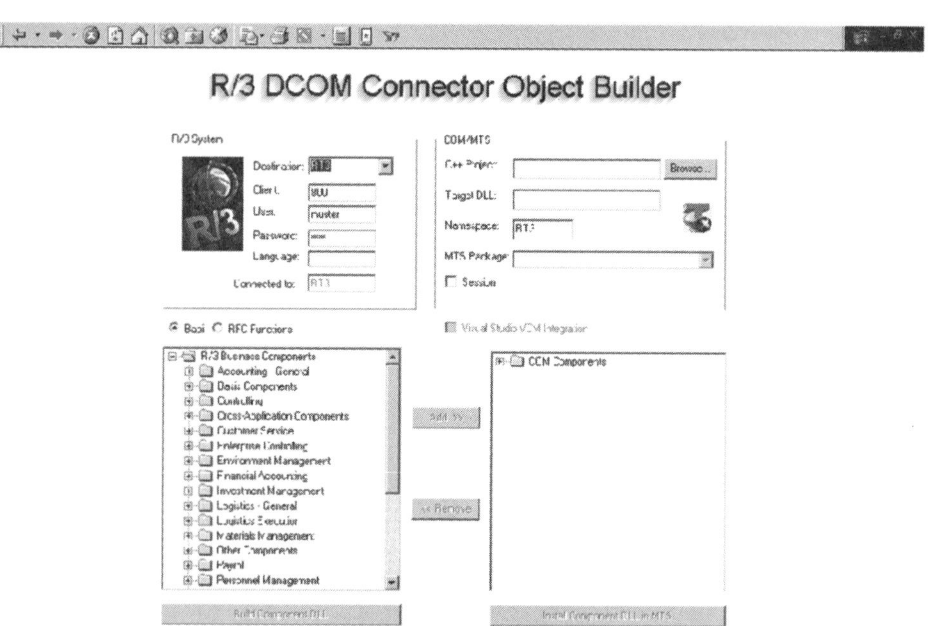

FIGURE 2-7 *Object Builder after logon*

As we will see later, one general and helpful BAPI is the Helpvalues Business Object in the Tree View. Find it, click on it, and click on the Add button. You may see results of this operation on the following diagram (Figure 2-8).

Now you can press the Build Component DLL button. If everything is installed right, the DCOM creates a C++ project and, using the scripting language, compiles it, generates and registers the DLLs. The system will return a dialog box, as shown in the following Figure 2-9.

Bidirectional DCOM

Since release 4.6D, SAP has included a component called COM4ABAP that enables ABAP programmers to access the COM world without using the

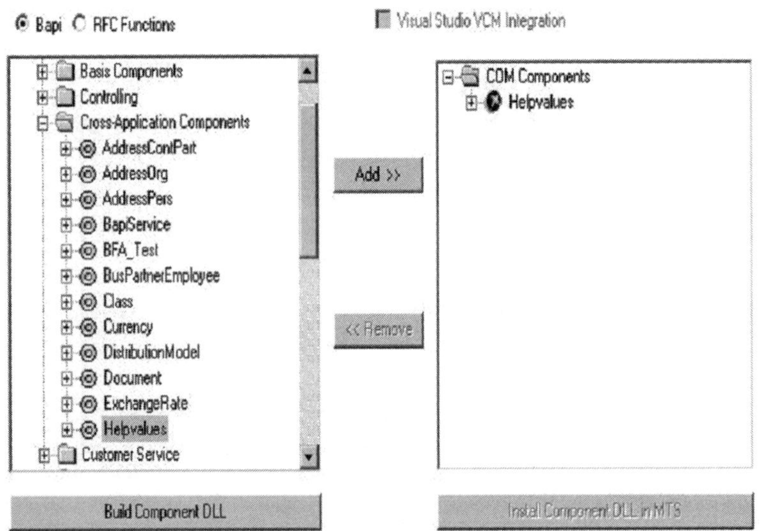

FIGURE 2-8 *Helpvalues BAPI*

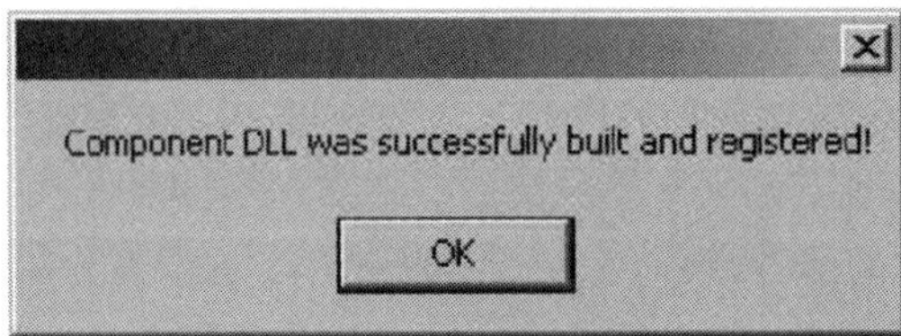

FIGURE 2-9 *Dialog box with DLL registration*

SAPGUI. With this functionality, ABAP programmers can access plenty of COM objects available in server mode, like access to external databases, hosts, SMS messaging systems, and whatever your imagination suggests to you.

Up to this release, you could also perform such integration, but with extra programming: You could create an RFC server and integrate the COM object in it. Then you could call functions of the RFC server from ABAP and with these functions map the call to the COM world. Your program also should be able also to map the ABAP variables to the COM data types.

COM4ABAP is implemented as a Windows NT service, where you just have to say which R/3 system should connect to and whether you want a default COM object (if you just want to use one object, this simplifies the calls from R/3). So, no code from COM side, just customize. The syntax for the service is:

```
com4abap -install [ -a RFC Server Program ID ] [ -g gateway host ] [-x gateway
service] [-r repository path] [ -c default class] [ -t default class type library ]
```

These parameters are stored in the registry under the key `HKEY_LOCAL_MACHINE\SOFTWARE\SAP\COM` for ABAP service.

You can then just start the service from the Windows NT Control Panel and check the connection from R/3 with transaction SM59. Create a destination of type R (Registration) with the same name as the -a parameter in the service definition and click on Test. This server is implemented as a multithreaded server, so you can access in parallel from one or even from more than one R/3 system in your installation.

To help the server to map the ABAP variables to the COM variables, you can (and should) define a TypeMap library where the mapping between the variables is done. This is especially necessary for Tables and ABAP structures. The mapping is saved in an XML file in order to transform the ABAP variable in a COM variable. In order to create such an XML document, you can use the available program typemap.exe. This program shows you a list of available registered DLLs. From each variable two methods are shown: GET-property and SET-property. This is because the properties are not directly accessible from ABAP, only through these methods. The program tries to define an ABAP type for each of these variables. In the case of structures, you should check the type of each of the fields of the structure.

You save your map in a directory defined as your repository path parameter in the COM4ABAP service. Figure 2-10 shows the typemap.exe program.

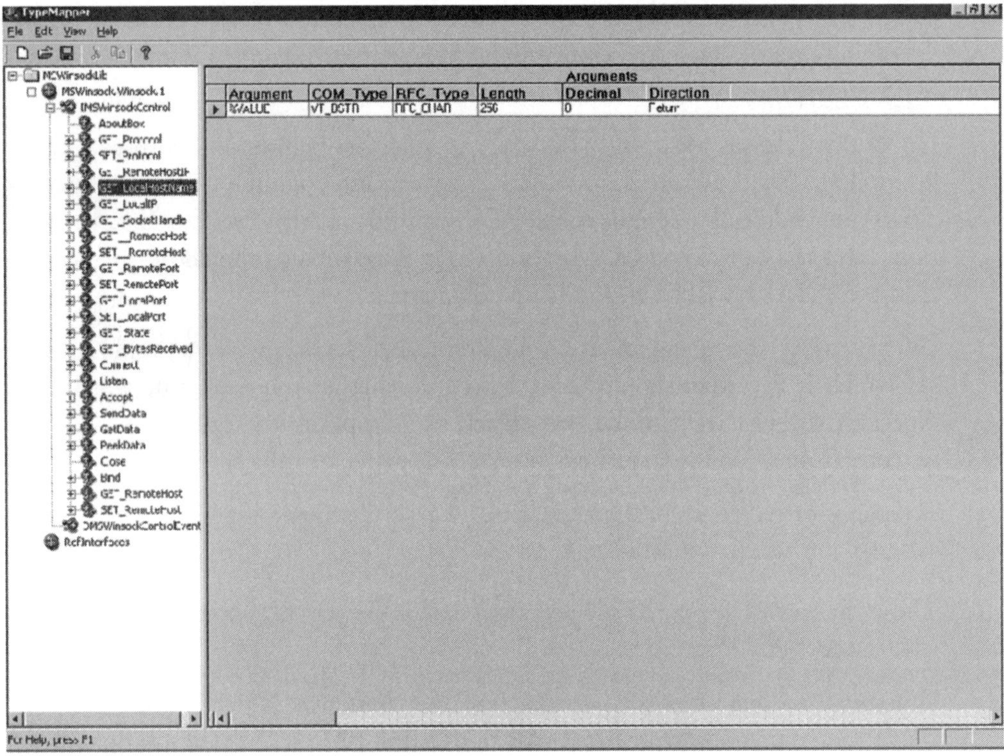

FIGURE 2-10 *Example of TypeMap with the Winsock DLL object*

XML and the Business Connector

Business Connector is the SAP XML enabler. The Business Connector allows SAP systems to send and receive documents in XML format through the Internet. Business Connector is based on software from the company webMethods (**www.webmethods.com**) and is included free of charge in the standard SAP software; it can also be downloaded from **http://service.sap.com/connectors**. Business Connector is a general Internet middleware and is licensed to SAP customers in scenarios where one of the partners is a SAP system.

XML in the Business Connector

As we have already mentioned, XML is the new standard for sending documents through the Internet. One of the advantages of XML is the reuse of existing Internet technology already in place like a language similar to HTML, HTTP as transmission protocol, and using the proxies and firewalls already working in most of the current companies.

There are several substandards for XML in the ERP industries. Ariba has cXML, Microsoft defines the BizTalk initiative, RosettaNet has a multivendor initiative, and so on. So if your system wants to speak XML, it will need a translator from your internal document representation to the XML standard your partner speaks. And here is where Business Connector appears.

What Is the Business Connector?

Business Connector is Java-based software that speaks standard Internet protocols like HTTP, HTTPS, FTP, or SMTP (e-mail). It is also able to receive SAP IDOCs and transform them into XML or vice versa, receive an XML document and send it to the SAP system as an IDOC.

Business Connector also has the possibility to receive XML BAPI calls and send them to SAP as RFC calls and vice versa, receive a RFC call from SAP and transform it into an XML document to be sent through the Internet to the next Business Connector and SAP system. It has built-in RFC client and server capabilities on one side and Internet protocols like HTTPS on the other side.

webMethods B2B Integration Server

Business Connector has two main components: the server and the developer. The server is a server program that is listening to HTTP, HTTPS, or FTP at customizable TCP/IP ports and listens to RFC calls on the other side from your SAP systems. You can administer the server from a Web server and define there which protocols and SAP systems it should use. Also, you define the security environment like user, user groups, and ACLs (*access control lists*) in order to define who can access which Business Connector services or functions.

The server also has routing capabilities. When the Business Connector server receives an XML document or a BAPI call, it determines how to route this by looking at the source, destination, and document type information. In the route definition you specify which protocol should be used and how to address the real target. For example, you can say that for IDOC types ORDERS from the SAP system C11 to the receiver SUPPLIER1, the FTP protocol should be used and determine which is the FTP server and user/password at the supplier side.

The server also has cache functions, used to improve the performance. For example, in order to call a function module in R/3, the server needs the interface specification (export/import parameters). This is saved in the cache to save time in the future calls. Another example is the typical Internet cache like Web browsers when accessing to Web server functions. Cache use is defined service by service as well as the expiration time for the cache.

The developer is the second component in Business Connector. It is a graphical Java-based developer environment where you can define or modify existing services in the Business Connector server. The developer connects to the server usually by HTTP, so it can be installed in a different machine. The developer allows you to define the so-called flow services. You can define flow services graphically, linking existing services at Business Connector.

Business Connector has a lot of defined services, for HTML, HTTP, or RFC, for example. Theses services are grouped in interfaces, and the interfaces are grouped in packages that correspond to a Java class from the technical point of view. You can include MAP functions in these services, define input and output records, and graphically link the fields between both records with arrows. You can define records based on existing DTD, DTD stored in a Web server, or by hand. In this way, it is very easy to map the SAP XML to the XML to be used in the conversation. You can also define new services with Java, C/C++, or even Visual Basic.

From ALE/IDOCs to XML

SAP Business Connector is able to receive XML from a SAP system and transform it automatically in SAP XML. In this way, Business Connector can be used to connect ALE logical systems through the Internet reusing your firewall and proxy settings and a cheap communication media to send and receive the XML messages between the systems.

On the other hand, Business Connector can send and receive IDOCs in other scenarios, like in supplier/vendor relationships, and transform the incoming XML in an SAP IDOC or vice versa. In this way, XML is expected to be a substitute of EDI in SAP systems.

From BAPIs to XML

With the XML RFC and XML BAPI specification, you can send an RFC call to the Business Connector, which is in charge of routing the call in an XML RFC document to the next Business Connector, which transforms it in an RFC call to the target system. The result is back in XML again and transformed in standard RFC at the end. In this way we can call functions between SAP systems (or external RFC servers or clients) using XML and HTTPS as the protocol through the Internet. Here you can see what an XML RFC call looks like.[1]

The following is an example of a XML RFC call from Business Connector.[1]

```
<SAP-RFC>
  <header/>
  <call>
    <TRAIN415_RFC_GET_CARRIER>
      <CARRID t='chars'>LH</CARRID>
      <CARRIER t='table.SCARR'/>
    </TRAIN415_RFC_GET_CARRIER>
  </call>
</SAP-RFC>
```

Example of XML RFC answer:

```
<SAP-RFC>
  <header/>
  <return>
    <TRAIN415_RFC_GET_CARRIER>
      <CARRIER t='table.SCARR'>
        <SCARR>
          <MANDT t='chars'>000</MANDT>
          <CARRID t='chars'>LH</CARRID>
          <CARRNAME t='chars'>Lufthansa</CARRNAME>
          <CURRCODE t='chars'>DEM</CURRCODE>
        </SCARR>
      </CARRIER>
    </TRAIN415_RFC_GET_CARRIER>
  </return>
</SAP-RFC>
```

Business Connector also allows you to call a BAPI or RFC from a Web browser and get the result back, merging the parameters with an HTML template. If you

[1] *From BC SAP Documentation. Reprinted with permission*

want to call BAPIs or RFCs from a browser, you should also have a look at the ITS functionality, because it is more powerful for this specific issue.

Web Automation

Another functionality within Business Connector is the possibility to execute actions in a Web server and examine the resulting page. Imagine that you want to know the delivery status of your order and your courier company has a Web server where you can log on, enter the delivery number, and get the information. You can automate these steps in a service in Business Connector and call this from ABAP, for example. This is a nice feature if your courier company has not XML-enabled the delivery status functionality. On the other hand, a change in the Web server can force a change in your server definition. That's why XML is useful to standardize dialogs between systems.

Use of XML in mySAP.com

XML is the language that the Internet marketplaces use to send and receive documents between the different connected partners. We are going to discuss more about the SAP Marketplace solution included in mySAP in Chapter 6, "mySAP Marketplace."

XML is used in other SAP solutions like BBP for procurement with a browser with Internet catalogs to send and receive orders. In general, XML and the Business Connector are used in any SAP business scenario where documents are exchanged through the Internet.

The Business Directory and Document Exchange

The SAP Marketplace solution included in the mySAP initiative has two important pieces. The Business Directory allows finding partners in the Marketplace that can help you in your transaction. For example, if you want to buy tins, you would like to know companies in a certain area that produce tins. In the Business Directory, you can get a list of the selected companies and other information like the URL where the company has its catalog on the Internet. Clicking on the URL, you get transferred to the vendor catalog, where you can select the products you want and transfer them to your shopping basket with a protocol called OCI

(*Open Catalog Interface*). Then you create your Purchase Order in your Purchasing system, which sends an XML purchase order to your Marketplace mailbox.

Then the document is passed in the Marketplace to the Business Document Exchange, another important piece of software in the Marketplace. It routes the order to the recipient mailbox and later will create a sales order in the vendor back-end system. The Business Document Exchange is used in other scenarios like auctions (public or closed) and routes the documents to the relevant mailboxes.

Functions of Business Connector in mySAP.com Portals

In fact, Business Connector is also used in the SAP Marketplace solution in order to send and receive XML documents with your partners. Also, the Business Connector you install in your system already has an entry for mySAP Marketplaces in order to configure the transport very easily. If you want to connect your SAP back-end system to a mySAP Marketplace, you need only to configure in a screen in your Business Connector the URL of the Marketplace and the logon information, like the mailbox assigned to you in the marketplace. It is only a matter of hours to be connected to a mySAP Marketplace with the Business Connector.

Extended Integration

The Internet and the Marketplace solutions will create new scenarios where the back-end systems of the partners will be integrated. New business processes will appear that go through systems as well as the business processes in your company go through modules or departments. For these scenarios, new software is needed in the marketplace and in the back-end systems to allow a seamless integration.

Collaboration Technologies

Up to now, the main scenarios used in the marketplace are sell/buy scenarios, increasing step by step to dynamic pricing scenarios, like auctions. But other scenarios are appearing based on collaboration between companies. Collaboration to join purchases to get better conditions is clear, but there is also collaboration to transport the purchased products together or to forecast together with our partners. The integration of processes can be done at different layers, like at the presentation layer, the application layer, or even the database layer.

Presentation Level

Presentation level means that a user connects to the partner portal and interacts with it. In this case, the user creates a document in the partner system, but has to create also the document in his own system. Technologies like mySAP Workplace will allow us to create Enterprise Portals with personalized interfaces in order to support this scenario for our customers, suppliers, or resellers.

Application Level: WebFlows

The integration at application level is based normally on exchange of XML messages between the partners or between the marketplace and the partners. WebFlows or Workflows through the Internet will appear to enable the systems to send Workflow requests between them, also based on XML standards. This is the most integrated approach with the application logic and is what all vendors are trying to supply.

Data Distribution Level: Web Projector

The other possible integration layer could be at the database level. The possibility is to update database records or objects directly through the Internet using XML SQL messages. Some databases are already allowing this, but the integration between different companies will be more difficult at this level because it requires the knowledge of the internal representation at database level. This case could be successful for internal use in a company.

EnjoySAP and SAP R/3 Release 4.6

EnjoySAP, introduced in Chapter 1 (particularly Figures 1-7 and 1-8), is the SAP initiative with the user at the center. As a friendly and more ergonomic interface, EnjoySAP has become the mySAP user interface.

The EnjoySAP interface can be used with any release of SAP R/3 above 3.1I. However, it is only fully functional with releases 4.6 and upward, which are the releases ready for supporting role-based scenarios, personalization, Web access from the Favorites menu, and so on. Because of the tight integration between the EnjoySAP interface and release 4.6, at the beginning (in 1999) release 4.6 was also known as the EnjoySAP release; however, it must be noted that EnjoySAP is the interface and must not be confused with the R/3 release.

First releases of SAP R/3 4.6 included basically the same application functionality of the previous 4.5 releases but with many technical advances. The kernel (programs at the operating system level) of 4.6D was, for a long time, the basis system for most of the mySAP components until the arrival of the SAP Web Application Server. In the next sections, some of the typical SAP Basis components are introduced briefly for a better understanding of the system.

With the arrival of new Web technology and the possibility of having a Java-based, platform-independent GUI, the strategy for user interfaces changed with the new world of mySAP.com e-business solutions. Let's first review the user interface strategy, but take into consideration that no matter the platform or the implementation of the GUI, the look and feel of each of them is EnjoySAP, that is, with a common graphical environment, personalization facilities, and so on.

User Interface Platforms

Over the years, SAP, in its tremendous effort to be open and supportive of all platforms, has provided the traditional SAPGUI in all available graphical environments, such as Microsoft Windows, OS/2, MacOS, OSF/Motif, and finally browser support. In all these cases, the SAPGUI offered a common look and feel for all those platforms and behaves exactly the same from an application point of view.

It has always been very important that the users could perceive the system as friendly and as easy as possible, as well as having as many personalization capabilities to make the daily tasks as efficient as possible. The user acceptance of the system often had to do with how they perceived this graphical interface. The continuous improvement of the interface, and the SAP personalization project back in late '90s, were key to the release of the EnjoySAP interface.

The EnjoySAP interface is centered on the usability of the systems. The EnjoySAP interface is supported in the classic SAPGUI for Windows, the SAPGUI for HTML, and the Java GUI. Other previously supported platforms must now use one of these interfaces; for instance, there is no more development for the Mac or the Motif platforms because they can use either the SAPGUI for HTML or the Java GUI. Let's briefly review in the next sections some of the features of these GUI platforms.

SAPGUI for Windows

The SAP graphical user interface, known as SAPGUI, acts as the presentation server, and it was typically available in all Microsoft Windows operating systems, Motif, OS/2, and Macintosh. They all look identical whatever underlying system SAPGUI was running on. Since release 4.6 of R/3, and now with releases 6.10 and later, this interface will only be available on the Microsoft Windows platforms such as 98, NT/2000, or XP.

The SAPGUI includes all graphical capabilities of modern Windows interfaces, with push buttons, menu bars, toolbars, hypertext links, on-focus descriptions, right-clicking options, tab strips, and so on. The graphical design and functionality is homogeneous across the entire system, which makes training easier and straightforward for all levels of SAP users. Figure 2-11 shows an example of the SAPGUI for Windows.

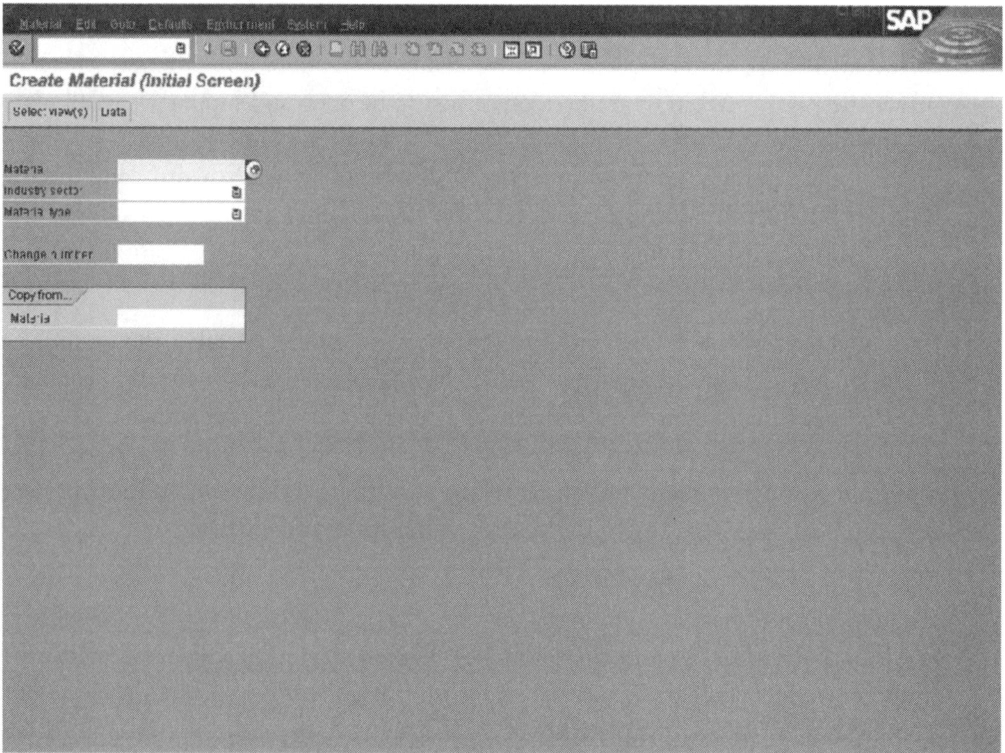

FIGURE 2-11 *Example of classic SAPGUI interface*

Depending on which R/3 application or processing tasks are going to be run, screens can be very simple or can contain multiple fields and graphical elements. Customers can also customize and create new menus and screens with the help of the Development Workbench or with the personalization functions available. The SAP R/3 presentation interface behaves very similarly to any other typical Windows application.

Before EnjoySAP, there were some shortcomings of the traditional SAPGUI, such as:

- Partitioned screens
- Limited personalization possibilities
- Many screens for single transactions

With EnjoySAP, the interface provided a new interaction design where it was possible to access full transactions from a single screen, to have many personalization possibilities, tab-based screens, and to have role-based scenarios, so that different types of users could have just the needed functionality in their screens. It was even possible to have different fields in the same transactions for different types of users.

SAPGUI for HTML

The SAPGUI for HTML refers to the ITS on the server side together with a Web browser at the desktop. With the SAPGUI for HTML, almost all business functions of SAP applications—including business functions for professional power users—can be accessed. The ITS, and thus the SAPGUI for HTML, are also part of the mySAP Workplace. The SAPGUI for HTML requires no additional software on the desktop besides a Web browser. SAPGUI for HTML automatically maps the screen elements in business transactions to HTML using Business HTML functions available within the SAP ITS. As a result, SAP ITS can dynamically generate a HTML version of a business transaction screen that is similar in layout.

To enhance the platform availability of the ITS, SAP has taken the first steps toward providing a W-Gate for the Apache Web server on both Windows NT and Linux platforms. This means that the ITS now supports a third Web server-specific protocol Apache module in addition to ISAPI (*Microsoft Internet Information Server*) and NSAPI (*Netscape Enterprise Server*) or any CGI Web server.

As of ITS 4.6D, the W-Gate architecture has been changed completely. The new W-Gate configuration means that you no longer have to attach each virtual ITS to a separate virtual Web server. Furthermore, one W-Gate can now communicate with more than one A-Gate, and these A-Gates can either be installed on the same machine or different machines. Figure 2-12 shows an example of the SAPGUI for HTML.

SAPGUI in Java

The development of GUIs in environments such as Motif for UNIX systems, Mac or OS/2 evolved into the *Platform Independent GUI.* Platform Independent (Platinum) GUI is the new generation of SAPGUI, which is being designed with the objective of having the same appearance and working in exactly the same way, no matter the underlying platform and operating system. It also has the design goal

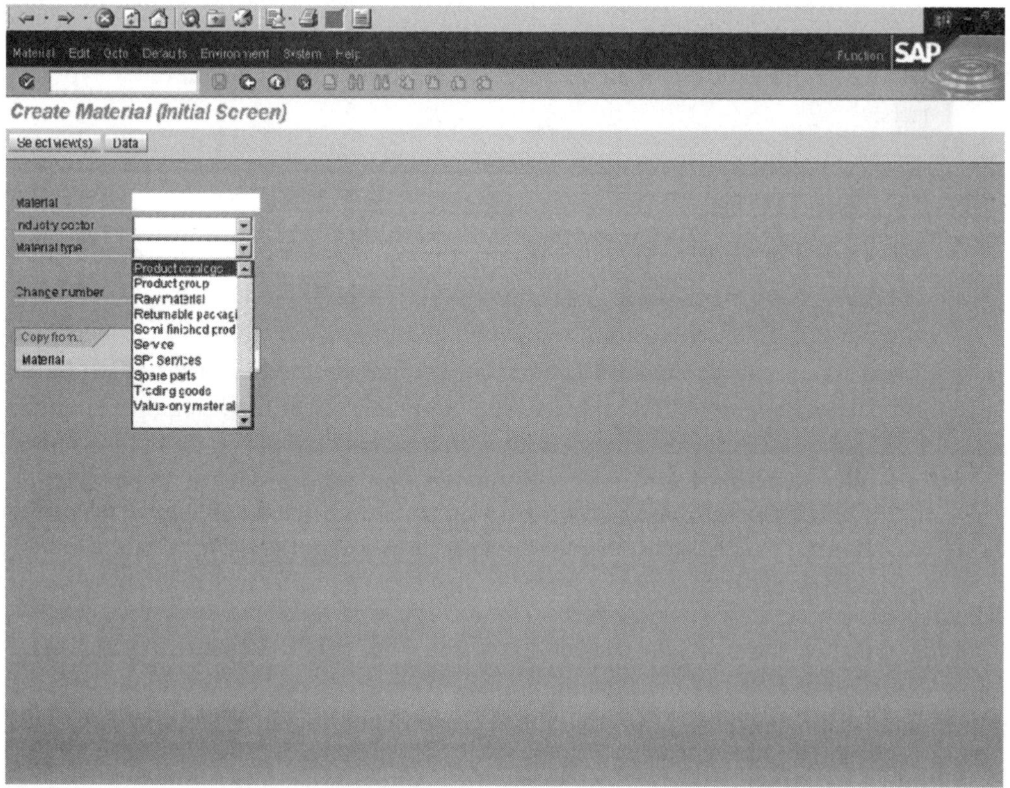

FIGURE 2-12 *SAPGUI for HTML*

of integrating all new available technologies within the user interface. Java SAPGUI is the R/3 interface for connecting to the system through an intranet or the Internet[JC1][JAH2], with the fundamental advantage of providing a great degree of independence on the platform when executing transactions.

EnjoySAP Navigation

With the introduction of the EnjoySAP interface, users have many additional possibilities for easy browsing and navigation through the SAP systems. The user-specific entry point into the SAP systems is provided through the SAP Easy Access, which is the user menu provided by the system administrators to the users according to their roles. Easy Access is the standard entry screen displayed after logon. If users are not assigned a particular menu, they can have a complete transaction tree of SAP functions by selecting Menu/Standard Menu. There are options for changing the look of the tree structure under the Extras/Settings menu. Users can also select which transaction will be the default when first logging in by selecting Extras/Set start transaction and entering the transaction code. Figure 2-13 shows an example of the SAP Easy Access menu.

The navigation options through the EnjoySAP interface still include most or all of the typical facilities found on classic SAPGUI interfaces before EnjoySAP, such as moving around the system with transaction codes, the context function menu, and others. When using the SAPGUI for HTML platform, some navigation functions are not available.

Personalizing the Favorites

You can create a Favorites list of the transactions, reports, files, and Web sites you use most. You can add items to your Favorites list by using the Favorites menu option or by dragging and dropping. You can also create your own folders in the Favorites list, move Favorites, and change Favorites' text as desired. Figure 2-14 shows an example of Favorites.

In addition to selecting functions from a Favorites list, user menu, SAP standard menu, or the menu bar, you can still select functions using transaction codes.

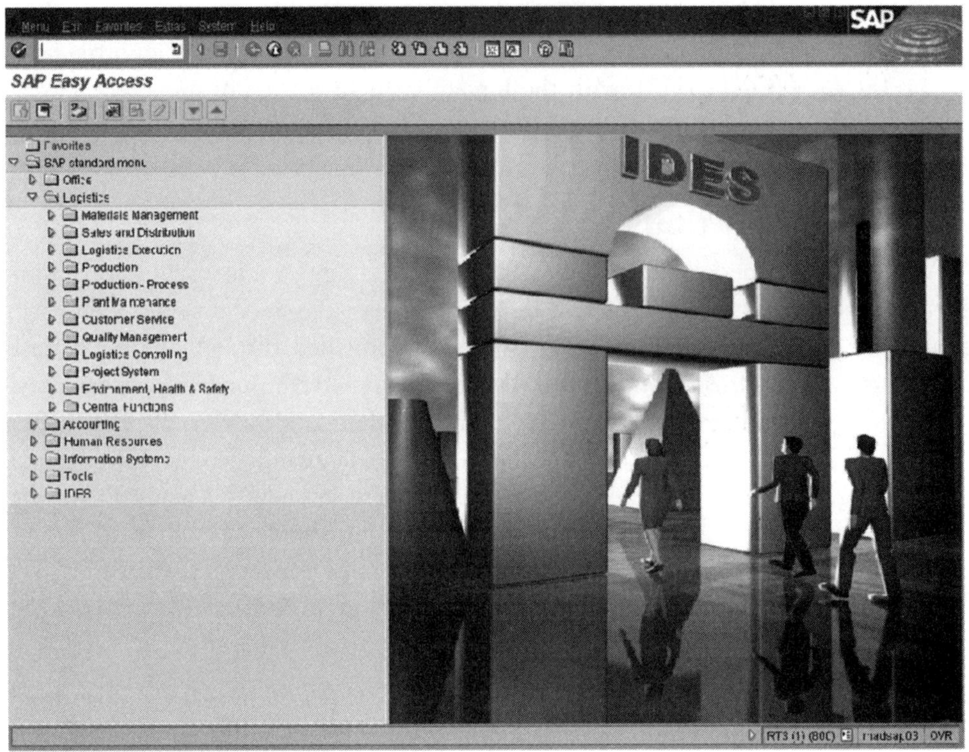

FIGURE 2-13 *SAP Easy Access*

Getting Help

The way to get help in the EnjoySAP interface is still quite similar to the traditional help functions, except that better contextual help information is provided and the interface has changed. You still use the traditional F1 and F4 key functions to access help options. Use F1 for help with fields, menus, functions, and messages. The F1 help also provides technical information on the relevant field. This includes, for example, the parameter ID, which you can use to assign values to the field for your user.

Use F4 for information on what values you can enter. You can also access the F4 help for a selected field using the icon immediately to the right of that field. Tabs allow you to select the search criteria you require. The icon to the right of the tabs allows you to choose the available search criteria. If input fields are marked with a small icon with a check mark, you can only continue in that application by enter-

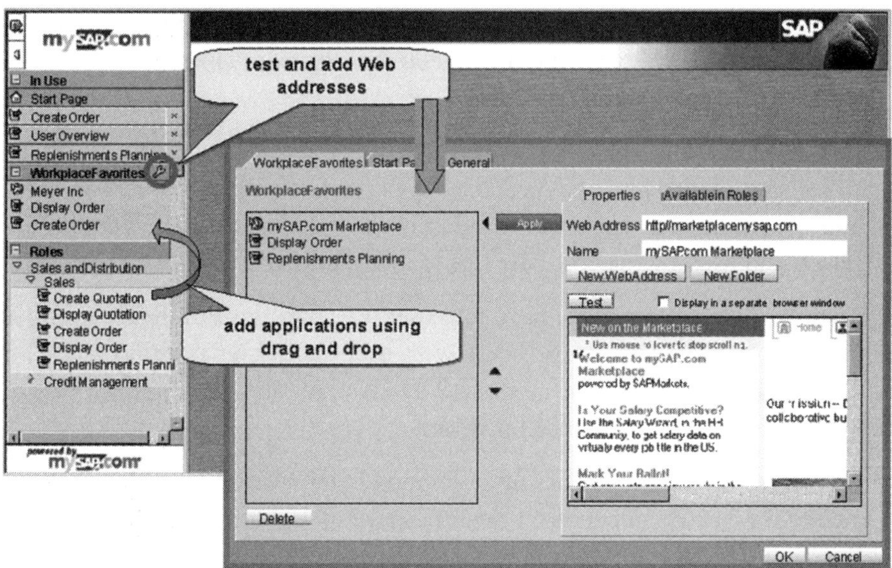

FIGURE 2-14 *Example of Favorites*

ing a permitted value. You can mark many fields in an application as either required entry fields or optional entry fields, or hide them using transaction or screen variants or Customizing.

The newly designed EnjoySAP transactions offer quick-info text for additional information about the current transaction. You can choose to hide or show this help as required.

Role-Based Scenarios

A growing majority of SAP users are not just professional users. Rather, an ever increasing percentage of a company's employees are using SAP products as occasional users. Realizing that these occasional users come from different departments and perform different jobs led to the creation of user roles. Though the interfaces are tailored to the user in each case, both still ultimately use the same back-end functionality. From R/3, role-specific scenarios were extended into SAP's New Dimensions and ultimately into mySAP.com solutions.

A role describes a set of logically linked transactions. These transactions represent the range of functions users typically need at their workstations. Users who have been assigned to an activity group can choose between the user menu and the SAP standard menu. Selecting the user menu icon displays the user menu in place of the SAP standard menu.

The authorizations for the activities listed in the menus are also assigned to the users using activity groups. With release 4.6, predefined activity groups (user roles) from all application areas are included in the standard system. These can be displayed and used by selecting the Other menu button.

Activity groups (user roles) have to be set up using the Profile Generator so that users of the SAP System can work with user-specific or position-related menus. The Create menu, Assign users, and Documentation buttons provide access to Activity Group Maintenance functions.

Note: The availability of the Other menu, Create menu, Assign users, and Documentation buttons depends on the user's authorizations.

System Administration for mySAP Systems

The following sections introduce the basics of administering mySAP systems. As you already know, most components that need to be managed come from the good old SAP R/3 Basis system. For those of you familiar with earlier releases of R/3, there are sections on specific topics of the Basis system, such as the printing system, batch handling, monitoring, CCMS, and database management. New functionality that was added on the latest R/3 releases is also introduced and explained.

In the mySAP.com age, we see an ever increasing complexity in SAP systems because of the number and type of logical and physical systems, Web servers, ITS, many Basis systems, several databases, and so on. It can be said that these systems have evolved from traditional R/3 administration to complex mySAP.com system landscape management.

The next sections introduce some of the available facilities and tools found on traditional R/3 systems that are still available on most mySAP.com software solutions. On the attached CD-ROM you can find demos and additional information on other more advanced tools specially suited for this type of complex system management.

System Administration Assistant

In order to make the administration of complex system environments a little easier, since release 4.5 of R/3 SAP included a comprehensive utility for system management tasks known as the System Administration Assistant (transaction SSAA).

With the System Administration Assistant, a system manager could perform such administrative tasks from a single point as

- Monitoring processes and users
- Performing daily checks and tasks
- Verifying the status of the database

The System Administration Assistant includes support for defining daily tasks, periodic tasks, and occasional tasks, and can be used to manage not only one single system but a system landscape, for example, both the development and the production systems.

The System Administration Assistant offers the system manager four different views: Work lists, Entire view, Selective view, and Alert view. Figure 2-15 shows an example of these views.

When the transaction is started, the Work lists display only the pending daily tasks. Once these tasks are performed, the light becomes green. If you leave the transaction and enter it again, those performed tasks are not shown any longer. This facility allows for checking the tasks as already performed, for instance, in the case of having performed them outside the SSAA or when performing several different checks or tasks from a single transaction. If a specific task must be performed several times in a day (for instance, checking ABAP dumps, lock entries, and so on), system managers can establish or reset the status of a task from the Entire view. The general or Entire view displays all the tasks regardless of whether these tasks are already performed or not.

The Selective view is useful for defining certain filters based on functions or periodicity, while the Alert view shows those tasks in which an alert is triggered. Figure 2-16 shows an example of a Selective view.

It is possible to define customer tasks and to do this based on SAP tasks as templates. These customer tasks are preserved even after a release upgrade. However, it is not possible to modify the SAP-defined tasks. As stated before, it is also

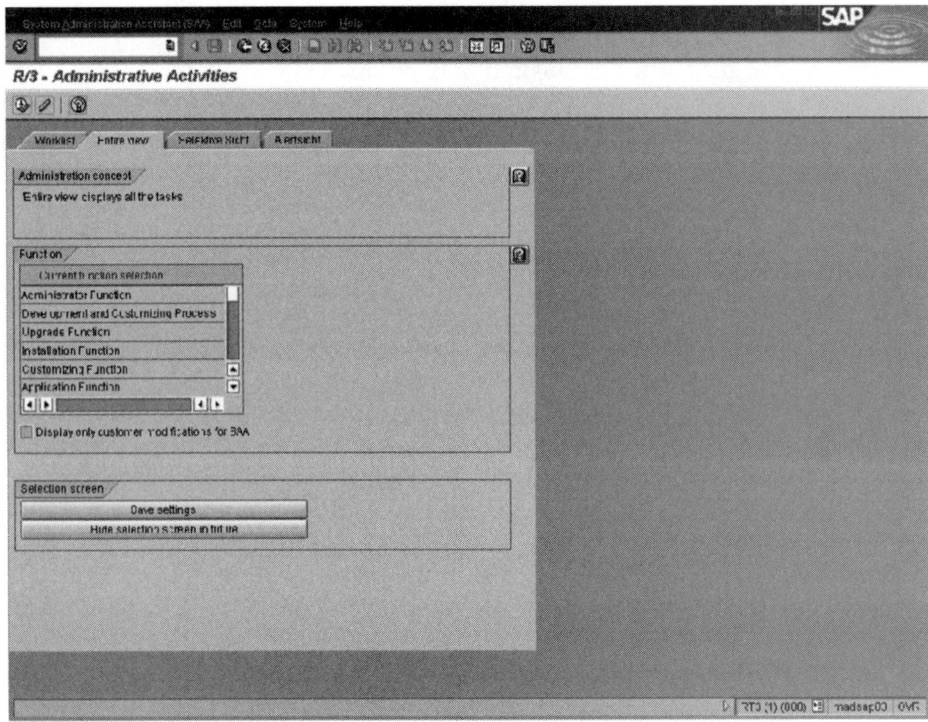

FIGURE 2-15 *System Administration Assistant views*

possible with the SSAA to control and monitor the development system from the productive system by means of remote access.

The Printing System

SAP has typically provided its own spooling and printing system embedded in the R/3 systems and applications, enabling all printing functions from a homogeneous interface and independently of the system platforms supporting both the printing devices and the application services. The printing services were handled and supported by the SAP spool work processes, which are in charge of formatting lists, documents, or any other output and passing them to the host spool systems.

More information on all the features of the SAP printing system can be found in the SAP Online Library under the CCMS section or in previously published works on SAP Basis systems. The following paragraphs introduce some of the new

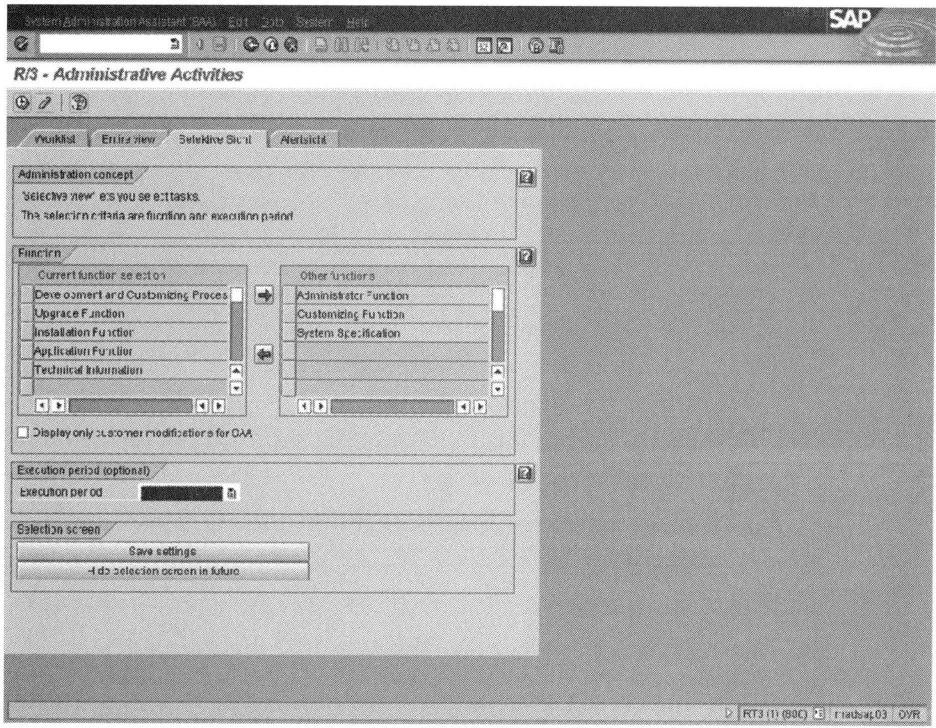

FIGURE 2-16 *Selective view within the SSAA*

features that were available on latest R/3 releases and can be found on mySAP components.

With release 4.6, we find the following new features and enhancements to the classic R/3 printing system:

- The spool administration transaction (SPAD) is much easier to handle and printing administration becomes simpler and more user friendly. Administration can be started from SSAA or directly from the SPAD transaction.
- Improved and new access methods:
  - Access method E substitutes to the Z access method (command interface for SPOOL exit); it is meant for the command interface or RFC interface to OMSs (*Output Management Systems*).

  - Access method P: Pool Printing can be used to print to several printers (these printers must be local to the server).
- Printer pools and spool servers have support for load balancing. Spool logical servers can be used for specifying a real alternative spool and to balance the load among them, as well as the transport of the printing architecture (it is enough with updating the real servers associated to a logical server).
- The spool process now handles front-end printing. In earlier releases, it was handled by a dialog process, which caused many troubles in several application components that were tightly integrated with the handling of printing through the spool work process. It is possible to limit the number of spool processes for front-end printing; it cannot be used in batch, but it is possible in update.
- New naming convention, page formats, multitray printers, and more have been added.
- Logical spool servers are offered.
- Transport of device types directly from the SPAD transaction is now available.
- Support for OMS is available using the XOM API (*External Output Management System API*); this is the API available for linking SAP with external printing management systems.
- Better maintenance of the spool data base is offered.

Computer Center Management System (CCMS)

The CCMS is the SAP set of system management tools that are used for monitoring, configuring, and tuning the SAP systems. As such, it includes a comprehensive set of graphical monitors and management tools that could be used specifically for:

- Managing SAP instances: defining instances, managing instance profiles, tuning instance parameters, starting and stopping SAP instances, configuring operation modes, and so on
- Monitoring and analyzing the systems workload: SAP systems, database, operating systems, and network
- Configuration of alerts and alerts thresholds for problem detection
- Configuration of the logon load balancing

- Centralized monitoring of the data archiving processes
- Centralized management of administration tasks (SSAA)
- Management of the background processes and the printing system

The CCMS monitoring and management utilities provide a large amount of technical, workload, and control information that requires experienced and knowledgeable system managers to fully take advantages of the provided facilities.

Already in 1998 with the release 4.0 of SAP R/3, the CCMS Alert and Monitoring architecture changed to an object-oriented one, with the possibility of defining centralized monitoring of a group of SAP systems. With the CCMS object-based architecture, the monitors and alerts are individually configured with their own analysis tools. SAP provides default monitor sets in the CCMS, but customers have the ability to define their own sets of monitors, as well as to define remote monitoring. For remote monitoring, system managers will need to define RFC destinations (transaction SM59), define monitor sets, and then select the MTEs and Notes.

Refer to the SAP Online Library for more information on how to configure and use the CCMS tools.

The Background System

The SAP background system present in all *former* (pre-mySAP) Basis systems, as well as in the Web Application Server, is in charge of handling the background or batch processes so that users can launch the execution of programs in batch, or in other words, work noninteractively with the systems. Submitting programs for background execution is handled by the SAP background work processes.

The planning and execution of programs (ABAP or external) in the background is handled using the so-called background jobs. The SAP Basis system includes many utilities and functionalities to behave as a comprehensive batch system, with lots of possibilities for planning and scheduling jobs at the most convenient time, after the successful or unsuccessful execution of other jobs, or by the reception or *events*.

The latest releases of R/3 systems also had many improvements found in the management of the background systems. For instance:

- The introduction of *Job Wizards* for making it easier to define and plan jobs

- For monitoring jobs, SAP introduced:
  - A redesigned and enhanced SM37 transaction
  - The possibility of performing job selections using additional criteria such as steps, periodicity, and others
  - An enhanced graphical job monitor (transaction RZ01)

The Transport System

The transport system is a complete environment of the SAP system landscapes, made up of a set of tools, applications, and operating system programs. It is used to manage and perform functions such as the management and control of new development requests, modifications to development objects, the configuration of the development classes, development versions management, and documentation.

In a distributed classic mySAP development environment, the transport system and related tools such as the Workbench and Customizing Organizers are in charge of transporting (moving) development and customizing objects between SAP systems, normally between the systems used to perform development and customizing work, QA (*quality assurance*) systems, and productive systems.

The transport system utilities also take care of logging the result of transports and determining the reasons for possible failures. Although the transport system has been managed through the STMS transaction since release 4.0 of R/3, the transport to the appropriate target system takes place at the operating system level using the transport control program *tp*, which is automatically invoked from within SAP systems.

For those readers familiar with the former R/3 transport systems, let's briefly review the evolution of the TMS (*Transport Management System*).

- R/3 releases 3.x
  - Introduction of the Workbench Organizer, common transport directory, tp control program, R3trans, STMS in beta
- R/3 release 4.0
  - Introduction of productive TMS: Transport Domains and Transport Domain Controller
  - Centralized CTS configuration, change requests, transport routes
  - Transport among systems without a common transport directory

- R/3 release 4.5
  - Enhanced definition of the QA system and the transport procedure for these QA systems
  - Enhanced and centralized configuration for the tp transport control program
  - New options for system modifications such as local objects, number ranges, and others
  - R/3 release 4.6
  - Client-specific transport routes for consolidation and delivery systems
  - Enhance options for transports to the QA systems
  - Approval procedure for the QA systems
  - "Not approved" change requests are not transported to the productive systems
  - Selective imports of project-based change requests
  - Batch scheduling of import process
  - Workflow for approving special (individual) transports

More information on the transport system can be found in the SAP Online Library. Additionally, the CD-ROM in this book includes a demo of a third-party advanced TMS application that further eases the process of managing transport requests in mySAP system environments.

Chapter 3

mySAP Cross-Industry Solutions: CRM, E-Procurement, Business Intelligence

In this chapter, readers will find an overview and reference information about some of mySAP Cross-Industry Solutions, all of which are in constant evolution and full of technological and application enhancements in every new release.

The objective of this chapter is to present and synthesize the main features and characteristics of the mySAP Cross-Industry Solutions so that readers have a clear picture of the mySAP solutions. In order to get further knowledge or information about the mySAP components introduced, visit the SAP Service Marketplace Web site (**service.sap.com**) or the public Web site (**www.sap.com**).

It is not the purpose of following sections to show how to install, set up, and customize these solutions, because for that purpose, a specific and deep knowledge of the relationship between all the components is required, which is beyond the scope of this book. In order to learn how to install or configure a mySAP application, there are specific training courses and several manuals and guides. Nevertheless, the following sections will help readers to better understand the purpose of these solutions and whether they apply for their e-business needs.

As has been mentioned, in any case, the business model is always the key to succeed in the Web age. What is really needed for configuring these solutions is a solid knowledge about actual e-business processes and how companies do e-business.

mySAP Customer Relationship Management

mySAP.com, as the collaborative e-business platform, is a comprehensive, integrated, and natural framework for deploying CRM (*Customer Relationship Management*) solutions. CRM is a term that, on first impression, could mean how a company manages the relationship with its customer in a unidirectional manner. In fact, CRM software is meant to facilitate the common job of employees, customers, and business partners in any situation, moment, or location.

There are many definitions about what CRM really is, and probably all of them are quite valid. But out of all of them, the one that I particularly like and found from a contributor on the **crmguru.com** website is: "Customer Relationship Management is a GLOBAL business strategy, designed for optimizing . . . benefits, income and customer satisfaction, organizing the company around different customer segments, and linking all the business process from the customers to the providers." The technology that can accomplish this strategy is known as CRM technology.

The key of the investments in CRM technology is to provide a better knowledge of the customers by increasing the contact and providing a better interaction and by using all the communication channels, integrating the company back-office functions and business processes with those of the customers.

The CRM domain comprises three big technology areas:

- TES (*technology enabled selling*)
- CSS (*customer service and support*)
- TEM (*technology enabled marketing*)

TES is also known as sales automation and is referred to the applications that enable selling using all the required sales channels. The components include: sales of products and services outside the boundaries of the company or SFA (*sales force automation*); telesales within the company and using the available resources such as Web, phone, fax, and e-mail; sales of partners' products (e-partners); Web-based selling (e-sales); and retailing. The objective of TES is to integrate technology with optimum business processes to provide a continuous improvement of the efficiency of the sales team by optimizing every sales channel.

CSS is the technology in charge of the postsales process: it is responsible for retaining, maintaining, and extending the relationship with the customer once the product or service is sold. Components within CSS are call management, Web-based self-service, technical support, and contact center, including any contact channel with customers, such as voice, Internet, e-mail, fax, video, traditional mail, and so on.

TEM is also known as marketing automation, that is, the analysis and automation of the marketing processes. The traditional metrics of market share and penetration must be correctly complemented with other figures, such as the life cycle or customer profitability. TEM components include: tools for generating consistent and valid data and information, software for data analysis, and a CMS (*Campaign Management System*) for the design and follow-up of campaigns using multiple channels.

CRM and mySAP

Under the solid umbrella of the business process concept and the complete functional chains of the SAP R/3 systems, CRM within the mySAP.com strategy is an open solution that supports all those tasks that are customer driven, both operational and analytical, using three fundamental channels: the Internet, the global relationship center (contact center), and personal contact.

The mySAP CRM solution links electronic commerce, the supply chain, financial management, and human resources with the global business strategy and the integration level provided by the back-end OLTP (R/3) systems. The mySAP CRM solution includes a central CRM server (a mySAP Basis R/3 system or a SAP Web Application Server in later releases), which is linked to one or several OLTP (R/3) systems and has the possibility of integrating other mySAP components and several extensions for supporting several ways of accessing the system. Depending on the channel or channels of approaching customers and the requirements of every company, not all CRM components need to be installed. Figure 3-1 shows the big picture of the possible connections of the mySAP CRM system.

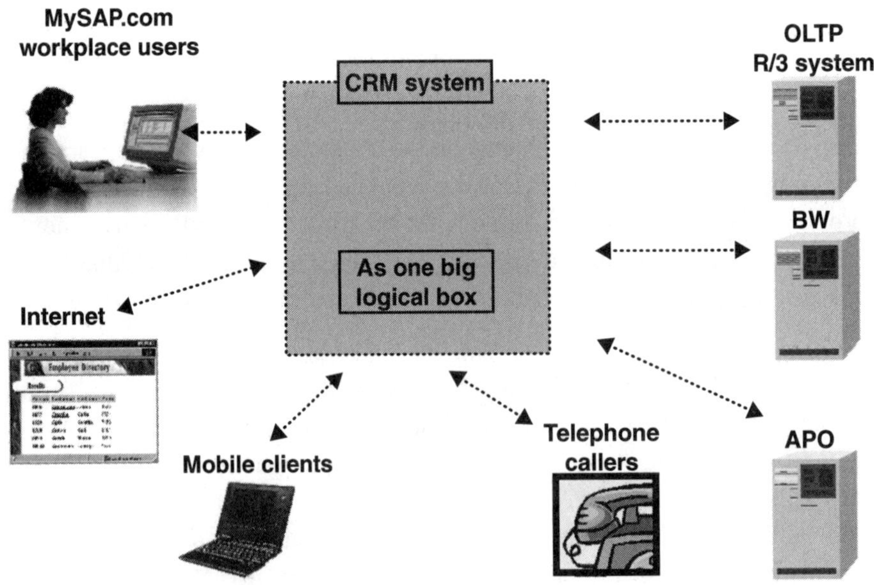

FIGURE 3-1 *Possible connections of mySAP CRM*

As seen in the picture, the CRM system can be accessed in several different ways:

- Directly from the traditional SAPGUI interface, just like any other R/3 system, by the company employees
- Through the mySAP Workplace portal and using the specific roles within mySAP CRM
- Using the Internet to configure and buy both products and services using the CRM Internet components
- Sales representatives or service engineers using their portable devices to exchange information
- All channels, including phone, fax, and e-mail, for contacting sales representatives or service engineers using a complete contact center

mySAP CRM System Architecture

The mySAP CRM system is built over a SAP Basis (SAP Web Application Server) system, including the traditional R/3 tools such as User Interface Builder, ABAP Editor, Data Modeler, ABAP Dictionary, Debugger, Report Builder, Multilanguage Support, Performance Monitor, or the CATT (*Computer Aided Test Tool*).

Above the R/3 layer, there are two different components, as shown in Figure 3-2.

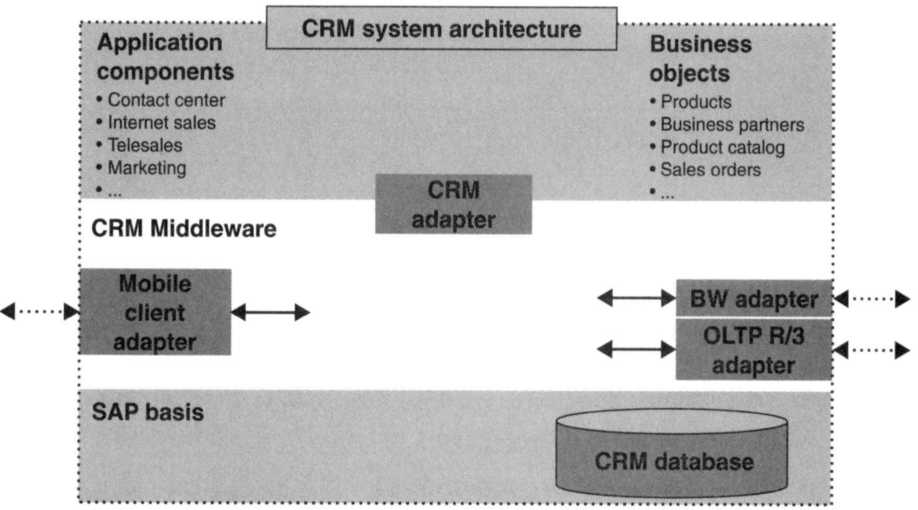

FIGURE 3-2 *Layers of the mySAP CRM architecture*

These are the main functions of these two main components:

- One component or layer supports data exchanged with other systems: mobile clients, back-end systems, and the business warehouse. This component is known as the *middleware*. For the mobile clients, a replication mechanism ensures, in a consistent manner, the update of the data to local databases. A special mention must be made to the adapters, which can be used for linking the CRM system to other external systems, validating and normalizing different data formats.
- The other component is the Application layer, including Internet sales, telesales, call center, campaign management, and others that manage business objects, such as customers or prospects, activities, opportunities, products, and catalogs.

The three scenarios into which the full mySAP CRM solution is commonly divided are:

- Internet sales
- Mobile sales
- CIC (Contact Information Center)

Let's take a closer look at each of these components.

Internet Sales

Since release 3.1H, SAP R/3 included the Online Store as an IAC (*Internet Application Component*), and therefore had functionality for selling through the Web. It is obvious that as electronic commerce evolves, the Web-based selling scenarios must cover both the actual realization of selling as well as other selling characteristics, such as the marketing campaigns and so on. That is, it must also include those tools and facilities included within the mySAP CRM solution, such as:

- Product catalog
- One-to-one marketing
- Promotions
- Shopping basket management
- Registration for new customers
- Payments
- Order tracking

From a technical point of view, those transactions for searching, browsing, and handling of multimedia files are clearly positioned outside the SAP R/3 back-end systems.

The Internet sales is a four-tier architecture: Logistics Execution, Business Service, Interaction, and Presentation. The components for these levels are shown in the following Figure 3-3.

The following list summarizes the components for the Internet Sales scenario:

- To provide the functionality for an Internet browser, the system requires at least an ITS (*Internet Transaction Server*). (Extensive information about ITS can be found in Chapter 4, "SAP Internet Transaction Server").
- The products catalogs are exported from the CRM system to an external index server for faster access. Those catalogs and multimedia files are stored within the CRM system in the component known as SAP Knowledge Provider (KPRO) before being published in the index server.

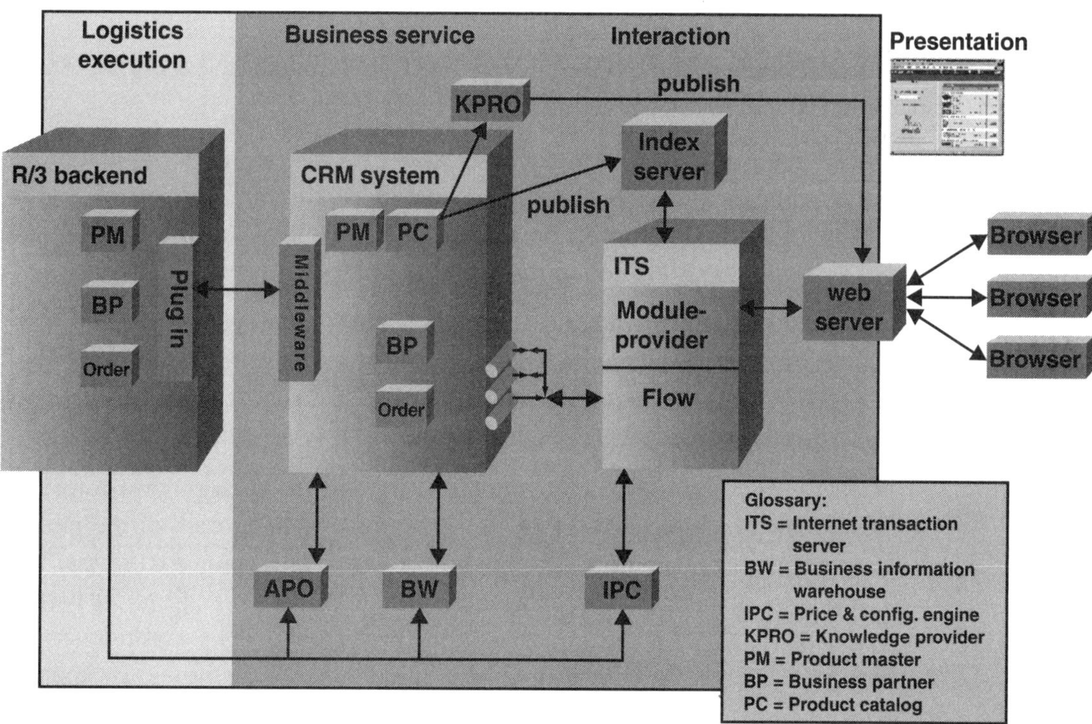

FIGURE 3-3 *mySAP CRM logical four-tier architecture*

- The IPC (*Internet Pricing and Configurator*) component provides the price and configuration options for the products. This information is obtained from the back-end SAP system, ensuring the faster access required for Internet-based scenarios.
- The IPC component and the CRM system are connected indirectly by the ITS. The changes in the configuration and prices once the initial download from the R/3 is completed are performed in an incremental way.

Mobile Sales: Services

Mobile sales is the scenario designed for supporting the sales force activities, as well as other company employees linked with those selling activities. In these types of scenarios, it is common that users work in *offline* mode using portable computers or PDAs (*personal data assistants*).

Every mobile device has its own application to perform tasks such as activities, opportunities, promotions, campaigns, and so on, besides having all the information about customers, contacts, products, and catalogs. The application is unique in content for each of the mobile devices. The CRM middleware component is in charge of synchronizing and updating that information.

The individual configuration of contents to be received for each of the mobile devices is performed using a component known as Admin Console (see Figure 3-4). It must be observed that those replication rules that are managed by the Admin Console are also stored in the CRM system.

The look and the user interface, as well as the definition of new business objects, is designed using a component known as WorkBench Application Studio (see Figure 3-4), and there are standard mechanisms for the distribution of new releases or support packages for the mobile devices.

The CRM system includes the functionality and tools for managing the information flow, which maintains the status of that information for each of the mobile devices. In this way, every time that one of those devices is connected to the central CRM system, there is an exchange of information both ways, from the mobile device to the CRM system and the other way around. The communication between the mobile devices and the CRM middleware is performed by another component known as the Communication Station (see Figure 3-4).

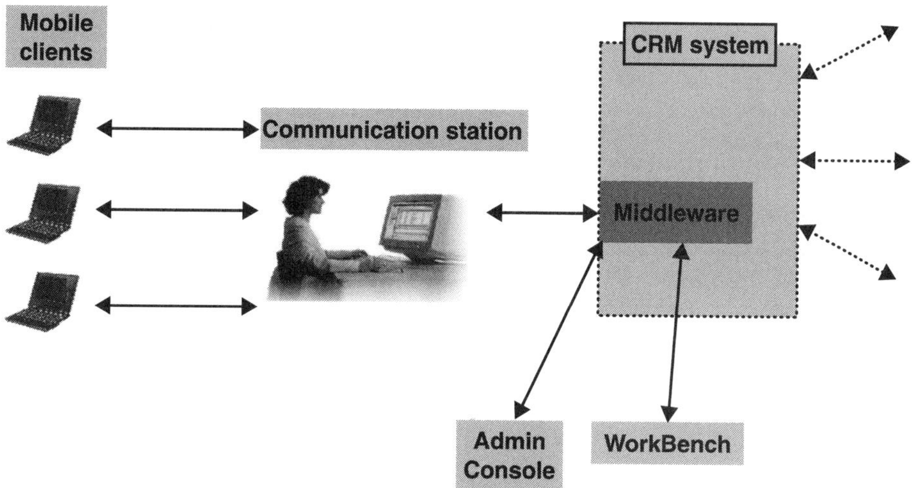

FIGURE 3-4 *Mobile sales components*

CIC

CIC is the most common and traditional scenario in the CRM application world. It allows for the interaction of the business partners with the customer information and support center, using all available channels such as phone, fax, mail, and so on.

mySAP CRM provides the integration of standard components from the Basis middleware such as SAPphone and SAPconnect, which are in charge of providing the communication support which are initiated from inside or toward the outside (see Figure 3-5).

SAPphone acts as the interface among the application components, the complex CTI (*Computer Telephony Integration*) middleware, and the telephony components for providing direct access from phone systems and the CRM system. For the CTI interface to work with guarantee, the providers of CTI solutions must be certified by SAP through the CSP (*Complementary Software Program*).

The SAPconnect interface is used together with the SAP Business Workflow to support the complete e-mail process. SAPconnect directs the mail to the SAPOffice component as an integral part of the mySAP CRM. Depending on the recipient address and the Workflow definitions, the mail is directed to a predefined set of queues, and the sender can receive a delivery notification.

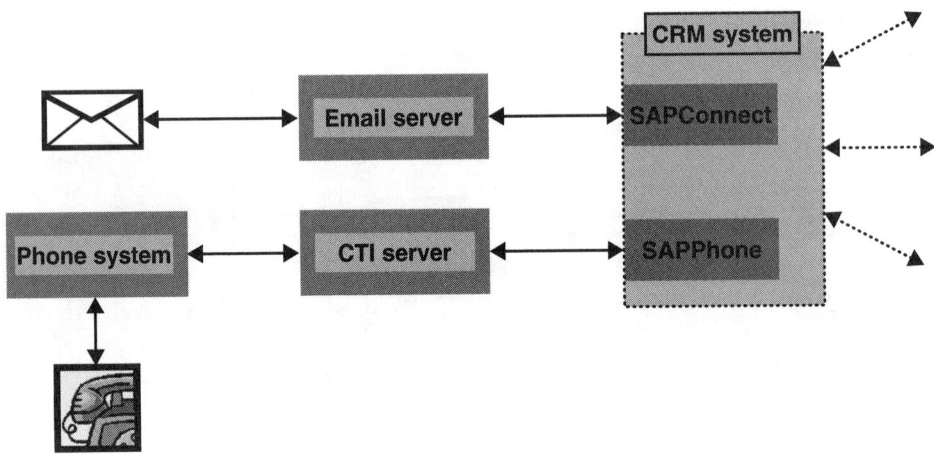

FIGURE 3-5 *Communication support for mySAP CRM*

The contact center solution provides knowledge management tools such as an SDB (*Solution Database*) and an IIA (*Interactive Intelligent Agent*). The SDB provides not only a structure of solutions, but also a search engine based on fuzzy logic and an index compiler.

mySAP CRM Services: Functions and Professional Profiles

Around the CRM world, there is a complete set of services to cover the design, building, implementation, and operation of both business processes and systems. In the market, there are four big areas of CRM services: application consulting, systems integrators, outsourcing, and training.

According to market data compiled by prestigious analysts IDC, CRM services in 1998 approached $32 billion, with a projection of an annual growth rate around 22 percent or more, which could represent a revenue of $89.7 billion in year 2003 (*The Global CRM Services Market: Major Players and Market Forecast, 1998–2003*, IDC #20207, September 1999).

For those services and projects around CRM, SAP has built a specific ASAP for CRM based on the AcceleratedSAP methodology in which it makes a distinction among five different consulting functions in order to categorize the different activities or tasks to be performed in a CRM project. From the SAP point of view, of the required specific knowledge, those five consulting functions are as follows:

- Strategy consulting (project management)
  - Generalist for SAP products in general and CRM products in particular
  - Generalist for CRM implementation projects
  - Expertise in project management
  - Expertise in CRM implementation strategies and methodologies
  - Understanding of the other CRM functions
- Application consulting
  - CRM scenarios (mobile sales SD and mobile services CS)
  - CRM business processes
  - Implementation methodology
  - Analysis, specification, and tests of customer requirements
  - Customizing through Workbench
  - Database queries
  - Reading and understanding ABAP, VB, and HTML programs
- Technical application consulting
  - Software engineering
  - Detailed conception of customer requirements
  - Customization of middleware through Workbench and Admin Console
  - Database design
  - Use programming language (ABAP, VB, HTML)
- Basis consulting
  - Design of system architecture
  - Installation and administration of systems
  - Database management
  - Complex programming
- Specialist
  - Detailed knowledge of specific components (APO, BW, B2B, ITS, and so on)

In order to achieve those tasks, ASAP distinguishes up to nine different roles that directly have a function in a mySAP CRM project: Project Sponsor, Project

Manager, Application Consultant Lead, Application Consultant, Technical Application Consultant Lead, Technical Application Consultant, Basis Consultant Lead, Basis Consultant, and Specialist.

An approach to handling projects in the mySAP.com world is presented in Chapter 9, "mySAP Projects."

mySAP E-Procurement

Under the umbrella of the mySAP e-procurement Cross-Industry Solution, SAP includes the procurement solutions that have jointly developed with Commerce-One in their SAPMarkets alliance. These e-procurement solutions are based on the Enterprise Buyer software, which has two flavors: Desktop and Professional.

Enterprise Buyer Professional is the evolution of the SAP Business-to-Business Procurement (BBP) solution, which is described in the following sections.

SAP BBP

There is no doubt about the need of an enterprise to buy goods or materials as part of its supply chain. Thinking about a Web-based automation solution for purchases—beginning with nonproduction materials and services—has become the strategy of the supply-chain management. At this point, I should classify materials into two groups: *direct* and *indirect* materials.

With direct materials, I am considering those that are integrated in the company's production planning processes, like raw materials—wood, metal—auxiliary materials, or components for the production. In other words, direct goods are the components of manufactured products. On the other side, with indirect materials, I could consider those referred to maintenance, such as services, or operations, such as office supplies. Indirect materials are normally known as MRO (*Maintenance, Repair, and Operations*) procurement. Business procurement is not simple and in fact comprises both direct and indirect procurement.

BBP As Part of mySAP.com

When talking about BBP, you can think about one of the business scenarios provided by mySAP.com solution. SAP BBP is the purchasing component of mySAP.com, presented as a Web-based e-procurement solution that supports companies with the procurement of direct and indirect materials. With BBP you can map the complete procurement process, from creating a requirement coverage request to the end of the process, presenting the invoice. For the fulfillment of the different tasks the user only has to use a simple Web interface. The functionality provided by the SAP BBP solution is being incremented with the different product versions.

A Little Bit of History

Although everybody is talking about the new e-solutions that are in the market as brand new solutions, I can already talk about history. This short history reflects the revolution that e-business supposes for software manufacturers. Changes and continuous improvements are happening these days. SAP is not an exception, and mySAP.com scenarios are subject to changes that improve their functionality.

First Release BBP 1.0B

This release was prepared to provide an Internet solution to map the procurement process for indirect materials (operating supplies) and services. The process began with the creation of the requirement coverage request and ended with the invoice or service entry sheet. During the process, vendors and service providers entered the invoices or services provided in SAP system through a browser and by connecting with the system.

As you can see, the procurement process of nonproduction materials changes from the conventional way performed by a purchasing department. SAP BBP enables the employees to handle procurement of goods and services by themselves. That is, all the employees can carry out the following tasks from their desk:

- Search for suitable products that meet their requirements in catalogs
- Create a shopping basket and check requirement status
- Enter the goods' receipts for the materials
- Approve the invoice or service entry sheet

There are other roles in the procurement process. These roles are developed by different employees in the organization. In a very simple way, you have to suppose that BBP helps them to know which tasks have to be achieved by the different roles.

The way to automate the flow of information among the different employees involved in a procurement process is by means of SAP Business Workflow. It helps end users to know which tasks are waiting for a decision or a special action (for example, approval shopping basket action). Even in these earlier releases, BBP included some standard Workflows, like:

- **RCRs (*Requirement Coverage Requests*).** Workflow for one-step approval or no approval depending on conditions like amount of shopping basket items
- **Service sheet entries.** Workflow for one-step approval or no approval

Release BBP 2.0B

You have to consider that providing a Web interface to the end user that is strongly connected with the ERP (*Enterprise Resource Planner*) system is not enough to support an e-solution for the procurement process. You can summarize the main advantages of these releases in the following issues:

- The SAP BBP application can run either independently or connected with the R/3 Material Management system, allowing for more flexibility.
- Connectivity to multiple back-end systems or instances (SAP R/3 or non-SAP systems) is permitted.
- There are new role-based scenarios in order to adapt to business functionality (for example, accountant, administrator, vendor and bidder, employee, manager, component planner, professional purchaser, goods recipient, secretary). Users can have more than one role assigned to their user account. Role-based scenarios allow assigning different tasks to different users in the procurement process.
- As an example based on role scenario, professional purchasers are supposed to process and complete local purchase orders in the SAP BBP system. In addition, the professional purchasers have the new function of creating public or restricted bid invitations—in case bidders are known—for goods and services in the systems. The biddings received can be converted in a reverse auction, that is, buyers post their needs for a product or service, and then suppliers bid to fulfill that need. By this process, the administrator user can provide suppliers with a user account in order to log on to the BBP system and enter their bids.
- Another functionality based in role scenario is component planner. Plant maintenance orders that are created by the back-end PM (*Product Master*) module can be fulfilled by SAP BBP. It's now able to read the

PM orders directly from the PM system, and the component planner is able to search for product or services by external catalog and then update the PM system on the back end.

- As of release 2.0B, the one-step business in which you can integrate purchasing and sales in a single step is possible. For example, it's possible to send an XML message from the BBP system to the vendor when a purchase order is created, allowing the creation of a sales order in the supplier system.
- The SAP BBP provides an OCI (*open catalog interface*) to interact with external catalogs such as Requisite.
- It provides, as of release 2.0B, integration with the BW (*Business Information Warehouse*).

Enterprise Buyer 2.0 and SAP BBP 2.0C

Previous releases covered only MRO procurement. As of 2.0C, it is possible to procure direct materials using SAP BBP. You can consider now that it supports full integration with the company production planning process. Indeed, one of the new features is integration with SAP APO (*Advanced Planner and Optimizer*) solution.

For catalog access it provides a new XML interface for supporting formats such as Requisite, xCBL, and BMEcat. It's also possible to log on to the system from mobile devices using a WAP (*Wireless Application Protocol*) phone or a PDA with a WML (*Wireless Markup Language*) enabled browser.

From the architectural point of view, a SAP BBP application can be hosted on a single enterprise SAP BBP system on a marketplace. The business functions are used by one buying company to procure goods and services from connected vendors. The buying company can have, as with all SAP BBP installations, its ERP in a SAP or non-SAP system.

Advantages of SAP BBP

When talking about MRO procurement, imagine that the processing costs for purchaser orders created by a purchasing department are similar, independently of the cost of the goods procured. So, as an example, the transaction cost for our purchasing department should be reduced if employees were able to manage the procurement of office supplies, which on the other hand used to be low-cost items.

Nevertheless, MRO products are only a small portion of the products, services, and materials needed for the core business. The direct procurement process is more difficult, complicated by supplier contracts, custom-made products from raw materials, and the need of a detailed specification for a product. So there is no doubt that a Web-based solution that supports both direct and indirect procurement will help the organization to improve its supply chain management.

The benefits that a BBP solution provides buying organizations can be summarized in the following key topics:

- Reduction of costs due to better control over the supply chain as well as the significant decrease of administration costs.
- Better management of suppliers enabling realtime integration.
- Faster and more efficient procurement process that enables users to quickly deploy the system in a self-service fashion.
- Better pricing and conditions due to the possibility of comparing suppliers' offerings, Internet biddings, and reverse auctions.
- Integration with plant maintenance, allowing users to quickly order material for repairs, as well as the use of automatic ordering.
- Additional business possibilities for suppliers through the broadening of their potential buyer base by means of publishing and offering their products and services in online catalogs and marketplaces.

Processes

In the following sections is a brief description of some of the main business processes supported or included within the mySAP e-procurement solution, that is, functionality included in the Enterprise Buyer software.

Procurement Process

The diagram below (Figure 3-6) illustrates the typical process flow for the procurement process using SAP BBP.

1. Users log on to the SAP BBP. The initial screen for the procurement process appears with different possible functions depending on the role assigned to the user.
2. Create shopping basket. Employees can create shopping baskets in different ways: by product selection in a catalog, by product number that

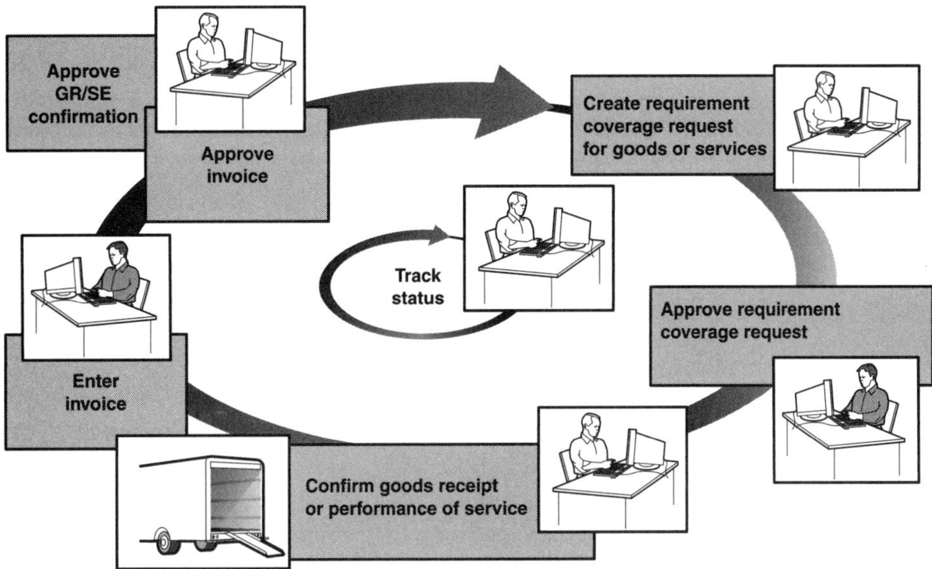

FIGURE 3-6 *Procurement process* Copyright by SAP AG

exists in the SAP BBP and can be downloaded from the back-end system, or even by a product description. Account assignment can be introduced when the shopping basket is created or when the purchase order or invoice is generated.

3. Create shopping basket with limit. Employees or purchasers can also create a shopping basket with a value limit and a validity period. In this case you can enter confirmations, services, and invoices up to this limit.
4. Approve shopping basket. Depending on the conditions configured in the Workflows provided by BBP, the shopping basket may need an approval. Depending on the amount of the shopping basket, it has to be one step or two step approved.
5. Process shopping basket. Employees can process RFQs for which no back-end document is created in order to change or delete shopping basket.
6. Check status. Employees can check status of shopping basket and if, for instance, it is not approved, change it according to comments and reroute approval flow.
7. Edit purchase order. Purchasers can edit or complete the purchase order if the employee has created an incomplete shopping basket, for example no vendor specified.

8. Purchase order output. The purchase order can be sent to the vendor by XML, EDI, mail, or fax.
9. Confirm goods receipt or performance of service. Employees can take this action when service or goods have been delivered. This action can also be performed by a central group of employees or even the supplier, if he can log on to the BBP system.
10. Enter invoice. Employees or even vendors can introduce invoices in the BBP system. The invoice may be subject to an approval Workflow. These invoices can be created locally for purchase order in the BBP system or in the back-end system through the BBP.

Tendering

If a company deals with a long number or RFQs (*Requests for Quotation*), tendering may be in the scope of a project for a BBP implementation. The following Figure 3-7 shows a typical bid invitation process.

1. Create bid invitation. Purchasers of an organization can create public or restricted bid invitations for materials and services. A bid invitation is a listing and description of materials and services to be procured. Bids with conditions are expected in response to a bid invitation. A public bid invitation is made accessible to all potential bidders through a marketplace. A restricted bid invitation is made accessible only to known vendors or business partners.
2. Submit bids. Bidders can log on to the SAP BBP system and create bids. They can see all open bid invitations in the system.
3. Process bids. Purchasers can compare bids and accept or reject them, notifying the bidder. Purchaser can directly create a purchase order from the best bid or convert the bid invitation into a reverse auction. Bidders are informed about this, and all bidders see the best price offered for the bid invitation. Of course, they can offer it at a lower price if they wish.

Component Planning with External Catalogs

If a company uses the plan maintenance module, you can configure the SAP BBP to use the component planning, as shown in Figure 3-8.

With this functionality, you can select additional components from Web-based catalogs for your maintenance or service orders. You can display order data from

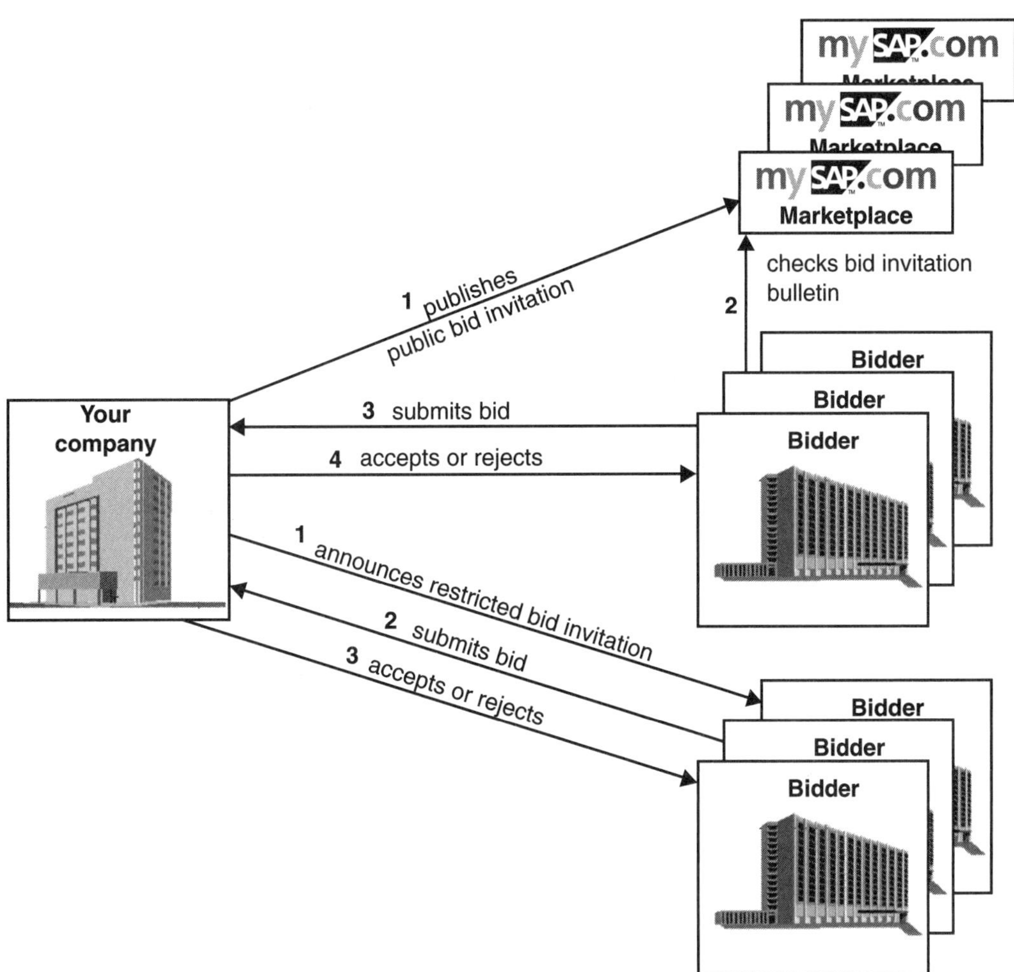

FIGURE 3-7 *Bid invitation process* Copyright by SAP AG

SAP back-end system in SAP BBP and enhance it. Once you have finished, data is transferred back to SAP back-end system.

Procurement Cards

Procurement Cards (PCards) are commonly used as a means of payment in different companies. In the SAP BBP you can specify PCards as a payment method when purchasing items.

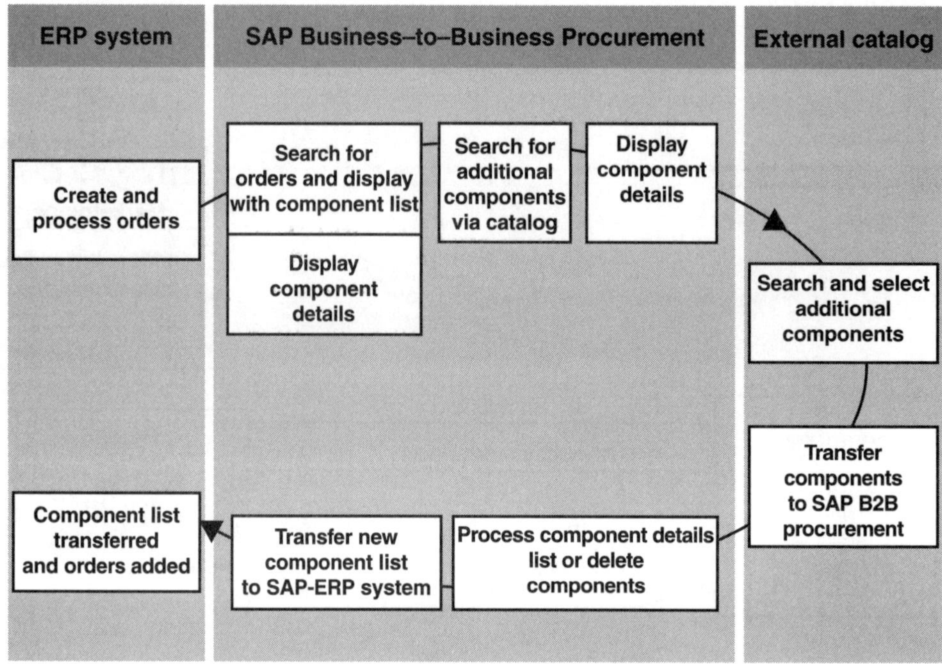

FIGURE 3-8 *Component planning process* Copyright by SAP AG

Implementation Scenarios

SAP BBP is a separate SAP system. Depending on its customizing settings, you can use it in a heterogeneous system environment with one or several back-end systems. The functionality to cover financial accounting and controlling must exist in the back-end system, whether it's a SAP or a non-SAP system. There are different scenarios that can be implemented with SAP BBP, with different customizing for each of them.

Classic Scenario

The SAP BBP system communicates the main Business Process to the ERP system where requisitions, purchase orders, goods receipts, service entry sheets, and invoices are created. This scenario supposes that all materials management functionality is mapped in the ERP system. Figure 3-9 shows this scenario.

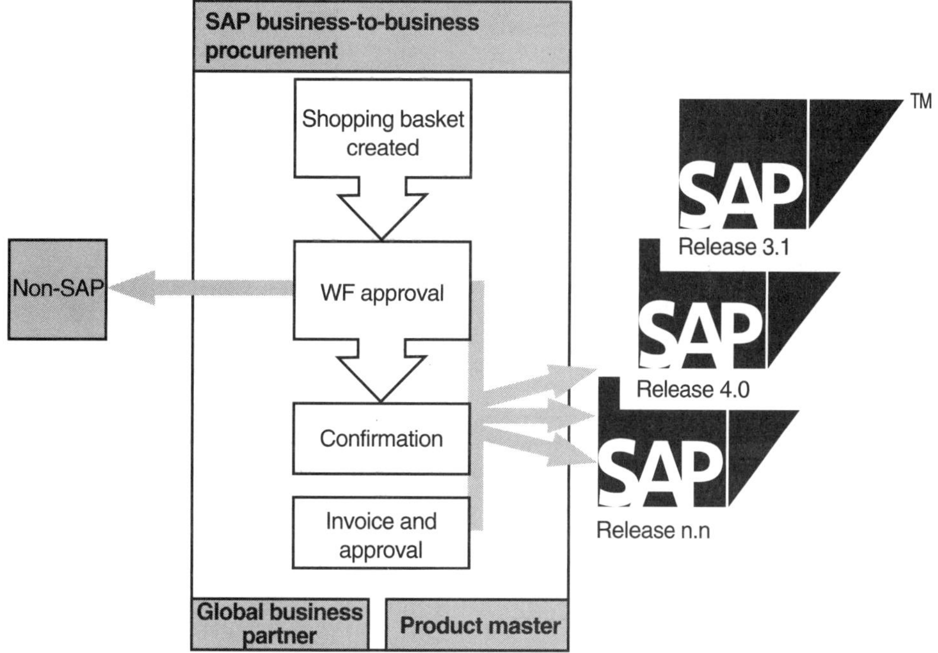

FIGURE 3-9 *BBP classic scenario with multiple back-end systems*

Standalone Scenario

In case your organization does not have the material management module installed, you can use this scenario. In this case, all materials management documents are generated in the SAP BBP system. The accounting process is performed in the back-end system. The BBP standalone scenario is shown in Figure 3-10.

Decoupled Scenario

If you mix both of the previous scenarios, you get the decoupled scenario. In this case, parts of the purchasing process are handled locally in the BBP system, and other parts in the back-end system. You can create shopping baskets for items contained in the BBP product master system that correspond to products replicated from your back-end system to the BBP. In this scenario, the materials management documents are created in the corresponding system. You identify which system corresponds depending on customizing settings and application data such as "Product Category." Figure 3-11 shows the BBP decoupled scenario.

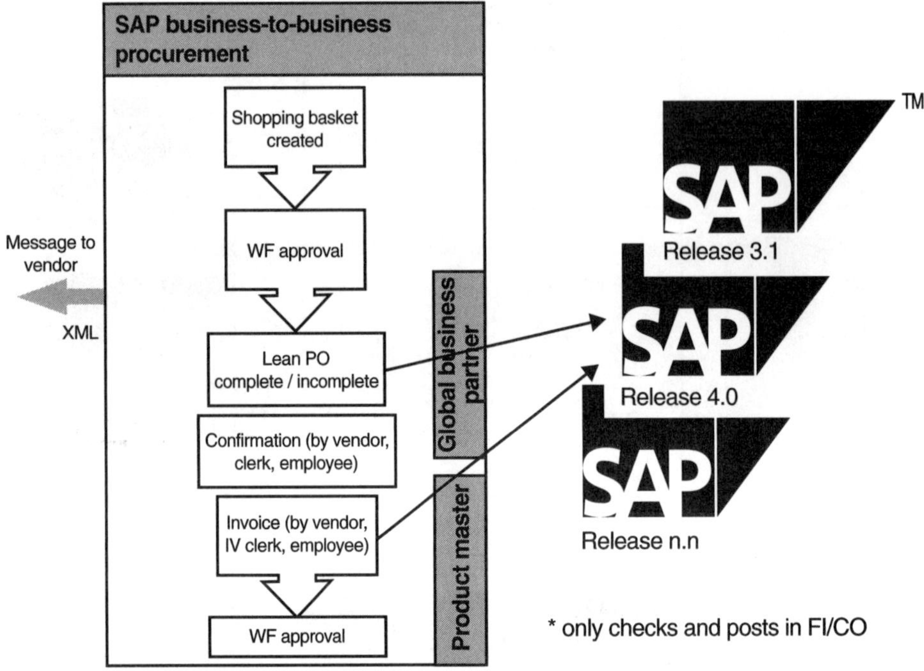

FIGURE 3-10 *BBP standalone scenario*

BBP Architecture

In the following sections is a brief introduction to the BBP (Enterprise Buyer) architecture.

Functional Components

From a very high level, SAP BBP presents a four-tier scalable architecture represented in the following Figure 3-12.

The following Figure 3-13 provides an overview of the functional components as of release 2.0B.

These functional components are:

- The software that interacts with the user and provides the Web interface referred to as Web browser.
- The software to provide access to the Web that interacts with the Web server referred to as the ITS. It allows interactive Web access to the SAP system.

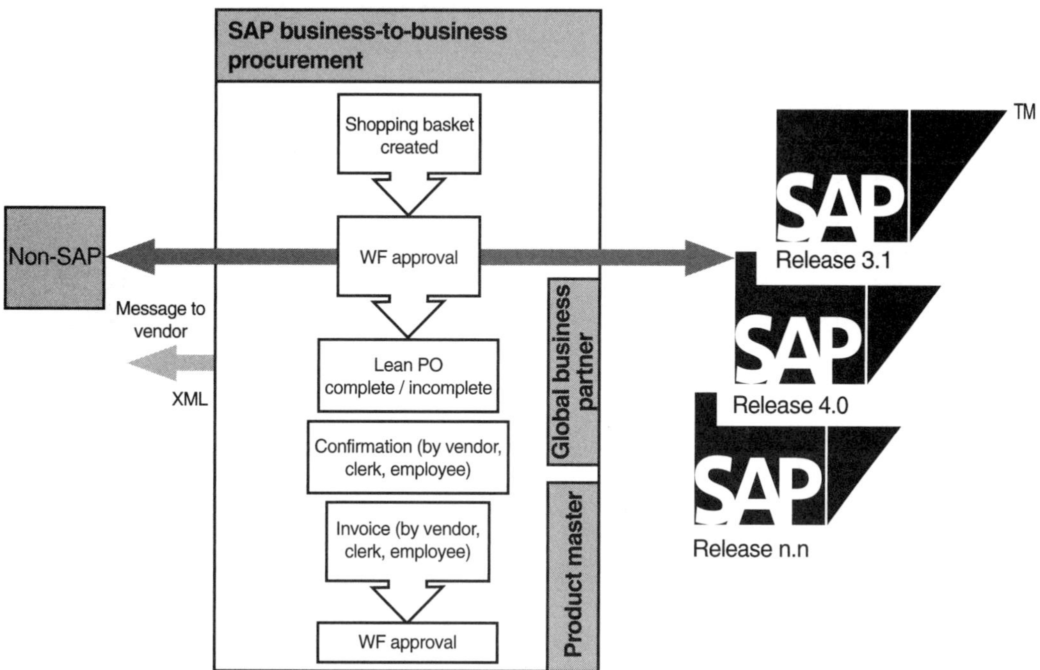

FIGURE 3-11 *BBP decoupled scenario*

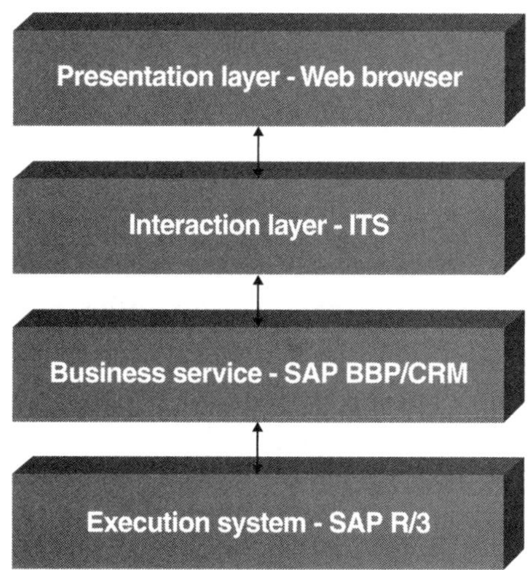

FIGURE 3-12 *BBP four-tier architecture*

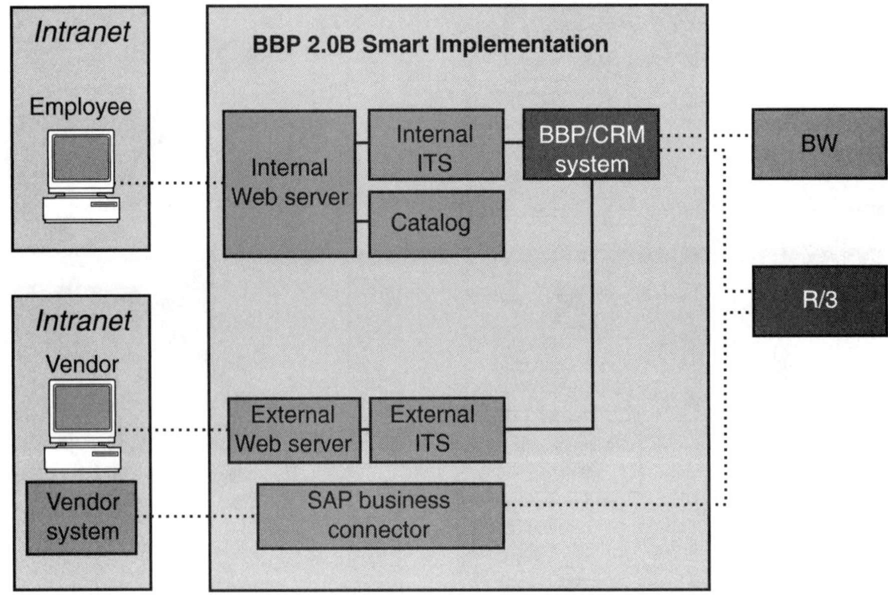

FIGURE 3-13 *BBP functional components* Copyright by SAP AG

- The software that provides the business service referred to as SAP BBP/CRM. This is a special SAP system based on the SAP system Basis release 4.6C (for BBP 2.0B). The BBP user interface and business process run on this system.
- The system where the ERP system runs is called the execution system or OLTP (*Online Transaction Processing*). You can have multiple connections to different back-end systems and non-SAP systems. With this architecture, the back-end systems, where you can have your core system, are protected from a high Internet/intranet user interaction.
- SAP Business Connector uses the Internet as a communication platform and XML/HTML as data format. In the BBP the Business Connector can be used for transmitting data over the Internet, like purchase orders, sales orders, shipping notifications, invoices, and catalog data.
- Catalog is for finding products in external electronic catalogs; requisite can be an example. Only remember that as of BBP 2.0C, formats such as Requisite (supports OCI), xCBL, and BMEcat are supported.

Technical Details

The following Figure 3-14 shows a more detailed diagram of the components, as well as the flow of information among them.

From this figure, if you look at flow of information between different components, you can describe the following components and interfaces:

- Plug in: If the back-end system is an ERP SAP R/3, you need to install a component in this system in order to be able to interact in a standard way with the OLTP system. The flow of information between the BBP system and the OLTP is by means of RFC (*Remote Function Calls*) and ALE (*Application Link Enabled*). SAP BBP is able to communicate with different back-end systems, SAP systems as well as non-SAP systems. For this reason there is an Abstraction layer that encapsulates the BAPI (*business application programming interface*) calls in the back-end system

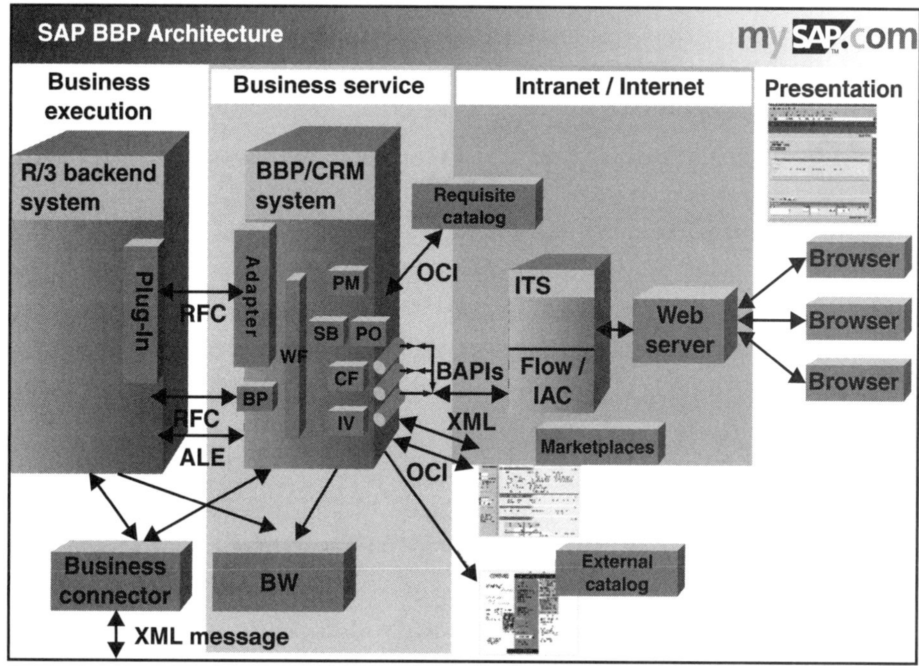

FIGURE 3-14 *Detailed components of the SAP BBP* Copyright by SAP AG

which are necessary to generate the back-end documents for RCRs. This Abstraction layer analyzes the customizing settings in order to know which driver it must call, which back-end system it is communicating with, and the back-end release. The driver module is the one that calls the BAPIs in the back-end system.

- The connection to the business service where the CRM and BBP software resides is enabled by the ITS. From the ITS by means of flow logic or IACs and using BAPIs, you get the BBP system where you can create the shopping basket (SB), Purchase Order (PO), Confirmations (CF), and Invoices (IV). This business process runs in the BBP component, and the automation is controlled by standard Workflows already implemented in the system. As you've seen, the flow between the BBP component and the OLTP system depends on the scenario you have chosen for your implementation.
- The shopping basket can be created with products from the PM, which means the products replicated in the BBP system from the OLTP system, or by accessing external catalogs. The access to external catalogs like Requisite is by means of XML messaging according to the published OCI interface, although I've already said that this has been improved in latest releases.
- From the BBP system or even the back-end system, you can exchange information with suppliers by means of Business Connectors whose output is XML messages. Through XML messaging, you can implement scenarios like receiving XML confirmations by the vendor or XML invoicing, where a vendor can log on to the SAP BPP system to enter an invoice and then download it to its own system with XML.
- We can integrate or communicate BBP with marketplaces by means of XML messages. XML messaging also offers the possibility for sending and receiving documents over mySAP.com or other software that supports XML.
- Also in Figure 3-14, you can see the integration with SAP Business Information Warehouse.

From a technical point of view, SAP BBP can be integrated as a component system into the mySAP Workplace.

mySAP Business Intelligence

mySAP Business Intelligence is the Cross-Industry Solution that aims to provide valuable information and knowledge about the company operations by integrating data and information from all the rest of the components of mySAP.com e-business platform and from non-SAP systems. The Business Intelligence solutions provide a general knowledge framework so that companies can better understand the operation's key figures, the performance metrics, having a strategic cockpit, or gathering and sharing the knowledge assets.

The mySAP Business Intelligence solutions have three different application components:

- SAP Business Information Warehouse (SAP BW)
- SAP Knowledge Management (SAP KM)
- SAP Strategic Enterprise Management (SAP SEM)

Together the applications within the mySAP Business Intelligence solutions are aimed to provide a comprehensive set of functionality for solving data warehousing, data analysis, strategic performance management, and knowledge management needs. The following sections briefly introduce these three components.

SAP Business Information Warehouse

The Business Information Warehouse (SAP BW) is one of the components of the mySAP Business Intelligence Cross-Industry Solution and has become a key solution component for other applications, such as APO and SEM.

SAP first introduced BW in 1997 as one of the major components of the Business Framework architecture and as one of the first New Dimension products. BW is the data warehousing solution, critical in the overall mySAP.com e-business platform.

The importance and use of data warehouse and data mining techniques generally have been increasing during the last few years in the search for business intelligence, particularly in the collection of tools and applications that support company-wide knowledge.

Data warehouses and analytical tools used for unleashing the meaning of huge amounts of data are thought of as an integral component of getting business knowledge feedback. The analytical processes supported by the SAP BW is key to provide a broader business knowledge that can give feedback on the continuous change and improvement on companies by providing key figures and taking business decisions.

Architecture of the BW

Figure 3-15 shows an overview of the SAP BW conceptual architecture.

SAP strategy is to position the BW as a ready-to-go warehouse, including all the components required by a global data warehouse architecture and all the tools for designing, extracting, building, and managing the system.

- **OLAP processor (server).** This includes the data and information models from SAP systems. SAP BW includes information models and report libraries for all the SAP business areas.
- **Metadata repository.** This manages and controls the full data warehouse environment.
- **Administrator Workbench.** This is the central data warehouse management tool, which can be used for maintaining and extending the BW.

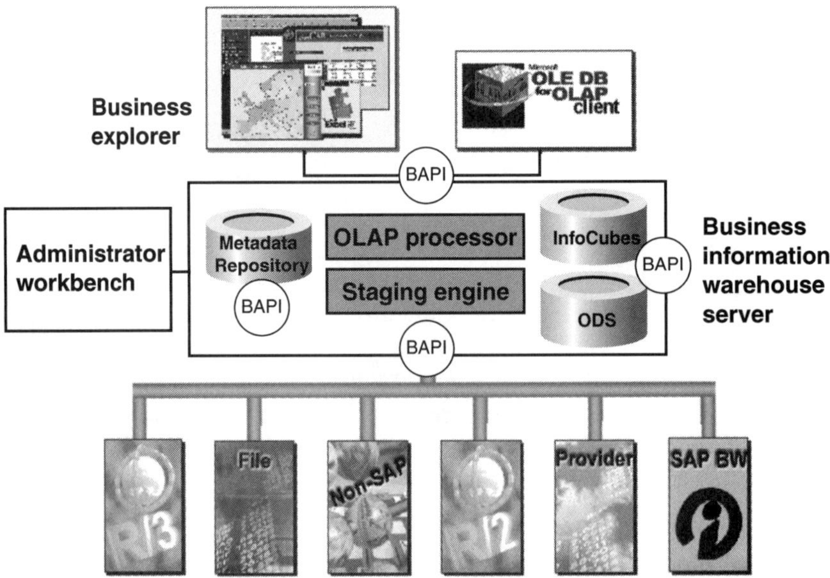

FIGURE 3-15 *SAP BW architecture* Copyright by SAP AG

- **Business Explorer.** This user interface is based on Excel and Internet technology and contains a large standard report library, as well as the required analysis tools. The Business Explorer works as an information catalog, allowing users to browse the available information from the business applications. The analysis tools that can support complex and multidimensional analysis based on different data views is also a central component of the BW.
- **Staging engine.** Additionally, the BW includes the processes that can automatically extract the data from the source SAP systems and from other external data sources. These are represented by a staging engine with integrated data staging routines that normally run in the background, supplying the BW with current data from data sources. These routines can run at predefined update intervals and are managed from the Administrator Workbench.

All the communication processes between the SAP BW and data sources are based on BAPIs, which provide a large degree of openness and extendibility so that the BW can be integrated with other applications, data sources, or tools.

The SAP BW systems can be used by all types of users. Besides its main purpose of providing business intelligence and historical performance and key figures to other mySAP components such as APO or SEM, it can also be an alternative or a complement to the standard SAP reporting options, and therefore it can help reduce the load and impact on performance of extensive online reporting.

The BW kernel is based on the SAP Internet Business Framework architecture and uses the traditional SAP Basis system and technology as the middleware, making it just as safe, open, and scalable as traditional R/3 systems. The next releases will possibly change the SAP Basis by the SAP Web Application Server.

Additionally, there is a smooth integration between the BW metadata repository and the ABAP repository, so changes in objects and processes can be immediately transferred to the BW. Users can use the provided and predefined BW reports or can use them as models and create their own. The use of Web browsers and Excel spreadsheets makes analysis and reporting quite easy and simple. Just like many other mySAP components, the BW also includes *wizards* for creating new reports, as well as much functionality for users to customize their own reporting and analysis environment.

Another key point of the SAP BW strategy is its very low implementation costs, because the kit includes all the needed models, configurations, and staging services for being able to work with data from other SAP systems right out of the box. This makes the need for data modeling only for special purposes or when loading the warehouse with external legacy systems.

SAP Knowledge Management

Because of the evidence that most of today's workforce is based on knowledge, knowledge management has been recognized as one of the company's biggest assets. The business goal for knowledge management is to transform individual knowledge into corporate knowledge. Knowledge is generically considered as both the technical abilities to perform and accumulated experience.

The SAP Knowledge Warehouse is the central software component of the SAP KM initiative for providing business and individuals with a continuous learning solution and knowledge transfer.

What Is Knowledge Management?

We are used to considering the economic indicators as the key figures to measure the success of companies. These indicators have been the result of the combination of three classical production factors: labor, capital, and assets (real estate, gold, and so on). The specific weight of these three factors has been evolving according to the different periods in which the economy cycles passed.

In the agricultural society, the real estate goods represented the most important aspect in the generation of wealth, whereas in the industrial society, it was labor. However, in recent periods, capital has passed over both previous factors. Nowadays, in the society that some authors have started to define as the knowledge society, it is not enough to create, accumulate, and maintain the labor, the capital, and the assets to become successful. It is becoming increasingly essential for companies to be able to grow their intellectual capital, which is the sum of the knowledge of the individual company employees, and make it accessible to everyone who needs it in the moment that they need it. That is knowledge management and its integration with the intangible assets of a company.

The definition of knowledge is classically defined by opposing the definition of data and information, because it could be relatively easy to misunderstand these concepts. A simple way to differentiate these concepts is:

- **Data.** Something represented in text, figures, drawing, facts, and so on, but always out of context
- **Information.** That data, but organized and presented in a specific context
- **Knowledge.** The information and the way to use it

Other more comprehensive definitions by the knowledge management gurus define knowledge management as the integration of the information management (known as explicit knowledge) of the processes (encapsulated knowledge), of the persons (tacit knowledge), of the innovation (knowledge conversion), and of the intangible assets or intellectual capital.

As important as the information stored in any type of media (explicit knowledge) is the tacit knowledge. For example, if someone asked a new hired employee about how she acquired certain vital information, the answer would most probably be that she asked a coworker. This typical situation shows a critical aspect of any knowledge management solution: organizations must be able to motivate their components to share the information, including also the informal ways of transferring that knowledge. All that means is that it's required that a certain business culture be achieved so that it allows the realization of that knowledge transfer; if this requirement does not exist, the solution will not reach the maximum degree of efficiency.

In summary, knowledge management is in charge of delivering knowledge to everyone who needs it at the moment they need it, covering the knowledge transfer, both explicit and tacit, and being able to transform the personal knowledge (tacit) into organizational knowledge (explicit).

Knowledge Management within the mySAP Platform

One of the most important features of the Workplace solution within the mySAP e-business platform is to provide the employees with all the required information and tools for performing their daily work, adapting that offer to the specific needs of different job positions (roles) that use that technology. Within that global offer it is also necessary to help people to find the information they need and provide access to other persons. These are the two main points that the knowledge management solution provides to the mySAP global solution.

An important challenge of any knowledge management solution is to determine who needs what type of knowledge. The solution to this problem is contained within some of the main features of the mySAP Human Resources solution, such as the employee profiles for their job position, the historical data of training received, the assessments and evaluations, and so on. By combining this information with the description of the job position and specifically with the roles to which the employees are assigned, it is possible to determine which information can be accessed by the employees through their personalized portal using the mySAP Workplace.

SAP Solution for Knowledge Management

The SAP solution for knowledge management is based in the tools that are contained within four main components:

- Knowledge Warehouse
- Performance Assessment Workbench
- iTutor
- Functionality within mySAP Human Resources

These four components provide the required environment to be able to perform the functions within the knowledge management processes in the company.

The Knowledge Warehouse

The Knowledge Warehouse is the main and most important part of the mySAP solution for knowledge management by providing the needed tools, which can be used to manage the creation, acquisition, modification, transfer, maintenance, and publishing of the information. This is also the repository for any type of information, both structured and not, which is susceptible to being stored in electronic format. By these means, the Knowledge Warehouse provides a knowledge portal with the required infrastructure for design in the form of an intranet, currently considered as the cornerstone of the information transfer within companies.

The content is stored in the form of *information objects,* which can be either physical or logical in a relationship of n to 1 (n:1) in such a way that the structure of the information can be contained in several physical objects that link to a single logical object. With this technique, the user can display only the content that fits a profile, such as the language, version, or any other characteristic defined. This profile is known as *user context.*

Among the main features of the Knowledge Warehouse are the following:

- Editing, creating, and modifying directly in the Web browser
- Possibility for modifying the design of the elements within the Web pages
- Structuring the information elements with cut and paste
- Access to the standard functionality of the SAP Business Workflow
- Integration with the mySAP standard authorization and role system
- Direct access to the information content from the online help of the SAP transactions
- Possibility for linking different documents using hyperlinks
- Workflow for translation
- Editing and modifying documents using the tools with which they were created

Beyond these possibilities, the latest releases of the SAP Knowledge Warehouse are meant to integrate seamlessly with the mySAP Workplace (especially because release 3.0 includes Web Content Management components) to support the design and creation of Enterprise Portals. The following Figure 3-16 shows what might be the building blocks of Enterprise Portals using mySAP solutions.

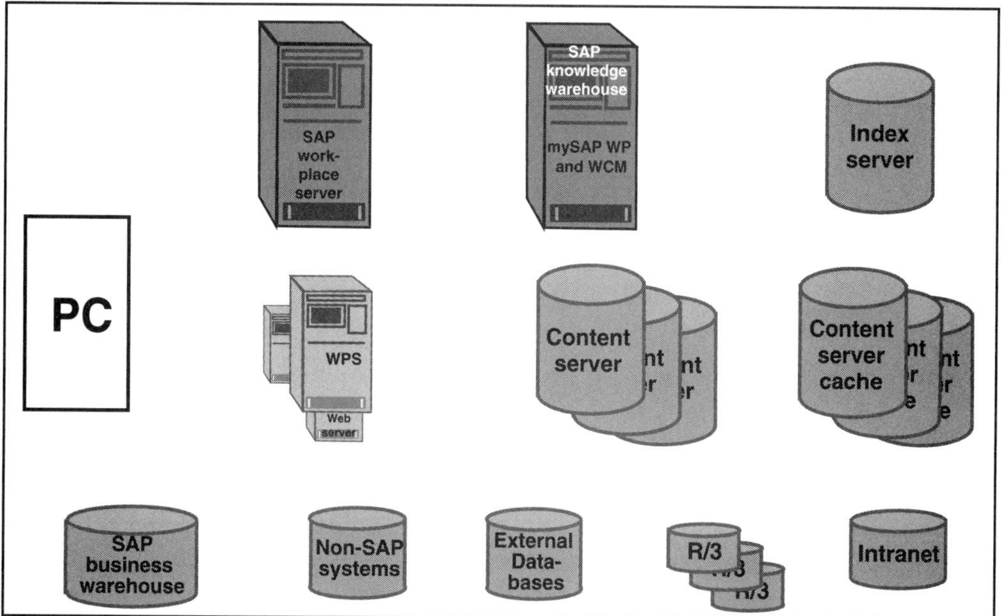

FIGURE 3-16 *Enterprise Portal with the mySAP Workplace and the SAP Knowledge Warehouse*

Performance Assessment Workbench

The PAW (*Performance Assessment Workbench*) provides the required infrastructure to check the efficiency of the received training using the mySAP knowledge management solution. With this tool, it is possible to create assessments before the knowledge acquisition (which are useful for assessing the employee skills in order to receive such training) and also after receiving the training or the information (in order to assess how usable the received training was).

The PAW can be integrated with the management of job profiles and competencies of the Human Resource application in order to establish the real competency level of the employee according to the result of such assessment.

The following are the main features of the PAW:

- Random selection of a question pool
- Multianswer questions
- Establishing different weights for the questions and even within the questions for those multianswer questions
- Utilities for adding text and images to the question design
- Direct link from the PAW to the knowledge contained within the Knowledge Warehouse

iTutor

iTutor is a tool for creating interactive learning units of any application that can be run in a Microsoft Windows environment, without the need for any programming knowledge. iTutor can be used for quickly and easily creating interactive tutorials, which, once integrated in the knowledge circle by means of the Knowledge Warehouse, can be repeated as many times as needed.

iTutor includes three main components: the recorder, the editor, and the viewer. The recording tool is used for fetching and recording in graphical format the application screens being used. The screen captures are done the moment in which the status of the screen changes, like a new screen, because a keystroke was pressed, or because there was some text entered in some screen field. The screens are stored in graphical format, but they provide an important storage savings, because it records those elements that made the status change. The editing component is the one that allows the fine-tuning the result of a previous recording with the introduction of text elements, additional screens, links to other documents, and so on. Finally, users can access and display the execution of the simulation using the viewer. The recorded screens, together with the text elements entered in the simulation, can be printed, which also allows for having a print tutorial of the recorded applications.

Functionality of the Human Resource Application

The functionality contained in the component PD (Personnel Development) of the mySAP Human Resources closes the circle for a full knowledge management solution. The main aspect is related to the management of job profiles and competencies of the employees in the training events management.

For instance, it is possible to link the required knowledge as stored in the KW, so that an employee is able to reach a required competency. Additionally, there is the possibility for linking the assessments contained within the PAW, that confirms that the employee has reached that level of knowledge or competency. Furthermore, the management of training events can also have the knowledge associated with the programmed training course or courses linked.

SAP Strategic Enterprise Management (SEM)

SAP SEM is basically a set of analytical applications within the mySAP Business Intelligence with the purpose of turning business strategy into action. One of the widely known tools or techniques in the world of strategic management is known as the *Balance Scorecard,* first introduced by Kaplan and Norton back in 1992. This tool is fully integrated into the SAP SEM solution. Because there is a close and traditional relationship between business strategy and financials, sometimes you might find the SAP SEM within the mySAP Financials solution. But as it is basically a set of analytical applications, it is better positioned within the mySAP Business Intelligence. Now let's have a closer look at some of the concepts mentioned so that you can get a better understanding of SAP SEM and the functions supported.

All companies must somehow define or formulate a *strategy* to make their business succeed in their market. But the difficult part comes when the strategy must be converted in the many activities to achieve the goals set by the strategy. It is not only a question of specific activities, because management gurus usually distinguish that strategic success comes from the right choice of those activities and the way to perform them.

As a set of analytical tools, SAP SEM includes functions for integrating meaningful financial, operational, and strategic information. The main problem is to transform the management strategic decision to specific and operational activities, and these in all the different business units, at all levels, and taking into account all the enterprise stakeholders. In order for the strategy to be homogeneously understood and implemented, there must be a set of well-defined strategic management processes that can really align the organization with the strategy so as to convert it into specific actions. It must also take into consideration a continuous change and learning process so that these activities can feedback the strategic decision process for further optimization.

In these strategic processes, financial figures are not enough anymore because they usually can tell only past performance, and comparison of planned and real figures of budgets is not a completely accurate measure. For improving some of the traditional shortcomings of traditional strategic analysis, there is a new approach for implementing strategy, which first appeared in 1992. This is the *Balanced Scorecard*, which is defined as the technique that can be used for translating strategies into terms that can be understood, communicated, and acted upon.

This technique is based on clearly defining strategic concepts such as value, customer satisfaction, growth, and others. When a clear strategy has been defined, it then is used as the organizational and management framework. Complementing the financial measures, upper management can monitor the drivers for performance and measure how the different units are creating value and how they could optimize their capabilities to improve their performance.

Based on the Balanced Scorecard concept and techniques, SAP SEM is meant to provide organizations with the solution for implementing strategic management processes. SAP SEM has been one of the first certified solutions from the Balanced Scorecard Collaborative, Inc. (the center of expertise of the Balanced Scorecard concept).

According to SAP, SAP SEM provides many benefits to organizations, enabling them to create value by identifying, simulating, managing, and realizing strategic growth opportunities by:

- Allowing management to control an enterprise internally
- Helping to translate corporate strategy into operational target setting
- Providing an end-to-end solution to support integrated enterprise management processes

- Improving significantly the communication process with stakeholder groups and helping therefore to realize stakeholder value
- Speeding up significantly the legal and management consolidation process by automation
- Enabling continuous and efficient simulation, planning, and forecasting processes across the entire organization
- Providing a powerful infrastructure for KPI (*Key Performance Indicators*) based performance monitoring
- Helping to find, structure, and edit relevant external (unstructured) competitive, market, or other information on an ongoing basis and to automatically distribute it to the appropriate information consumers
- Accelerating implementation through ready-to-use generic and industry-specific content for SEM excellence

Figure 3-17 shows the role of the SAP SEM within the general business processes.

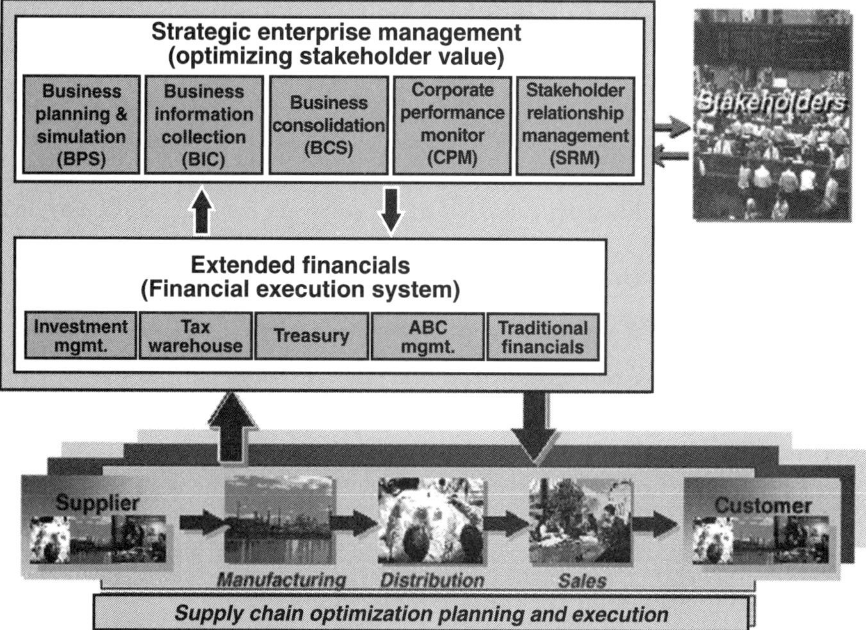

FIGURE 3-17 *SAP strategic enterprise management*

SAP SEM Software Architecture

As I have introduced, the SAP SEM is a set of analytical applications, and it is based on the SAP BW. The SAP SEM software does not require a link to R/3 ERP applications, although when there is a connection, the data collection is then made easier.

There are three different possibilities for installing the SAP SEM:

1. SAP SEM as a stand alone application

   Companies or business units that are installing the SAP SEM are not required to have a previously installed data warehouse (a BW system), since the needed BW functions for operating the stand alone SAP SEM are incorporated inside the SAP SEM. In this case, the SAP SEM will extract data for the backend ERP (such as R/3) or any other external source that might be needed.

2. SAP SEM as a data mart linked with a Data Warehouse

   This is the case of companies or business units wishing to use the SAP SEM separately, who already have an operational data warehouse running, which could be either SAP BW or other third-party software. In either case, the SAP SEM will be installed with the SAP BW technology, and will obtain data by extracting it from the operational data warehouse already in place, as well as from any other required external resource.

3. SAP SEM as a SAP BW application

   The company or unit installing the SAP SEM already is using the SAP BW, and would like to deploy the SAP SEM into or within the same system. In this case, the SAP SEM software can be installed to be run as an application on top of the already running SAP BW. The data needed for the SAP SEM will be provided by the BW and any other required external source.

In any of the above three cases, the SAP BW is the technical core for the SAP SEM. It is the SAP BW, the mySAP component in charge of storing the data and the metadata for all the application components within the SAP SEM. All the extraction, collection, administration, and updating of the data is done using the tools provided by the SAP BW. End users will be able to access the SAP SEM functions and reports from the Enterprise Portal provided by mySAP Workplace or from another solution from SAPPortals.

More information about the SAP SEM and the SAP SEM Applications can be found on the following URLs: www.sap.com/sem and service.sap.com/sem.

Chapter 4

SAP Internet Transaction Server

When the ITS (*Internet Transaction Server*) was introduced in 1996, it was the key component in the initial SAP strategy and offering for the Internet. It was launched with release 3.1G of SAP R/3. The SAP ITS is an extremely important element within the mySAP initiative, so it is part of most of the mySAP components that are accessible by Web browser.

The following sections introduce and explain briefly the most important concepts and aspects of the SAP ITS. The ITS architecture and components are introduced and explained, including W-Gate, A-Gate, SAP@Web Studio, OK, and the IACs (*Internet Application Components*). The chapter then deals with an overview of the installation procedure and how to configure and manage ITS.

SAP had the vision in 1996 that access to ERP (*Enterprise Resource Planner*) functions through a Web browser would be a key point in the following years. The ITS was designed at the beginning to be able to offer typical Internet and intranet scenarios with R/3 through a Web browser. In this way, SAP designed transactions in R/3 with a simple user interface in order to be used on the Internet. These transactions, plus the HTML (*Hypertext Markup Language*) templates used in the ITS to merge the result in a final HTML page, are called the IACs.

There are IACs for logistics, financials, and HR scenarios. Currently, there are more than 90 IACs. If a company wants to use one of these scenarios, the main task is the customizing of the IAC HTML templates provided by SAP with the company's logo and marketing standards. The IACs OK are designed mainly to be used externally (on the Internet), but some of them are also for internal use in a company with a Web browser-like creation and release of purchase requisitions.

An example of an IAC is the SAP-HR with ESS (*Employee Self Service*). ESS allows the employees of a company to access their data in the HR module with a Web browser. Latest releases also include some internal financial, logistics, and office applications. In the HR area, the employees can access their payroll and personal data information, travel expense and activities reports, job offers in the company, and training and event information and registration.

These scenarios increase the efficiency in the company, decrease the HR department's effort, save time and papers, and give quicker services to the employees than in the past.

Figure 4-1 shows an example of one of the screens of the SAP-HR ESS that is implemented as an IAC.

If there are no IACs for a customer scenario, or the customer wants to develop his own application, SAP provides the SAP@Web Studio in order to generate the HTML templates automatically from a customer R/3 transaction.

ITS was designed to be able to call functions in R/3. These functions should be designed to work with ITS because they should return a table with the HTML page (see the section "WebRFC and WebReporting" later in this chapter).

In release 4.6, a new type of ITS development appears with *flow files*. Flow files are text files in the ITS where you can program BAPI or RFC calls to R/3 and then evaluate the result: for example, call another BAPI and at the end merge the BAPI result with an HTML template. The main difference is that with IACs, the programming logic is mainly in the R/3 transaction and you use the text files (templates) in ITS to merge the result, but with flow files, the programming logic is in the ITS text files. The developer calls BAPIs in R/3 but then evaluates the results and decides to call another BAPI or merge the result with the final HTML template.

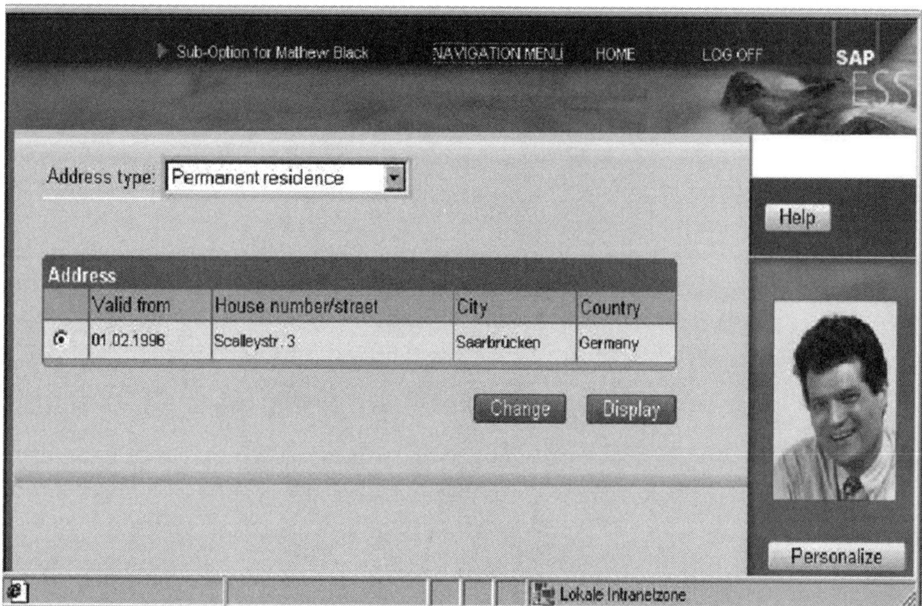

FIGURE 4-1 *Example of IAC with the ESS* Copyright by SAP AG

ITS and mySAP Workplace

With the R/3 release 4.6, SAP also released the SAPGUI for HTML for the ITS. The SAPGUI for HTML, also called Webgui allows the user to access SAP with a Web browser with the same look that the EnjoySAP SAPGUI has. The ITS was able to translate the SAPGUI protocol in DHMTL pages and R/3, and all of the mySAP components are available through a Web interface.

The following Figures 4-2 and 4-3 show a couple of examples of the Workplace with SAPGUI for HTML.

Moreover, the Workplace was developed as a new SAP product included in the mySAP initiative that allows you to create an enterprise portal based on user roles. In this portal, the user can access all functions, SAP and non-SAP, internal and external (Internet), through a Web browser, depending on the user's personal role in the organization. The Workplace service and portal generation are also included in the ITS.

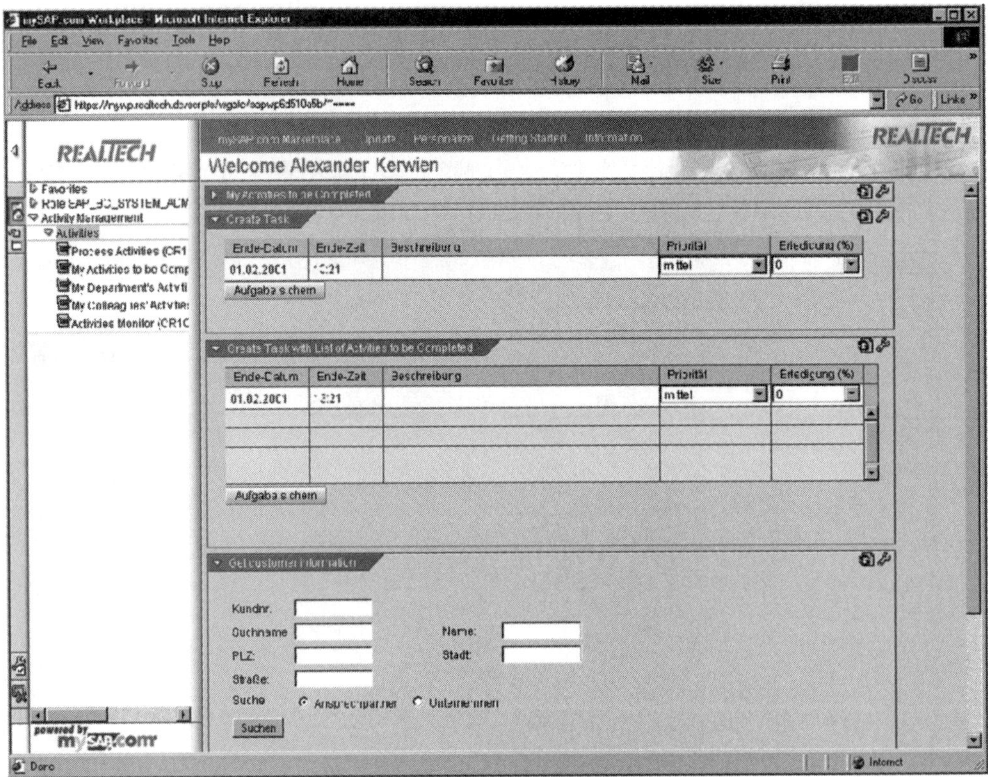

FIGURE 4-2 *mySAP Workplace with the SAPGUI for HTML*

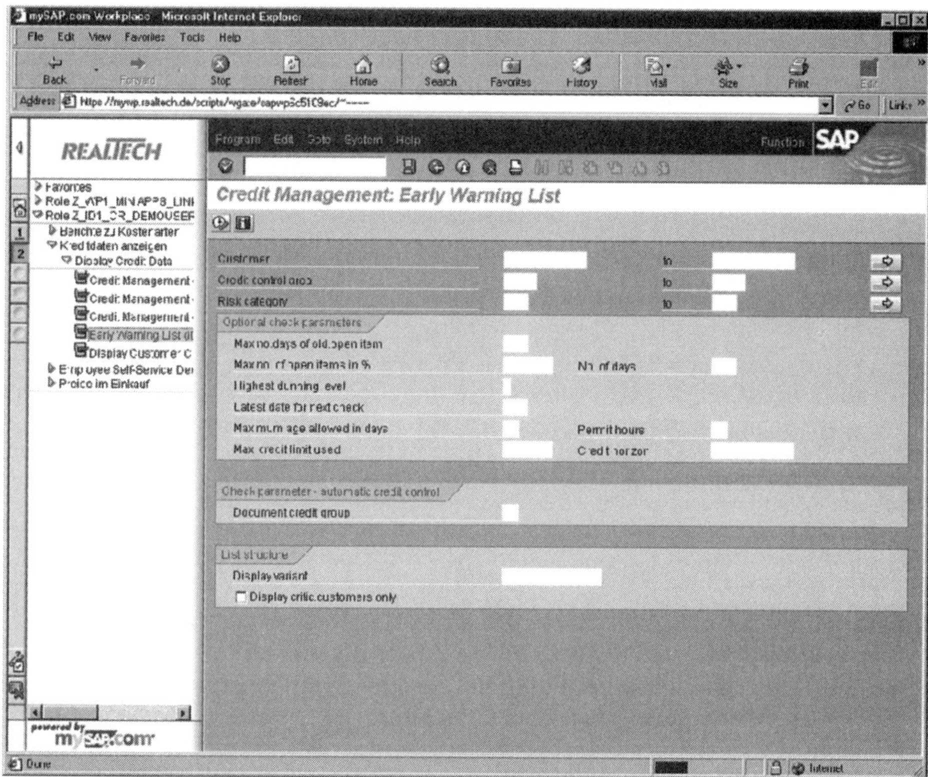

FIGURE 4-3 *mySAP Workplace with the SAPGUI for HTML*

Development Outlook

The SAP Web Application Server is the newest Internet solution from SAP. When this book was written, it was in the First Customer Shipment status (FCS). The SAP Web Application Server, with the SAP internal name "Roadrunner," is a SAP-native Web application server. In this case, the application server can directly speak HTTP, and the application server work processes can work with HTML pages with ABAP or JavaScript code. This new method promises a faster access from the Web to SAP and some of the new Internet scenarios. For example, Internet Sales 3.0 is being totally rewritten with the SAP Web Application Server. At the moment, it is only available on Windows NT/2000 or UNIX platforms with SAP-DB as a database.

Whether the SAP Web Application Server will replace the ITS in the future or not is something we will discover in the next two years. This new technological solution will be soon so important that there is a full chapter (chapter 8) about it. Let us now introduce the concepts and the secrets of ITS.

Internet Basic Concepts

Before going into details about the ITS architecture, the following sections introduce briefly some basic Internet and communication concepts, which are basic to understanding how all of the components work together.

TCP/IP

IP (*Internet Protocol*) is the protocol that allows two programs in two hosts to communicate with each other. IP assigns a so-called IP address to each host. In the current release, IP v4 is a 4-byte number that's usually represented separated with dots in decimal base, like 147.204.2.5.

TCP/IP (*Transmission Control Protocol/Internet Protocol*) is a protocol that guarantees the delivery of the IP packets to the program and tries to resend the packet if the destination has not acknowledged the packet reception.

Another protocol over IP is UDP (*User Datagram Protocol*). As opposite to TCP, UDP does not guarantee the packet delivery, but it has less overhead because of this. UDP is used on the Internet in, for example, broadcasting scenarios like radio or video applications.

The most successful protocol used in applications is TCP/IP. There are TCP/IP implementations in nearly every operating system, including UNIX and Windows.

A lot of programs were developed over TCP/IP in a client/server mode. For example, Telnet allows the UNIX user access to execute functions in the UNIX server from a remote computer (with the Telnet protocol); FTP (*File Transfer Protocol*) allows the user to transfer files from computers (based on FTP commands sent by TCP/IP); and the popular Internet mail is based on mail clients and mail servers based on POP3 (*Post Office Protocol*) or SMTP (*Simple Mail Transfer Protocol*) commands sent by TCP/IP. Also, TCP/IP is the protocol where the SAPGUI sends the SAPGUI commands between the SAP front end and the dispatcher at the application server.

TCP/IP is based on the concepts of the IP address and the network mask. The idea behind a network mask is that all of the hosts belonging to the same physical network have the same network mask. The network mask is also a 4-byte number like 255.255.255.0. As you probably know, 255 in binary is 111111111. The network mask is used to compare the destination host address with its own host network mask. The bits with 1 in the network mask should be the same in the destination address as the bits in the source address. In this case, the host is considered to be in the same network, and the packet is sent through the Ethernet, Token Ring, or local network adapter that is used. If not, the packet is sent to a new host called a *router* or a *gateway*.

The router has several network adapters to communicate with other networks, like ISDN cards, frame relay, or others. On the other side of this ISDN line is another router that knows its own networks, and there are protocols between the routers to exchange routing and network information in order for the routers to discover how to reach a specific IP address. It is beyond the scope of this book to analyze the protocols between the routes. Let's just say that there are open protocols that every router should know to communicate on the Internet, some routers also speak proprietary protocols (which are more efficient in the routing information exchange), and that the routers decide which protocol the other side can use. This is basically how the Internet works: lots of networks interconnected with routers and the IP packets traveling to reach their destinations.

We do not use the 4-byte IP address to reach a host. We assign to each host a so-called hostname. For example, we know the SAP Web site as **www.sap.com** instead of as its IP address, 204.154.71.132. A name resolution maps the hostname to the real IP address used in the IP protocol. This can be solved in a small network in a text file called "hosts" on each computer, but in larger networks, there are servers called DNS (*Domain Name Server*) that resolve the hostname to the IP address. The hostnames on the Internet have a hierarchical structure. For example, **www.sap.com** means that this host belongs to the domain ".com" (commercial companies), is in the "sap" domain, and the host is called "www" in the sap domain. The DNSs are also structured hierarchically. There is a DNS for the .com domain that knows the IP address of the .sap.com DNS, and the .sap.com DNS knows the IP addresses of their hosts. When the DNS concept was launched, some top-level domains were defined, like .com, .org, .edu, .mil (military), .es (for Spain), .uk (for United Kingdom), or .de (for Germany). When a new domain wants to be defined, the responsible DNS of the lower-level domain assigns it the name and registers the new DNS address in its DNS. In this way, we can find, with DNS resolution, the real IP address of a hostname on the Internet.

HTTP and HTML

Some of the most popular services on the Internet now are the Web services based on the HTTP protocol. HTTP is the protocol used between a Web server and a

Web browser. The Web server hosts text files called HTML pages, and the Web browser gets these pages from the Web server, reads the HTML code in the page, and shows it to the user. The Web browser sends an HTTP GET command to the Web server to read a page, the Web server sends this page written in a language called HTML, and the browser decides how to show the page.

HTML was designed to support hyperlinks. The idea was for a document to reference another document stored in the same Web server or in another Web server on the Internet. In this way, you can navigate from one document to another, always looking for the up-to-date document that is maintained by its owner.

At the beginning, HTML was used to show static information, like documents with text and graphic information. The first method to call a program and, in this way, to generate dynamic content was called CGI (*Common Gateway Interface*). CGI is the protocol (mainly used in UNIX Web servers) that specifies how to design forms in HTML and how to pass the fields in the form to a program in the Web server. In the first implementations, the Web server passed the fields like environment variables, which the called program could get and use to generate the next HTML page as standard output. Then the Web server sent this generated HTML page as the result to the Web browser.

Other programming possibilities appeared later, like ASP (*Active Server Pages*), where the Web server could have some special tags in the HTML code that it used to call the code at the Web server site.

DHTML (*dynamic HTML*) also allows you to include special tags, executed in this case at the browser site to provide special animation and integration features on the client side.

Java and JavaScript allow the browsers to interpret JavaScripts at the browser side. On the other hand, Java applets or servlets (client or server) side allow you to integrate the Java language in the HTML code at the client or server side.

ITS Architecture

The ITS is the SAP middleware to integrate the Web world with SAP applications. The ITS allows browser users to access Internet application scenarios designed by SAP and customized to the company specific requirements and to access mySAP components with the SAPGUI for HTML. It is the portal generator for the mySAP Workplace.

The ITS consists of two components: W-Gate (*Web Gate*) and A-Gate (*Application Gate*).

W-Gate is the component that talks to the Web server. Currently, three Web servers are supported: Internet Information Server (IIS) from Microsoft, Netscape Enterprise Server, and Apache Server. Additionally, a native CGI-W-Gate exists that can be used with any CGI-compliant Web server (for example, Lotus Domino). Supported operating systems include Windows NT/2000 and Linux. For a current overview of the supported platforms see the SAP ITS pages at **www.sap.com/sap-its**.

The W-Gate is called from the Web server using different interfaces: ISAPI for IIS, NSAPI for Netscape, a specific module for Apache Web Server, or native CGI.

The W-Gate isolates the A-Gate from the Web server. The A-Gate can be installed on the same machine with the W-Gate and the Web server, so-called Single-Host ITS, or on a separate machine, Dual-Host ITS. If W-Gate and A-Gate are on the same machine, they communicate with each other by local memory pipes, and if they are installed on different machines, they use TCP/IP. You can choose a so-called Dual-Host Installation for security, scalability, and performance reasons. If both components are installed on different machines, you can install a firewall in between, improving the security. (See Figure 4-4.)

A-Gate uses DIAG (the SAPGUI protocol) or RFC for communicating with R/3 application servers. A-Gate uses DIAG for executing IACs or SAPGUI for HTML; RFC is used for BAPI or Function Module calls as with ITS FlowLogic or WebReporting.

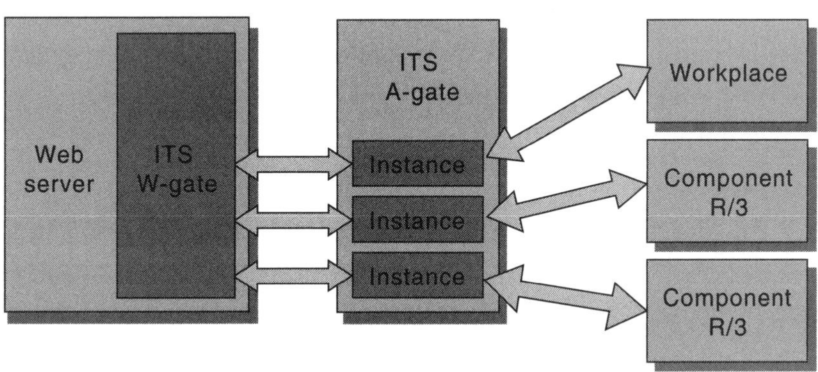

FIGURE 4-4 *ITS architecture*

Internally, the A-Gate includes a dispatcher thread, several worker threads, and shared memories for the sessions. HTTP is a stateless protocol, so there is no concept like the session in HTTP. On the other hand, transactional systems like SAP use a session concept and should know in which screen, values, and so on a user is. The A-Gate assigns a session to each request and maps this session to the user session in SAP R/3.

Instances

The ITS supports virtual instances. If you want to connect to different R/3 systems from one ITS, it is recommended to install separate ITS instances for all R/3 systems. It is also very common to have the ITS for development and quality assurance installed on the same machine. This way you can reduce the hardware requirements, because you do not need a separate server for each R/3 system you want to connect to.

The first time you install the ITS on a system, the physical installation takes place and one ITS instance is created. If you start the installation procedure again, only additional ITS instances are created on the server.

Services

The A-Gate can run different R/3 programs or transactions. For each of them a service must be defined. For example, the service for an IAC in logistics is called MEW0. The service definition in the A-Gate specifies which transaction is executed in R/3 and where. There are some generic services like the WebRFC that allows you to call RFCs in R/3 or the Webgui service that allows you to execute the SAPGUI for HTML in the browser.

In order to execute the service XXXX from a URL, you have to type into your browser **http://ITShost/scripts/wgate/XXXX/!** (in Microsoft IIS, other Web servers often use the directory "cgi-bin" instead of "scripts").

The service is defined in a text file with the extension ".srvc," which includes parameters such as system, transaction, and so on. You can find a subdirectory called Services on the A-Gate machine where you find all of the service files.

You can define all the default parameters for the services in the global service, called global.srvc. For example, if all of the services will point to the same R/3 system, you can put these parameters in the global service once. In Table 4-1, you can find typical parameters within a service file.

Table 4-1 Parameters for the ITS Service Files

~messageserver	Message server of the SAP system
~logingroup	Login group defined in the CCMS
~appserver	R/3 application server
~systemname	System name used to find the service sapmsXXX for the message server
~systemnumber	Used with the application server parameter to connect to a specific app server
~transaction	R/3 transaction to be executed
~client	Client in the R/3 system
~login	Some IACs use a default user to connect to the R/3 system, which can be specified here
~password	Some IACs use a default user to connect to the R/3 system, which can be specified here

Templates

Each service has a template subdirectory where the A-Gate can find the HTML templates to be used with that specific service. These templates can be grouped in themes (the default theme is 99) in order to have different looks for the same service (language, double-byte problems) or testing purposes. There are also parameters like client, user login, and password to specify a generic user in the service definition. If there is no user login in the service definition or in the global service, the ITS generates a HTML logon screen.

If you remember the URL to call a service, you just have to add the theme parameter in the call to use a specific set of templates. For example:

http://host/scripts/wgate/mew0/!?~theme=95

When you request the URL, the A-Gate logs on to R/3 with the user specified in the service and executes the transaction specified. As you know, the screens in R/3 are identified by the program name and the screen number. The ITS receives the first screen of the transaction from R/3 and looks in the template directory for a file called "program_screennumber.html," for example, SAPMMEW0_1000.html, and merges the R/3 data with the HTML template. In the HTML template, you can specify special tags for this merge; this script language is called Business HTML.

In release 4.6, a new type of ITS development appears with the flow files. Flow files are text files in the ITS where you can program BAPI or RFC calls to R/3 and then evaluate the result: for example, call another BAPI and at the end merge the BAPI result with an HTML template. The main difference is that with IACs, the programming logic is mainly in the R/3 transaction and you use the text files (templates) in ITS to merge the result, but with flow files, the programming logic is in the ITS text files. The developer calls BAPIs in R/3 but then evaluates the results and decides to call another BAPI or merge the result with the final HTML template.

SAP@Web Studio

SAP@Web Studio allows you to automatically generate the service templates from the R/3 transaction and screens. You just need to say the name of your R/3 transaction, and the screen names and the SAP@Web Studio will connect to R/3, get the screen definition, and generate the HTML templates with the R/3 screen field names already in place.

SAP@Web Studio can be installed on a Windows NT workstation or Windows 2000 machine for the developer. The installation process is a normal setup program where you have to specify where the ITS network shares are in order to send the generated templates to the ITS later.

All components within a Web transaction can be maintained using the Web@Studio:

- Service files
- Business HTML templates
- MIME (*Multipurpose Internet Mail Extensions*) objects
- HTRC language resource files

As of release 4.6 of the R/3 system, the functionality of the SAP@Web Studio is also included in the R/3. You can use the ABAP Workbench, Transaction SE80, to develop Internet applications, as well.

MIME objects are graphics or add-ons to your HTML pages. More important are the HTRC files. When you execute a SAP transaction, the screen appears in the user logon language. This also happens with ITS. If ITS finds a field label in the HTML template like KNA1-KTNRA.label, it substitutes it with the label coming from R/3 in the user logon language (or the logon language specified in the service definition). But sometimes you want to define some labels in the HTML template that do not come from the R/3 transaction. In this case, if you want to support multilanguage, you should use the HTRC files.

You can define text variables in the HTML template, like #Welcome, and then the ITS resolves the variable in the HTRC file. For example, if you log on in Spanish, the ITS looks for a file called servicename_ES.htrc, and in this file there is a line like this:

```
Welcome Bienvenido
```

And you get *Bienvenido* in the resulting HTML page.

With SAP@Web Studio, the developer creates a project on the PC. A project can include more than one transaction.

From the Web Studio we can:

- Create new empty files
- Create objects using wizards
- Export (publish) to the ITS or import from the ITS
- Export to R/3 for integrating with the CTS (*Correction and Transport System*)

To publish with SAP@Web Studio, you must define the Web site and ITS server you want to work with. When you define the site, the SAP@Web Studio asks you for the following parameters:

- **Web server.** HTTP ITS server name to test from Web@Studio
- **WebRootDir.** ITS share for MIMEs
- **URLwgate.** W-Gate name in the Web server, should be wgate.dll in Windows NT
- **ITS Host.** A-Gate hostname
- **ITS Data Directory.** Service and template share name (for the PUBLISH function).

Internet Application Components

IACs are ready-to-use applications—for example, the SAP Online Store—based on the ITS.

SAP has defined a lot of transactions in R/3 with a simpler user interface (normally this means fewer fields than in the standard transaction) and the corresponding HTML templates in the ITS. For example, there are IACs for purchase requisition and purchase release so that occasional users can execute the purchasing transactions from their Web browser. This is included now in an important intranet IAC called ESS where the employee can also access personal data like holidays, salaries, address modification, event and training registration, and so on.

There are more than 90 IACs in the 4.6 release; they are used for intranets but are mainly for Internet use by a company's vendors, customers, applicants, and so on.

The IACs are a quick way to connect your system to the Internet. You just have to customize the IAC if necessary and modify the templates supplied by SAP with your look and feel requirements. If you want to connect your SAP system to the Internet or an intranet, first have a look at the available IACs, because you could save time and money by using them.

If there are no IACs for a customer scenario or the customer wants to develop her own application, SAP provides the SAP@Web Studio in order to generate the HTML templates automatically from a customer R/3 transaction.

Figure 4-5 shows an example of SAPGUI for HTML.

On the other hand, with the SAPGUI for HTML, you could give access to nearly any mySAP transaction from a browser. Why should you use IACs then? Because for external users or occasional users, you do not want to use the same SAP functionality and look as for your professional SAP users. The SAPGUI for HTML is a very quick way to expose your whole R/3 system to the Internet but with the SAPGUI look, and this is not the case in most of the Internet scenarios you want to define. You would probably prefer more flexibility to customize templates for occasional and external users.

Operating ITS

Operating an ITS means installation of the ITS software first, but it also means administration and tuning of a running system.

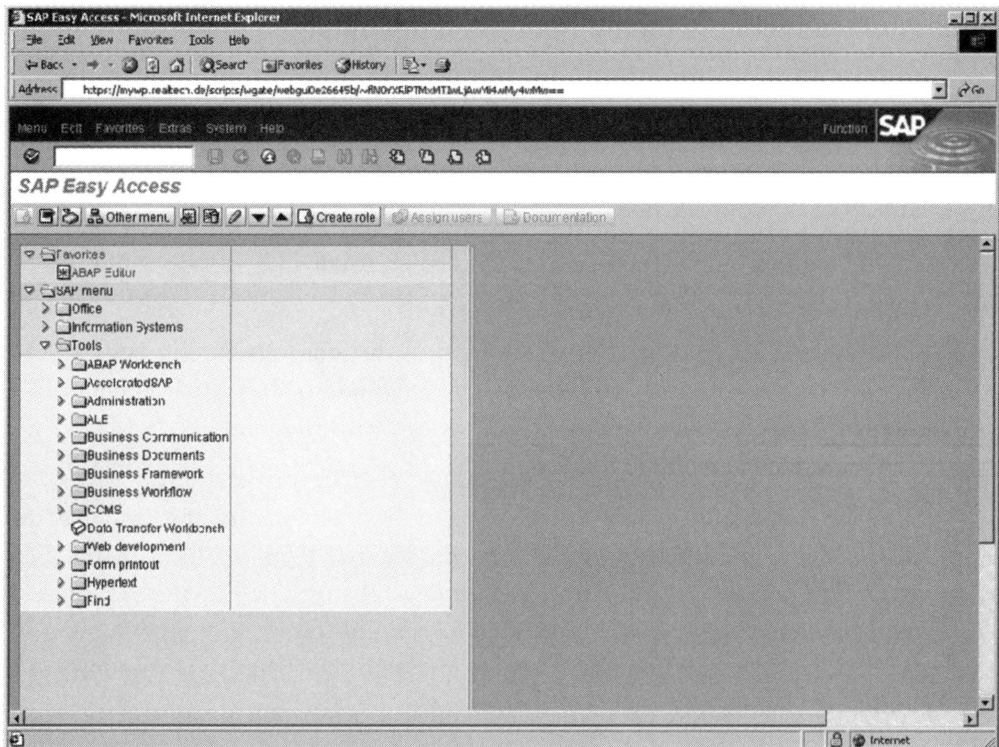

FIGURE 4-5 *Example of SAPGUI for HTML*

Installation

The installation process depends on the operating system (Windows NT or Linux) and is described in the installation guide. Here we are going to explain the internals of this process.

First of all, the Setup program is executed. This program calls the ITSinstall program. ITSinstall installs the software on the host. It then calls ITSVinstall (virtual ITS installation). With ITSVinstall, you create different subdirectories (templates, services, MIMEs, and so on) for each A-Gate installed on the same machine. In this way, you could, for example, install the A-Gate for development and quality assurance systems on the same machine.

Setup is an intelligent program that can be executed more than once. If it discovers that the software has already been installed, it only calls ITSVinstall in order to install another virtual ITS with the same software.

Then the Setup program calls ITSprotect, which asks you which permissions you want to assign to the directories and shares generated by the ITS. As already mentioned, the recommendation is to assign them to the developers group in your Windows NT domain in order to use the SAP@Web Studio later. ITSprotect could be called as a standalone later if you want to change the permissions or use native tools to do the same.

Other programs are ITSuninstall and ITSVuninstall ITS software and virtual ITS.

Each virtual ITS is assigned a name used in directory generation later and in TCP/IP services naming convention. In a Windows NT environment, ITS installs the A-Gate as a Windows NT service with the name "ITS Manager – XXX" where XXX is the ITS name.

After the installation, two network shares are created: one for the graphics, the MIME share, and another one for the service and template files. In the ITS installation, you also assign permissions to these shares. The ITS installation asks you if the permissions should be created for administrators only, a Windows NT group, or everybody. The normal way is to assign the shares to a Windows NT group that your developers are also assigned to.

Administration

Administration of the ITS can be done in different locations. You have to configure the W-Gate or the A-Gate, which can be done either in the configuration files, the registry, the service files, or with console commands. The following section describes the different possibilities of configuring the ITS.

ITS Administration Tool

From release 4.5, it is possible to install an additional virtual ITS called Administration ITS. This ITS has the service admin.srvc that allows you to manage other ITS from the Web browser. With the Administration ITS, you can see performance indicators and start/stop ITS instances, view log files, or change configuration settings with a browser-based Administration Tool. (See Figure 4-6.)

The Administration Tool offers you access to almost any configuration parameter of the A-Gate. In most cases, it is the most convenient way to make configuration changes with the Administration ITS.

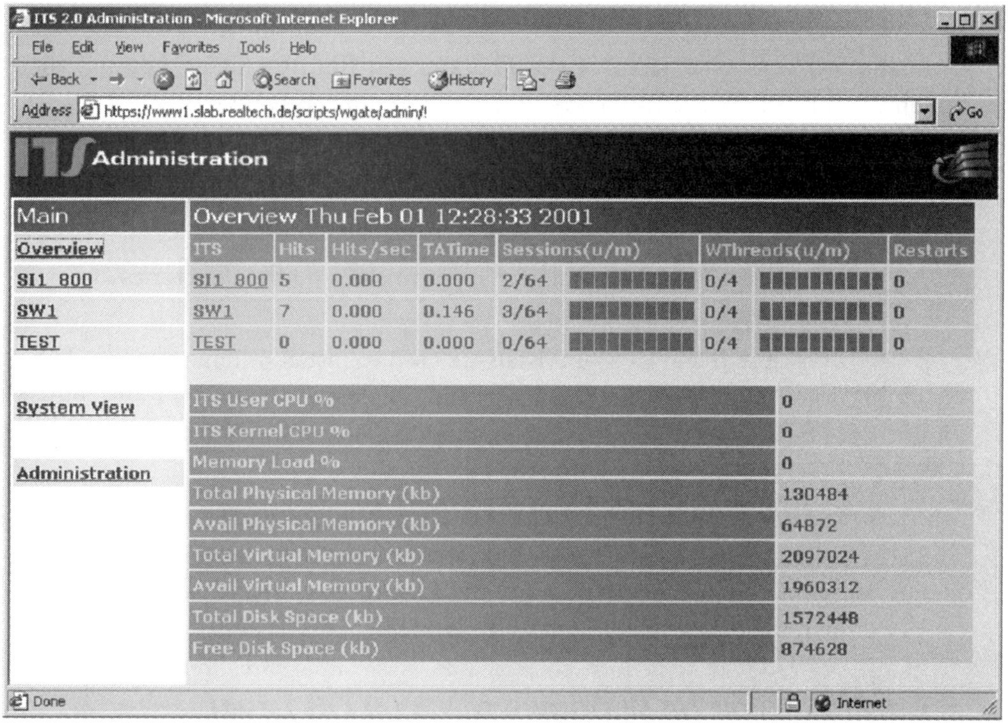

FIGURE 4-6 *ITS Administration Tool*

ITS Remote Diagnostics is not used very frequently, but it is useful if you want to have a look at the ITS log files from a remote location. You have to request the URL **http://Itshostname/scripts/wgate/?~command=diagnostics&password=keyword** in a browser window. Then the ITS sends you an HTML page with the log and configuration files from ITS. For this to work, you have to activate the following registry entries on the A-Gate machine first:

```
HKEY_LOCAL_MACHINE\SOFTWARE\ITS\2.0\programs\Agate
AdminEnabled = 1
HKEY_LOCAL_MACHINE\SOFTWARE\ITS\2.0\VITS\diagnostics
Password=PPPPP
Autolock=0,1(ask password each request)
Objects= files to show in the HTML response
(registry,*.srvc,agate.trc,wgate.trc,...)
```

ITS Console Commands

In the installation directory of the ITS you can find the folder Admin, where some command-line tools for the administration of the ITS are stored.

- ITSVcontrol is a command tool that allows you to start, stop, and change trace level to the ITS. The same can be achieved by starting or stopping the Windows NT service from the Control Panel.
- ITSprotect is used to change the permissions on the directories and shares generated by the ITS.
- ITSVinstall and ITSVuninstall are used to install or remove single ITS instances on the machine. In general, it is more convenient to use the ITS Setup Tool for installation and the Control Panel/Add/Remove Programs for uninstallation of ITS instances.
- ITSinstall and ITSuninstall are used to install or remove the ITS physically on the machine. In general, it is more convenient to use the ITS Setup Tool for installation and the Control Panel/Add/Remove Programs for uninstallation of ITS instances.

Configuration on Windows NT/2000 OS Level

In Windows NT/2000, an ITS instance appears as an entry in the Control Panel/Services dialog box. You can use this dialog box to start or stop single ITS instances. Starting and stopping of instances has no effect on other instances running on the same machine.

This dialog box can also be used for disabling single instances or to modify the behavior of the service at startup, for example, if you want to change the service to be started manually.

Configuring Windows NT/2000 Registry-Settings

The ITS creates a tree in the Windows registry where configuration parameters for the A-Gate are stored. ITS releases prior to release 4.6D also stored configuration information for the W-Gate in the Windows registry, since release 4.6D W-Gate configuration is stored in the XML-file wgate.conf. The tree in the registry for the configuration of the ITS is

```
HKEY_LOCAL_MACHINE/Software/SAP/ITS/2.0/<ITS Instance>/...
```

Here, the settings concerning memory, security, or debugging can be changed. The meaning of the parameters available here is explained in the document *ITS Administration Guide*, available from SAP.

After making changes in the registry, it is necessary to restart the ITS instance in order for the changes to take effect.

If it is possible to install the ITS Administration Tool (either as service or as separate instance) you should prefer making changes to the configuration with the Admin Tool, because it is more convenient and more secure.

W-Gate Configuration

ITS releases prior to release 4.6D stored configuration information for the W-Gate component in the Windows registry; since release 4.6D, the configuration of the W-Gate is made with the XML-file wgate.conf. The file is stored in the same directory where the wgate.dll is stored: usually .../SAP/ITS/2.0/SAP-WGate-Scripts/.

You can use the wgate.conf file to configure security settings and connection parameters to the A-Gate. Additionally, you can configure the W-Gate to connect to different A-Gates, depending on the hostname that was used to connect to the Web server; for example, workplace.company.com determines that the W-Gate should connect to the ITS instance for the Workplace system, and hr1.company.com determines the same W-Gate to connect to the ITS instance of the HR system HR1.

On Windows platforms, the installation of the W-Gate automatically installs a plug-in for the Microsoft Management Console (*MMC*) that can be used for the configuration.

ITS Sizing

ITS is very scalable. You can choose different configurations and install different machines for Web servers, A-Gates, and different application servers and mix them. The following considerations should be observed:

- Each W-Gate points to one or more A-Gates using *load balancing*. But several W-Gates could point to the same A-Gate.
- An ITS instance can use more than one application server by using load balancing to connect to the R/3 server. One ITS can connect to more

than one R/3 system. Several ITSs can connect to the same R/3 system. Several A-Gates can be installed on the same server.

- Virtual ITS allows for installing different ITS environments using one software installation (for example, development and test) and has been available since release 2.0 of ITS.

The number of worker threads and session memory created for an ITS instance determine the memory required for that instance. Each work process consumes about 1MB, and each session approximately 250KB. For example, if you expect 1,000 session users and 20 simultaneous hits, you need 20 * 1MB + 1,000 * 250KB = 270MB RAM for the ITS (plus the demands for the operating systems and other applications like the Web server).

During the installation, you can choose different configurations, but you can change the number of processes and sessions in the registry or with the graphical administration utility later.

You can also install several Web instances on the same machine with different W-Gates, or in the latest releases, one W-Gate installation can even serve multiple A-Gates. All this provides you with a very high degree of scalability, and you can choose just one machine to install several ITSs or a pool of machines, depending on your needs.

ITS does not require a lot of hardware. Here you can find some rules of thumb for the A-Gate:

Table 4-2 Rule-of-Thumb Approach to Sizing ITS

Up to 100 users	minimum 1 Pentium 133 and 64MB RAM
Up to 200 users	minimum 1 Pentium 133 and 128MB RAM
Up to 500 users	minimum 2 Pentiums 133 and 256MB RAM
Up to 2,000 users	minimum 4 Pentiums 200 and GB RAM
For more than 2,000 user	it's recommended to install and use several ITSs

ITS Security

When you speak about Internet access, security is always an issue. ITS has to access R/3, so you need a user and password in R/3; ITS can ask for the R/3 user or can use a generic R/3 user for access. In this case, the IAC should ask for a so-called Internet user (you define Internet users with transaction SU05). Internet users are pseudo-users in R/3 (like customer, vendor, bank, or applicant) that you define for your external users with limited authorization in that specific IAC.

ITS also supports standard security measures like HTTPS (HTTP over Secure Socket Layer), firewall support (you can set up a firewall between the Web Server and W-Gate, as well as from the W-Gate to the A-Gate), saprouter and also SNC (*Secure Network Communication*) with data encryption between ITS and the application servers. ITS also supports X.509 certifications for user authentication from SAP 4.5B on and Single Sign-On scenarios based on cookies or logon tickets for the Workplace.

Development with the ITS

Developing Web pages to interact with SAP systems can be based on HTML or Business HTML, which are introduced in the following sections.

Introduction to HTML

HTML (*Hypertext Markup Language*) was created at CERN (*Conseil Europeen pour le Recherche Nucleaire*, or *European Laboratory for Particle Physics*) with the aim of sharing up-to-date information between research centers. In this way, a Web server in Europe could host the documents in text files that could link to other documents stored in other Web server (in Australia, for example) in a transparent way to the user.

HTML is a tag language based on SGML (*Standard Generalized Markup Language*). SGML is a standard for how to specify a document markup language or tag set. SGML is a formal description of how you can define languages based on tags. HTML is a very specific implementation with a closed number of tags designed to format and show graphical and text information and the hyperlink tags. You can see the last HTML standard at **www.w3c.org**. HTML and the Web technology has become so popular that new standards have also arrived, like XML (*Extensible Markup Language*), to define documents based on tags (but this is another story; you can read about it in the "Business Connector" section in Chapter 2).

In fact, the latest HTML specification is called XHTML, and it is an HTML definition with the XML's more rigorous standards.

Every HTML page starts and ends with the <html> and </html> tags. The page is divided into a header (<header>) and the body (<body>) of the page. The header has some tags like <title> to specify general attributes for the page, and the body has the page content.

In the body area, you can find tags to define the size of the font (like <h1> up to <h6>) and other tags to include graphics, like <img src=/graphics/picture.jpg>

You can define hyperlinks with the anchor tag <a src=http://otherweb/otherpage.html> Other page</a>. In this way, the user sees "Other page" with underscores, and if the user clicks on the words, the user is redirected to the new page. The good thing with the tags is that they can be nested. For example:

<a src=http://otherweb/otherpage.html><img src=/graphics/picture.jpg></a>

In this example, a picture is a hyperlink, and if you click on the picture, you are redirected to the new page.

This address **http://otherweb/otherpage.html** is a URL (*Uniform Resource Locator*), a unique way to address a file in Internet. The general form of a URL is

protocol://host:service/directory1/directory2/file

protocols being either an ftp or mail.

Other important tags in HTML define tables to represent tabular information. This is done with the <table> tag and with the <tr> and <td> tags for the table row and table data fields. Tables are important in the SAP environment because they are frequently used in the SAP screens as so-called step loops and table controls.

The latest HTML browsers also support *frames*. The browser screen can be split in several subscreens, or frames. In each frame, a different HTML page can appear, and it is possible to interact with forms in one frame and change another frame's content.

A typical frame HTML page looks like this:

```
<html><head>...</head>
<frameset cols="30%,70%">
<frame name="Frame1" src="frame1.html">
<frame name="Frame2" src="frame2.html">
</frameset>
</html>
```

Business HTML

Business HTML is an SAP-specific scripting language for the ITS, similar to ASP or PHP scripting. In contrast to other Web scripting languages, Business HTML is not interpreted on the Web server, but on the ITS A-Gate.

Business HTML is a kind of SAP programming where you call ITS functions. This is a good approach because it does not require special plug-ins on the browser side. The resulting page is standard HTML that could be used in any browser.

NOTE

The SAPGUI for HTML and the Workplace are not browser-independent. The dynamic HTML pages only have their full functionality with Microsoft Internet Explorer 5 or higher.)

Business HTML commands appear in the HTML template in single quotation marks. For example, **'KNA1-KUNNR.LABEL' <em>'KNA1-KUNNR' </em>** is resolved by ITS merging the field KNA1-KUNNR from the SAP screen and the text label. Fields can be positioned in any place in the HTML template.

The following sections briefly introduce some of the main features of the SAP Business HTML.

Conditions

Business HTML allows you to set conditions in the programming logic of the page, for example, whether or not to include an HTML portion of the page depending on a field in R/3.

```
'if (KNA1-LAND1 == "ES")'

<i>Spain</i>'else'
<em>Other country </em>
'end'
```

Operations

The operations allowed in Business HTML are similar to C operations.

The SAP screens are converted to HTML forms by the SAP@Web Studio with the following action:

```
<form action='wgateURL()' method="POST">
```

This action is resolved at run time in the ITS into a URL like this:

```
action=/scripts/wgate/XXXX/~g1t5d3Xgt=j
```

The number at the end of the URL has the status that the ITS has given to this request. When the ITS receives the next HTML page, it's able to map the request with the open SAP session and execute the next screen in SAP R/3. This is done automatically by the ITS and the SAP@Web Studio.

Table 4-3 Business HTML Operations

+,++	ADD, increment
*	multiply
-,--	rest, decrement
/	division
%	integer module
||	logic OR
&&	logic AND
&	String concatenation without blanks
==	equal to
!=	not equal
>	bigger than
<	less than
<=	less or equal to
>=	greater or equal to

Some tips:

- **How to exit from a service.** You can set up a button in the HTML template like this: `<input type=submit name="~Okcode=/NEX" value='#end'>`

  When this button is executed, the SAP session is finished, and the ITS redirects the user to the URL specified in the parameter

  ~exitURL

  in the global or service file. Usually, this URL points to the home page or menu of the Web server.
- **To skip the first screen of the R/3 transaction.**

  ```
  http://host/scripts/wgate/xxxx/!?~OkCode=DISP&CARRID
  =LH&CONNID=0400
  ```

  where CARRID and CONNID are the mandatory fields of the first screen and DISP is the OK-CODE used to go to the display screen. If there is an error in the fields or not all the mandatory fields are filled, the first screen appears to solve the problem.

Synchronization Problem

If the user presses the Back button in the browser, the ITS doesn't acknowledge it, because it's a local operation in the browser. In this case, the ITS could receive a HTML page that does not correspond to the R/3 screen where the user is. The best solution for this is to hide the standard browser buttons when the scenario starts. If not, you have to program this possibility in your transaction logic.

ITS is able to detect that the HTML status does not match the SAP status and, in this case, sends a special OK-CODE to SAP: AWSY<program><dynpro>. The ABAP should accept this code and program a SET SCREEN to the chosen dynpro.

Here you can see a pseudo-code of how to program this in ABAP:

```
Case save_ok_code(4).
...
When 'AWSY'
len = STRLEN( save_ok_code ) - 4.
Scr = save_ok_code+len(4).
...
Leave to screen scr.
Endcase.
```

Step Loops

Step loops are widely used in SAP screen programming to show a list of records with the same definition. SAP@Web Studio is able to map the screen step loop to an HTML table if the transaction has standard paging implemented.

This means that the transaction should have PF21 to go to the beginning of the step loop and at least PF23 to go one page forward in the step loop. In this case, the ITS is able to send these commands to the SAP system until the screen doesn't change and it detects that the step loop is finished.

This is an easy way to map step loops in ITS. It is not as quick as desired because the ITS has to send several requests to SAP to get the whole loop. For this and for other situations (like matchcode or table check entries), it is also possible to send an ABAP internal table to the ITS in one step.

This method is used, for example, to send an internal table with allowed values for a field to the ITS in order to generate and select a field in HTML with the values. The call is done internally in RFC (*remote function call*) and is programmed in ABAP with macros. These macros are defined in the include AVWRTCXM, so every ABAP that wants to use this technique should have this include. The macros are Field-Set and Field-Transport.

```
·Field-set NAME INDEX VALUE.
·....
·Field-transport.
```

These macros are included in the PBO (*process before output*) of the dynpro, for example, to fill the internal table with the allowed values and then transfer it to ITS. This method gives better performance than the automatic method used by ITS for step loops.

A pseudo-code should look like the following example. Let's assume you have an internal table ISCARR filled with the flights from a table in R/3.

```
ABAP PBO
counter = 1.
Loop at iscarr.
Field-set 'CARRID' counter iscarr-carrid.
Field-set 'CARRNAME' counter iscarr-carrname.
counter = counter + 1
endloop.
Field-transport.
```

All the Field-Sets are stored in memory until you execute the Field-Transport. In this moment, all the tables are sent by RFC to the ITS. Let's see how you should program the Select field in HTML to show the allowed values:

```
<select name=SCARR-CARRID>
'repeat with j from 1 to CARRID.dim'
<option value="'CARRID[j]'">'CARRNAME[j]
'end'
</select>
```

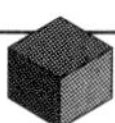

NOTE

In previous ITS releases, an additional field called AW-SESSION should be defined in the dynpro and in the ABAP in order for the macros to work. `Data: AW-SESSION(30).`

Debugging

ABAP programmers are used to executing debugging in the SAP system from the menu in the development transactions or with the /h OK-CODE. When debugging, the programmer can see step by step the execution of the ABAP, as well as displaying the values in the fields or replacing them.

Sometimes the transaction works in R/3 but the HTML template gives different information. You can start debugging also from any HTML page in R/3. First of all, you should enable the functionality in the A-Gate:

```
HKEY_LOCAL_MACHINE->SOFTWARE->SAP->ITS->2.0->VITS->Programs->Agate->AdminEnabled 1
```

Then you can execute the HTML scenario. When you want to start debugging, just start a SAPGUI against the ITS host, system number 00. A SAPGUI screen will pop up with the R/3 screen where your HTML browser is. Then you can enter /h in the OK-CODE and start debugging in R/3, have a look at the fields and internal tables, set breakpoints, and so on.

If you want to change the debugger port of the ITS to the other port, change the registry entry:

```
Agate->SAPGuiDebuggerPort sapdp00
```

This is a very nice functionality. Please be aware that the SAPGUI starts with the last ITS session without asking your username or password, so this functionality should be active only in development environments.

Frames

Subscreens are very useful in the Screen Painter in R/3. They allow the developer to split an SAP screen into different subscreens, each of them with its own processing logic.

SAP subscreens are mapped to HTML frames with SAP@Web Studio. Nearly all the IACs in SAP are programmed with subscreen frames. The only restriction when you program with frames is that HTML allows you to change one frame at one time, so the ABAP developer should change either only one subscreen at one time, or the whole screen.

For more information about Business HTML, refer to the help files provided with the SAP@Web Studio.

Some Function Modules Useful with ITS

Following is a list of some function modules that can be quite useful while working with ITS.

- **ITS_BROWSER_REDIRECT.** Allows you to redirect the user's browser to a new Web server page.
- **ITS_PING.** With ITS_PING, the ABAP developer can know if the transaction is being called from SAPGUI or from ITS and either execute or not some ABAP code in each case. For example, there is no sense to use the Table Transfer macros when the transaction is used with SAPGUI.
- **ITS_BROWSER_REDIRECT.** Like redirect, but allows you to send additional data to the new Web server, like a filled form.

Other function modules that relate to ITS programming can be found in the Group AWRT in transaction Function Builder SE37.

WebReporting and WebRFC

Up to now, we have been discussing the so-called WebTransactions: Transaction in R/3 plus the Business HTML templates to merge and evaluate the result. These transactions are easy to use, and the user should not need special training for them. Other possibilities with ITS are WebRFC and WebReporting (in fact, a special kind of WebRFC).

WebRFC

WebRFC allows you to call a function module in R/3 from a URL and get the next HTML page generated by the function module. So that the function module is designed for ITS, it should have a specific interface (export and import parameters and tables). One of the tables is called HTML and is the next HTML page that the ITS will send to the browser as a result. WebRFC is a service in ITS that always calls the WWW_DISPATCH_REQUEST function module in R/3, and this calls the function module we set in the URL. For an example of how to program and define the interface for such a function module, see the example WWW_HTML_ECHO in the Function Builder.

The URL to call a function module with the WebRFC service is:

http://host/scripts/wgate/WebRFC/!?_function=functionmodule[¶meter1=value¶meter2=value2]

The following parameters are special for the WebRFC service:

- ~RFCGatewayHost gateway host name
- ~RFCGatewayService gateway service (sapgw00)
- ~RFCSystemType SAP system type 3, 2 (ITS can be used with R/2)
- ~RFCTimeOut (in minutes)
- ~RFCDetailedError (detailed description of errors)
- ~RFCDebugginOn 1 allows SAPGUI debugging starting a SAPGUI in the same machine as the A-Gate

If you have a look at the interface in WWW_HTML_ECHO, you can see an internal table QUERY_STRING with a parameter and a value field. All the parameters passed in the URL are a record in the QUERY_STRING table. The function module should loop over this table to get the parameters and fill the HTML table with the next HTML page or the MIME table with the next MIME object.

There are some interesting function modules to create HTML pages from ABAP, like WWW_ITAB_TO HTML, to convert an ABAP internal table in HTML, or WWW_HTML_MERGER to merge a template HTML with ABAP values and others in the SURL group. For the MERGER, the template should be stored in R/3 in the table WWWDATA maintained with transaction SMW0.

Transaction SMW0 is also used to release a function module for the Internet. This is a prerequisite for security reasons.

WebReporting

WebReporting is a special case of WebRFC. SAP has already defined some function modules that allows you to execute any report with or without a selection screen, with or without variant.

The function module WWW_GET_SELSCREEN can execute reports with or without selection screen, with or without variant, that does not use the ABAP instructions:

```
CALL TRANSACTION, CALL SCREEN, CALL SELECTION SCREEN, SUBMIT REPORT.
```

WWW_GET_SELSCREEN calls the function module WWW_GET_REPORT to execute the report and returns the list in HTML. You can set the following parameters in the URL to call these function modules:

```
_report
_variant
_template_set.
```

The standard template_set is called WEBREPORTING_report or WEBREPORTING_selscreen. It can be copied to NAME_selscreen in order for WWW_HTML_MERGER to merge the result with the template. These template sets are maintained with transaction SMW0.

Other parameters in the selection screen include:

```
SELECT-OPTIONS:
sel<type>_<name>-low (high)
PARAMETERS:
par<type>_<name>
Check Box o Radio button
```

```
cboc_<name>
radc_<name>
```

Interactive Reports

Since ITS 2.0, if a report uses the instructions HIDE, AT LINE-SELECTION, or AT USER-COMMAND, the function module WWW_GET_REPORT generates JavaScript automatically in order to insert buttons in the HTML page and code that simulate the double-click on a report line and get a new sublist, like in R/3. In this case, Internet Explorer 4 is needed for the JavaScript.

If you want to work with other browsers, you have to program the interaction by hand with the help of the function module WWW_SET_URL. For example, if you want to create a hyperlink in ABAP on the word *realTech* pointing to the real-Tech Web site:

```
write: / 'welcome to realTech'.
Call function 'www_set_url' exporting offset =  12
length = 8 funct = 'http://www.realtech.de'.
Welcome to <a href="http://www.realtech.de">realTech</a>
```

You can, in this way, write icons in your list and create a hyperlink for them pointing to the new report.

Report Trees

It's also possible to execute reports in report trees with the function module WWW_GET_TREELIST. The report trees have to be released for the Internet, also from transaction SMW0. For report trees, the templates used for merging the result are

WEBREPORTING_TREE_LIST

WEBREPORTING_TREE_NODE

Chapter 5

mySAP Workplace

The mySAP Workplace is the fundamental component within the mySAP.com strategy, because it acts as the single access point to the role-based Enterprise Portal.

The objectives

- What is an Enterprise Portal?
- What is the mySAP Workplace?
- When and why should you use the mySAP Workplace?
- Architecture and technical infrastructure
- mySAP Workplace configuration basics
- The role concept and implementation tips

mySAP Workplace Basics

There are always two ways to see a portal: from the inside and from the outside. From the inside view, you can reach all information, applications, and services inside and outside your company. This can include SAP systems and non-SAP systems, as well as the mySAP Marketplace or any other Internet services. You can use your personal portal for your daily work to access all applications you need, such as Microsoft Outlook or mySAP Business Information Warehouse.

From the outside view you can reach all relevant information you need, for example, to work with your partner. That could include access to an SAP system or any other internal information that is connected to the portal.

Within the mySAP.com strategy, SAP delivers the capacity for building a personalized business portal by deploying the mySAP Workplace. This portal provides access to all SAP functions, as well as the full range of Internet applications, services, and communities. The mySAP.com portals are ways of accessing all of the services and benefits afforded by the mySAP.com strategy.

The mySAP.com Workplace is tailored to individuals, companies, and industries. It puts the business solutions, knowledge, and services they need to succeed in their daily business activities at their fingertips. The users, through their Web browsers, can access functionality that is most relevant to their roles and then configure their personal desktops to suit their individual work styles.

As has been introduced in previous chapters, one of the mySAP.com targets as a full e-business solution is to provide the right information, functions, and applications to employees as well as to business partners. mySAP Workplace provides a customizable and role-based interface for their requirements.

- Access to business solution applications, both SAP and non-SAP
- Access to services available on the Internet
- Access to internal corporate information, reports, press releases
- Instant push information when logging on (MiniApps)
- Access to any user applications
- Access to SAPMarkets and other Marketplaces

Figure 5-1 represents how the Workplace provides access to all required functions within and beyond the company boundaries. mySAP Workplace is therefore the interface to all SAP products: collaborative, front office, and back office. SAP's

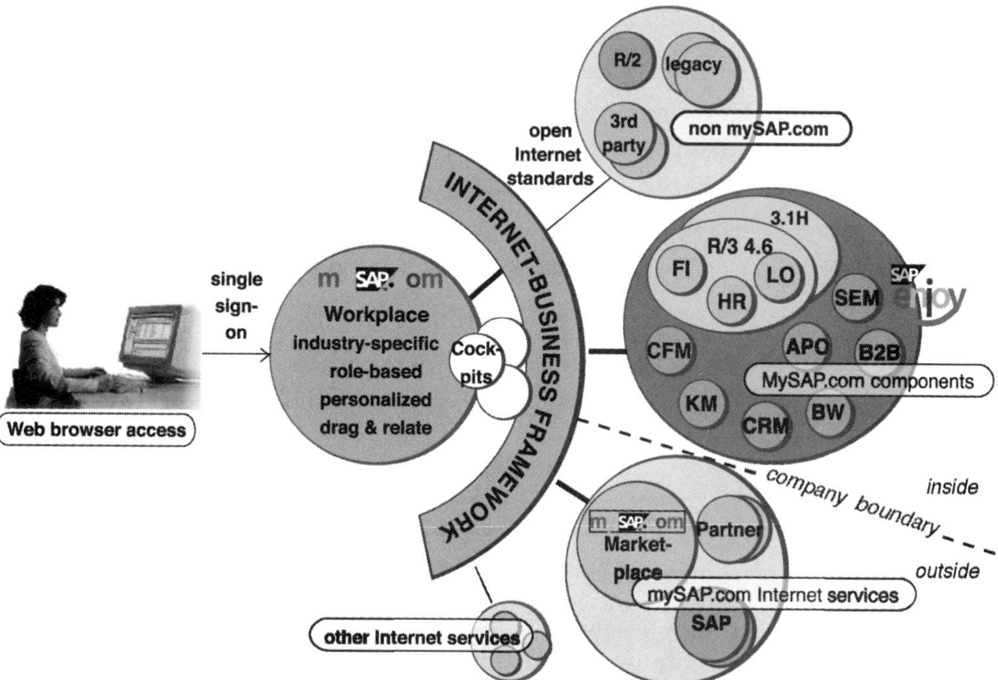

FIGURE 5-1 *mySAP Workplace as Enterprise Portal* Copyright by SAP AG

vision is to continue to provide complete, integrated solutions. SAP is committed to creating all of its applications to work in an integrated mode in a similar move as that which made R/3 such a success.

mySAP Workplace: Main Features

The mySAP Workplace is the browser-based environment through which the user can access a set of business applications. This access is provided by a common and unique interface for all the functions required by the users according to their roles, no matter on which platform, system, or application the business process is run.

In order to accomplish this objective, SAP has included unique features within the Workplace that, combined, provide the power to become the strategic interface for accessing different application components and business processes, including those that are non-SAP. Some typical components that can be found within the mySAP.com strategy are:

KW *(Knowledge Warehouse),* BW *(Business Information Warehouse),* CRM *(Customer Relationship Management),* BBP *(Business to Business Procurement),* and APO *(Advanced Planner and Optimizer).*

The Workplace's main features are:

- Web browser access to all business functions
- Role-based user menu, security, and application access
- SSO (*Single Sign-On*) for accessing all applications with only one authentication process
- MiniApps for providing instant and useful information according to role
- Drag&Relate functions to easily integrate data and functions among different applications and Internet services
- EnjoySAP user-friendly interface that can be tailored and customized by the user
- Standard and advanced Web technology

Why Deploy the mySAP Workplace

There are many reasons for deciding to implement and deploy the mySAP Workplace. First of all, it is the pivotal entry point into mySAP world. As has been introduced in previous sections, there are many other advantages and benefits as well, which are described in the following table.

Table 5-1 Benefits of the mySAP Workplace

For the user:	For the company:
◆ Easy browser access, navigation, and use ◆ Easy browser access, navigation, and use ◆ Role-based access, interface, and menu ◆ Push information (MiniApps) ◆ Accessible from anywhere ◆ SSO ◆ Drag&Relate function ◆ Customizable, including adding favorite Internet links or files	◆ Low cost of ownership and maintenance ◆ Zero installation, only need for an Internet browser ◆ Standardization, easy and convenient user interface facilitates training ◆ Simple maintenance and installation, only the Web browser might be required to be updated
◆ Open Solution ◆ Standard and universal front end through Web browser ◆ Integration of SAP and non-SAP components and applications ◆ Standard role definitions and utilities for enhancing and extending them	◆ Security ◆ Centralized administration ◆ Controlled access ◆ Support for certificates, encryption, and CUA *(Central User Administration)*

Workplace Architecture

This section discusses the architecture, technical infrastructure, and main components and elements that make up the mySAP Workplace.

Workplace Elements

Figure 5-2 shows an example of the mySAP Workplace once the user has logged on.

- The *LaunchPad* on the left side, which shows the personalized role-based menus and functions for the user. This can be considered the *pull area* of the Workplace, that is, where users make requests to business processes or services.
- The *WorkSpace* on the right side contains either the MiniApps (also known as the Home Page) or the business transactions or services as

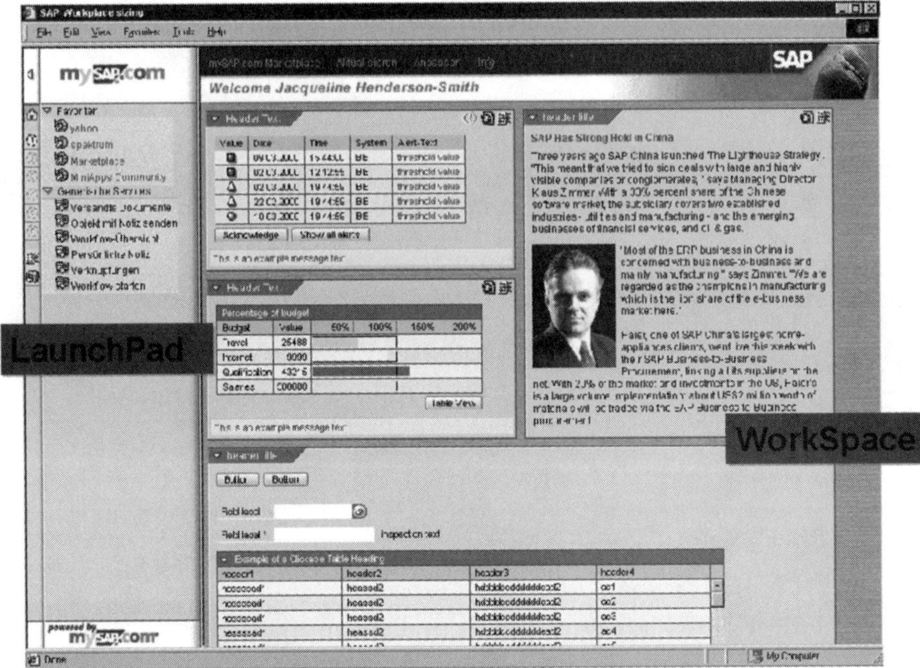

FIGURE 5-2 *Example of Workplace 2.11*

required through the menus and functions. The Home Page (MiniApps) is also considered the *push area* because it proactively sends information to the user automatically as programmed.

The initial access or login to the Workplace is done through a URL *(Uniform Resource Locator)* request to the Workplace server, which can be accessed using a predefined link to the URL or by typing it directly in the browser. An example of URL request to the Workplace server is:

<protocol>://<Web Server>:<port>/scripts/wgate/sapwp/!

For example:

https://mywp.realtech.de:443/scripts/wgate/sapwp/!

This naming convention is based on the ITS (*Internet Transaction Server*) architecture (for reference and information on ITS, see Chapter 4, "SAP Internet Transaction Server").

The LaunchPad is personalized based on the user role that connects to the Workplace. It contains specific activities that are relevant for the user's job position. It can include the business functions of mySAP components, as well as non-SAP systems, applications, and services, as long as they can be called or referenced by a URL. This is further explained in the sections about role definition later in this chapter.

The LaunchPad can include multiple roles for each user. It also permits the customization or personalization of some parts. For instance, the users can add their favorite Internet links or access their most frequently used documents or files.

The Workspace can display the results of the MiniApps as they have been assigned to the user, as well as the result of SAP transactions or business scenarios. The MiniApps provided by the Workplace are dependent on the user roles. Some examples of MiniApps include Internet links, new mail, to-do lists, pending orders, news, reports, alerts, Workflow items, and so on.

Additionally, the Workplace includes the Drag&Relate functionality, which is used for linking business objects from different transactions or applications and passing the values from one object to another. There are different scenarios for linking objects through the Drag&Relate technology.

Technical Background

From a logical point of view, the Workplace architecture is based on three levels, or layers.

- **The *client* or *browser* installed on the user's workstation or any other device that supports an Internet browser.** This component is used for communication with the Web server. Currently, the only browser supported for working with the Workplace is Microsoft Internet Explorer 5.0 or higher, but other options might be available in the future. Besides the browser, some applications might require the installation of a different GUI (like the traditional SAPGUI for Windows, the Java GUI, or Citrix) because the SAPGUI for HTML does not support some features. Transactions supported by different GUIs are defined in the Workplace customizing table TSTCCLASS.
- **Workplace Middleware.** The Workplace Middleware is made up of a Web server and an ITS. The connection established from a Web browser must be in dialog with a Web server that is part of the Workplace

Middleware. The Web server communicates with the *component systems* or *back-end systems* through the ITS. Both components make up the Workplace Middleware. If the Drag&Relate functionality is going to be enabled, other elements will be required, such as the SAP DCOM (*Distributed Common Object Model*) and the Drag&Relate Servlets.

- **Back-end systems that are integrated in the Workplace.** The main system that has to be connected is the Workplace server, a special SAP system (based on the mySAP Basis Middleware like R/3 release 4.6). From there, users and roles are administered, as well as the RFC (*Remote Function Calls*) connections to other component systems. All supported systems that are accessed through the Workplace—such as R/3, BW, KW, and so on—are normally known as component systems.

Figure 5-3 shows a basic view of the mySAP Workplace architecture, and Figure 5-4 shows the same architecture but with a deeper technical view.

Special applications or transactions that cannot be displayed, handled, or converted into HTML format—in other words, that can only be executed using SAPGUI for Windows or SAPGUI for Java—are directly displayed using their corresponding front-end software components.

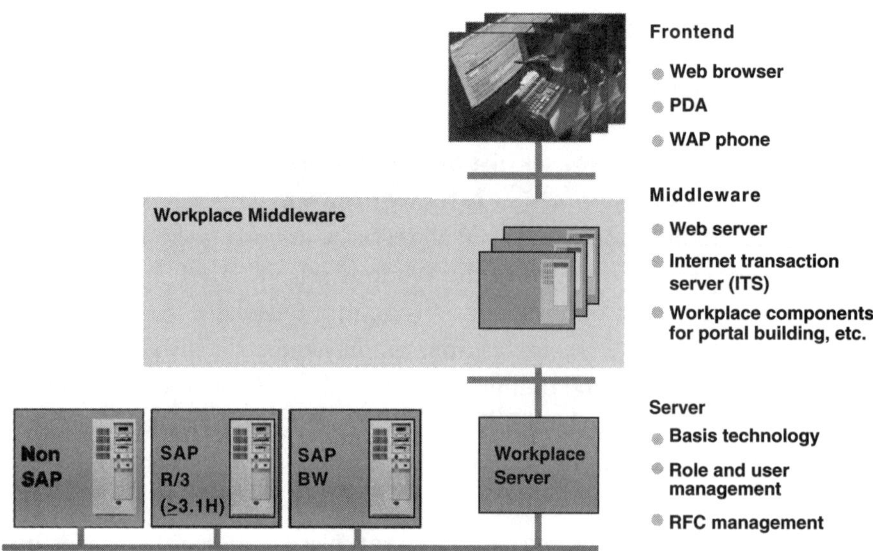

FIGURE 5-3 *Basic view of the Workplace architecture*

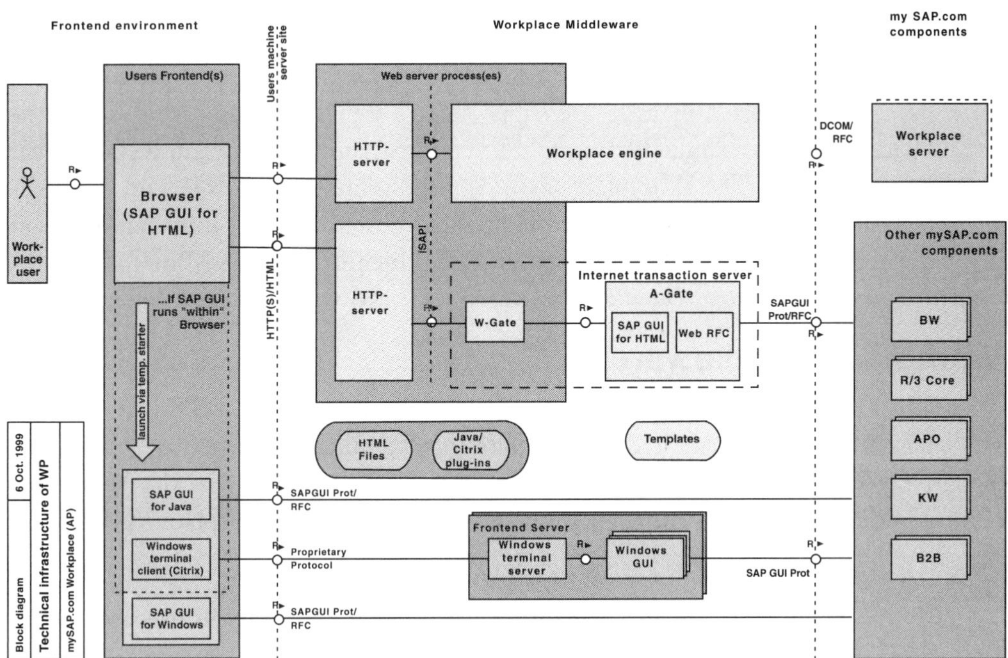

FIGURE 5-4 *Detailed view of the Workplace architecture*

Not all transactions work with the SAPGUI for HTML. As part of the customizing process, the transactions are classified (table TSTCCLASS) depending on which GUI type they can be run or displayed in. This customizing table is already provided by SAP as standard. Customers can further modify or classify it, normally by adding their own transactions.

The Java SAPGUI is executed within the WorkSpace window and does not require additional software, except that the Java plug-ins must be provided from a server, normally from the same Web server. When the transaction is going to be executed using SAPGUI for Windows, the system launches the SAPGUI in the WorkSpace of the browser window. In both cases of SAPGUI for Java and SAPGUI for Windows, the transactions (the process logic) are executed in the corresponding component system. There are some exceptions, though.

For a user to access a Workplace, all that is needed is a workstation (normally a PC), Internet Explorer release 5.x or higher, and a valid username and password.

Workplace Server

The Workplace server itself is a SAP R/3 4.6 Basis system. All platforms and databases supported by SAP are supported, as well. If you are using CUA, the Workplace server should be your CUA server, because it is the central system that knows all users. The Workplace server is responsible for user, role, and personalization management, as well as content. The content includes information about the activities that can be reached from the LaunchPad and the MiniApps.

Workplace Middleware

The Workplace Middleware consists of the Web server and the ITS with the Portal Builder Engine. If Drag&Relate or Terminal Services are used, the Drag&Relate Servlet and the Citrix Terminal Server belong to the Workplace Middleware as well. Figure 5-5 shows a better view of the Workplace Middleware.

The ITS uses so-called HTML template files to generate the HTML files with the R/3 data. The template files contain placeholders and ITS instructions in the SAP scripting language Business HTML.

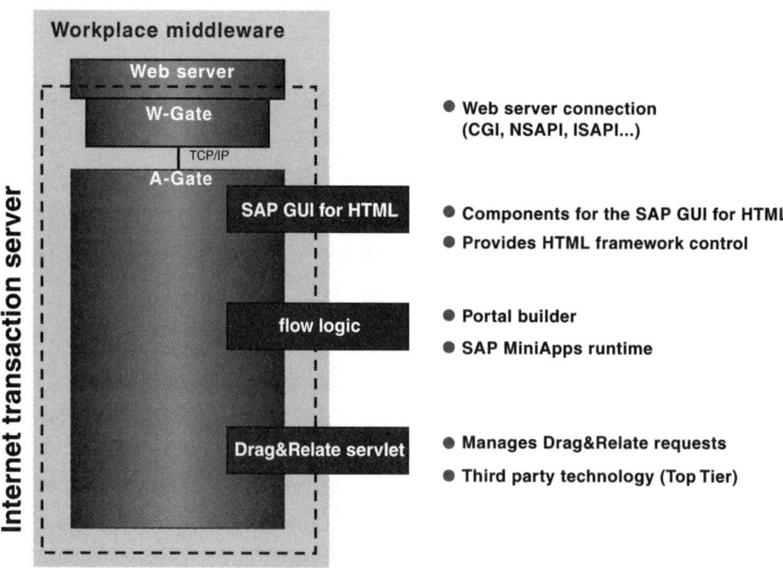

FIGURE 5-5 *Workplace Middleware* Copyright by SAP AG

The ITS supports different programming models: Easy Web Transactions, ITS flow logic, SAPGUI for HTML, and WebRFC.

Easy Web Transactions are simple R/3 transactions developed for use with the ITS. In contrast to standard R/3 transactions, these transactions offer a reduced functionality. The data from Easy Web Transactions is merged into HTML templates that can be displayed in the Web browser. The whole application logic remains inside the R/3 system; the ITS is only needed for generating HTML pages with the templates and data from the R/3 system. This scenario is often called Inside Out.

Contrary to Easy Web Transactions, applications developed with ITS flow logic only use RFC and BAPI (*business application programming interface*) calls to the R/3 system and are not based on a transaction in the R/3 system. Similar to Easy Web Transactions, HTML template files are used to define the design of the application, but the flow of the application is determined with so-called flow files. Flow files define which screens are displayed and which RFCs and BAPIs are called. This scenario is often called Outside In.

The standard for R/3 applications in the mySAP Workplace is the SAPGUI for HTML, often called WebGui. The SAPGUI for HTML looks like a classic SAPGUI for Windows, but it is running in the Web browser and is based on HTML. Most of the transactions can be used in the SAPGUI for HTML without problems, but certain transactions require a SAPGUI for Windows or a SAPGUI for Java. Figure 5-6 shows an example of the different GUIs.

The fourth programming model for the ITS, WebRFC, uses RFC calls to get HTML pages directly from the R/3 server. So the generating of the HTML pages takes place on the R/3 application server and not on the ITS itself.

The Workplace Engine is a service, *sapwp*, running on the ITS instance for the Workplace server. If the user logs in to the Workplace, the LaunchPad, WorkArea, Channels, and MiniApps are generated by the sapwp service. If a user clicks on an entry in the LaunchPad to start an application on a Workplace-component system, she or he connects directly to the ITS of the component system. The ITS service of the Workplace is not involved in this step.

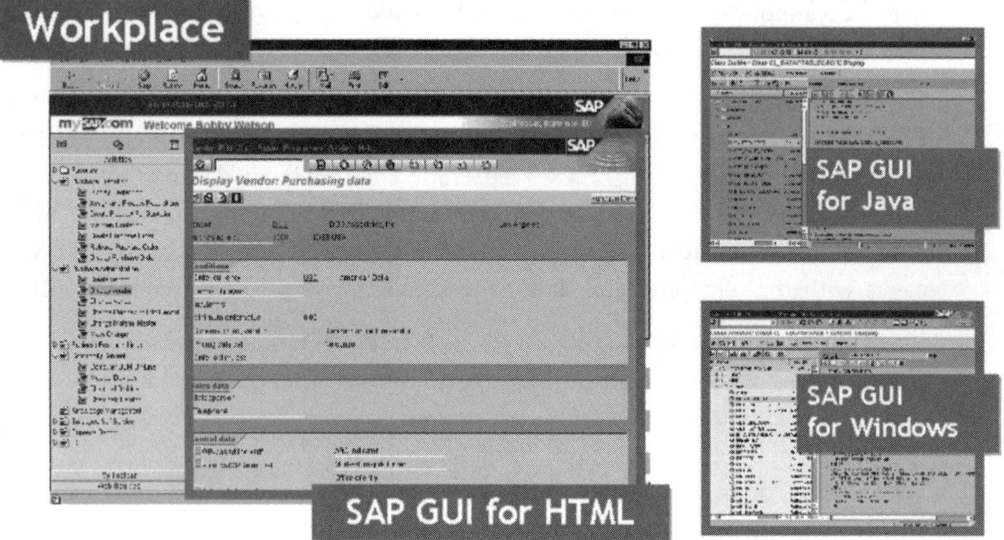

FIGURE 5-6 *GUIs available for the mySAP Workplace*

User Management in mySAP.com

mySAP environments can become complex from the point of view of user management because of the number of component systems, as well as the complexity of synchronizing them. User management involves creating new users; deleting users who leave the company; updating or modifying the master records; managing the component systems, connections, and the ALE (*Application Link Enabled*) configuration; and so on.

Users from the R/3 world know well that the users' master data is client specific. Each client must be independently managed within a system landscape. For each SAP R/3 system and for each client there is the need for creating users that are going to work in that environment. Additionally, users need authorization profiles for having access to the required transactions. These must also be maintained.

Normally with the SAP R/3 system, users could be copied across clients or across systems with the transport tools or the client copy tools by using the SAP_USER copy profile, which supports the duplication of all users and their authorizations (their activity groups). There are no synchronization mechanisms or utilities for having all user masters updated across clients.

All this decentralized and laborious work, which requires a large amount of time and management resources, has been greatly simplified in mySAP environments using the CUA utility. This tool is also available independently in R/3 systems since release 4.5. This point is quite important because, although the Workplace can connect component systems from release 3.1I and higher, systems with a lower release than 4.5 cannot make use of or be incorporated within the CUA functionality.

Background of R/3: Overview of the SAP Authorization Concept

The traditional SAP and R/3 authorization system was in charge of enforcing the right security methods so that users could access the business transactions and information they needed. The SAP systems always provided a comprehensive, complex, and flexible way of securing data and transactions against unauthorized use.

Since the introduction of the release 4.6 of R/3 and the role concept as one of the backgrounds for mySAP, the authorization system has slightly changed to make it easier to implement, more adjustable to specific users' needs, and with more options for personalizing and fine tuning. However, the foundation of the role concept is still completely based on the traditional SAP R/3 authorization concept.

SAP R/3 users are defined in *user master records*, where they are assigned one or more authorization *profiles*. These authorization profiles are made of a set of *authorizations*, which provide control accesses or access privileges for the running or accessing of the different transactions and objects of the SAP systems. Further down, authorizations refer to *authorization objects* that contain a range of permitted values for different system or business entities within the R/3 system.

The implementation of the authorization concept never was technically complicated, although it could be very time consuming. It was, however, a big issue within implementation projects due to the organizational aspects of it. This type of implementation should always be a joint project and effort between the SAP functional and the technical people. The reason is that usually SAP system managers or technical consultants do not have to deal with such things as giving access to certain users to specific cost centers, accounts, sales organizations, or production plants. It is typically the role of the key users, customizing specialists, developers, or business consultants to define the transactions, objects, or entities that should be protected by means of authorization objects and to assign or create the corresponding authorization profiles.

The following sections introduce a closer look at the traditional authorization SAP R/3 system.

Authorization Profiles

An authorization profile contains a group of authorizations, that is, a group of access privileges. As indicated above, profiles are assigned to users in the user master records. A profile could represent a simple job position because it defines the tasks for which a user has access privileges. Every profile might have as many access privileges (authorizations) as desired. Profiles can contain authorization objects and authorizations. Changing the list or contents of the authorizations inside a profile will affect all users who are given that profile when it is activated. It becomes effective the next time the user logs on. The change is not effective to the currently logged on users.

Composite Profiles

Composite profiles are sets of authorization profiles, both simple and composite. A composite profile can contain an unlimited number of profiles. They can be assigned to users just like profiles in the user master records. Composite profiles are suitable for users who have different responsibilities or job tasks in the system. These profiles are sometimes known as *reference* profiles for assigning a larger group of access privileges and having the possibility to better match users with several responsibilities. This concept is technically very similar to the current role concept.

Making modifications to any of the profiles in the list included in the composite profile will directly affect the access privileges of all users having that composite profile in the user master record. When displaying profiles in the different SAP screens, there is a flag indicating whether the profile is simple or composite.

Authorizations

The SAP systems use authorizations to define the permitted values for the fields of an authorization object. An authorization might contain one or more values for each field of the authorization objects.

An authorization object is like a template for testing access privileges, consisting of authorization fields that finally define the permitted values for the authorization. An authorization is identified with the name of an authorization object and the name of the authorization created for the object. An authorization can have many values or ranges of values for a single field. It is also possible to authorize for every value (entering an asterisk "*") or for none (leaving the field blank).

Authorizations are entered in authorization profiles with the corresponding authorization object. When an authorization is changed and then activated, it will immediately affect all users having a profile containing that authorization in their user master records.

The technical names for authorizations and authorization objects have a maximum of 12 positions, but usually they display in the system using short descriptive texts. For customer-created authorizations, the only name restriction is not to place an underscore in the second position of the technical name. Additionally, every customer-created system object should comply with the SAP standard style guide and begin with either a *Z* or a *Y* to distinguish it from the SAP original objects, thus avoiding the possibility of being overwritten by a system upgrade.

Authorization Objects

An authorization object identifies an element or object within the SAP systems that needs to be protected. These objects work like templates for granting access rights, by means of authorization fields, which allow for performing complex tests of access privileges. An authorization object can contain a maximum of 10 authorization fields. Users will be permitted to perform a system function only when passing the test for every field in the authorization object. The verification against the field contents is done with the logical AND operator. A user's action will be allowed only if the user authorization passes the access test for each field contained in an object. With this mechanism, the system can perform multiconditional tests. As with authorizations, when maintaining authorization objects, the system does not display the names, but a descriptive text for each object.

Authorization objects are grouped in object classes belonging to different application areas that are used to limit the search for objects, thus making it faster to navigate among the many SAP system objects.

SAP predefined authorization objects should not be modified or deleted, except if instructed by the SAP support personnel or a SAP note. Deleting or changing standard authorization objects can cause severe errors in programs that check those objects. Before an authorization object is to be modified, all authorizations defined for that object must be first deleted.

If you want to use the OR logic for giving users access to certain functions, you can define several authorizations for the same object, each time with different values. In the user master records, you assign each of these profiles, which are linked with the OR logic. So, when the system tests whether the user has access privileges, it will check each authorization to see if the assigned values comply with the access condition. The system will allow access with the first authorization that passes the test.

Authorization Fields

Authorization fields identify the elements of the system that are to be protected by assigning them an access test. An authorization field can be, for example, a user group, a company code, a purchasing group, a development class, an application area, and so on. There is one authorization field that is found in most authorization objects: the *Activity* field. The Activity field in authorization objects defines the possible actions that could be performed over a particular application object. For example, activity "03" is always "Display." So if an authorization contains two fields like "company code" and "activity," and the company code field is "*" (which means all company codes), it means that the user with that authorization can only display the company codes.

The list of standard activities in the system is held on the SAP standard table TACT. The relationship between the authorization objects and the activities is held on table TACTZ. Not all authorization objects have the Activity authorization field. Authorization fields are the components of authorization objects. Fields are also part of the standard ABAP function call AUTHORITY-CHECK.

When maintaining authorization, the system does not display the real names (technical names) for the fields, instead it shows a description for each field. Table TOBJ contains the fields that are associated with each authorization object, which is how the SAP system knows which fields belong to an authorization object. The fields in an object are associated with data elements in the ABAP data dictionary. Authorization fields are not maintained from the user maintenance menu, but have to be defined within the development environment. Normally, users do not need to change standard authorization fields, except if they are adding or modifying system elements and want those elements to be tested with authorizations.

The Profile Generator

Creation, modification, and assignment of authorizations and profiles used to be a complex task within SAP projects. This task is often underestimated in the planning charter. In order to overcome the problem of missing authorizations and the inability for working normally, there is a natural tendency to assign full privileges to many users, which might create problems and also seriously threaten security and control.

Time and effort needed for authorization tasks, together with customer requests, made SAP design a tool for reducing the time needed for implementing and managing the authorizations, decreasing the implementation costs. This tool is known as the *Profile Generator*.

The Profile Generator is an SAP utility available since release 3.0F and productively since release 3.1G. Its goal is to facilitate the users' authorizations and the management of users' profiles. It can be used for automatically creating authorizations and profiles and assigning them easily to users.

The Profile Generator is the predecessor of the Menu Maintenance and Role Maintenance function from releases 4.6 or mySAP Workplace. It can be accessed by entering transaction code *PFCG* in the command field.

The Profile Generator only generates simple profiles. When these profiles have been automatically generated with the Profile Generator, they can not be maintained manually.

When profiles are manually maintained, the administrators must select the authorization objects, group them into profiles, and then assign them to users. With the Profile Generator, administrators select functions and tasks—*transactions*—and the system automatically selects and groups the authorization objects.

The definition of profiles with the Profile Generator is based on the possibility of grouping functions by *activity groups* in a company menu, generated by using customizing settings, that will only include those functions selected by the customers. Activity groups form a set of tasks or activities that can be performed in the system, like running programs, transactions, and other functions that generally represent a job role. The activity groups and the information they include are what make the profiles able to be automatically generated.

Central User Administration

When the Workplace is used as an Enterprise Portal, all users of the component systems must be defined within the Workplace server (WPS). So the WPS becomes the perfect place for the centralized administration of users from the mySAP component systems.

The objective of the CUA tool is to use a specific client in a system. From this client, it is possible to manage the user master data for all clients within a complex system landscape such as mySAP. For each individual user, it has to be determined to which clients and on which systems the user will connect. Usually, users do not need to connect to all component systems within the Workplace.

The CUA tool also allows defining which data from the user master records can be centrally managed and which data can be managed locally. The interchange and synchronization of data is possible using the ALE technology. ALE can be used for configuring and operating distributed applications within SAP environments.

Using CUA, the following data can be distributed:

- User master data such as address, logon information, default values, and so on can be distributed.
- The assignment of users to simple roles is possible. Composite roles and profiles must be done in each of the component systems. The advantage of using CUA for these assignments is that it is not required to connect locally to each system that will contain these assignments. It can be performed in a centralized manner from the Workplace server.
- When a new user is added, the initial password is distributed to the component systems for which the user is defined.
- Besides the normal locking mechanisms for users (logon failures, session lock, manual lock) there is a new *global lock*. This lock is effective in all component systems where the user is defined and can be unlocked either locally or globally.

In the case of roles, either simple or composite, and the authorization profiles, this data is usually maintained locally and not centrally. This is because the systems could have different releases, and customizing is typically different in component systems. In order to use the CUA tool for SAP, R/3 systems release 4.5B or higher is required.

Data is exchanged between systems using ALE technology with transactional RFC. The objective is to guarantee the consistent distribution of data among all systems, even in the case that a component system is temporarily unavailable.

Steps for Configuring ALE

The following are the required steps for configuring ALE in order to use CUA:

- First, the name of the component systems must be known; the Workplace server must know the name and location of every component system. Likewise, every component system must know the name of the Workplace server.
- Because the communication is established using RFC calls, the RFC connections must be defined in every component system that will take part of the mySAP landscape.
- Within the WPS, the ALE distribution model must be defined. This model defines which data (data types) is exchanged and among which systems this is performed. It defines how many systems exist, how the data flows, and the documentation between them.

ALE Configuration

The systems that take part in the mySAP Workplace landscape are defined within an ALE scenario based on an *alias,* which is defined using *logical systems.* A logical system corresponds exactly to one client within a SAP system. For each system and client that should be enabled for connection, a logical system must be defined. This definition is client specific so that the client is directly related to the logical system. Within the Workplace server, all component systems have to be defined as logical systems. In the component system, the same system and the WPS system have to be defined as logical systems.

Logical systems can be defined using transaction SALE: Sending and Receiving Systems/Logical Systems/Define Logical Systems (See Figures 5-7 and 5-8). SAP recommends to use only uppercase letters for the names and suggests also the following naming convention:

```
<SID>CLNT<Client number>
```

The table that contains the definition of the logical system is client independent.

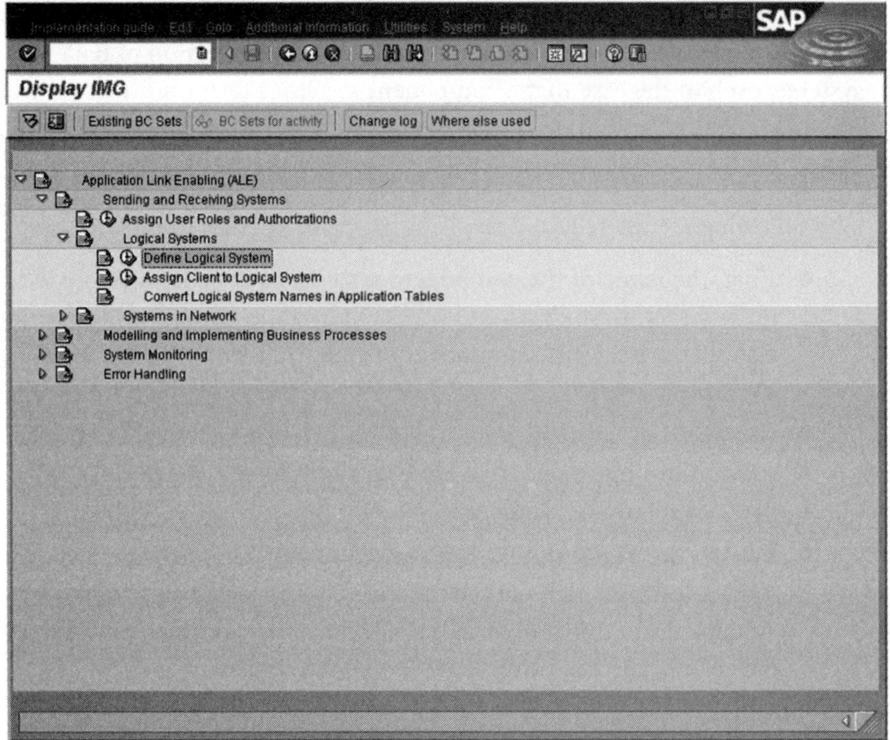

FIGURE 5-7 *Overview of transaction SALE*

The following step is to assign the logical name to the clients, which is done using normal transaction for client maintenance such as the SCC4. For defining the RFC connections, the transaction SM59 is used. Figure 5-9 shows an overview of transaction SM59.

Because the WPS will need to connect to every component system, all RFC connections to these systems must be defined. This is not required in component systems that only need to define the RFC connection to the WPS for this purpose. The definitions of RFC connections are client independent and are held in table RFCDES. The name of the RFC connection must match exactly that of the logical names of the component systems. The connection type is "3," which indicates that it is an R/3 connection (Basis). Detailed definition of an RFC connection is sown in Figure 5-10.

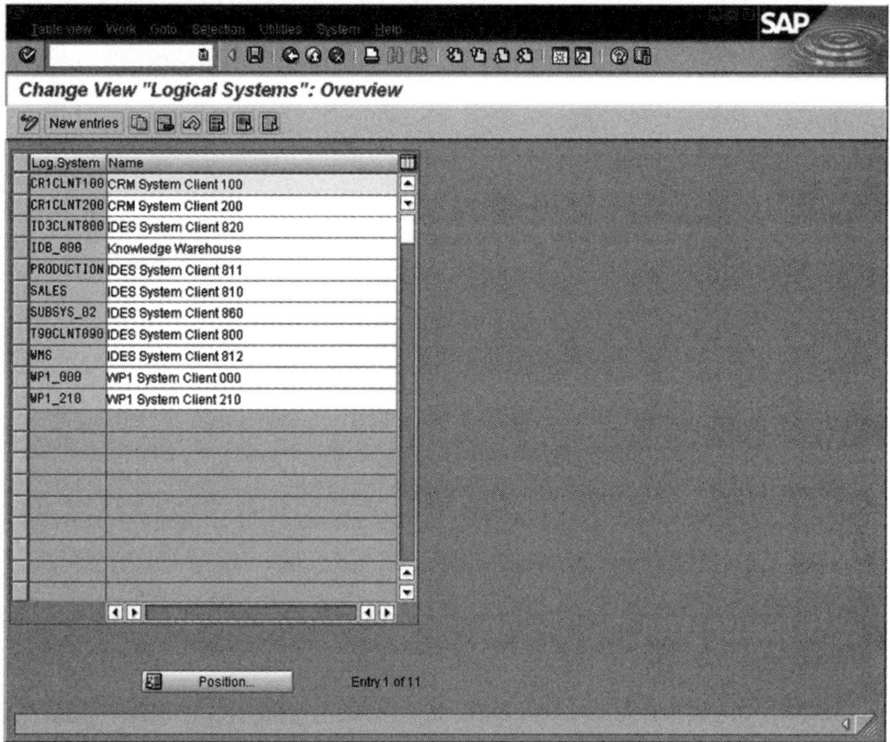

FIGURE 5-8 *Defining logical systems with transaction SALE*

Additionally, SAP recommends using the *load distribution* feature for these connections.

For the RFC communication to function properly, it is required to define a CPI-C user for each of the component systems with the SAP_ALL authorization profile. This user should be defined at the beginning of the customization process.

ALE Distribution Model

The ALE distribution model is first defined in the WPS and later distributed to each of the component systems. This configuration is a three step process that can be performed using transaction BD64.

1. First, while in change mode, select option Create model view for creating a new ALE distribution model. This model will be identified by a

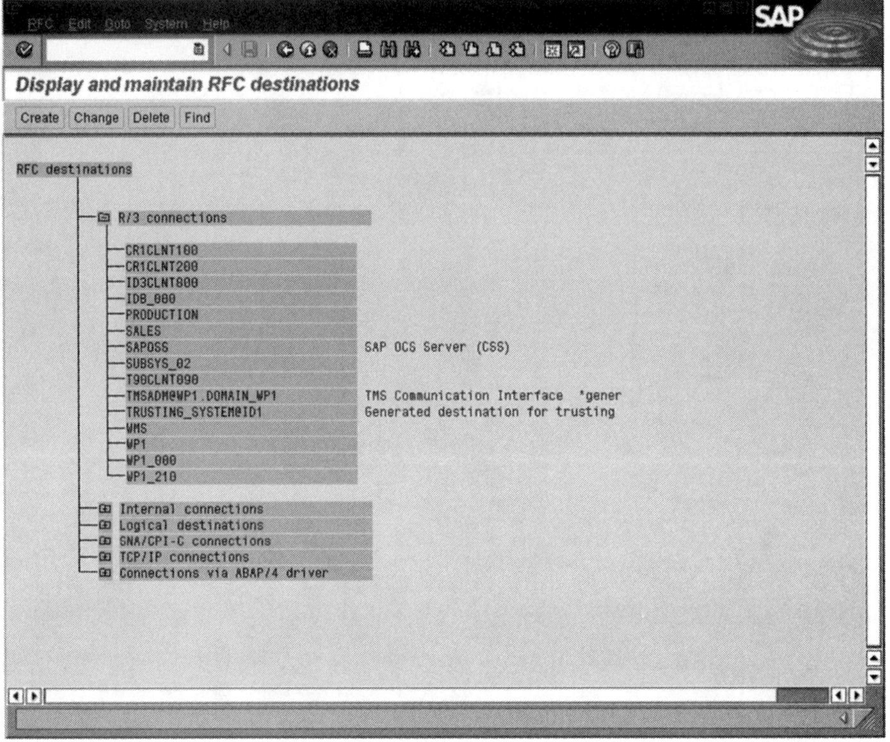

FIGURE 5-9 *Overview of transaction SM59*

technical name. Then select option Add BAPI to add the following BAPIs to the model:

USER.Clone	(user data)
UserCompny.Clone	(company data)

2. The logical system of the WPS is defined as the sender and the logical name of the component system is the receiver.
3. The next step is to generate the *partner profile*, which is required for the ALE distribution. This is accomplished by selecting Environment/Generate partner profiles from the menu.
4. Next, the model must be distributed to the component systems. This is done by selecting Edit/Model view; then the ALE distribution model

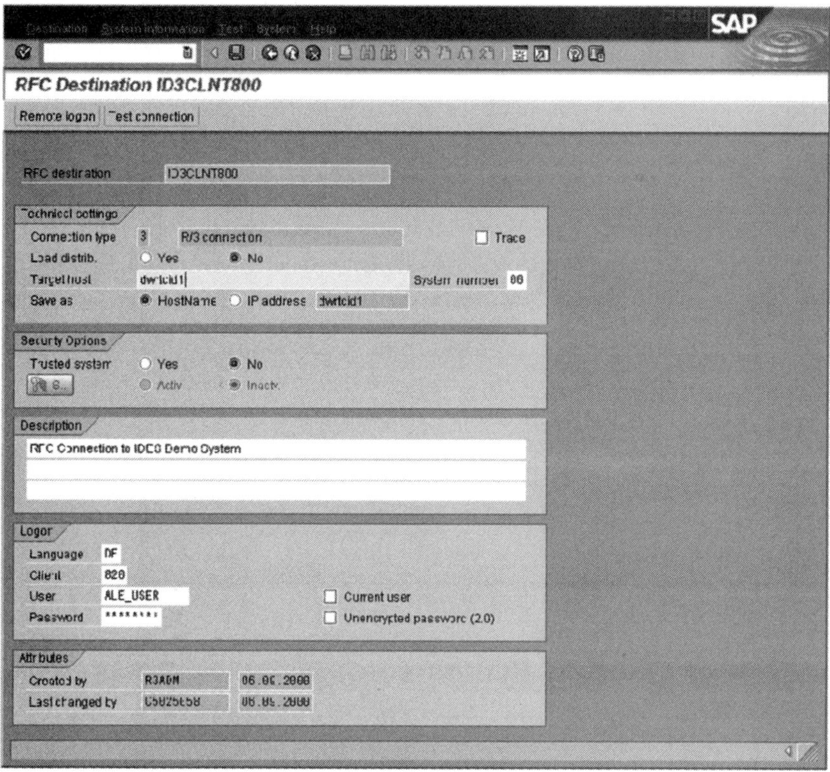

FIGURE 5-10 *Detailed definition of an RFC connection*

and all the logical names of the component systems are selected. The partner profiles must also be generated in the component systems.

CUA Configuration

The CUA utility is activated within the WPS using transaction SCUA. For each of the elements of the user master data, you can define whether they are going to be maintained globally from the WPS or locally from the component system. This is accomplished using transaction SCUM. For each of the fields of the user master record that can be found using transaction SU01, a field attribute can be defined. Possible values are as follow in Table 5-2.

Table 5-2 Field Attributes for User Master Records

Attribute	Meaning
Global	The value can only be maintained in the Workplace. The data is distributed to the component system as soon as it is saved in the Workplace. In the component systems these global fields cannot be changed and can only be displayed.
Proposal	An entry in the Workplace is distributed to the component systems. These fields can be maintained locally but without reverse distribution (toward the Workplace and the other component systems).
Retval	The field data can be maintained both locally and globally. If the data is modified in a component system, this change is transmitted toward the WPS and from there to the rest of component systems.
Local	It can only be maintained locally and there is no distribution to other systems.
Everywhere	The data can be maintained in any system but without distribution to other systems.

Integrating Existing Systems

There are two ways of implementing CUA with existing systems:

- Starting from scratch, creating all user master records
- Using the existing user master data that can be migrated to the CUA environment

In the first case, the consistency for the data to be distributed is guaranteed. In the second case, in which CUA is implemented when there are already user master data records, there must be a migration process to reuse this information, which will need to be modified and validated in the Workplace server. Likewise, both the simple and composite roles as well as the user assignments to these roles or activity groups must be known to the WPS. The assignment of authorizations to simple roles must still be maintained in local systems (component systems).

Migration Tool

The migration of user master records from the existing component systems to the Workplace server can be performed using the transaction SCUG (option Transfer users). The migration is done only once for each of the component systems. After data is transferred (migrated), the user master records can only be maintained within the WPS according to the field attributes which were defined (see previous section). A user account (user master record) should have the last and first name in all the component systems using CUA where the same user must be defined.

When transferring users using the Migration Tool, three cases are possible:

- **The user account in the component system does not exist in the Workplace server.** In this case, the migration can take place without problems.
- **The user account already exists in the WPS with the same first and last name.** In this case, the account can also be transferred without problems.
- **The user account in the component system exists in the WPS but has a different first or last name.** In this case, before transferring the data, the ambiguity should be resolved. If the name on the WPS is the correct one, the data can be migrated. On the contrary, the username in the WPS should be modified before using the common user maintenance transaction SU01.

Once the CUA utility is activated, the appearance of the SU01 transaction changes slightly. In the WPS there is an additional tab Systems. This tab will contain the logical systems where the user data should be distributed. The user is only available in those systems. In the tabs Roles and Profiles, there is also a Systems column. In this way, the assignment of users to simple roles, composite roles, and profiles can be defined individually for each of the component systems. When the option Save is selected, the data is distributed.

The creation and maintenance of simple and composite roles takes place in the component systems. For assigning these roles or authorizations that are only known in the component systems, the option Text comparison for child systems must be selected in the folders for profiles and activity groups. The names of the roles and authorization profiles are replicated to the WPS. From that moment, these names will be available in the WPS (use the help function F4). Because this information can be modified at any time and in any of the component systems, the replication operation should be repeated regularly.

CUA Log System

Each change in the user data is distributed asynchronously to the component system. These systems respond to each change by sending a message to the WPS. This message can be a successful, warning, or error situation. This is displayed using transaction SCUL. (See Figure 5-11.)

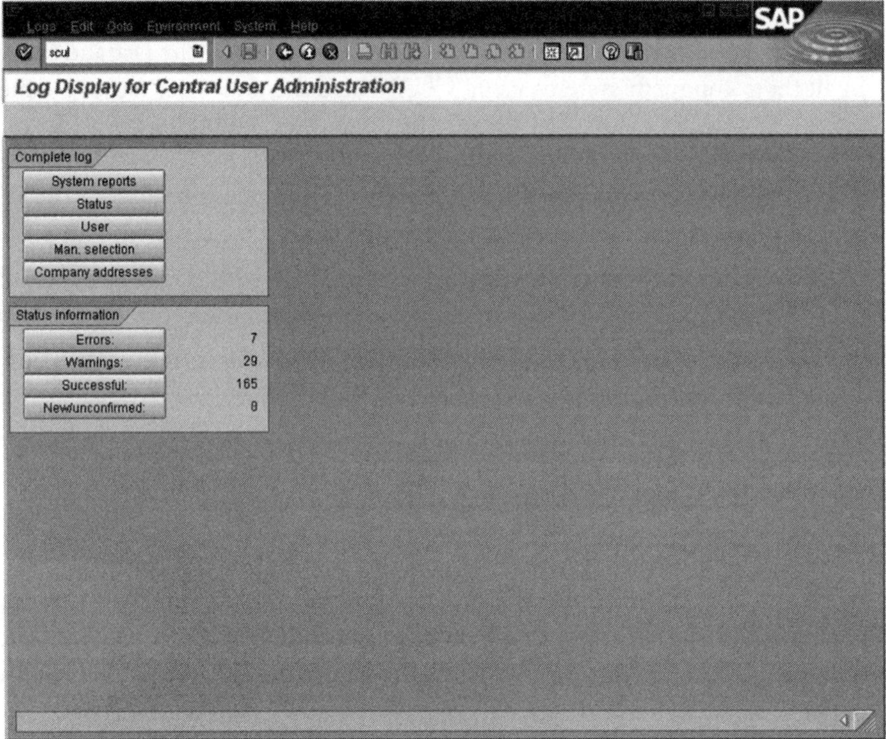

FIGURE 5-11 *Initial screen of transaction SCUL*

Managing Roles in the Workplace

Within the mySAP strategies, actual application components are provided by means of Business Scenarios. These scenarios are provided on a role basis so that customers can choose SAP functionality for the jobs they need. Users can have several roles within Business Scenarios or can participate in different ones. For instance, a user might be a professional purchaser, but at the same time needs the Employee Self Service functionality or access to parts of the financial accounting. This is a real-life example of why the concept of roles is so important and fundamental within mySAP. The functionality of the roles is handled in the Workplace.

The mySAP Workplace includes a large set of predefined roles ready for use or for copying and adapting to particular company needs. The following Figure 5-12 shows the role map provided by SAP.

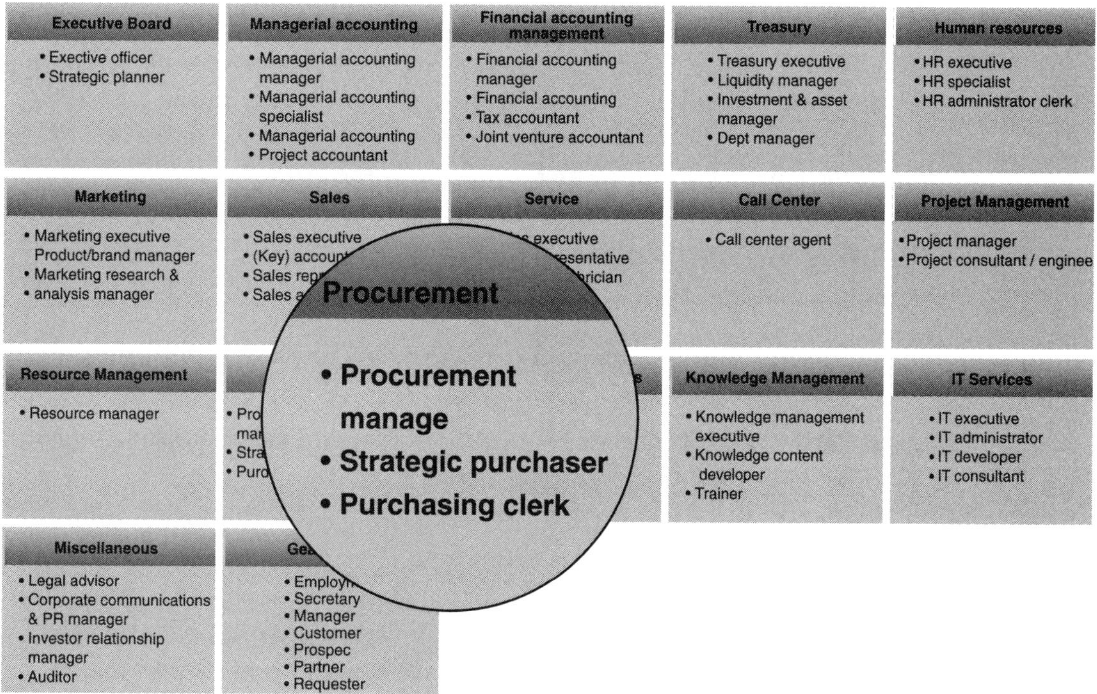

FIGURE 5-12 *Role Map*

From a logical point of view, a role is the description of a job position, function, or responsibility within a company organization. The entire working environment of the mySAP strategy is focused on the role concept. That is, every user defined within the mySAP Workplace must have one or several corresponding roles. From a technical point of view, a role is made up of a collection of transactions, Web links, reports, MiniApps, non-SAP applications, and so on. Additionally, a role is associated with the required authorizations to be able to start and execute the functionality associated to the role. Basically, roles define which transactions, which information, and what services are available for the users of the Workplace.

Defining Roles

The first question that must be answered within a Workplace environment configured with several component systems is, Where are roles managed? Depending on the role type, roles are defined and managed in the component systems or in the WPS.

- **Single roles.** These are created and managed in the component systems and are later transferred to the WPS.
- **Composite roles.** These are created and maintained only in the WPS. With this type of role, the administrator configures the appearance of the LaunchPad for the user logging in to the Workplace.

Defining Roles: Steps

The following are the basic steps for role definition:

1. The first step for defining a role is to define to which systems the user having such a role will have access.
2. Next, the roles (menus) are created, and the authorizations and profiles are generated for each role defined.
3. Once roles are generated, they must be assigned to the corresponding users. How and when this assignment takes place depends on whether the CUA is used or not. If the CUA is not being used, the roles must be assigned to the users, and then the administrator must perform a *user comparison* for transferring the authorization values to the user master records. If the CUA is used, the role assignment is done later in the WPS.
4. Next, the role definitions and the user assignments are transferred, in the case of not using the CUA. For configuring the Workplace, the users and roles must be available to the WPS.
5. The composite roles are defined within the WPS. If the CUA is enabled, the administrator must assign the users to the systems to which they need to have access.
6. The final step is to assign composite roles to the WPS users.

Defining Simple Roles

Simple roles are first created and maintained in the component systems, to be later transferred to the WPS. Roles can be created from scratch. However, SAP provides a large collection of standard roles that can be imported and later copied and used so that customers can adjust their needs without starting from scratch.

There is a standard report, RSUSR070, which provides a list of user roles that are provided by SAP. You can also use the SUIM (user and authorization information system) to generate a description of available roles.

Menu Design

The role administration is performed using the classic transaction for the Profile Generator: PFCG. You can also access the utility by selecting Tools/Administration/User Maintenance/Roles.

The user menu options (LaunchPad) can be adapted to user requirements by adding or deleting transactions and folders, including reports, Internet links, files, and MiniApps. When a report is included within a role, the Profile Generator creates a user-defined transaction code so that the user can start the report.

Generating Authorization Profiles

Roles are maintained using the Profile Generator transaction PFCG, which automatically generates the authorizations corresponding to the transactions that are previously selected using a menu tree for the user role. There is, however, some manual maintenance for these authorizations because there are values that must be defined by the customer for each case: for instance, the organization structure allowed, activities, and so on.

When maintaining and generating profiles to be assigned to roles, the screen shows a yellow light right by the object if the authorization objects are not completely maintained (do not have values assigned). When all values are assigned, the light becomes green. Once all values are adjusted for the authorization objects according to the user requirements (the authorization project), the profile can be generated just by clicking on the Generate button.

Working without CUA

When the CUA is not activated, the assignment of users to roles must be manually performed in each component system to indicate how users will have access to those systems. This assignment is also performed using the role administration transaction PFCG. As has been mentioned, it is possible (and even quite common) to assign more than one role to users. It is also possible and typical to assign the same role to several users.

The assignment of users to roles does not automatically activate the authorizations for them. For this process to take place, it is required to execute the operation known as a user comparison. By using this program, the system compares the actual user master record with the record as it has been defined with the assignment of the role. This process can be launched either individually or massively, either interactively or in a batch job.

Assigning Users to Composite Roles

When the CUA is not activated, the assignment of users to composite roles must be performed in the WPS. As indicated in the previous section, the assignment of a simple role to a user must be performed in each of the component systems. When using the CUA utility, it is only required to assign the user to the composite role in the WPS. In this case, the simple roles are automatically assigned to the users in each of the component systems. In both cases, with or without the CUA, updating the user master records must be performed using the user comparison utility in each component system.

Once the composite roles are assigned to users in the WPS, the users can log on to the Workplace. The users can select from the transactions or services offered within the LaunchPad. All transactions will be executed on the corresponding component system.

Authorization for Connecting to the Workplace

All users who are going to connect to the Workplace are also required to have the authorization S_RFC with all values assigned (that is, the wildcard "*"). Additionally, to allow users to personalize their access to the Workplace, they must also have the SAP_WORKPLACE_USER assigned. With this role, the users can customize their MiniApps and their GUIs.

Configuring the mySAP Workplace: Overview

Implementing a mySAP Workplace as an Enterprise Portal is an exciting project, which requires a great deal of preparation, analysis, design, and implementation. There are many technical details and tasks that should not be overlooked and must actually be performed in order to set the basic functionality of the mySAP Workplace. These are the customizing settings required for defining such topics as general settings, Web server definitions, connections, classification of transactions, and so on.

In the following section "Overview of Customizing Tables," there is a table of the Workplace customizing tables and their purpose. Later, Chapter 8, "The SAP Web Application Server," includes a detailed overview of activities and task lists in order to implement a mySAP Workplace.

Considerations Before Implementing the mySAP Workplace

Before starting the mySAP Workplace configuration, you must check that the system (Workplace server) is correctly and completely installed. This basically means having the mySAP Basis (just an R/3 system) and the Workplace plug-in. If the SAPGUI for Windows or SAPGUI for Java is going to be used, the corresponding front-end software or Java plug-ins need to be loaded.

Technical requirements are as follows:

- As browser, Microsoft Internet Explorer 5.0 or higher is necessary. Check in the SAP Service Marketplace for the availability of other browsers. If this release is not used, the Drag&Relate and drag and drop functionality is not available.
- An ITS instance is required for the Workplace and all the R/3 component systems to which users will connect from the Workplace.
- The Workplace server will be a standalone system from which to execute the main functions. These include:
  - Role management
  - CUA
  - Configuration or development of MiniApps
  - SSO
  - Definition of RFC connections and logical systems
  - Generation of transaction URLs
  - Drag&Relate
  - Customizing
- Workplace Middleware server (an ITS server with specific services for the Workplace) is needed.
- Server for the Drag&Relate functionality is required.

Central Settings for the Workplace

The following list reflects the basic tasks that must be defined for the Workplace. These tasks are achieved with some of the transactions described earlier, as well as by filling up some of the customizing tables.

- ◆ Registering logical system
- ◆ Creating RFC connections
- ◆ Registering an ITS server
- ◆ Creating individual roles (adding transactions, reports or Web addresses)
- ◆ Creating authorization for single roles
- ◆ Assigning a user role (without CUA)
- ◆ Transporting role to mySAP Workplace using a transport request
- ◆ Importing roles from component system by RFC
- ◆ Entering the destination system in a single role (adding MiniApps)
- ◆ Creating composite roles
- ◆ Assigning a user role

Creating and Configuring MiniApps

MiniApps refer to any kind of application, information, or service that can be visualized in a Web browser frame. The MiniApps are shown in a push mechanism in the home page of the user of the Workplace. Users will see the MiniApps that have been assigned to them according to their role. The previous Figure 5-2 showed the WorkSpace with the MiniApps.

These are the main features and characteristics of MiniApps:

- ◆ The set of MiniApps provided in the mySAP Workplace depends on the role of the user.
- ◆ MiniApps are self-contained Web documents that are provided by a URL, managed by the mySAP Workplace server. The resource itself can be anywhere on the Web.
- ◆ MiniApps proactively provide information to the users.
- ◆ Examples of MiniApps are e-mail or calendar access, alerts, reports, search engines, company news, stock tickers, BW reports, help, banners, and so on.
- ◆ MiniApps are open to any custom development.

There are several ways to create MiniApps. Some of them are as follows:

- Because they are always called using a URL, the easiest way is to set a URL link to a Web service or document. If this is the case, there is no development at all.
- They can be developed using popular environments such as Visual Basic (Visual Studio), Visual Age, and so on.
- They can be created by linking a BW Web report using the ITS flow logic.

The way to integrate a MiniApp in the Workplace is by just including the URLs in the user's role. This is performed by selecting Goto/MiniApps from the Role Maintenance screen.

In order to facilitate and increase the number of MiniApps that can be deployed within the mySAP Workplaces, SAP has created the MiniApps Community at the following site: **http://www.sap.com/miniapps**, this is displayed in Figure 5-13. SAP maintains the MiniApps Community for customers, partners, and other parties, in order to create interest in the development of MiniApps, as well as to share information, ideas, and programs. On the MiniApps Community Web site, there are all of the required materials for MiniApps development, such as:

- Downloads
- Information
- Books
- Chat
- Examples
- Tricks
- Interesting links

Integrating Non-SAP Systems

The integration of non-SAP systems depends on the type of application that should be integrated into the Workplace. Web applications based on HTML can be integrated very easily, but it is also possible to integrate applications using a browser plug-in, applications installed on the local client, or by running on a Citrix Terminal Server. Web-based intranet or Internet applications can be integrated into the Workplace by adding their URLs to a role. Standard Windows applications can be installed on the local client, or the application can run on a Citrix

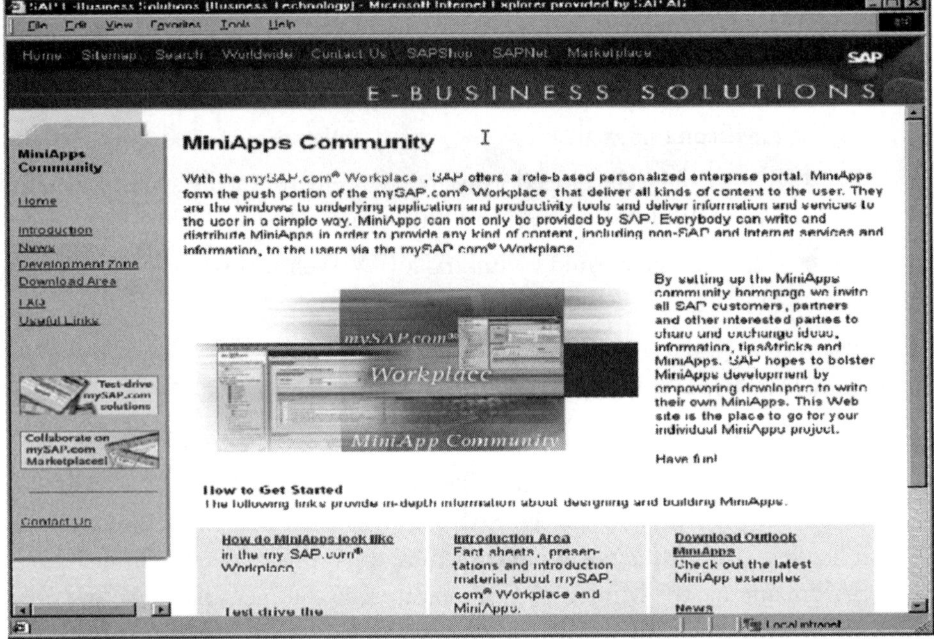

FIGURE 5-13 *MiniApps Community*

Terminal Server and be displayed with a browser plug-in in the WorkArea of the Workplace. This also applies for the SAPGUI for Windows.

You have to decide on which way you want to integrate non-SAP applications into your Workplace. You can either include them by link in the LaunchPad of the user or execute them as MiniApps in the WorkArea. Applications integrated in the LaunchPad can run in the WorkArea of the Workplace or can start in a separate window. MiniApps have to be called with a URL, so they should be either based on a HTML Web application or run as a Java applet or ActiveX control.

Just adding links to non-SAP applications to the LaunchPad or embedding them as MiniApps does not fulfill the requirements of real integration, because third-party applications often require an additional login process. So you have to think about enabling those applications for SSO.

If you are using SSO cookies, this integration is very restricted, because SSO cookies only work with the ITS or the SAPGUI for Windows. For using SSO

Tickets, SAP AG offers a library (sapsecu-lib) for checking SSO Tickets in third-party applications. This way, existing intranet applications can be integrated into the Workplace, and SSO will work.

Client certificates (X.509) are qualified for SSO solutions in heterogeneous environments with SAP and non-SAP systems. X.509 is a public standard and is supported by a wide variety of applications. Additionally, it is possible to verify the certificates using a central directory service such as LDAP (*Lightweight Directory Access Protocol*).

Overview of Customizing Tables

Normally, the customizing tables are maintained by importing the Workplace add-on (Workplace server) or the plug-ins (components). The tables TWPURLSVR, USRURLSVR, TWPLGRPLNG, TSTCCLASS, THRPCLASS, THRSCLASS, and USRURLPRS generate URLs. The tables TSTCCLASS, THRPCLASS, and THRSCLASS classify transactions, IACs (*Internet Application Components*) and Workflow tasks in the component systems (see Table 5-3 below).

Table 5-3 Workplace Customizing Tables

Table	What gets configured?	Where does it get configured?
VWPCUSTOMC	Central settings for the mySAP Workplace	mySAP Workplace
TWPURLSVR	Web server definition for Workplace components	mySAP Workplace
USRURLSVR	Logical Web server for logical systems of a given user	mySAP Workplace
TWPLGRLPNG	Mapping from logon language to logon group	mySAP Workplace
USRURLPRS	SAPGUI specifications for a given user	mySAP Workplace
TSTCCLASS	SAPGUI classification for a transaction	Component system
THRPCLASS	SAPGUI classification for a Workflow object (customer)	Component system
THRSCLASS	SAPGUI classification for a Workflow object (standard)	Component system

mySAP Workplace Release 3.0

With the introduction of release 3.0 of the mySAP Workplace, SAP aims to become a big player in the market for corporate portals. In order to achieve this strategic goal, SAP is leveraging the current Workplace offering with new layer for MiniApps Development and technologically advanced content management. Figure 5-14 is an overview of the design for the new Workplace architecture.

The key piece of the release 3.0 of the Workplace is the component known as the WCM (*Web Content Management*), which will be in charge of joining knowledge management-based technology with the role concept and making the inclusion, search, formatting, and storing of the content a faster and more technically advanced process.

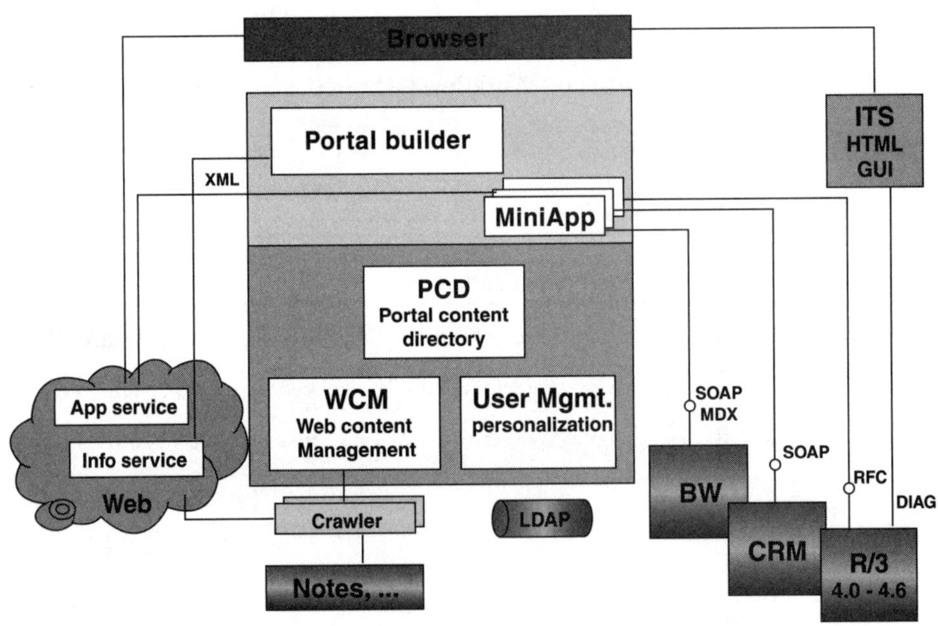

FIGURE 5-14 *Architecture for the mySAP Workplace 3.0* Copyright by SAP AG

Chapter 6

mySAP Marketplace

The mySAP Marketplace is an important component within the global mySAP.com e-business platform, because it is the major player in the collaborative business-to-business arena, providing a set of advanced services that can be used by many other mySAP solutions.

The need for collaboration and cooperation among the information systems of different companies has always existed. But the tremendous infrastructure provided today by the Internet and Web protocols has enabled collaboration among businesses like never before. Virtual marketplaces, also known as *e-marketplaces*, are today the maximum expression of that collaboration.

An e-marketplace is a concentrator for interenterprise communication. Through an e-marketplace, the documents generated by the information systems of different companies are exchanged. The e-marketplaces also provide added value services for businesses, such as buying and selling, bidding, news, bank services, logistic operators, and so on.

There are horizontal virtual marketplaces in which companies from different industry sectors do business. And there are vertical ones, in which only companies from the same industry collaborate. There are also private marketplaces where only a company and its business partners (providers, main customers, and so on) do business together.

In May 2000, SAP created a new company with the mission of promoting marketplace software and projects. This company is SAPMarkets, devoted to spearheading all marketplace efforts of the SAP Group. One month later, in June 2000, SAPMarkets reached an agreement with the company CommerceOne for the joint development, support, and sale of the software for the creation and operation of virtual marketplaces. As a result of this joint venture, SAPMarkets launched its software solution for e-marketplaces known as MarketSet.

MarketSet Overview

MarketSet is the SAPMarkets open solution for horizontal, vertical, and private e-marketplaces. As such, MarketSet is the main application solution for the mySAP Marketplace component.

MarketSet can be used for designing, implementing, and managing virtual marketplaces that potentially deliver added value to businesses and business partners. Examples of added value services include the possibility for reducing inventories' cycle times and improving an efficient communication channel between buyers and suppliers so that the supply chain becomes integrated into a fast and efficient collaboration process.

The virtual marketplace is also a place where there is a greater transparency between business partners, allowing for simultaneous interactions, the publication of requests for proposals, or demand planning. Therefore, suppliers participating within marketplaces can respond faster to buyer needs compared with other competitors outside the marketplace.

In summary, e-marketplaces can be one of the most efficient collaboration resources for business and trading partners. The exchange of information in real-time allows for a great optimization potential for saving costs and for streamlining the supply chain and thus the time to market or the product or service availability. Therefore, e-marketplaces will directly benefit businesses and end-customers, and companies can effectively turn this collaborative relationship into a great opportunity for generating revenues and profit.

With the goal and focus of getting that efficiency out of collaborative communities, SAPMarkets created the MarketSet platform. It is a collaboration platform that can provide those added value services by also joining processes and exchanging documents across multiple information systems. The MarketSet is therefore a step forward in the traditional procurement processes and applications and can handle both direct procurement and complex supply chain management.

As you will see in the rest of the sections in this chapter, the MarketSet infrastructure is based on and designed using standard technologies, making it an open solution that provides the platform, tools, and services for creating a solid virtual marketplace.

From a software point of view, the MarketSet provides all the needed pieces to design and build a virtual marketplace that can provide collaborative business services such as selling and buying, auctions, catalogs, planning, and so on. As an open platform, e-marketplace operators can expand their service offerings by incorporating additional services by other providers.

Figure 6-1 shows the basic components of release 2.0 of MarketSet.

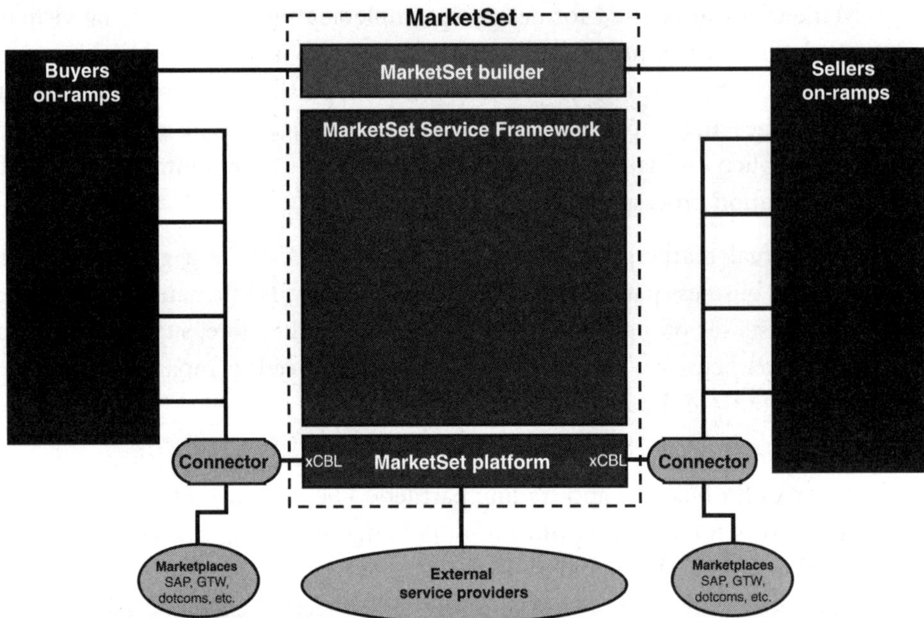

FIGURE 6-1 *MarketSet 2.0 basic structure* Copyright by SAP AG

MarketSet Internal Blocks

Within the internal components of the MarketSet, the first thing you should look at is the *MarketSet Service Framework*. This is the component in charge of holding the different services supported by the MarketSet. The Service Framework is a collection of rules, methods, APIs (*application program interfaces*), and tools, which are in charge of managing and controlling the way in which those services must be placed within the e-marketplace.

The SAPMarkets document "Business Service Framework Cookbook" includes detailed aspects of some of those rules, such as the ability for user registration and administration, specific interfaces based on xCBL (*XML Common Business Library*) documents, common user interface, Single Sign-On, tracking, billing, and others. Figure 6-2 shows the different interfaces for those services that are to be hosted within the MarketSet.

As stated earlier, the MarketSet Service Framework is a completely open environment, and therefore it can contain two types of services: those included within the MarketSet or from third parties. The included services will be described with

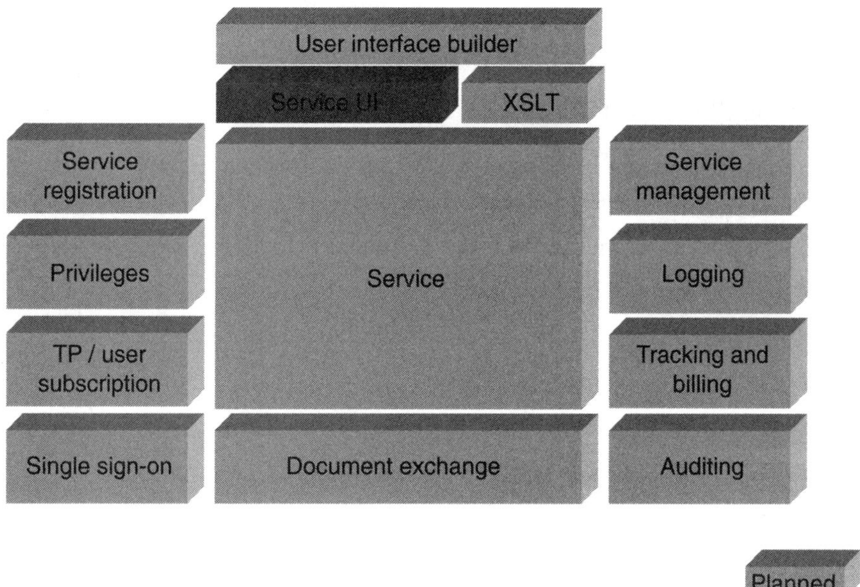

FIGURE 6-2 *MarketSet service interfaces* Copyright by SAP AG

detail in the following sections of this chapter. Of the third-party types, only several examples will be introduced.

The services of release 2.0 of MarketSet include:

- MarketSet Procurement
- MarketSet Order Management
- MarketSet Dynamic Pricing
- MarketSet Catalog
- MarketSet Analytics
- MarketSet Bulletin Board
- MarketSet Life-Cycle Collaboration
- MarketSet Supply Chain Collaboration

Some types of third-party services include:

- Logistic Services
- Transport Arrangement
- Transport Settlement

- Legal Services
- Foreign Trade Atrium
- Import/Export Control
- Sanctioned Party List Screening
- Customs Determination
- Export Documents
- Financial Services
- E-payment
- Escrow
- Orbian Credit
- Credit Risk Evaluation
- Factoring (Selling of Debts)
- Purchasing Cards
- Credit Risk Insurance
- Security Services
- Personal Identification
- Content Setup Services
- Auction Execution Services

MarketSet Builder

The *MarketSet Builder*, also known as the User Interface Builder, is the component in charge of generating the HTML interface for the users. It is technically based on an open source solution that includes role and personalization functions, as well as support for document exchange based on both XML and xCBL. For administrators, it also includes a framework for handling transformations, styles, and other management tools.

From a functional point of view, the MarketSet Builder is in charge of providing a common look, personalization services, and the user interface framework for the integration of the MarketSet services. To facilitate the creation of e-marketplaces for market makers, the MarketSet Builder includes:

- Templates
- System for user/policy management

- Role-based and user-based personalization
- Methods for trading partner registration and user login

Figure 6-3 includes a basic diagram of the MarketSet Builder components.

In the upper part of the figure, you can see the Jetspeed 1.2 component. This is maybe the most important one within the MarketSet Builder, because it allows for joining several HTML sources into a single one without using frames. The Jetspeed component provides compatibility with any browser and, at the same time, quick downloads. More information about Jetspeed, as well as about Cocoon and Turbine, can be found at the following URL: **http://jakarta.apache.org/jetspeed/site/index.html**.

MarketSet Platform

The MarketSet Platform provides the technology foundation for the MarketSet. The functionality can be divided into three main aspects: security, connectivity, and management.

Regarding security, the MarketSet Platform provides the single logon functionality for all the services integrated within the MarketSet: role-based access control

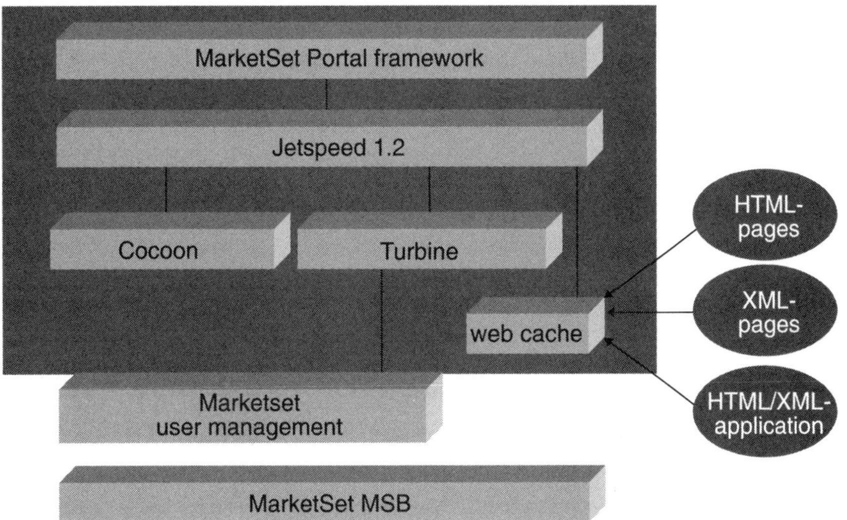

FIGURE 6-3 *Architecture of the User Interface Builder*

through the user management interface Netegrity, PKI (*public key infrastructure*)-based authentication support with x.509 CA both for user and XPC authentication, and multilevel user and role management through user management interface.

The connectivity component is in charge of managing all the communication with the trading partners, the integration with their applications, EDI (*Electronic Data Interchange*) communications, and support for the RosettaNet standards. This component must also guarantee the correct routing of xCBL documents (**www.xcbl.org**) within the Marketplace, in both the order and the delivery of those documents. The main component for the connection with the trading partners is the MarketSet Connector, which is part of the MarketSet Platform layer. This piece allows for the mapping and transformation of data, as well as the connection of virtually any system. Regarding SAP environments, the MarketSet Connector is able to translate classical SAP interface mechanisms, such as RFC (*Remote Function Calls*), IDOC (*intermediate documents*), or BAPIs (*business application programming interfaces*), to xCBL.

The MarketSet Connector is based on the classical Business Connector with XPC (*XML Portal Connector*) add-ons, an XML integration software provided to virtual marketplaces by CommerceOne and fully integrated in the MarketSet. The MarketSet Connector uses protocols such as HTTPS (*HTTP over Secure Sockets Layer*) or more normally SonicMQ, which is an implementation of a queue system that uses SSL (*Secure Sockets Layer*) over TCP/IP and allows such characteristics as high availability, load balancing, and scalability.

Figure 6-4 shows an example of possible connections within an e-marketplace.

Finally, the management components include features for performance tuning of each of the services, providing with an administration console for the complete management of the marketplace.

On-Ramps

All those systems behind the firewalls of the companies that operate in the e-marketplace are known as *On-Ramps* systems. These systems can be either classical ERPs (*enterprise resource planning*) such as SAP R/3 or other buying and selling applications, from any software vendor or developed in-house. In any case and whichever type of system, it will be able to communicate with the MarketSet

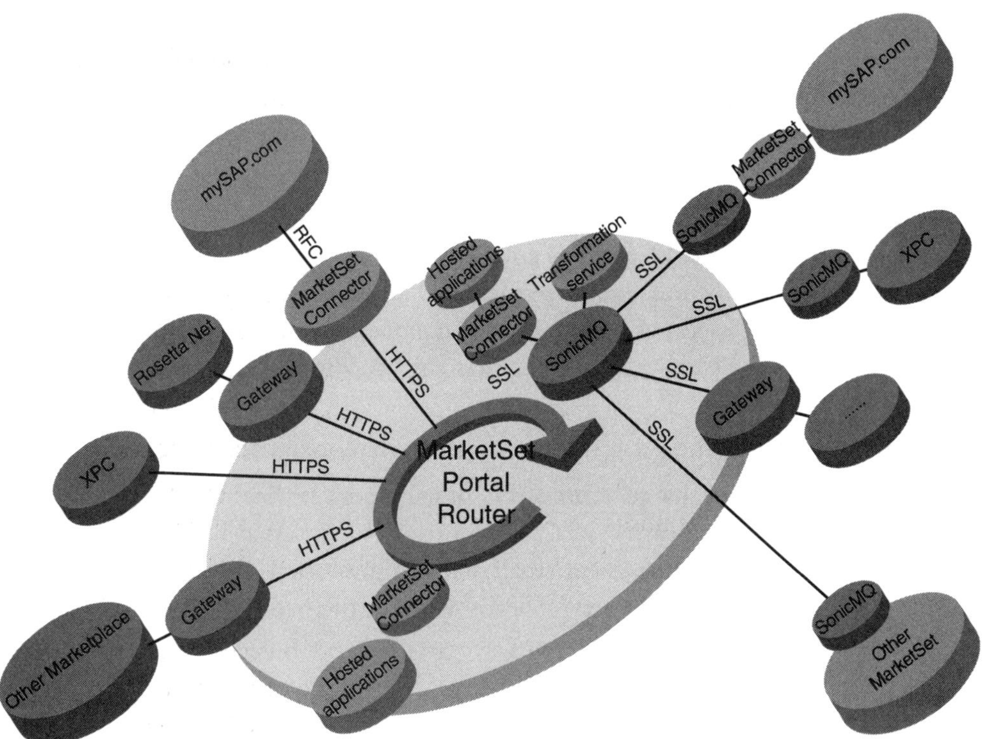

FIGURE 6-4 *Connectivity of the MarketSet Platform* Copyright by SAP AG

using the MarketSet Connector. For instance, procurement systems will be able to access catalog services, planning tools will be able to collaborate with other applications through the marketplace services, selling applications will be able to receive orders, and so on. In summary, any type of system within the companies that operate in the e-marketplace will be able to integrate into the MarketSet.

MarketSet Business Framework

The MarketSet Business Framework hosts all the different services that can be supported by the MarketSet 2.0. A service is a specific application that provides added value to the trading partners that use it. A user from a company can be subscribed to one, several, or all the services provided within the MarketSet. The next section introduces these services with some detail.

MarketSet Procurement

One of the most typical services provided by the MarketSet is purchasing or procurement, which enables users to create purchase requisitions and automate the purchasing processes, such as the order or the approval. One of the additional benefits for companies is the possibility for consolidating the procurement needs across multiple divisions, departments, plants, or geographies, and all without needing to install or configure any additional applications. With the possibility of linking efficient procurement processes based on an e-marketplace with the planning and design process of direct goods, companies have an excellent environment for improving the supply chain by exchanging documents and information with business partners.

The MarketSet Procurement, as one of the services of the MarketSet, is a Web-based application in charge of providing procurement services to those companies that take part of the e-marketplace. The procurement services are ideal not only for large companies, but also for small and medium-sized companies, which can take part in a solid procurement solution without the need to install and configure their own hardware and software.

The next sections contain a detailed description of some of the most important functionalities that are supported by the MarketSet Procurement.

Shopping Basket Functions

Within the MarketSet Procurement, there are several functions for working shopping baskets.

- **Create Shopping Basket.** There is the possibility of using existing shopping baskets as templates. This can be useful for defining reference templates that users and employees can use quickly. For instance, depending on the procurement needs, you could define shopping basket templates for procuring standard configuration of computing equipment such as PCs. With templates, often users only have to change the quantities.
- **Fill Shopping Basket.** For filling shopping baskets with products or services, users can select them from the MarketSet Catalog, and if they cannot find them, they can also post a description of their requirement.

  Users can display details for items in the shopping basket and, if necessary, change them. The details include the basic data, as well as internal notes. Furthermore, users or employees can enter additional information to the next level of approval, like their managers or the purchasing department. These notes are not sent to providers, but are only for internal use.

- **Finish Processing.** Users can assign a name to their shopping baskets so that they are easier to find. Users always have the possibility of ordering the products or holding them for later processing. When choosing the Hold option, a requirement coverage request is created in the MarketSet Procurement. When choosing the Order option, additionally to the requirement coverage request, a Workflow is also started, which will check whether that coverage request needs to be approved.

  In the case that no approval is required, the system creates the follow-on documents (for example, purchase order) according to the data on the request and the customizing of the system.

  If an approval is required, the people responsible for approving the request will receive a work item in their Inbox. If the request is approved, the system will create follow-on documents.

- **Change Shopping Basket and Check Status.** Users can continue processing their requests as long as no follow-on documents have been created for them.

  Users can also check the status of individual items in their requirement coverage request, allowing them to check whether the items:

  - Have been approved or are waiting for approval
  - Still need to be processed
  - Have been rejected

  Users can see information about the item details, for example, the approval process, the document history, and the delivery. They also have the possibility for changing their approver by themselves, when the system is configured for it. This might happen when there is some change in the approval responsibilities.

- **Delete.** Users can delete their shopping baskets and the individual items if they need to do so. However, this process is not always possible in case follow-on documents have already been created, for example, if the purchase order has already been sent to a provider.

Bid Invitations, Reverse Auctions, and Bids

The marketplace users can create public and restricted bid invitations for materials and services. Bids with conditions are expected in response to a bid invitation.

Public bid invitations are made accessible to potential bidders publishing on the MarketSet Bulletin Board, for example. Purchasers can also inform known bidders by e-mail. The bidder can reach your Web page directly from the marketplace via a hyperlink, log on to MarketSet, and enter a bid. *Restricted bid invitations* are only made accessible to known bidders by e-mail.

Once bids have been submitted, the marketplace user can check these (once the opening date has passed) and accept the best bid or bids. If marketplace users want to have the opportunity to receive a better bid, they can convert the bid invitation into a reverse auction. The previous bidders are informed of this and can then check their bids once again. All bidders see the best price per item and can undercut this price, if they so wish.

MarketSet users can create simple or complex bid invitations. To give bidders explanatory or graphical information (for example, technical drawings), users can include long texts and upload documents from their PCs. Users can do the following with the bid invitation:

- **Hold.** The system saves the bid invitation without checking it.
- **Delete.** This is only possible if the bid invitation has not yet been published.
- **Complete.** The system checks the bid invitation and—if it does not contain any errors—saves it. This makes particular sense if you have finished processing the bid invitation, but do not yet want to publish it.
- **Download to Excel.** You can download the bid invitation locally to your PC and view it in Excel.
- **Publish.** The bid invitation is sent to the bidder or MarketSet Bulletin Board.
- **Convert to a reverse auction.**
- **Close.** If no more bids are expected for the bid invitation, users choose this function. The bid invitation can then no longer be changed.

MarketSet users always have an overview of which data needs to be added to make the bid invitation complete. This takes the form of a checklist.

If the bid invitation is changed after it has been published, users must decide whether they inform all previous bidders or marketplace bidders of the changes by e-mail or just certain ones. It makes sense to choose the latter if, for example, only certain bids come into question and users only want to inform those bidders.

Once bids have been submitted, users can check individual bids or display and compare all bids submitted for the entire bid invitation using Excel. Bid comparisons are also possible with the MarketSet Analytics. If information is missing from the bid, for example, users send the bid back to the bidder for further processing.

Once MarketSet Procurement users have accepted the best bid, the bidder receives the acceptance automatically by e-mail. The bidder can accept more than one bid. Users send the other bidders a rejection. If users do not want to accept a bidder's entire bid, they can reject individual items.

MarketSet Order Management

MOM (*MarketSet Order Management*) is a hosted Web-based application offered through a service from MarketSet, which enables suppliers to manage orders simply and publish content through a Web browser. MOM allows suppliers to transact with MarketSet-enabled procurement applications, such as Market Buyer, using just a browser and access to the Internet.

MOM allows the participation of small or specialized suppliers that were previously priced out of the B2B commerce market because of high costs. With MOM, the buying customer can access unique products from a full range of suppliers, irrespective of their technical infrastructures.

For the operator of the marketplace, MOM provides an efficient and easy-to-administer solution to enable suppliers and automate the transaction process. At the same time, the operator is able to administer and monitor transaction-related activities to ensure high service quality for the MarketSet solution.

MOM supports multiple suppliers with their own users, products, prices, business partner relations, orders, shipping notification, and invoices. These documents can be created and changed with xCBL messages (sent by the customer) or with order/shipping notification/invoice management User Interface (UI) (manual step from the supplier).

One of the most important transactions in the MOM is the *Order Management.* Order Management enables suppliers' users to manage orders over the Web using MOM. Orders are received by MOM and stored in an internal database. At the time of receipt, MOM sends an e-mail notification to the supplier. The supplier can view the orders at any time.

With MOM, suppliers can:

- View orders online
- Respond to orders
- Change order status
- Change order data, like item price and delivery date
- Export an order to another format
- Print orders (PDF file)
- Download order as either a CSV (*Comma-Separated Value*) or as an XML document in the xCBLv3. format
- View, print, and download attachments similar to orders

Self-service within Order Management allows suppliers to set up and edit their user preferences in various areas, such as the following:

- E-mail configuration (e-mail addresses and notification intervals) for incoming orders
- Order validation against item prices and availability
- Automated order acceptance
- Ability to set infinite inventory availability (when enabled, this feature will always return the quantity that the customer is asking for when an availability check is requested)

Another important transaction is the *Change Order*. An order change can be triggered by either the customer or the supplier. The customer can trigger changes with an xCBL order change message. The supplier manually changes an order with the MOM user interface.

With the *Order Response* function, whenever necessary the supplier can send an order response to the customer. The order response can be sent at any time in the business process and as many times as needed. It is not dependent on a certain status of the order. The MOM user interface will be used to trigger the sending of order responses.

The *Order Status* function includes the status request and status result for orders through xCBL messages. This area is completely automated and no human interaction is required. The order status result informs the buyers about the processing status of their order.

A *Shipping Notification Document* is sent from a supplier to a customer. It informs the customer that goods either have been or will be shipped on a specific date. The document also contains additional shipping information. MOM supports the creation of a shipping notification in reference to an existing order. This is done by allowing the supplier to import an order into an open shipping document. Suppliers are able to modify data in the new shipping notification, such as quantity on a line item, adding or removing a line item, and so on. Suppliers can search shipping notifications on the basis of several criteria (for example, order number or period of time).

MOM supports the creation of *invoices* in reference to existing orders. This is done by allowing the supplier to import an order into an open invoice. Suppliers are able to modify data in the new invoice, such as quantity on a line item, adding or removing a line item, and so on. Suppliers can also create an invoice without any reference to another document. The MOM then leads the supplier through a step-by-step process, starting from the customer's information. Suppliers can search invoices on the basis of several criteria (for example, order number, invoice status, or period of time).

MarketSet Dynamic Pricing

Prices freely move in online marketplaces because of variable supply, demand, competition among buyers and sellers, and the customary nature of the product. In dynamic pricing—as opposed to fixed pricing, such as from a catalog—the price is negotiated instead of just being accepted or rejected. The negotiation rules, the starting point for the price, and the evaluation criteria for negotiation such as timeliness, quality, service, and so on all vary, giving rise to a combination of dynamic prices. To benefit from this variety and movement, marketplace participants need to use a variety of dynamic pricing mechanisms. MarketSet provides access to the full range of dynamic pricing mechanisms with the following MarketSet Services: *Auction*, *Exchange*, *RFP/RFQ*, and *classified advertisements*. These four services are collectively referred to as DPS (*Dynamic Pricing Services*) and are linked to a core DPE (*Dynamic Pricing Engine*).

The DPE determines winners by continuously matching multiple parameters that govern the auction, exchange, or RFP/RFQ. DPE is unique in its ability to handle structured specifications of products (for example, Bill of Materials (BOM)); this allows the user to specify a large complex product as a hierarchy of subproducts. DPE further increases the ease of use by providing a central point to, as SAP documentation puts it, "publish once to be available to all" and to "change once to be available to all." DPE has been implemented in pure Java (version 1.1.7) and is fully standards compliant, allowing easy integration to back-end systems.

DPS allows creating, displaying, modifying, and describing the details of exchanges, RFP/RFQ, and several types of auctions. These services are capable of handling a variety of scenarios: full and broken lot sizes, existing and new products, and fixed or computed end dates.

MarketSet Catalog

The tool to create and maintain catalogs is the Content Engine. The Content Engine addresses all the critical needs of a Net Market Maker to create, operate, and maintain a commerce-ready catalog.

The Content Engine combines unique data aggregation capabilities with an easy-to-use, powerful search engine that enables Net Market Makers to offer a multi-supplier catalog that could potentially contain products and information from thousands of suppliers. The Content Engine also allows Net Market Makers to link third-party data (ratings, data sheets, regulations information) or self-created content to product information to provide a unique value-added search experience for their community. Content Engine (in the past, also called iMerge) is composed of several components that form a unique architecture for e-commerce catalogs.

Catalog Creation Capabilities

The Content Engine (iMerge) is an application for building catalogs. You can build these catalogs from existing data sources, or you can author content directly in Content Engine (iMerge). Content Engine (iMerge) has connectors to support input from files (XML, CSV, TXT), LDAP (*Lightweight Directory Access Protocol*), or relational databases (Access, SQL).

When you aggregate multiple data sources into a single Content Engine (iMerge) catalog, you do not have to transfer data from the data sources into a single physical catalog; you simply map the existing data sources to a master schema in the Content Engine. To the end user browsing it, the catalog appears as a single, unified catalog.

Search Capabilities

Content Engine (iMerge)'s patented PCCS (*Parametric Cross-Category Search*) provides multiple search capabilities to allow buyers to locate exactly the suppliers or items they are looking for.

- **String search.** Content Engine (iMerge) provides the ability to find products that match a word in a description or other field.
- **Taxonomic search.** A taxonomic search is a search through a classification system or *taxonomy*; it enables users to find all instances of a particular category or subcategory. A taxonomy or ontology defines a structure for creating a classification of objects. Companies and industry organizations are developing similar structures to define products within certain vertical markets, such as electronic components and industrial components. Taxonomic search provides the ability to traverse a structure by following the appropriate links. Users specify a category to search by clicking its name, for example, Writing Instrument. Content Engine (iMerge) displays all instances of the Writing Instrument category in the catalog, for instance, all specific pens, pencils, and markers. Users can quickly narrow down the list by clicking a subcategory.
- **Parametric search.** A useful supplement to taxonomic search is parametric search, which enables users to search for items based on their *attributes*, such as color, size, manufacturer, and so on. Specifying a category (through taxonomic search) brings up a list of attributes meaningful for that category; users can then enter values for any of those attributes, asking Content Engine (iMerge) to find instances that match those values. For example, to search for blue pens, a user selects the category Pen. This brings up a list of attributes for Pen (such as Color and Type). In the Color attribute field, the user chooses the value "blue" and submits the search. Parametric search takes advantage of the fact that data is structured; the results are usually closer to the user's needs than conventional string search.
- **Cross-category search.** Cross-category search enables users to search parametrically *across* categories. In the process of creating the

Commerce-ready Catalog and the associated mappings, Content Engine (iMerge) relates product data in many ways and creates relationships to other nonproduct information that can be used for searching. In the situation that multiple products meet the technical specifications, other information, such as supplier reliability, quality, dependability, and location, need to be considered before making a final selection. For example, suppose your catalog has a Product category and a Manufacturer category. Cross-category search enables users to ask a single question that transcends category boundaries, such as, "What are all products whose manufacturers are based in Spain?"

User Interface

Users access Content Engine (iMerge) and its catalogs through a Web browser. This Web-based interface provides the following benefits:

- As long as users know the catalog's URL and have been granted the appropriate access rights, they can access the catalog from any computer with a Web browser.
- No other application needs to be installed on a user's computer. Content Engine (iMerge) automatically generates catalog pages each time a user accesses the catalog.
- Any changes made by the administrator or to the source data are immediately reflected on catalog pages.
- Users navigate the interface through familiar Web techniques, such as searching and following hyperlinks.

Administration

Administrators use an interface similar to the one seen by end users. The difference between end-user interfaces and the one used by administrators involves the *types* of items seen and the *actions* that can be performed on those items. In short, administration interfaces are for creating and managing catalogs, whereas end-user interfaces are for searching catalogs. The administrator can create other administration interfaces; for example, it is possible to divide up administrative responsibilities by roles, using a different interface for each role.

All kinds of things in Content Engine (iMerge) (including classes, relations, agents, chores, and others) are classes. Administrators can create, modify, search for, and delete classes and instances of classes. Administrators can also customize the appearance and behavior of existing classes. For example, you can control the order and styles (check boxes, menus, and so on) of attribute relations appearing on classes.

Building a Schema and Defining a Reference Schema

One of the key tasks in using Content Engine (iMerge) to create catalogs is to build *schemas*. The real power of Content Engine (iMerge) comes from the ability to aggregate catalogs from multiple data sources, which requires designing a reference schema. Finally, you can create user schemas, which are subsets of the reference schema.

A schema determines which objects users see and which pieces of information they can view and update. It consists of a set of classes and a set of relations. A schema could comprise a collection of classes, their attributes, and some tables.

Information organized in different schemas poses some challenges, particularly in searching and updating. Content Engine (iMerge) integrates a wide range of schemas into a flexible, accurate, and responsive information source. By enabling you to create a single catalog out of multiple catalogs (each with its own schema), Content Engine (iMerge) resolves two types of heterogeneity:

- **Physical heterogeneity.** Data is distributed among different locations and stored in different formats.
- **Conceptual heterogeneity.** Problems of conflicting terminology, different structures, and missing information exist.

Writing Rules

One of the most powerful aspects of Content Engine (iMerge) is the way it handles rules, which allow you to express relationships between tables. Rules play a key role in solving the integration problem. They also help you enforce constraints; for example, you can implement business rules and check for data-entry errors.

No programming is necessary to build a catalog in Content Engine (iMerge). The administrator defines rules in Content Engine (iMerge) through a point-and-click interface. This approach is more modular and makes it much easier to write and debug rules; you approach each problem case by case. Changes in data or rules for a vendor or buyer do not affect other vendors and buyers. Also, if one vendor's data source goes down, only that vendor's data goes down (unless the catalog is cached in Content Engine [iMerge]).

View Management

Content Engine (iMerge) enables various groups of users to see different views. Whereas the overall experience is similar for all users, some groups require different levels of access than other groups. The catalog administrator controls access. For example, the catalog administrator can:

- Create a view that displays price information and another that does not
- Prevent users from accessing a view that they are not authorized to see by using some of the security mechanisms available in Content Engine (iMerge)

Relational Logic Aggregation

The RLA (*Relational Logic Aggregation*) in Content Engine (iMerge) is unique in its ability to address catalog issues. Relational logic extends the relational algebra found in commercially available databases with functions to handle missing or incomplete information. RLA extends this powerful relational logic to deal with business rules and data from heterogeneous sources.

RLA contains a browser-based mapping facility that allows nonprogrammers to add new supplier mappings, discrete buyer mappings, and other necessary specifications without any programming. Through a series of dialogs, the issues dealing with data sources, incomplete or missing data, and data access are all addressed.

RLA addresses differences in data format. A multivendor catalog must deal with the fact that different vendors store catalog data in different formats, including relational databases, XML (obsolete), tab-delimited text, and Web pages. Even if a single common format could be found, requiring vendors to switch to a single format would not be desirable or practical. With its unique tools, iMerge enables vendors to keep most of their data in the original form. iMerge can:

- Connect to data in relational databases directly, without importing the data
- Import data in many structured formats
- Extract data from unstructured sources

Dynamic Sourcing Architecture

What makes the RLA and the PCCS usable is the unique DSA (*Dynamic Sourcing Architecture*) of Content Engine (iMerge). DSA consists of three components:

- In-memory object-relational database engine
- Dynamic caching
- Powerful query optimizer

Let's briefly review these components.

Content Engine (iMerge) has a unique in-memory object-relational database engine. This in-memory architecture eliminates the overhead normally associated with disk access and complex relational databases. When dealing with hundreds or thousands of buyers and suppliers, the fast response time and scalability provided by Content Engine (iMerge) are critical.

The in-memory engine also permits the administrator of the Content Engine (iMerge) application to dynamically change the way data is accessed without changing the applications using the database. More specifically, data can be cached locally rather than accessed from a distributed site simply through point and click. The catalog administrators have the flexibility to deal with issues such as security, network performance, availability, and backup/recovery.

Content Engine (iMerge) uses the metadata for the Commerce-ready Catalog and the mappings for suppliers and buyers to implement the latest *query optimization* techniques. Content Engine (iMerge) knows if data is cached or remote and, more importantly, which suppliers may potentially have the correct information. Access plans are calculated to provide the best access to the data. Data is then passed to the in-memory database for processing and presentation to the user.

DSA for Catalog Updates

Another challenge in aggregating data from multiple sources is keeping the data in the master catalog fresh even as vendors update information in their own individual catalogs. Content Engine (iMerge) uses *dynamic sourcing* to ensure data currency when the data is not stored in Content Engine (iMerge). Through dynamic, realtime queries to individual sources with changing structures, Content Engine (iMerge) maintains a constant flow of accurate information. A related challenge overcome by Content Engine (iMerge) is keeping the catalog running as vendors are added and removed. Because of Content Engine (iMerge)'s modular architecture and the rule-based way in which relationships in a catalog are defined, administrators can remove a vendor's catalog without disrupting the master catalog; no software needs to be recompiled, so the catalog can operate with no downtime. Similarly, adding a new vendor's catalog is largely a matter of writing rules that map the new source to the master catalog. The changes are immediately visible in the application. Finally, if one of the sources goes down because of site-specific technical problems, users can continue to get answers from the remaining sources.

Other components of the catalog are:

- **ACP (*Auto Catalog Publisher*).** ACP creates catalogs out of supplier texts and pictures and deposits the created catalog on MarketSet. e-mails are sent to the supplier, to registered buyers, and eventually to Content Refinery if conversion is requested.
- **Content Refinery/XCP (*XML Content Pipeline*).** XCP changes formats of the catalog, for example, from Requisite catalog to another format.
- **MarketSet Analytics.** The BIConnect (*Business Intelligence Connector*) component from SAPMarkets converts XML documents into BWXML, a format compatible with the SAP BW (*Business Information Warehouse*). This allows marketplace owners to easily apply the powerful analytics and reporting capabilities of BW to the marketplace data. BIConnect is based on SAP Business Connector with new Java services for integration with the different data sources from the marketplace.

Figure 6-5 shows a view of one of the analytic reports you can get with a Web browser.

MarketSet Bulletin Board

The Bulletin Board (BB) enables businesses to rapidly share and locate information of any kind, including business opportunities (for example, auctions, RFP/RFQ processes, exchanges, classified advertisements) from the DPE. Any XML-enabled application can post communications on the Bulletin Board with a fixed XML format.

The Bulletin Board supports the full life cycle of broad-based business communications, from posting and publishing through tracking and retiring. Each of these postings is called a "note," like a note posted on an actual bulletin board. Initiators (marketplace users creating a note) may use the Bulletin Board directly or

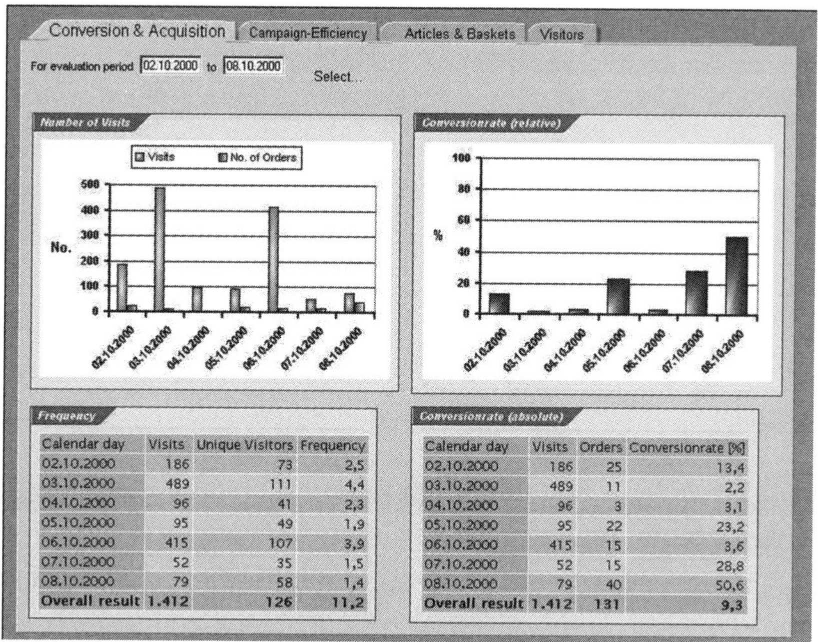

Calendar day	Visits	Unique Visitors	Frequency
02.10.2000	186	73	2,5
03.10.2000	489	111	4,4
04.10.2000	96	41	2,3
05.10.2000	95	49	1,9
06.10.2000	415	107	3,9
07.10.2000	52	35	1,5
08.10.2000	79	58	1,4
Overall result	**1.412**	**126**	**11,2**

Calendar day	Visits	Orders	Conversionrate [%]
02.10.2000	186	25	13,4
03.10.2000	489	11	2,2
04.10.2000	96	3	3,1
05.10.2000	95	22	23,2
06.10.2000	415	15	3,6
07.10.2000	52	15	28,8
08.10.2000	79	40	50,6
Overall result	**1.412**	**131**	**9,3**

FIGURE 6-5 *View of analytic report* Copyright by SAP AG.

another service or application to create and post notes to the Bulletin Board. Respondents (marketplace users interested in finding and replying to a note) may browse or search for notes in a variety of ways using the Bulletin Board.

The Bulletin Board is scalable to the needs of the largest electronic marketplaces and fully supports integration with other marketplace services. In addition to being implemented using servlets, JSPs (*Java Server Pages*), and EJBs (*Enterprise JavaBeans*), the Bulletin Board communicates with other marketplace services using XML messages passed with XML Commerce Connector (XCC). These XML messages are written to the xCBL standard published by CommerceOne. Because XML messages are designed for transport over the Internet, the Bulletin Board can receive messages from services on other marketplaces or from enterprises. This allows one marketplace to aggregate listings from a host of marketplaces or companies.

The Bulletin Board is constructed in a three-tier architecture.

- The presentation layer provides an intuitive interface and a uniform way of creating notes.

- The business logic layer manages the note life cycle.
- The data layer stores the data.

This architecture allows owner/operators to scale their system from setups as small as one machine for all layers, up to one or more machines for each layer. In addition to scalability, this architecture also provides application flexibility and service manageability.

Bulletin Board Features

The following are the main features of the Bulletin Board:

- Connectivity with any marketplace service on any marketplace enabled with a fixed XML format
- Standard integration with MarketSet EnterpriseBuyerPro and MarketSet DPE
- Readily available integration with enterprise back-end systems, for example SAP R/3
- Enabling free-form communication (note descriptions) and advertising by qualified parties in a controlled environment
- Analysis of respondent requests for each posted note
- Full life cycle support for initiators
- Templates that speed creation of postings
- Bookmarks and Favorites for a more personalized experience

BB Process Flow

The following steps describe the process flow that takes place in the Bulletin Board.

1. Initiator posts a note either interactively, with the Bulletin Board, or by another service or application. Each note may include the title, description, beginning and expiration dates, an industry classification, and a URL link to additional information for the note.

NOTE

Initiators must be with a registered company in the Trading Partner Directory.

2. Initiator publishes notes to the Bulletin Board, which creates an accurate record or "paper trail" of notes for financial and legal purposes. For notes that are eventually removed from the system, the statistical information is still available and serves the purpose of financial and legal tracking, as well. This allows analysis of performance and success for individual postings.
3. Respondents locate notes on the Bulletin Board through simple or advanced searches, browsing industry hierarchies, or by corporate portals.
4. Respondents may respond to notes in several ways: link to an auction, exchange, or RFP/RFQ process on the marketplace; a Web link to additional information or another Web site (if included in the note); or e-mail (if an address is included in the note).

Additional functions available to the initiator include viewing a summary of postings, modifying or deleting existing notes, viewing statistics related to each note, creating notes from templates, and withdrawing published notes.

MarketSet Life-Cycle Collaboration

MarketSet Life-Cycle Collaboration offers various components and services:

- Hosted, Web-accessible environment with user access through a standard Internet browser.
- Secure document management system

As the design service is beyond the OEM's (*original equipment manufacturer*) and the supplier's firewalls, security is particularly important. The following features are implemented:

- **Data vault.** The data vault, together with the document folders, is designed to share documents across the team. It helps to protect information while simultaneously sharing it with the trading partners. Data residing in the enterprise systems behind the firewall is replicated at the exchange. The original version is locked to establish the baseline.
- **Version control at the project folder level.** The version controller at the folder level tracks document changes. Successor folders are tagged to the original folder to keep the data consistent.
- **Text search for documents using metadata.** The user can search for documents in the collaborative design environment using metadata (such as keywords, user names and document types).

- **Full-text retrieval.** When retrieving a document, the user can access the entire contents of stored documents using an add-on search engine.

Offline Processing of Collaboration Documents

To facilitate the exchange of documents between two or more collaborating business partners, it is often convenient or even necessary for the participants in the collaboration to use their systems behind the firewall to edit collaboration documents. Examples include marking up and commenting on potential solutions. Visualization and marking up of 2D and 3D data are critical features in the collaborative process. To accommodate the huge diversity of CAD and media formats, the MarketSet Life-Cycle Collaboration viewing tool supports 24 different data formats. It is delivered by a plug-in. Multimedia files can be added to the document folder, and the relevant application can be started from there. Applications that support these activities are provided with the product.

WebFlow: The Workflow Engine

Establishing and supporting business process workflows is a crucial function of life-cycle collaboration. MarketSet Life-Cycle Collaboration uses SAP WebFlow to provide an efficient tool to coordinate and control collaborative workflows. You can easily define information items and approval steps and send them to all participants involved in a specific exchange scenario.

Interface to MarketSet Collaborative Sourcing (eRFQ/eRFP)

MarketSet Life-Cycle Collaboration provides crucial hooks into the MarketSet supplier discovery and sourcing processes. This significantly reduces the scope for human error and the time required to process the bid. Collaboration can be initiated by attaching document folders.

The interface to Supplier Evaluation Data also provides an interface to the personal Tendering Partner Directory, allowing you to view evaluation data of potential trading partners. The interface to the Bulletin Board permits exchange participants and their employees to rapidly share and locate product-related information and business opportunities. The Bulletin Board can also handle other free-form postings from any XML-enabled application or service.

What is the difference between MarketSet Life-Cycle Collaboration and mySAP Product Lifecycle Management (PLM)? MarketSet Life-Cycle Collaboration is a fully-integrated service of MarketSet 2.0 and represents a separate set of functionality with a strong focus on collaboration processes on private and public exchanges. mySAP PLM provides a complete and collaborative solution to manage all product and asset information over the complete life cycle, from first idea to design, production, and maintenance.

CEP (*Collaborative Engineering and Project Management*) allows a one-to-many communication of PLM data with internal and external business partners tightly integrated within the PLM backbone.

MarketSet Life-Cycle Collaboration complements and integrates with Product Data Management (PDM) systems, such as mySAP PLM, to provide a platform for strategic sourcing and collaborative product design in private and public exchanges. It does not cover high-end project management and PLM functions such as product structure management, routings, and process management.

MarketSet Life-Cycle Collaboration allows the development of virtual communities with many-to-many relationships between business partners and easy integration of new partners to a public marketplace or a private exchange. New partners participating at the marketplace can subscribe to all offered services, including the design services of MarketSet Life-Cycle Collaboration. Once they have subscribed, they can initiate collaborations. An example of such a live marketplace can be found at **www.ec4ec.com**.

MarketSet Supply-Chain Collaboration

The key to collaborative planning in the marketplace is allowing business partners to exchange information to improve the planning process. Until now, planning data has been exchanged by phone, fax, mail, or e-mail. However, the unstructured nature of the process limits the collaboration activities possible. In some cases, EDI is being used to transfer data , but the high cost and rigidity of EDI technologies restrict both the number of partners you can deal with and the type of collaborative activities possible.

The Internet and associated technologies such as XML promise to revolutionize interenterprise business processes by enabling seamless information exchange between business partners. High volumes of data can be transferred at low cost, and even minor business partners can exchange information in an economical manner. Interactive access to common planning data can be achieved easily with conventional Internet browsers. Internet technologies enable enterprises to establish secure, scalable, and dynamic collaborative commerce networks with their business partners at a low cost. The Collaborative Planning application enables enterprises to plan logistics activities together, including collaborative supply and demand planning.

The goal of supply chain management has always been to increase customer service and simultaneously to reduce costs. Supply chain costs are driven by inventory along the chain (finished goods, work in progress, and so on) and the capital investment required to meet expected demand.

Now Collaborative Planning extends the boundaries of supply chain management to include all relevant business partners and enable collaborative business processes across the network. The distinct entities in the network, such as suppliers, manufacturers, and retailers, will be able to cooperate and act as a single entity focused on delivering enhanced customer value while reducing costs throughout the entire chain.

The direct fiscal benefits include lower inventory levels, higher inventory returns, improved cash flow, and reduced capital investment. Enterprises can increase their profitability and their market share at the same time. The indirect benefits include tighter relationships with customers, leading to higher customer satisfaction. Leading-edge companies perceive collaborative abilities as a significant competitive advantage that will help them retain existing customers and acquire new ones.

Collaboration removes the divisive barriers that formerly separated the distinct links in the chain: procurement companies, production companies, and so on. Though the supply chain partners are still distinct entities, they cooperate at an unprecedented level because they realize the mutual benefits. The results of real-time collaboration and true partnership include low inventory levels, high inventory returns, an improved cash flow, and a drastic reduction of the bullwhip effect.

The goal of Collaborative Planning is to help enterprises carry out collaborative supply chain planning activities with their business partners. Thus, relevant input from business partners can be taken into account to synchronize planning across the network and leverage the APS system behind the firewall to generate optimized plans based on data from the supply network. Enterprises can now focus on enhancing customer value by enabling true business collaboration across business partners in their networks.

Collaborative Planning was designed to:

- Enable exchange of required planning information with business partners
- Allow the use of a browser to read and change data
- Restrict user access to data and activities
- Support consensus planning process
- Support exception-based management
- Generate one number for supply chain planning across networks
- Be used with SAP APO or any other APS system behind the firewall (including no APS system at all)

Collaborative Planning leverages Internet technology to enable collaboration across business partner networks. The salient features include:

- Display and change access to data through a browser
- Multiple partner access
- User configuration of negotiation process as a series of activities
- User-configurable screens and workplaces
- Authorization to restrict partner/user access to selected data and activities
- Easy selection of products and data to be used for collaboration
- Alerts of business partners to exceptions by Internet e-mail with relevant data
- Link to partner systems using XML technology over the Internet
- State-of-the-art Internet security technology

The Collaborative Planning components were developed as a repository for information that can be stored on the marketplace in a so-called planning book. Planning books are highly configurable. They allow the user to view and change information such as marketing activities, sales order forecasts, shipment plans, and so on. The flexibility of the planning books facilitates the implementation of the collaborative processes between partners based on the CPFR (*Collaborative Planning Forecasting and Replenishment*) guidelines. The Alert Monitor informs the partners about exceptions triggered by predefined business criteria. Forecasts, plans, decisions, and exceptions can also be broadcast to different partners within the supply chain with e-mail and attachments using Microsoft Excel format. All of this is executed with a simple Internet browser.

Consensus-based forecasting and exception-based management form the backbone of the Collaborative Planning application. Collaborative Planning enables the following scenarios:

- Consensus-based forecasting
- CPFR-compliant collaborative forecasting
- Vendor-managed inventory
- Supplier collaboration

Each of these processes is described in more detail in the next sections, but it is important to note that these are only examples that illustrate the variety of ways in which enterprises can collaborate with their partners.

Internet-Enabled Consensus-Based Forecasting

Consensus-based forecasting allows you to create plans for different business goals (strategic business plan, tactical sales plan, operational supply chain plan, and so on) and integrates them into one consensus plan that drives your business. You create a joint business plan, together with your supply chain partners, that drives your business as well as theirs. The necessary tools include planning books and advanced macros. Several parties are usually involved in creating a consensus-based forecast, among them the central planning department, which creates a consolidated forecast for all products; the key account manager, who creates a forecast for a specific retailer or wholesaler; and the sales department, which forecasts its own demand. Each of these parties bases its forecast on specific information. The goal of consensus-based forecasting is to consolidate the various forecasts into a common time series to be used for further planning. A typical consensus-based process, using forecast data from different sources, is described as follows.

Department-specific forecasts are made. Departments involved include:

- **Sales.** Created for a combination of product and customer, goals are tactical: maximize sales, focus on promotions, orders, POS data, competitive information, customer information.
- **Logistics.** Created for combination of product/item and location, goals are operational: minimize costs, fulfill orders, focus on shipments, material and capacity constraints.
- **Marketing.** Combination of product family/market zone, focus on promotions and events, causal relationships, and syndicated POS data, goals are strategic: increase demand, reduce stock.

A team meeting is held to reach consensus. A special planning book is used for this purpose. Time specifications include a planning horizon (short to medium term), time buckets in days, and a specified frequency (once weekly). Manual adjustments can be made. An accuracy of forecast is checked against actual sales data.

Planning books are created for each of the necessary planning steps, and macros are used for implementing consensus rules. Planning books can be accessed through an Internet browser. This enables the user to include business partners in the consensus forecast development process. Business partners can view each other's forecasts, make changes, and agree on a consensus-based forecast using just an Internet browser.

Collaborative Forecasting

CPFR is one of the fastest-growing technologies for both retail and consumer goods firms. It is hailed as the next great advance in inventory and customer relationships. CPFR is a cross between CRP (*continuous replenishment programs*) and VMI (*vendor-managed inventory*). Analysts agree that VMI has been successful in many cases, but inaccurate forecasts and unreliable shipments have been major obstacles to higher performance. Collaboration requires redefinition of a company's goals and direction. It requires trust between partners. For it to succeed, partners must be willing to share their promotion schedules, POS data, and inventory data. Although redefining a company's direction is no easy task, for those companies that do manage the leap across traditional barriers, the benefits can be great. Consumer goods companies can expect major sales gains and a reduction in inventory, and retailers can count on increased in-stock customer service, leading to higher sales and optimized promotional costs.

The CPFR Process

Buyer and seller develop a single forecast and update it regularly based on information shared over the Internet. It is a business-to-business workflow, with data exchanged dynamically, designed to increase in-stock customer stock while cutting inventory. The basic process consists of seven steps.

1. Agree on the process. Define role of each partner, establish confidentiality of shared information, commit resources, agree on exception handling and performance measurement.

2. Create a joint business plan and establish products to be jointly managed including category role, strategy, and tactics.
3. Develop a single forecast of consumer demand based on combined promotion calendars and analysis of POS data and causal data.
4. Identify and resolve forecast exceptions. This is achieved by comparing current measured values, such as stock levels in each store, adjusted for changes, such as promotions against the agreed-upon exception criteria (in-stock level, forecast accuracy targets).
5. Develop a single order forecast that time-phases the sales forecast while meeting the business plan's inventory and service objectives and accommodating capacity constraints for manufacturing, shipping, and so on.
6. Identify and resolve exceptions to the forecast, particularly those involving the manufacturer's constraints in delivering specified volumes, creating an interactive loop for revising orders.
7. Generate orders based on the constrained order forecast. The near-term orders are fixed while the long-term ones are used for planning.

The CFR process can be implemented in Collaborative Planning. The steps in the CPFR process are modeled as a series of activities using planning books. Collaborative Planning allows multiple partners to be involved in each of the planning steps. Each screen can be customized to show chosen data and allow updates only to selected data. Thus, a business partner will be allowed access only to relevant data, ensuring confidentiality of information.

Making CPFR Work

Mutual trust and open communication are key to CPFR success. Ingrained fears and the tendency to maintain secrecy and promote aggressive competition must be overcome. Many companies are loath to share planning data for fear that competitors will somehow gain access to confidential information. In fact, security is a major concern.

Questions like who gets what portion of the generated savings must be answered before the collaborative process begins. An understanding of each other's data and performance measurement is needed. Management must take the lead in creating working alliances and combating adversarial relationships. New systems and methods must be learned. And last but not least, one trading partner alone will not bring in big benefits. The key is to involve a large number of partners.

Supplier Collaboration

Just as the exchange of forecast and sales data between retailers has mutual benefits, the planning process can be improved even more if suppliers and customers engage in an early exchange of planned dependent requirements and production quantities. In the automotive industry, strong integration between supplier and customer is already widely accepted. Suppliers are connected to their customers, in this case, car manufacturers, by EDI. That solution, however, requires large investments on the side of the supplier.

Marketplaces offer an economical alternative to traditional EDI, allowing the inclusion of smaller companies that deal with more limited amounts of data. Planning books on the marketplace allow users to have an interactive role; for example, if the delivery of the dependent requirements cannot be made in time, an alternative date can be suggested.

Using the SAP Business Connector, Collaborative Planning can directly communicate with partners' systems using XML messages over the Internet. This allows system-to-system communication, enabling users to be involved only in exception situations. Thus, Collaborative Planning on the marketplace enables synchronized planning across business partners. Partners' systems must have the capability to receive and process XML messages.

Other MarketSet Applications

This section briefly introduces other applications and services available with the MarketSet. These include the MarketSet Information Services and Demand Aggregation.

MarketSet Information Services

Information Services contains the following components:

- **NewsFeed.** The NewsFeed application allows the generic connection against news agencies and the collection and grouping of incoming news. Additionally, it allows for searching for news in the archive using several search algorithms.
- **AdvertisementFeed.** The AdvertisementFeed allows the management of advertisement banners as well as their visualization inside of the MarketSet portal solution.

- **WebSearch.** The WebSearch application allows the indexing of the intranet sites based on a crawler technology. Additionally, it allows for searching this automatically generated page index.

Demand Aggregation

DA (*Demand Aggregation*) focuses on uniting buyers and sellers of commonly purchased and sold materials and services. DA aggregates buyer demand for a wide variety of businesses and industries within and across vertical markets. It provides single access to low-cost transactions and efficient trade executions. An integrated search engine makes it easy to find and match the buying and selling power among different units (purchaser, departments, projects, and even companies) with the same interest.

Through its open catalog interface, it supports a wide variety of catalog services. DA has built-in XML document interfaces, allowing rich collaboration scenarios with other engines and services.

MarketSet Additional Software

Just to give you an idea of the additional software and the technical knowledge needed to install the Marketplace software, I have included a list of the additional software (non-SAP or CommerceOne) necessary for the core component of the Marketplace.

- Microsoft Internet Explorer 4.01SP1 or Netscape Navigator 4.5 or later
- XPC 3.2.1, needed by Bulletin Board
- IBM WebSphere 3.5 including IBM HTTP Server 1.3.12, needed by Bulletin Board
- SUN SDK 1.2 or SUN SDK 1.3, needed by Bulletin Board
- IBM DB2 7.1 Universal Database, Enterprise Edition, needed by Bulletin Board
- SAP R/3 Gateway, minimum release 4.6C, needed by SAP DrFuzzy (part of SAP KPRO installation, on CD SAP Server Components)
- SAP Index Management Service (SAP-IMS), minimum release 4.6C, needed by SAP DrFuzzy (part of SAP KPRO installation on CD SAP Server Components)

- SUN JRE 1.3, SUN JDK 1.1, or SUN JDK 1.2, needed by Information Services
- Allaire Jrun 3.0 or iPlanet Webserver 4.1, needed by Information Services
- Microsoft SQL-Server 2000, needed by Information Services
- Netegrity Siteminder, needed by SAPMarkets Single Sign-On Service
- SUN JDK 1.2, needed by SAPMarkets Single Sign-On Service
- Allaire Jrun 3.0 or iPlanet Webserver 4.1, needed by TrustCenter Service Integration
- SUN JDK 1.2, needed by TrustCenter Service Integration
- Allaire Jrun 3.0 or iPlanet Webserver 4.1, needed by User Management for SAPM Java Applications
- SUN JDK 1.2, needed by User Management for SAPM Java Applications

Before starting, you are recommended to read the SAP Marketplace deployment guide as described in the installation note 369337 in order to plan and configure your system infrastructure.

Chapter 7

Dealing with Security within mySAP Environments

Security is increasingly being considered one of the key points to boost e-business over the Web. Only when we all, consumers and businesses, feel safe and confident can we really appreciate the advantages of the Net economy and start using the Web as the global village to do business. The mySAP.com strategy is well aware that security is one of the hottest topics on Web-enabled applications. Every professional involved in modern mySAP projects is aware that leveraging security technology and measures and having a sound security policy is mandatory.

The information stored in the systems ranks among a company's most important and valuable assets. Moreover, addressing security during and after an SAP implementation not only protects valuable business information, but also ensures continuous and stable systems operations.

Because mySAP.com has been the SAP natural evolution for e-business, security is based on the sound security services available in R/3 systems, plus the latest security technology. Therefore, this chapter first includes an introduction to traditional SAP's traditional security concepts and other general security concepts and options, relating back to issues dealt with in previous chapters, such as the authorization concept, the roles, and the central user administration. It then takes a deeper approach into Single Sign-On solutions, the SNC (*Secure Network Communications*) interface, digital signatures, data encryption, PKI (*Public Key Infrastructure*) technologies, and privacy protection for user data. There are additional sections explaining available security options for user authentication, such as cookies, X.509 certificates for Internet connections, standards such as HTTP-SSL (*Secure Sockets Layer*), and new Web security services. The chapter finally includes an overview of the security services available for the mySAP Workplace and the mySAP Marketplace.

Security within mySAP.com

Because mySAP.com is, according to SAP, the place for doing business over the Web, it must also be the safe and confident place for doing so. It is well known that the most important barriers to the boost of electronic commerce in everyday life are lack of trust of security and privacy. For fighting those barriers, collaborative business processes among companies require a full range of security measures and technologies so that business data integrity and privacy is protected against unauthorized access. Security is, more than ever, increasingly important, considering how data and business processes expand beyond intranet levels into Web collaborative scenarios that are often quite transparent to end users.

With these and many other considerations, SAP and its partners provide a full range of security services to make mySAP.com, in SAP's words, "the secure place to do business."

Objectives of mySAP.com security include:

- Set up of private communication channels
- Use of strong authentication mechanisms
- Implementation role concept for users
- Providing evidence of business transactions
- Enforcement of auditing and logging

Among these objectives, the security services available for mySAP.com environments are:

- The use of client and server certificates for user authentication
- SSO solutions to access the full range of mySAP.com components
- The role-based concept based on activity groups and authorizations
- Deployment of firewalls between systems and networks, as well as secure protocols such as HTTPS
- SNC and SSF (*Secure Store and Forward*) for compliance with security standards
- Its own Trust Center

Before going into specifics of what the available options and implementation considerations for mySAP.com security are, the following sections introduce readers to common security concepts. These sections will also go into the background of traditional SAP security services from the R/3 age, most of which still apply into mySAP.com scenarios.

Overview of Security Concepts

Traditional SAP implementation projects usually considered security just as the design and realization of the authorization concept. At the *application level*, the authorization concept (user masters, profiles, authorizations, activity groups, roles) are key to providing access to needed transactions and ensuring secure access to sensitive data. As such, it is extremely important within the SAP security infrastructure. However, systems within mySAP.com do have many other levels that could be potentially attacked, and therefore, a consistent security strategy must also consider all these other layers and components of the SAP systems.

Security can be defined from two different perspectives, which have in common the objective of protecting the company systems and information assets. These two perspectives are:

- Security as the protection measures and policies against *unauthorized accesses* by illegitimate users (both internal and external). An attack is considered internal when a SAP user tries to access or perform functions for which she or he is not allowed.
- Security as the protection measures against hardware, software, or any other type of environmental *failures* (disasters, fires, earthquakes, and others) using safety technologies (backup, restore, disaster recovery, standby systems, archiving, and so on).

In this chapter, only the first perspective is dealt with. This chapter will explain some of the most common and practical concepts of SAP security components and security infrastructure to protect the SAP systems from unauthorized accesses. It must be noted that a global security policy includes other non-SAP-related components, which can be defined as *peripheral security*, such as the measures that must be taken to protect workstations, servers, and networks from the many types of outside attacks such as viruses, denial of services, password cracking, sniffers, and others.

Security Policy Basics

Companies must implement some type of security policy to protect their assets, most importantly, but they are also required to comply with their country's legal obligations, business agreements, and industry laws and regulations. For instance, many countries have some form of laws for protecting confidential data of employees. It is also very important to keep all financial records for the tax authorities. And in terms of business partners, it is of great importance to ensure the confidentiality of commercial agreements with vendors or customers.

Modern information systems and technologies are both the means and the containers of the strategic and operative business information. They are the known but hidden treasures of companies, and everyone wants to keep their coffer away from mean pirates.

The *Security policy* is the set of procedures, standards, roles, and responsibilities covering and specifying all of the security and organizational measures that must be followed by the companies to protect the business from threats and vulnerabilities.

An approach to security will have the objective of building a strong security policy. It should start by assessing a risk analysis to later implement, monitor, and enforce such a policy. It is very important to realize the fact that security implementation never ends and must be continually updated, reviewed, communicated, implemented, monitored, and enforced.

The security strategy and risk analysis must first consider these basic issues:

- **What is to be protected?** Companies must identify those assets—such as critical information (customer lists, employee personal data, contracts), hardware, software, intangibles (hours of operation, cost of nonrevenue and nonproduction), or others—that require some type and some degree of protection against unwanted and unauthorized access that could damage or destroy such assets.
- **What are the possible threats?** The second security issue is to identify the possible sources of attack on your assets, as well as the degree of vulnerability of your infrastructure. Threats are of different types and natures and are sometimes unknown. They are often intentional, but they can also be unintentional. They can be external threats or can be internal (for instance, by other geographical locations or by burned-out or frustrated employees).
- **What protection measures can be taken?** Finally, the risk analysis and the security policy must identify the best security measures to efficiently implement and enforce such a policy. Measures can be standard measures included in the information systems capabilities, additional and external security infrastructure, and also behavioral rules. For instance, a basic and strong security measure is the password that users must provide to access systems; however, it is almost impossible with technical means to know whether someone told her or his password to someone else.

Efficiency in a security policy means that measures should by no means include such awkward procedures so as to obstruct or make the users' jobs more difficult. Security policies always follow a principle of controls, which means that the security strategy must approach the balance between the risks and the control measures.

As indicated earlier, security is a continuous process because new assets, new threats, or new technology can be identified and some threats or assets become obsolete and no longer need to be protected against. These facts will make the security policy a living entity, which also includes the retraining of employees.

In the following sections, the SAP security infrastructure is discussed so that you can better identify threats and vulnerabilities. You will also learn which are the standard and nonstandard measures that can be applied to better protect and secure your assets.

Risks and Vulnerabilities

The increasing need for broad and open connectivity within complex SAP system landscapes, the number of components within the architecture, and the options for external communications introduce risks of systems being attacked. The systems are more vulnerable when a security policy is either insufficient or nonexistent at all. In these cases, people trust that standard measures will be enough, but normally this is not the case.

Just as an example, the following is a brief list of threat types:

- External network attacks to make systems unavailable
- External password cracking attacks
- Internal sabotage to make systems unavailable
- Internal attacks for collecting confidential data
- Unintentional internal attacks or misbehavior
- Trojan programs
- Intentional internal breach of security policy
- Unintentional breach of security policy
- Unknown attacks

As there are more risks and fewer security measures in place, the systems and therefore the company assets are more vulnerable. They could be easily attacked.

Security Basic Processes

The following sections introduce some of the basic processes that are common when dealing with security and that you will find referenced continuously during this chapter.

Authentication

Authentication is the process that is used for verifying that users, programs, or services are actually who they say they are. Authentication is the cornerstone of any security infrastructure or technology.

SAP's standard user authentication verifies a user's identity through the use of logon passwords. Unsuccessful logon attempts will cause the session to terminate and activate user locks. As standard security measures, SAP provides several login profile parameters and an initial set of password rules which you can expand according to your needs. Standard security measures already provide a moderate to high degree of protection. User authentication applies mainly at the presentation level, but a breach will affect other layers as well.

Limitations on SAP standard authentication have to do with the legal export rules of different countries when including encryption software and algorithms. SAP overcame these limits by including SNC in the kernel.

Additional security measures to raise your system to the highest protection level include:

- **Using external security products that support encryption.** Any such products, however, must be SNC compliant (see the discussion later on SNC).
- **Using techniques such as client certificates or logon tickets for Web user authentication security.** However, these methods can only work if other security layers, such as the network and the Internet, are also properly protected over secure protocols such as SSL.

Further references for SAP User Authentication can be found on the SAP online help, the Security Guide, and the SNC user's guide, which can be found at **http://service.sap.com/security**.

Smart Card Authentication

SAP's standard smart card authentication allows a safer authentication process. The users use cards, smart cards, instead of passwords to log on to the security system. No password information is transmitted over the communication lines. Because the smart cards are often protected with a password or PIN, it is much more difficult for someone to compromise a user's authentication information.

The use of hardware devices such as smart cards is normally configured using an external security system based on the SNC interface.

The smart cards that can be used for login to the mySAP Workplace are actually holders of the private keys of users, so they work as digital certificates that authenticate the holder.

Authorization

Authorization is the process that is used for determining what accesses or privileges are allowed for users. Authorizations are enforced by means of *access controls,* which are in charge of restricting user accesses.

SAP's User Authorization Concept

SAP's standard User Authorization secures user access to business data and transactions, ensuring that only preauthorized users gain access to data and processes. User authorizations are defined by authorization administrators in coordination with key business users in authorization profiles that are stored in the SAP user master records. An initial set of authorization profiles is predefined by SAP; you can modify or add to these profiles and you can use the Profile Generator to create new profiles automatically based on user activity information. Authorization applies mainly to the application level, but remote communications, operating system commands, and the CTS (*Change and Transport System*) must also be taken into account.

The SAP authorization system is very comprehensive, but it's hard to implement fully to achieve the strictest security standards. It is hard to implement and maintain because it has a great deal of organizational projects where users, key users, managers, and technical consultants are involved. Therefore, it is a must to audit and monitor critical system authorizations. The SAP online documentation and the SAP security guide provide a good basic understanding and methodology for implementing the authorization concept.

You can increase the security level of SAP's User Authorization system by including well-defined developing standards along with a quality control that filters programs that do not implement the necessary security and authorization checks.

Privacy

Privacy is the process that can be used for ensuring that data or information sent over a network or communication line is not accessed or read by unauthorized persons. A usual way of granting privacy is by using *cryptography* technology. Both authorization and privacy ensure the confidentiality of data and information.

Within mySAP landscapes, privacy can be considered the highest security level that can be set by technological means. It can be enforced by means of digital signatures, digital envelopes, and the use of the SNC and SSF components.

Integrity

Integrity is the process that verifies that nothing or nobody modifies data from a source to a target. Similar to the privacy within mySAP landscapes, integrity can be enforced by means of digital signatures, digital envelopes, and the use of the SNC and SSF components.

Proof of Obligation

Obligation, or proof of obligation, is necessary for confirming and guaranteeing that a business message is correct so it can be considered a business transaction between business partners. For this reason, in electronic commerce, there must be enough security mechanisms to guarantee the *nonrepudiation* of business messages.

Auditing

Auditing is the process of collecting and analyzing security data for verifying that the security policy and rules are complied with. *Accounting* is a way of measuring or restricting the use of system resources and, as such, is a form of authorization.

Cryptography

Cryptography is the technique based on mathematical algorithms and other methods to encode data, thus preventing it from being read or disclosed. Cryptography is commonly defined as the science of secret writing.

SAP's encrypted communications secure the exchange of critical data. This is an important security aspect in e-commerce communications. You can use SAP's SNC or SSF solutions and the SSL (*Secure Sockets Layer*) protocol to encrypt the data being transferred over HTTPS connections. Data encryption ensures that the data being exchanged is secured end-to-end and protected from being intercepted.

SAP does not directly include encryption software within their solutions, but it provides the possibility of external security products that are compliant with SNC and SSF, so it can be used for authentication, Single Sign-On, digital signatures and envelopes, and so on.

If security measures are not taken seriously, the manipulation and disclosure of information or digital documents is relatively easy with the aid of the current technology. Most of the advanced security measures are based on cryptography technologies. The next sections discuss common topics in modern cryptography applied to information technology.

Public Key Cryptography

Public key cryptography is based on mathematical functions in one direction, meaning that it is impossible to reverse the results.

With this type of system, each user who originates communications or messages has two keys:

- A private one that is secret
- A public one that is distributed to communication partners

Every message that is sent with one key can only be decrypted using the other key.

Let's make an example of how this system works. For instance, suppose that these keys are the keys for a wooden box. From one of the keys there is only a master copy that you have kept securely, from the other one you have as many copies as you want and you give them to all of the people who want to communicate with you. The messages are boxes that have two locks (one opens with the secret key and the other one opens with the public one), with the special feature that if the box is closed using one of the keys, it can only be opened using the other one. Because of this procedure each communication partner has its own private key and the public keys from other partners.

If a person (sender A) wants to send a private message to another person (receiver B), the procedure would be as follows: the sender will introduce the message in a box, which would be locked with the public key of the receiver so that only the receiver will be able to open it with a private key.

Then there is the following question: Once the message is received, how does the receiver knows that the message comes from the person (sender A) and not from another person who has the public key? This is the type of problem that digital signatures try to solve.

Digital Signatures

Digital signatures are special appendixes that are added to the digital documents to show the authenticity of the origin and the integrity of those documents.

A digital signature is equivalent to the traditional handwritten signatures on paper documents. When someone tries to illegally modify a handwritten signature, it usually leaves clues that can be detected by physical means. This is usually what guarantees the authenticity and integrity of data and information contained.

The digital signature must guarantee the same elements, although using technological means. The first important point is that each digital signature will be different in every document, otherwise, it could be quite easy to copy and falsify them. For this reason the digital signature will depend on the document that is being signed using a mathematical function so that this relationship allows for a later verification of the validity and authenticity of the document.

The impossibility to falsify any type of digital signature is based on using characteristics or knowledge owned by the sender (the one that signs). Every time a person uses its analogical (handwritten) signature, it generates a very similar graphic using its inherent graphological characteristics. In the case of digital signatures, the signatory uses its secret private key. This is a very secure mechanism, because even if the message is intercepted and someone wants to modify its content, he or she must also modify the signature. That cannot be done without knowing the secret private key.

In order to guarantee the security of the digital signatures, it is required that the digital signatures have the following characteristics:

- **Unique.** Only the signatory can generate digital signatures.
- **Unfalsifiable.** In order to distort the signature, the criminal should resolve very complex mathematical algorithms (considered computationally safe).

- **Verifiable.** They should be easily verifiable by the receiver or by a competent authority.
- **Nondeniable.** The signatory can not deny its own signature.
- **Feasible.** They should be easily generated by the signatory.

Several different protocols based on private key cryptography were proposed in standard organizations. However, currently it has been concluded that the public key cryptography is safer. Digital signatures in use and according to the above characteristics are based on the RSA signature and the DSS (*Digital Signature Standard*) signature.

In certain countries, digital signatures can already be used legally as if they were handwritten. In terms of security this means proof of obligation and nonrepudiation. For this reason, the use of digital signatures based on PKI can raise the system to a high degree of security.

Cryptography in the SAP Systems

Since release 4.0, the SAP Basis (R/3) systems include the SSF mechanisms as mechanisms for protecting some of the data within the system. The SAP applications can use the SSF layer for securing the integrity, authenticity, and privacy of certain data. The key point of the SSF is that the data is still protected when it leaves the SAP systems. The first applications using SSF are:

- Production Planning–Process Industry
- Product Data Management
- ArchiveLink II

SAP is committed to providing further applications that support SSF. SSF uses digital signatures and *digital envelopes* for securing the data. The digital signature identifies the sender and ensures the data integrity, whereas the digital envelope ensures that the message can only be opened by the receiver.

Besides those features, the SSF includes others that are quite relevant and important for electronic transactions:

- **SSF is asynchronous.** The creation, transmission, reception, processing, and confirmation of business transactions are different steps that can take place at different times without locking or affecting the applications in charge of the process.

- **Independence of the transport.** It should be possible to use different transfer mechanisms, such as public networks, Internet, online services, magnetic disks, and so on, as well as different protocols and communication services such as HTTP, FTP, e-mail, EDI, and so on.

In order to perform these functions, SSF requires the use of a third-party security product. Since release 4.5 of SAP R/3, the system includes the SAPSECULIB (SAP Security Library) as default provider for SSF services. SAPSECULIB is a software solution, but the functionality is limited to digital signatures. In order to support specific cryptographic hardware such as smart cards or for supporting digital envelopes, SSF needs to be complemented by an external product that must be certified by SAP.

To use digital signatures effectively, it is necessary to maintain a PKI. Because there is not an accepted worldwide PKI yet, this infrastructure is required to be established in a secure provider domain. Digital signatures are available in SAP systems and the SAP Business Connector and can be used to secure business documents in mySAP.com.

SAP's standard digital signatures authenticate the R/3 data that is being transmitted and ensures that the senders (signatories) can be clearly determined. The subsequently assigned digital envelope ensures that the data contents will only be visible to the intended recipients. On SAP systems, digital signatures are based on SSF.

SSO (*Single Sign-On*)

With SAP's standard SSO solution, users need to enter their passwords only once when they initially log on to the security system or the operating system. The security system then generates "credential" information so that the users can later automatically log on to other systems, such as R/3 or other mySAP component systems, without any password information being transmitted over the communication lines.

With SAP R/3 and further with the mySAP.com system, there are many possibilities for SSO, although not all of them provide the same level of service. Some of these features are:

- External security product that's compliant with the SNC interface
- Uses central administration
- Trusted systems

- Windows NT security provider
- Cookies
- Client certificates (X.509)
- Integration with LDAP servers
- mySAP logon tickets

The SSO feature of the mySAP Workplace is discussed in the section "Security and SSO in the mySAP Workplace" in this chapter. You can find extensive information on the SSO solution on the security page of the SAP Service Marketplace (**http://service.sap.com/security**), in the online documentation, and in SAP note 138498.

LDAP (*Lightweight Directory Access Protocol*)

LDAP is a directory access protocol that provides defined criteria to search, read, or write within a directory. Known for a long time (for example, Novel Directory Services NDS, Netscape Directory Server), directories are having a comeback with the introduction of PKIs that require a LDAP server to store the users and certificates and have them accessible for search and verification requests. Also, Microsoft introduced LDAP functionality with the new Windows 2000 OS and its ability to use Active Directory Services.

Originating from the OSI DAP (*Directory Access Protocol*) introduced to the Internet community in August 1991, the X.500 LDAP is specified in RFC1777 from March 1995 as a read-only access protocol to the X.500 protocol suite (LDAP v2). The word *lightweight* is derived from the fact that this directory access protocol provides read-only access to the main topics, variables, or features using TCP or another transport. This means that not all accessible values are represented using LDAP and that the corresponding layer is the transport layer, bypassing much of the session/presentation overhead required for DAP. An update of LDAP can be found in RFC2251 from December 1997, which specifies LDAP v3 that has, besides other enhancements, writing capabilities within the directory.

Single Sign-On Protocol

HTTP is the default protocol for transferring files in the World Wide Web. HTTP transports Web sites as plain-text files, so it is possible that a third party having access to the network can read or alter the data sent. The protocol has no proper mechanisms to ensure authentication and confidentiality for the data. For that purpose, SSL encryption can be used. The HTTPS protocol transfers HTTP over an SSL connection. HTTPS offers options to encrypt the data and to identify the other party by its digital certificate.

SSL and HTTPS provide confidentiality and integrity of the data transmitted and authentication of the user.

- Confidentiality is ensured through strong encryption. The information transmitted cannot be decrypted by anyone other than the intended recipient and is unreadable to third parties.
- Data integrity ensures that a third party did not alter data sent through the network.
- Authentication is provided through digital certificates, which are very difficult to falsify.

When an HTTPS communication is set up, client and server first agree on a protocol version and define the encryption algorithms. Then they authenticate each other and use encryption techniques to generate the session information.

The following steps provide an overview of the steps required to set up a HTTPS connection:

1. The client sends a request to the SSL-enabled server.
2. The server sends its public key and its certificate to the client.
3. The client checks whether the certificate of the server was signed by a certificate authority whom the client trusts. Otherwise, the client will abort the connection to the server.
4. The client compares the information from the certificate with those it just received about the server: domain name and public key. If the information matches, the client accepts the server as authenticated. At this point, the server might request a certificate from the client as well.
5. The client creates a session key, encrypts it with the public key of the server, and sends it the server.
6. The server receives the session key and decrypts it with its private key.
7. Client and server use the session key to encrypt and decrypt the data they send and receive.

SAP's Security Infrastructure

As indicated earlier, SAP systems security often is only seen as the implementation of the authorization/role concept. However, SAP solutions based on open multitiered client/server and Web-based architecture include many components that can exchange or are used for exchanging data and information with other components, applications, or systems. Each of the elements needed for the communication and exchange of information is a layer of the SAP security infrastructure also known as a security service. Figure 7-1 shows a big picture of typical SAP systems components.

Security must be addressed at all of these layers. Here is an introduction to each of them, which will be further covered in following sections.

- **Presentation level.** This level is represented by all forms of front ends used for accessing mySAP systems. This is typically the SAPGUI for Windows, though other options are available, such as the SAPGUI for HTML, the short cuts, Session Managers, and other front ends that can be programmed with the SAP Automation and other utilities. At the presentation level, the main security service is the *User Authentication*.

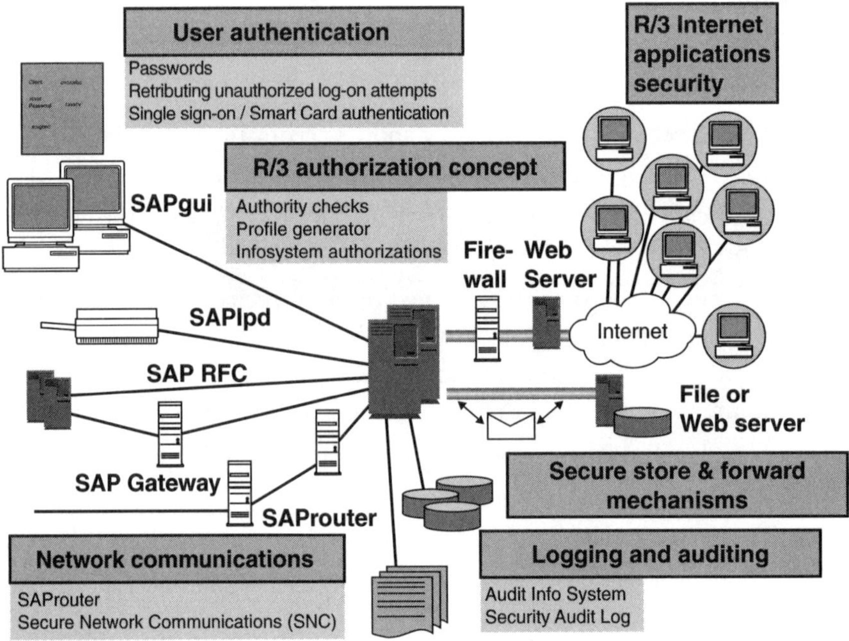

FIGURE 7-1 *SAP's traditional security infrastructure* Copyright by SAP AG

- **Application level.** This level includes the application logic that is run by the ABAP programs. The role-based and authorization concept is the main security service located at this level.
- **SAP databases.** These are the containers of all the business information, as well as the metadata, data models, and object repository. They must be protected against unauthorized accesses, which can come from direct or remote accesses. It is very important to recognize and protect the most critical system tables. This is the level of data access protection.
- **Network.** The network is the de facto backbone of computing, and there is no business or collaborative application that can work without it. mySAP systems are a complex set of networked servers and applications both inside and outside the companies. As such, the network is the enabler that must be protected. Since SAP R/3 release 3.1G, the system includes the SNC interface that can be complemented with third-party security products to further enhance and protect the mySAP network communications. The network is located at the access security level.
- **Remote communications.** The natural openness of the mySAP systems and the endless possibilities of communicating and exchanging data between them and other systems requires also a security analysis from the point of view of external or remote communications, mainly in the areas of the RFC and CPIC protocols that are used in other interfacing techniques, such as the BAPIs (*business application programming interfaces*).
- **Internet.** The Internet represents the biggest opportunity and natural marketplace for e-business and, at the same time, the riskiest place if security measures are not in place. mySAP systems are extensively based on Web technology and are Internet enabled. Internet security is very extensive and would require a book on its own. In the case of mySAP systems, care must be especially taken using firewalls, protecting the ITS servers, and using SNC and other cryptographic technologies.
- **Operating system.** The mySAP solution naturally includes a large collection of software applications. Access protection to SAP files and directories and the operating system commands must also be properly in place.

Additionally, security must also address the overall system landscape: development system, quality assurance system, productive system, and any connected complementary system, whether belonging to the SAP Business Framework architecture or not. Security also implies the CTS.

All security aspects on mySAP systems components are based on restricting the access to each of the system's layers to authorized users or authorized external systems only. A security infrastructure must also include all the logging and auditing possibilities because these mechanisms are required for monitoring and enforcing the security policy.

Standard Security on SAP Systems

The mySAP systems include many security features, the majority of which are not often applied in most customers' installations. On one hand, it is easy to think that in order to reach SAP systems, you must first leak into the network, the operating system, or the database. Although sometimes this is true, it is also true that if internal threats are considered, standard security measures will certainly not be enough.

The SAP Basis Middleware (R/3) includes basic and generic security measures based mostly on passwords for user authentication, as well as the authorization concept for user access to business data and transactions. But SAP Basis comes with other powerful security features such as support for SNC, SSF, and digital signatures, allowing the use of external security products, SSO solutions, smart cards, and many other options to suit the needs of the most exigent businesses and chief security officers.

Improving SAP Standard Security

If you understand the security components and infrastructure, there is a lot you can do to improve the R/3 systems' security without compromising the normal user's operation. You can improve security by:

- Designing and implementing a secure systems infrastructure by means of firewalls, settings, password policies, and parameters
- Setting the most appropriate values for security-related instance profile parameters
- Using external security products
- Establishing a security policy and efficiently communicating it
- Creating a security checklist that can be periodically tested either manually or automatically so you can evaluate the efficiency of your security policy

- Enforcing the security policy by means of logging and auditing
- Monitoring security alerts and locating threats
- Establishing a procedure for constant update of the security policies

The Multilayer SAP Security Infrastructure

Take a moment to get acquainted with the various layers of the SAP security infrastructure shown in Table 7-1. These layers must interoperate to form a cohesive security strategy. That cannot happen unless you understand what each layer is supposed to do. That is what we will explore in the following sections.

Security at Presentation Level

Presentation level security addresses all forms of front ends used for accessing SAP systems. This is typically the SAPGUI, though other options are available, such as the SAPGUI for HTML, SAPGUI for Java, the short cuts, the mySAP.com Workplace, the Session Manager, and other front ends or logon programs that can be programmed with SAP Automation and other utilities. The primary security service at the presentation level is user authentication. When security fails at this level, it is typically because:

- The security policy is weak, not well communicated or enforced, or not existing at all.
- The profile parameters that enforce basic security measures are not set.
- The passwords of standard users have not been changed.
- Basic protection measures at the workstation are not taken.
- Advanced security methods such as SNC, SSO, client certificates that allows encryption, or smart login devices have not been implemented.
- Security auditing and monitoring is scarce.

As a result, you see unauthorized users logging in with privileged user accounts, many unsuccessful logon attempts or users using other people's accounts.

Once I was starting a security analysis for a customer, and he gave me access to a PC. I asked him for a username and password to enter the SAP systems (they had many systems), and he went out for a few minutes to ask someone else for a username. When he came back, I had successfully logged in to every SAP system using the well-known privileged username and password. I said, "What SAP instance do you want me to stop?"

Table 7-1 The SAP Security Infrastructure at a Glance

Layer	Components	Readily Available SAP Security Measures	Performed By
Presentation	GUI Front-end PC Web GUI Shortcuts mySAP.com Workplace Session Manager SAP Automation SAP MAPI Client Other developed user interfaces	Access Controls User Authentication Profile parameters SNC Smart cards Single Sign-On Client Certificates LDAP integration User Exits Security Audit Log CCMS Security Monitor Audit Info System (AIS)	Basis administrator User administrator Security department IT department
Application	Application modules Work processes Enqueue server Local developments	Authorization System Profile Generator Predefined Roles Access Controls AUTHORITY-CHECK Security Audit Log CCMS Security Monitor Audit Info System (AIS) Object Locks	Authorization administrator User administrator Application administrator SAP developers (ABAP, BAPI, others)
Database	Relational database Remote database connections Critical Tables SAPDBA	Access Controls DB User Authentication SAPDBA Expert Mode Backup Administration	Database Audit Basis administrator DBAs OS administrator
Operating System	UNIX, Linux Windows NT OS/400, OS/390 External SAP commands	Access Controls User Authentication Authorization System OS Monitors OS Logging and Auditing	OS administrator Basis administrator
Network	Network Services Topology SAPnet Public access (Modem, RAS, others)	Access Controls SAProuter Routers Firewalls SNC Log Book	Network administrator Basis administrator

(continued)

Table 7-1 *(continued)*

Layer	Components	Readily Available SAP Security Measures	Performed By
Transport System	System landscape Objects Transport	Client Concept TMS Workbench/Customizing Organizers SSCR Access Controls	Basis administrator Customizing users SAP developers
Remote Communications	CPIC RFC ALE BAPIs Trusted Systems OLE Remote printing	SAProuter SNC Access Controls Authorization System Gateway Monitor	Network administrator Basis administrator SAP developers
Document Transfer	Electronic mail Media exchange Document Management Application Modules	Public Key Infrastructure SSF Smart cards Digital signatures Digital envelopes SAP Security Library Trust Centers	Security department Legal department Basis administrator
Internet	Web browsers Web servers ITS mySAP.com Workplace	Access Controls SNC Firewalls HTTPS SAProuter Client certificates (X.509) Single Sign-On Trust Centers	Web administrator Network administrator Basis administrator

It is mainly the job of the Basis administrators and user administrators, together with the IT department and the security manager, to define a clear authentication policy, to set in place all the standard SAP security measures, and if needed, to add any advanced measures to protect the system at the presentation level.

Application Level Security

Security at this level addresses the application logic that is run by the ABAP programs. Here the main security service is the user authorization concept, which grants or denies access to business objects and transactions based upon a user's authorization profiles. When security fails at this level, it is typically because:

- The authorization system has been poorly implemented.
- Critical authorizations have not been defined.
- Local development did not include appropriate authority checks.
- Administration of authorizations and profiles are not properly distributed and protected.
- The user and authorization information system is rarely used.

As a result, you see unintentional transaction executions by unauthorized users, performance problems, display or modification of confidential information by unauthorized users, or even deletion of important data.

Several times, it happened to me that a user who was not supposed to have such an authorization had unintentionally deleted or changed parts of the number range table (NRIV), and because of the legal implications of this, we had to make a point-in-time recovery of the whole system.

It is the application administrator's job to define which users have access to what data and transactions. These definitions must later be technically implemented by the user and authorization administrators. It is also very important that every developer follows a programming methodology that includes security checks.

Security at the Database Level

The SAP systems' databases are the containers for all the business information and the metadata, data models, and object repository. They must be protected against unauthorized accesses. At this level, security services must grant access protection to R/3 data. When security fails at this level, it is typically because:

- Standard passwords have not been changed.
- Access to the operating system is not properly protected.
- Remote access to the database is not secure.
- Auditing has not been activated on critical tables.
- The authorization system at SAP level is poorly implemented.

As a result, you see modifications at the database level that compromise system integrity and consistency, uncontrolled access to confidential information below the application level, or system unavailability.

In one of my customer installations, the operator (who additionally did not understand English very well) started a tablespace reorganization instead of adding a new datafile to a tablespace. The system was stopped for some hours.

It is the job of the database administrators, together with the OS system managers and the Basis administrators, to take appropriate security measures at this level. Some of the measures are changing the passwords of privileged database users, protecting SAPDBA with expert mode, restricting external remote access to read only mode, auditing critical tables, setting the S_TABU_DIS authorization object correctly, and others.

Operating System Level Security

Security services must guarantee access protection to SAP files and directories, as well as the operating system commands and programs. At this level, security services are provided by the operating system features themselves. When security fails at this level, it is typically because:

- Permissions on files and directories are not properly set.
- The password and user policy at the OS level is static and widely known.
- Logging and monitoring is scarce.

As a result, you see deletion of important system and application files, software malfunctions, or experience unavailability.

Though fortunately not too often, I have seen a system operator deleting critical system files by mistake, like the database files that were fully unprotected. A restore and recovery was necessary in order to have the system up and running again.

It is the job of the operating system manager to implement security measures at the operating system and to monitor the main log files of the audit system. Some measures to include: implementing a security password policy at the user level, not creating unnecessary users or services, monitoring SETUID programs, setting ACLs (*Access Control Lists*) in critical files and directories, and protecting external commands from being executed from SAP.

Network Level Security

Networks are the de facto backbones of computing. There is no business or collaborative application that can work without one. SAP systems based on a client/server architecture are no exception. Starting with release 3.1G, SAP Basis (R/3) systems now include the SNC interface, which can and, in most cases, should be complemented with third-party security products to further protect network communications. When security fails at this level, it is typically because:

- There are too many unprotected network services.
- Network topology is poorly designed.
- There is little or no network monitoring.
- Routers, filters, or firewalls are not correctly configured.
- SAProuter configuration is not properly set.
- There is no automatic intrusion detection system.
- Data is not travelling in encrypted form.

As a result, you see users, like hackers, or programs trying to log on to unauthorized systems, users logging on to the wrong servers, unbalanced system loads, or even sniffing. One example of security violations in the network environment is when end users log on directly to the database server when it has an administrative instance. Another one I have seen many times is when the *rlogin* service is completely unprotected and users have logged on through the network and stopped the wrong servers.

It is the network administrators' responsibility to design and implement a security network topology that takes into consideration an automatic monitoring and intrusion detection system.

Transport System Level Security

SAP has provided the CTS as an environment for coordinated customizing and team development that protects the modification of objects and settings across an SAP landscape. Unfortunately, CTS is a facet of the SAP enterprise that is often undersecured. When security fails at this level, it is typically because:

- System landscape settings are not properly configured.
- Repairs are freely allowed.
- There are no filters that control which objects are being transported.

- Authorizations are not completely implemented.
- Transport monitoring is not a periodic task.

As a result, you see software failures, transport of copied programs without security checks, or problems when upgrading your system.

It is the task of the Basis administrator, together with users in charge of customizing and developers, to properly set the system to basic security standards and to define a security policy that makes sure that there is some type of filtering and monitoring within the CTS.

Secure Network Communications (SNC)

SAP's standard SNC provides protection for the communication links between the distributed components of an R/3 system. SNC is built on the R/3 kernel based on standard GSS API V2 and allows you to increase the level of your SAP security with external security products: for example, SSO, smart card authentication, and encrypted communications. SNC can raise your system to high security standards because it can cover several layers, such as the presentation (authentication and SSO) layer, the remote communications layer, the network layer, and even the Internet layer.

Remote Communications Level Security

The natural openness of the SAP systems and the endless possibilities of communicating with and exchanging data between SAP and other systems requires stringent security analysis from the point of view of external or remote communications mainly in the areas of the RFC and CPIC protocols, which are used in other interfacing techniques such as ALE (*Application Link Enabled*) or BAPIs. When security fails at this level, it is typically because:

- The authorization system is poorly implemented for remote communications.
- RFC communications include the passwords in their definitions.
- There is scarce monitoring at the gateways.
- OS and network security is also weak.
- No encryption software has been used.

As a result, you see unexpected connections or program executions from other systems, software failures, or access to confidential information.

It is the job of Basis administrators, together with network administrators and developers, to implement standard security measures to avoid leaving holes at the remote communication level.

Some standard measures include: do not create more RFC destinations than those necessary, include AUTHORITY-CHECK within the programs that can be remotely called, protect table RFCDES, use standard interface techniques, periodically monitor the gateway server, ensure that the *secinfo* file exists, and others.

Document Transfer Level Security

SAP security services must guarantee the integrity, confidentiality, and authenticity of any type of business documents such as electronic files, mail messages, and others. At this level, SAP provides SSF mechanisms, which include digital signatures and digital envelopes based on public key technology. These mechanisms can be deployed using external security services like digital certificates and digital envelopes.

When security fails at this level, it is typically because:

- Certificates and encryption are not used or implemented.
- Private keys are not properly protected.
- There is scarce tracing and monitoring.

As a result, you see documents intercepted by unauthorized persons or access to confidential information.

It is the job of the Basis administrators and expert security consultants with the help of the legal department to define and implement secure mechanisms, like encryption methods for protecting the secure transfer of documents.

Introduction to SSF

SAP's standard SSF provides the required support to protect R/3 data and documents as independent data units. You can use the SSF functions to "wrap" R/3 data in secure formats before the data is transmitted over insecure communication links. These secure formats are based on public and private keys using cryptographic algorithms.

Although SAP provides a Security Library (SAPSECULIB) as a software solution for digital signatures, as well as standard support for SSF in certain application modules such as PDM or ArchiveLink, a high degree of protection is achieved only when private keys are secured using hardware devices such as smart cards.

Despite the fact that the communication infrastructure might be well protected, it is also necessary to protect the private keys that are used in digital signatures and envelopes, because if this information is intercepted, the cryptographical strategy will be useless. This includes SAP components such as the application servers when these act as the senders of the messages and therefore hold the private keys.

Besides the risk that exists in case the private key is known to get into the wrong hands, it must also be considered that criminals can be interested in sabotaging the communications and could modify the public keys repository for the partners with whom the company systems communicates.

Protecting Private Keys

There are two main ways for storing and protecting private keys:

- **Hardware.** The best solution for protecting SAP users' private keys is the use of an individual smart card for every user. With individual smart cards, there is no way to reveal the private key that it holds. Additionally, the users must identify in their smart cards using biometric means (such as a fingerprint, the eye print, and so on) or by the use of a secret number such as a PIN, a password, a question that only the user knows, and so on. Users are responsible for securely keeping their cards and avoiding losing them.

  If this method of protecting private keys is selected, the companies should develop a communication campaign so that users are informed of the importance of not sharing or letting others use their smart cards.

  From the point of view of the server and in order to improve performance, the recommendation is the use of a crypto box instead of a smart card.

- **Software.** The software solution is not as safe as when specific hardware is used. If a file holding the keys is used, it is very important to protect this file from unauthorized accesses.

Protecting Public Keys

If the security products use an address book for holding the public keys, just as in the case of the private keys, securely protecting the files to avoid unauthorized access or modifications is required. An alternative is to use certificates that are issued by a trusted Certification Authority (CA) to grant the authenticity of those certificates.

There are already several countries that have regulated the use of cryptography and digital signatures. However, these rules or laws generated a big amount of controversy and even change frequently. Some countries already accept the digital signatures as a valid proof of obligation and therefore they can be used for secure business.

Internet Level Security

Last, but by no means least, is what I call the "Internet level," which addresses the interactions that take place between an SAP system and browsers, Web servers, ITS, Workplace, firewalls, and so on. Figure 7-2 shows a basic diagram of security at the Internet level.

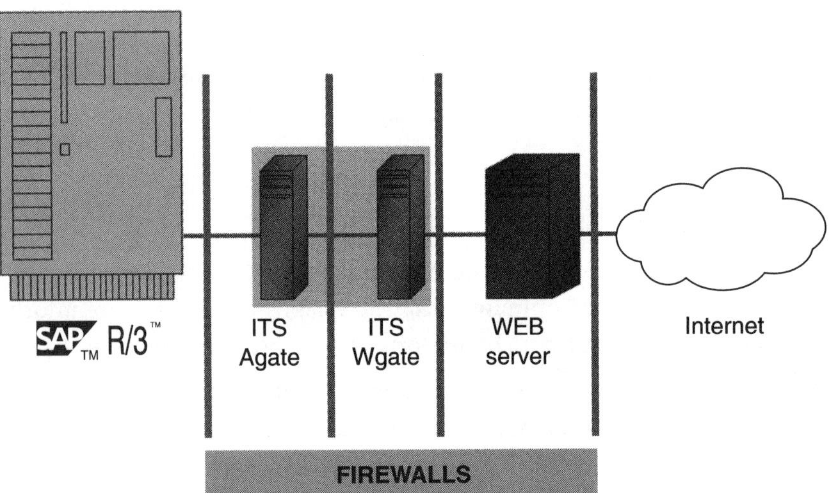

FIGURE 7-2 *Security at the Internet level*

When security fails at this level, it is typically because:

- Secure protocols are not properly set.
- Encryption and certificates are not used.
- Remote debugging of ITS is not disabled.
- Service files are not protected.
- Firewalls and authentication might not be properly configured.
- Security measures at Web servers are weak.
- Monitoring is scarce.

As a result, you see many types of attacks on Web servers that might make systems unavailable or compromise critical information.

Thousands of Internet security incidents and break-ins are reported; some of them make the CNN headlines. Dozens of books and hundreds of Web sites cover security, hacking, and protection software. You could start, for example, at **www.securitynews.org**.

It is the job of the Basis administrator, network administrator, and Web administrator to set in place a system design for implementing the best security measures to protect against attacks to the SAP systems that are tightly connected to the Internet.

A comprehensive security strategy limits access at each of these security layers to only authorized users or authorized external systems. It also accounts for the overall *system landscape*: development systems, the quality assurance system, the productive system, and the CTS that operates between them, in addition to any connected complementary systems, whether they belong to the SAP Business Framework (or Internet Business Framework) architecture or not. You want to be sure that certain protective procedures are set in place to guard against insecure programs or Trojan horses that may travel from one system to another.

Logging and Auditing

Finally, a security infrastructure must include robust *logging and auditing* capabilities: the mechanisms you will need to monitor and enforce your security policies. Logging and auditing address the efficiency of the security measures and the capacities of the system for detecting weaknesses, vulnerabilities, and any other security problems. There are logging and auditing facilities in the SAP security infrastructure at every level. These facilities are implemented mainly in the Security Audit

Log, the AIS (*Audit Info System*), the security alerts within CCMS, and the Users and Authorization Info System (SUIM). These tools are complemented by other logging facilities like those available at the operating system level, database auditing statements, network and Internet monitoring and management, and others.

The difficulty of monitoring the whole SAP security infrastructure is that there is no single tool for doing it automatically, although the evolution of the CCMS and the AIS tools make us think that it might happen. A comprehensive checklist for auditing security can be found in volume III of the SAP Security Guide, which can be found at the SAP Service Marketplace (**http://service.sap.com/security**).

Security and SSO in the mySAP Workplace

Protecting the mySAP.com Workplace against attacks requires security measures that must be based on the Workplace architecture and components installed.

The mySAP.com Workplace offers users a single point of access to all functions, information, and services needed to accomplish their daily tasks. Links to back-end and legacy applications, self-service applications, company intranet services, and Internet services are all readily available in the user's Workplace. Because the borders between company intranets and the Internet are blurring, comprehensive security is vital to protect the companies' businesses.

The security features used in the mySAP.com Workplace include:

- SSO, using either user identification and passwords or X.509 client certificates with the SSL Internet protocol
- Role-based authorization concept
- Simplified maintenance using central user administration
- Data encryption using the SSL protocol and the SAP SNC layer
- Secure business document exchange with digital signatures

mySAP Workplace Role-Based Authorization Concept

The mySAP.com role concept is based on the SAP authorization concept. When users log on to their Workplace, they receive the personalized LaunchPad, containing links to the information and services for their daily work and MiniApps containing information from accessible applications. Here, *accessible applications* means applications that the user has the right to access. The users' personalized menus and the corresponding authorizations are assigned based on the roles they have in the company. Central user administration helps in creating, assigning, and distributing roles and authorizations. Existing activity groups can be assigned to roles. Users can individually design the content of the LaunchPad and the MiniApps, but they cannot change the role definition for security reasons. Only administrators can change the role definition to set activities and related MiniApps. For more details, see the section "Background from R/3: The SAP Authorization Concept" and the following pages in Chapter 5.

SAP Trust Center Services

The focus of the SAP Trust Center Service is to provide global one-step authentication and digital signature technology for enabling collaborative business scenarios. The trust infrastructure relies on already existing business relationships between SAP and its customers. The SAP Trust Center provides more trust than any other existing trust center because others do not typically rely on existing business relationships. This service provides a smooth migration from password-based authentication to certificate-based authentication.

The Trust Center Service works with the customer's internal mySAP Workplace to distribute digital certificates—called SAP Passports—to individual users. The SAP Passport is based on the X.509 certificate standard and enables data to be encrypted and transmitted safely over intranets and open Internet connections. mySAP.com customers using the Trust Center Services can be sure that only authorized partners and employees are accessing information and conducting business in mySAP Marketplaces.

If SAP users wish to apply for a SAP Passport when they log on to their Workplace, their UID (user identification) and password is used. The Workplace server transfers the user as well as the company's identity to the Web browser of the user. The Web browser then automatically generates an asymmetric public/private key pair. After receiving and verifying the certificate request containing the user's and the company's identity and the public key from the Web browser, the Workplace Server approves the certificate request with its digital signature. The Web browser then sends the approved certificate request to the SAP Trust Center Service. The SAP Trust Center Service verifies the certificate request against the agreed naming convention. Then the Trust Center Service CA creates an X.509 certificate and transfers the certificate back to the Web browser. The SAP Passport is now ready for use.

mySAP Workplace SSO

As was extensively explained in Chapter 5, the mySAP Workplace provides an intranet and Internet portal, which greatly facilitates a large amount of services, business processes, and information for users. These services and information are provided by systems that can be both mySAP and non-SAP and might each have different access and administration policies.

One of the main advantages of the mySAP Workplace is the possibility of logging in only once (SSO) to access all services. This login process takes places in the Workplace system, and from there, the users can work with the services and applications as defined in their role and that might be distributed across different systems. This means that with the SSO, the users can navigate through the different functions and services from the Workplace without requiring to log in every time they access the different systems that might be supporting the applications or services provided.

This has obvious security considerations for systems and for access restrictions. mySAP Workplace can resolve this security issue with several different methods:

- **SSO based on user ID and password.** This method has the advantage of using the existing authentication process in SAP R/3 systems. The users log in to the Workplace and identify themselves using the same username and password. Once correctly authenticated, the users receive their personalized role-based menus. They do not have to further identify themselves (in SAP systems).

  The mySAP Workplace supports two different SSO mechanisms based on user ID and password.

  - SSO cookies
  - SSO Tickets
- **SSO based on certificates (X.509).** This method uses digital certificates to identify the user logging on to the Workplace.

  The Workplace can be customized so that the SSO feature is not enabled. In this case, the users must authenticate in every system that they want to access.

SSO Cookies

To configure the SSO environment, the Workplace server provides the user identification to the rest of component systems that make up the company portal. This is done by using a *cookie* that the system locates in the user's Web browser. This cookie will be available for the rest of the systems and is used to correctly identify the users as they navigate through the component systems. When users log off of the Workplace, the cookie is removed and is not available for the Workplace anymore. When the users want to connect again, they will have to authenticate first.

The requirements for SSO are:

- The users must have the same username and password in each of the component systems accessed from the Workplace. If this is not the case, the users must identify themselves in each of the systems they want to access.
- Users must configure their Web browsers so that they can accept cookies. Normal Web browser configurations have this default setting. However, if the security options within the browser are set to high, then normally the browser does not accept cookies.

There are also some restrictions to be considered:

- The SSO cookie is held on the user's Web browser memory. If the user closes the browser, the cookie is lost and the user has to identify if she or he wants to connect again to the Workplace.
- The cookie expires after some time (default value is 60 hours). If it expires while connected, the system will require the user to authenticate again in the Workplace.
- The SSO method using cookies works within the same domain (the Internet). It means that the cookies established by a Web server are only sent to Web servers that are in the same domain.

For security reasons and ease of maintenance, SAP recommends that the Workplace Web servers be configured using the HTTPS protocol.

When a user first connects to the Workplace, the corresponding Web server (as defined in the Workplace architecture) sets a cookie in the user's Web browser. When the user accesses any of the component systems that are integrated within the Workplace (and for which she or he has access), the cookie stored in the Web browser is sent to the system. This cookie provides the target system with the required user credentials for authentication and therefore for logging in (executing the report, transaction, or service).

The process flow for identification using SSO cookies is covered here. Two phases can be established:

Initial connection

1. The user enters the Workplace URL in the Web browser or clicks on a link to it.
2. The request is sent to the Workplace server through the Workplace Middleware (Web server).
   - The server requests the user to identify with username and password.
   - The Workplace server validates the information. After validation, the Workplace sends the user its personalized role-based menu, which is displayed in the Web browser, and the Web server sends the SSO cookie to the user's Web browser.
3. Access to the component systems after initial connection:
   - The Web browser sends the cookie to the system the user wants to access (it could be using both ITS and SAPGUI for Windows).
   - The target system verifies the user information that is contained in the cookie. If the information is correct, the system allows the user to access without needing to authenticate again (so she or he does not need to provide login information). If the information is not correct (for instance, the user password is different in the Workplace server and the system being accessed), then the system requests the user for login information (username and password).
4. Cookies are not sent to systems whose domain is different from the domain of the Web server of the Workplace.
5. Some security settings that are available and some default work for protecting cookies include:
   - The cookies are only sent to systems within the same domain as the Workplace.
   - Cookies are not persistent, which means that they are not held on the workstation hard disk but in memory.
   - Cookies include an expiration time (default is 60 hours). The parameter that sets this limit is ~usertimeout. This parameter is set in the

global service file of the Workplace Middleware (ITS). This file is *global.srvc*.

- The *cookies'* content is encrypted.

SSO Tickets

SSO Tickets improve the security of the SSO environment and eliminate some of the restrictions that apply to SSO cookies. SSO Tickets are cookies that are stored in the browser as well, but the data stored in the Ticket is different from the data stored in SSO cookies. If you are using SSO Tickets, users have to have the same user ID in all of the systems, but they are not required to have the same password for these accounts.

In contrast to SSO cookies, SSO Tickets do not store the password of the user. The tickets contain the ID of the user and additional session information. This information is digitally signed with the private key of the Workplace system. The component systems can use the public key of the Workplace server to check the signature of the ticket.

The SSO Administration Wizard (transaction SSO2) assists you in setting up SSO with Tickets and can automatically import the public key of the workplace server by means of RFC.

The process flow for identification using SSO Tickets involves two phases.

Initial connection:

- The user enters the Workplace URL in the Web browser or clicks on a link to it.
- The request is sent to the Workplace server through the Workplace Middleware (Web server).
- The server requests the user to identify with username and password.
- The Workplace server validates the information. After validation, the Workplace sends the user its personalized role-based menu, which is displayed in the Web browser. The Workplace server creates the client's logon Ticket, signs it with its private key, and sends it through the Workplace Middleware to the user's Web browser.

Access to the component systems after initial connection:

- The Web browser sends the Ticket to the system the user wants to access.

- The target system verifies the Ticket with the public key of the Workplace server. If the Ticket is correct, the user ID stored in the Ticket is used for logging on without needing to authenticate again. If the information is not correct (for instance, the user has a different user ID in the system being accessed), the system requests the user for login information (username and password).

SSO Based on Digital Certificates (X.509)

Digital certificates work like digital signatures, as previously explained in this chapter. The public key certificate acts as the digital identification that authenticates a person or application.

The certificate of a holder contains all the required information for identifying the digital signature (the public key) and the algorithm that will be used.

The information contained in the X.509 standard is:

- General information
  - Version
  - Serial number
  - Validity period
- Certificate owner's information
  - Owner's name
  - Owner's distinguished name
  - Owner's public key
  - Hash algorithm used for the owner's signature
- CA information
  - CA's name
  - CA's distinguished name
  - CA's public key
  - Hash algorithm used for the CA's signature
  - CA's signature

As a reminder to create a digital signature, the signatory has a pair of keys: one public, which is supplied to all target or partner systems, and one private, which is used by the signatory to generate the digital signature. None of the keys must be obtained in any mathematical way from the other.

The public key must be known to those systems or receivers in which the digital signature should be verified. Normally there is a special entity known as the CA that securely generates and distributes these keys and assign them to users, servers, or signatories. It can be compared to the public administration in charge of providing passports to citizens.

To digitally sign a document, the signatory uses her or his private key and the mathematical algorithm to process the document to be signed. The receiver of the digitally signed document must verify the authenticity of the signature by using the signatory public key, which must have been previously received. Both the signature and the document integrity are verified in order to test that the content has not been modified in the transfer process.

There are several questions that can be deduced from this process. For example:

- How do you know which public key belongs to whom?
- How do we obtain the public key from communication partners?

The answer is basically that the public key is normally generated by a CA and provides the pair of keys to a signatory by issuing a digital certificate, which contains the required information to ensure that the public key belongs to the correct person. This certificate is used by senders to identify themselves to other partners. The public key is normally distributed by mail or by using other services like the X.500 Directory Services.

Use of Certificates in the mySAP Workplace

The user certificate using the X.509 standard for connecting to the Workplace is processed and verified by the Web server using the SSL protocol. With this type of connection, there is no need for entering a username and password.

In the mySAP environment, the CA is known as a *Trust Center.* SAP has enabled its own Trust Center. Because the protocol used is SSL, the connection between the Web browser and the Web server must be HTTPS. When certificates are used for connecting different SAP system components, such as the ITS W-Gate, the ITS A-Gate, and the Application Server, it is necessary to use the SNC protocol.

The requirements are as follows:

1. Establish a PKI or use a Trust Center (CA) for getting the certificates.
2. Configure the Web servers for managing HTTPS connections.
3. Configure the Web servers for accepting user certificates.

4. Activate and configure the systems for using SNC.
5. Configure the mySAP systems for using X.509 certificates.
6. Establish the mapping between the user certificates and the usernames (identification) within the SAP systems.
7. The users additionally must import or install their certificates within the Web browser.

Chapter 8

The SAP Web Application Server

As you will see, the SAP WAS (*SAP Web Application Server*) is one of the main technical foundations of the mySAP.com strategy. It fully integrates Internet and Web connectivity into the suite of the mySAP.com e-business platform. The SAP WAS is the platform of choice for creating dynamic, scalable, and collaborative Web applications based on the mySAP.com infrastructure.

The World Wide Web technology has completely changed the business landscape in the last several years. In order to keep pace with this constantly changing environment, SAP has been offering Web-enabling technologies to its suite of products since the beginning of the Web era. But this is the first time that the Web way of doing things gets fully integrated in the traditional SAP application server architecture. This achievement is of such importance that the main part of the SAP system, formerly called SAP Basis, is now known as the SAP WAS.

In the following pages, I give an overview of the changes and new features offered by the SAP WAS. I mostly focus on the new Web-oriented development model, which gives enough power to create the most reliable and scalable Web-centric portals and other common Web applications.

I assume that the reader has a basic knowledge of HTML and the Web development model in general. An introduction to the fundamentals of the Web environments and protocols is given in the following section, "The Web Environment," to allow readers who are not fluent with the peculiarities of Web terminology to be able to easily follow the chapter. The following section gives an overview of how the SAP WAS integrates in the technical architecture of the SAP system. The chapter also includes extensive details about the application development model and locates the different components. A summary of the profile configuration options that affect the SAP WAS is provided at the end of the chapter. The last section shows the roadmap to the definitive first productive release of the SAP WAS.

The Web Environment

Under this section, you will find an overview and the basic terms for a correct understanding of the World Wide Web and the Web environment in general.

Brief History of the World Wide Web

The World Wide Web was born in the '80s as a research project carried out at CERN (*European Organization for Nuclear Research*) by Tim Berners Lee, a British computer scientist who was working there at the time. His idea was to create a cross-referencing document model that was called *hypertext*. A hypertext document was defined as a document that should be able to contain not only plain text, but also references to other documents that could be located anywhere in the network. This hypertext model was built upon three things:

- A hypertext reference markup language, which allowed the generation of documents containing cross-references to other documents, was called HTML (*Hypertext Markup Language*).
- A way of uniformly locating or identifying resources in the network. The result was a locating scheme known as URL (*Uniform Resource Locator*) or URI (*Uniform Resource Identifier*).
- An application layer client/server TCP/IP-based network protocol, which allowed the effective access to information through the network. This protocol is the HTTP (*Hypertext Transfer Protocol*).

The World Wide Web thus provided the basis for a powerful way of sharing information and collaboration. At the beginning of the Web era, the client used to access information was the Line-mode Web browser developed by the CERN. This client was not especially user-friendly, as it did not have the features that are expected today and was text-mode based. CERN provided a universal access to this browser by Telnet on one computer connected to the Internet called **info.cern.ch**. This original way of accessing the Web was available until 1995, when graphical browsers had become mainstream and CERN felt there was no more demand for this service to justify keeping it running.

The first graphical client, what we usually know today as a Web browser, was Mosaic. It was developed by the NCSA (*National Center for Supercomputing Applications*), a computer research center of the University of Illinois at Urbana-Champaign. Mosaic added to the hypertext the possibility of showing images inserted in the text. The most used Web browsers today, Netscape Navigator and Microsoft Internet Explorer, are in some ways descendants of this first Mosaic.

Since 1994 the Web has grown at a fast pace. From the 500 *information servers* that were available at the end of 1993 to the more than 29 million Web sites that exist today, the Web has became an integral part of our lives, like the telephone or the television. Companies offer access to their data to prospective clients, technical information, product brochures, and online support centers. People can very easily set up a Web server to host their family photos, and anybody can publish her own book on the Web. Web-based applications allow business-to-business commercial relationships and sharing of information. We are now witnessing how the Web is becoming the common interface for distributed data access, even replacing legacy interface programs for that function and in the process easing their maintenance and installation tasks.

How the Web Works

The HTTP protocol is based on a request/response model. The exchange of information starts when a Web client opens a connection to a Web server and sends a request. When the request is finished, the Web server sends a response, and the connection is finished. I mean that the connection is finished at the logical level and not necessarily at the physical level because the client can ask the server to keep the connection alive in order to use it to send more requests. This is the same as saying that no application state is maintained in the connection (it is stateless). This makes it difficult to maintain users' sessions, and some kind of workaround has to be defined in order to convert them in stateful connections.

HTTP requests and responses have two parts: a header and a body. They are separated by a blank line. A Web request doesn't always have a body, but a response always has one, even if it is empty. A usual HTTP conversation goes as follows: The client starts a request for a resource identified by **http://some.server.com /somepage.html** saying:

```
GET /somepage.html HTTP/1.1
Host: some.server.com
[blank line]
```

The meaning of this request should be obvious: The client wants to get somepage.html located in the Web server called some.server.com, and he or she understands version 1.1 of the HTTP protocol. The server knows that the request header is finished when it sees a blank line. Because the request is done with the GET method, it doesn't expect a request body to follow, so it sends a response like this if the resource is found:

```
HTTP/1.1 200 OK
Content-type: text/html
```

```
Content-length: 99

<html>
<head>
<title>Some Page</title>
</head>
<body>
    This is some page you asked for.
</body>
</html>
```

This HTTP response has the following meaning: The server understands version 1.1 of the HTTP protocol, the server has the resource you asked for, and you are authorized to get it from me, so the server sends it to you (code 200, which could be read as "OK"). The resource is of type text formatted in HTML and its length is 99 bytes. Then, a blank line goes for indicating that response headers are finished and the body containing the document requested is sent to the client. The HTML content type indicates to the client that it should show the HTML page in the browser window.

If the resource that the client asked for was not found in the server, the response would be something like this:

```
HTTP/1.1 404 Not found
Content-type: text/html
Content-length: 84

<html>
<head>
<title>404 Not found</title>
</head>
<body>
The resource you asked for has
not been found in this server.
</body>
</html>
```

This conversation shows the minimal header fields that the clients and the servers should always send. The following table sumarizes:

Table 8-1 Client Requests and Server Responses in HTML

A client request header always needs:	And a server response header always has:
A request for obtaining a resource using some method	A response numeric code followed by a human-readable explanation of it
A way of identifying the host this resource has located	A field indicating the type of document it is going to send (Content-type)
A blank line (actually two sequences of carriage-return line-feed ASCII characters) indicating that the header is finished	A field indicating the number of bytes the client should read from the server in order to obtain the resource (Content-length)
	A pair of CR/LF (Carriage Return/Line Feed) characters to finish the header

Normally a response header is followed by a content body. This body is the resource requested by the client or some automatically generated information text in case an error occurs.

Up to now, this scheme only shows a one-way method of sending information: from server to client. If you want the Web to be a bit more useful, some method of allowing the client to send data to the server has to be defined. First, let's see how the client would send some data using the GET method:

```
GET /getform.cgi?name=Alfred+Stephen&age=32 HTTP/1.1
Host: some.server.com
[blank line]
```

This way of sending data in the request consists of adding an encoded string that contains all the data. This encoding schema is known as *urlencoded*, meaning, in fact, that the data has to be encoded like a continuous string so it can be added to the URL.

The urlenconded string consists of an unlimited number of name=value pairs. The string is separated from the resource request by a question mark character (?). The resource called in the request (in this case, getform.cgi) is a CGI (*Common Gateway Interface*) program or a page that behaves like one; it is in charge of decoding the string, creating the variables specified in it, and assigning to them the values. This kind of tedious and repetitive task is one that is resolved by the Web application server and thus the programmer doesn't need to worry about it.

The GET method for sending data has some inherent limitations; the most important of them is that the maximum length of the string is not enough for sending lots of data. To avoid this and allow the Web browser to send data of arbitrary length, there is the POST method. A POST request that sends the same data that the GET request above is:

```
POST /postform.cgi HTTP/1.1
Host: some.server.com
Content-type: application/x-www-urlencoded
Content-length: 84

name=Alfred&age=32
```

The most visible difference is that the encoded string is not appended to the URL. It is instead sent as part of a request content body, whose type and length are specified in the request header, very much like a server response. When a server receives a POST request, it knows that it should read a content body after the blank line. The same processes to decode the data explained above should be done, in this case by the postform.cgi program.

The system explained above with its two methods is commonly known as the CGI. The CGI was defined simply as an interface that would allow a Web browser to send data to a Web server and a protocol for the Web server to create an execution environment in which to run a program that would process the data. Historically, the processing of the data was done by external programs that had to be launched by the Web server. This caused a lot of system overhead in case of heavy loads, because the Web server had to fork a new program to handle any new request received. To avoid this, Web application servers came into life. Web application servers extend the functionality of Web servers so they can be programmed and can directly process requests.

As can be inferred from the explanations above, the HTTP protocol does not provide any means of keeping session state. So it may seem at first sight that the protocol is not adequate for critical things on which state should be kept, like transactions. Actually, the methods of passing data from client to server can be used to pass back and forth a variable containing a session identifier. That way, a foundation for state keeping is created, and the application that processes requests will be in charge of providing a way to keep session relevant data. The common system for keeping state is done with cookies. Cookies are unique session identifiers and are passed in a special header: Set-cookie for the server to set a cookie in the client, and Cookie for the client to send back the cookie to the server. Nowadays it is becoming more common to pass cookies as a variable that is part of a GET or POST request. This way the problems associated with cookies, like their use being dependent on the user's will to accept them, can be worked around. The SAP WAS provides the basics for cookie handling, but at the moment of this writing, another method should be directly implemented by the programmer.

What Is a Web Application Server?

When you take into account all the components of a Web installation, it is easy to see that keeping a good development model is quite a complex task. The ample choices of server operating systems, page layout styles, Web embedded programming languages, database access and more, while giving a great range of flexibility, have an implicit set of problems quite difficult to deal with effectively. This is the point when a web application server comes to help us.

It is usual to talk about a three-tiered or three-layered architecture as the foundation of Web application servers. Those three layers could be summarized as follows:

- A presentation layer
- An application layer
- A database layer

For each of these layers, there should be a special program intended to fulfill each task:

- A Web server program
- An application server program
- A relational database management system

This division of tasks is often considered a good way of separating different parts of a development project instead of an actual installation of software (even if there are a number of products in the market that try to mimic this division).

In the presentation layer, I am talking about page layout, style sheets, static images, and all the elements that don't have any (or at least don't have a lot) of program logic.

The application layer is the place where you should put the business program logic. The idea behind this separation is the easing of maintenance of programming and layouts and the avoiding of interference between the designing team and the development team. Designs and layouts change very often in the Internet, so a modification in the design should never affect the business logic in the application.

The database system provides the basis for data storage and retrieval using some kind of query language, normally the SQL (*Structured Query Language*) if a relational database management system is in use. Other types of databases in widespread use today are systems based on directories, like the LDAP (*Lightweight Directory Access Protocol*).

I could define a Web application server in general as a system that integrates an environment to serve and develop Web applications while separating program logic and presentation layout and providing a uniform and consistent method for data access.

The SAP WAS has the following characteristics in order to fulfill this definition:

- A generic TCP/IP multithreaded server that is able to implement different protocols with the use of plug-ins. The HTTP, HTTPS (*HTTP over Secure Sockets Layer*), and SMTP (*Simple Mail Transfer Protocol*) protocols are available at the moment of this writing, but the hooks to program other protocols are there in order to leave the system open to further enhancements.
- A complete development environment (the Object Navigator) based on the SAP 4.6 Development Workbench that offers version control, transport requests, and concurrent work in a project.
- A development model that offers a clear separation between page layout design and program logic. The ABAP (*Advanced Business Application Programming*) language has been extended and now has objects that directly deal with HTTP requests and can be embedded inside HTML tags. The Server Side JavaScript language for embedding inside HTML tags has been made available; for the first time, it is possible to create an application running inside a SAP system in a programming language other than ABAP.
- A MIME (*Multipurpose Internet Mail Extensions*) Repository provides easy tracking and maintenance of static documents and binary objects that are related to a Web project. The MIME repository is used to add images, sound or video files, PDF or Microsoft Office documents to a given project, and so are parts of its transports requests.

- The powerful time-proven and well-established SAP Basis system provides the foundation for reliable data management.

In conclusion, the SAP WAS is a complete system specifically optimized for the development of Web-oriented applications and is fully compliant with the accepted requisites for an optimal Web application server design.

The Architecture of the SAP WAS

The technology behind SAP Web Application Server can be considered as an improvement on the SAP application server technology basis. Its aim is to provide a framework that will enable the SAP technological foundation to process HTTP requests and requests coming from other Internet protocols. This converts any SAP application server into a full-featured Web server that can directly accept connections from Web clients and send responses to them. The SAP WAS can also work as a Web client, generating requests to other Web servers and processing the responses sent back by them.

This enhanced functionality of the SAP WAS is handled in the SAP kernel by means of an additional process. This process is the ICM (*Internet Communication Manager*). From the internal SAP architecture, the ICM could be seen as a special work process that is in charge of handling connection requests from external clients and creating requests directed to external servers when asked to by a program running in any of the work processes. It is designed as a multithreaded server, and it communicates with the rest of the work processes by memory pipes located in shared memory.

Figure 8-1 shows a graphical description of the ICM integration in the traditional SAP architecture.

The ICM is an external process that is launched by the dispatcher if the system is configured to do so in the instance profile. The internal server architecture of the ICM is a prelaunched pool of worker threads to allow optimal dealing with a lot of simultaneous Web requests. The detailed ICM architecture is shown in Figure 8-2.

The components of the ICM shown in Figure 8-2 are also implemented as threads. Their description is given as follows.

- **Thread control.** This thread accepts incoming TCP/IP requests and calls a worker thread (or creates one if there aren't any available) to process the request.

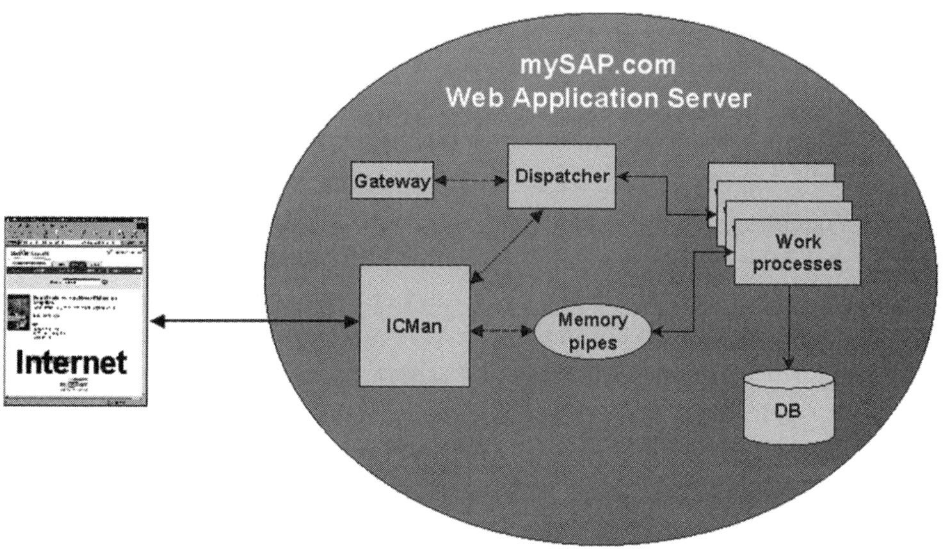

FIGURE 8-1 *The SAPWeb Application Server architecture*

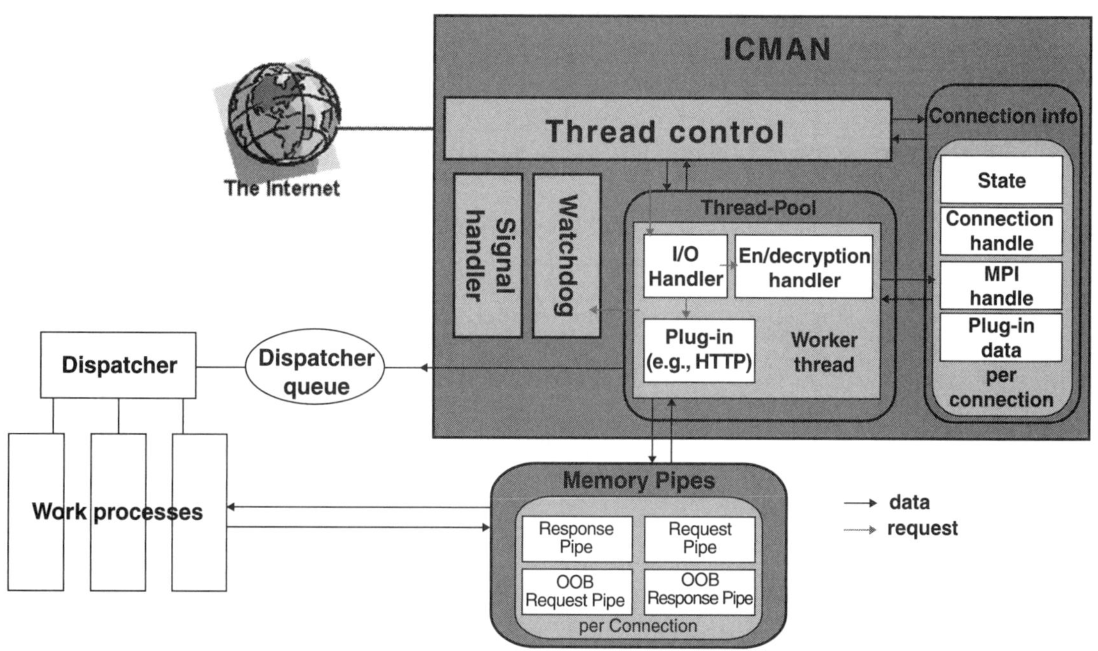

FIGURE 8-2 *Internal ICM architecture* Copyright by SAP AG

- **Worker thread.** This thread is in charge of handling the request and the response of a connection. The way a working thread will handle a connection is determined by the plug-in. The plug-in will define the protocol under which the processing of the connection is to be done (HTTP, SMTP, or others).
- **Watchdog.** This thread is responsible of watching for timeouts and idle time of working threads. If a timeout occurs (usually when ICM is waiting for a response), the watchdog will take hold of the connection and inform the thread control that the working thread is free for other tasks and when a connection has been received.
- **Signal handler.** This thread will process signals sent by the operating system or from another process.
- **Connection info.** This table will keep information about the state of every existing network connection, such as memory pipes or plug-in data.
- **Memory pipes.** These are memory-based communication objects. They handle the communication of data between the ICM and the work processes. There are four pipes for every connection: one for the request, one for the response, one for control information, and one out-of-band pipe.

The SAP WAS Development Model

The SAP WAS is based on a Web-oriented development model. This model has the following characteristics:

- **Page-based development model.** This means that Web applications are built around Web pages.
- **Event-driven model.** The events are usually generated by navigation actions taken by the user, such as clicking on a link or pushing Submit buttons.
- **Server side scripting.** That is to say that programming code can be inserted in Web pages. This is necessary for the dynamic generation of Web content in response to user input. This code should normally be presentation-related code, and no business logic should be in it.

- **Event-related programming code.** This should be in handler programs intended for that function. This also provides a way of eliminating presentation tasks from the programming language by leaving most of the presentation to the HTML layout.
- **Static (non frequently changing) objects and documents in non-SAP format.** For example, Microsoft Office documents are stored in a repository in order to keep track of them and to relate them to the application.

The integration of all these characteristics is done around the BSP (*Business Server Pages*). Actually, a BSP application is the normal method of developing programs within the SAP WAS. BSP applications are not screen (*dynpro*) based SAP programs; instead, they are meant to be accessible not through the SAPGUI, but through a Web browser.

The SAP WAS development model also includes predefined ready-to-use Web controls that are meant to ease and give a consistent aspect to Web page design. These controls are gathered together in the WCF (*Web Control Framework*) and include programming structures to create tables, forms, buttons, and other presentation elements.

The basis for the Web-oriented development model inside the SAP system is the enhancement of the traditional ABAP programming environment with objects that allow the direct handling of low-level HTTP requests. This provides an infrastructure for extending SAP Web functionality even outside the BSP application. Actually, the BSP runtime is nothing more than a big ABAP program (the BSP processor) using these Web objects. This extension of the ABAP language is the ICF (*Internet Control Framework*).

This development model has been introduced in the SAP system, adopting the technologies for Web development that have been proven in other environments, notably the Microsoft IIS (*Internet Information Server*) ASP (*Application Service Provider*) development model and the JSP (*Java Server Pages*) technology present in most modern Web server programs. The details of the SAP WAS BSP-based model are explained in the following sections.

Business Server Pages

In the following sections, I review one of the main aspects of the SAP WAS development model, based on the BSPs.

Introduction: The Web Application Builder

BSP applications are the core component of the SAP WAS development model. They have access to the full functionality of the SAP system; for example they can access BAPIs (*business application programming interfaces*), make RFC (*Remote Function Call*) calls, and access the database. They consist of the following set of elements:

- **BSP pages.** These are pages (normally defined with the HTML language) that contain the layout of the presentation. These pages have code in either ABAP or JavaScript used to insert the application data. BSP pages could have dedicated event handlers and parameters. The system distinguishes between two types of pages: proper pages and page fragments. Page fragments contain small pieces of data that are intended to be inserted in normal pages such as page headers and footers.
- **Navigation structure.** It defines the navigation flow that is used to direct requests to Web pages.
- **MIME objects and themes.** This group contains all the static objects, namely images, documents, and so on, that belong to the BSP application. MIME objects are handled in the MIME Repository. A theme is a container for MIME objects that are used to customize the appearance of the Web application. Themes are based on CSS (*Cascade Style Sheets*) and should be used to clearly separate the appearance from the application and presentation logic. A theme is created as an independent object and therefore can be assigned to several BSP applications.
- **Application Class.** This is a global ABAP class that encapsulates the business logic necessary for the BSP application. The Application Class should provide interfaces (for example by BAPI calls) to the functions it defines. All the components of the class (attributes, methods, and so on) are directly accessible by the BSP application. The Application Class holds the business core logic of the application and therefore is the key element to consider if you are migrating from previous *dynpro*-based applications. These applications should provide a method to make business functions available for use within BSP applications.

The work center for creating BSP applications is the Web Application Builder. The main interface of the Web Application Builder is the SAP Development Workbench, which has been enhanced to provide all the functionality necessary for Web applications building. The Web Application Builder is started with transaction SE80. Figure 8-3 shows the Application Building starting screen.

FIGURE 8-3 *The Web Application Builder*

The screen of the Web Application Builder has three areas. The big area in the right side (showing a photo in Figure 8-3) is the working area. This area will hold the programmer's editor and all the attributes and configuration screens related to each of the different components that are parts of the BSP application. The left side is split in two areas. The top left area allows the user to go to the different parts of the SAP development system. The bottom left shows a browser allowing access to the object hierarchy. The Repository Browser button will allow you to access the zone of the builder that contains the BSP objects.

A BSP Application Example

In this section, I am going to show an example of developing a very basic Web application. Note that a complete Web application is normally a lot more than a set of BSP pages. Application Class interfaces are very important to allow access to business functions from BSP. Traditional SAP programming techniques and principles are still valid and should be the core of any high-quality Web application. As this knowledge can be acquired from a number of sources, in this chapter I will give an introduction to the use of the Web Application Builder, focusing mostly on the development of BSP pages.

The first thing to note with this version of the Web Application Builder (as opposed to the previous ABAP Development Workbench) is that it is no longer possible to create a Development Class. This may come as a surprise to the experienced ABAP developer, but the concept has not disappeared: the former Development Classes are now called Packages. Packages are exactly the same thing; therefore, they act as containers for every kind of object in the SAP Development Workbench, including Dictionary Objects, ABAP Classes, and so on, but in addition to all that, there are now Web Objects.

So, the first step of our example will be to create a Package that will contain all the elements of the application. For that, select the Package option in the object type list box in the top left area and fill in the name of the package that you want to create (in this case, I name it ZWEBAPPS). Press the Enter key and the system will check if a package with the given name already exists in the system. If this is not the case, the dialog box shown in Figure 8-4 will appear, asking confirmation to create the package. Just answer Yes and assign the package to a transport request to create it.

The next steps will create a BSP application. The procedure goes as follows:

1. Right-click on the newly created entry for the package (ZWEBAPPS).

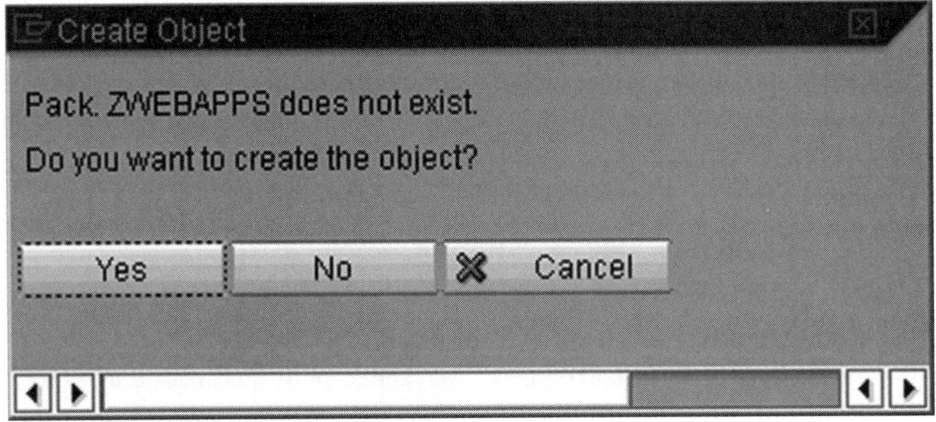

FIGURE 8-4 *Create a Package*

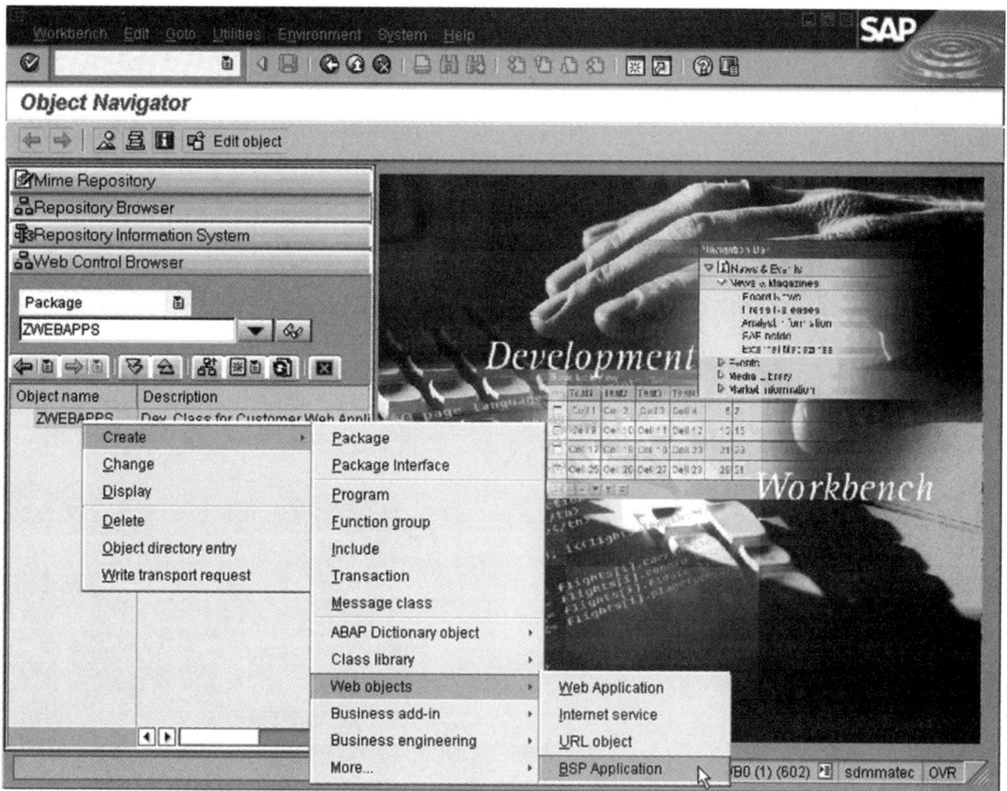

FIGURE 8-5 *Creating a BSP application*

2. Select the option Create/Web Objects/BSP Application in the pull-down menus (see Figure 8-5).
3. In the dialog box, choose a name for the BSP application (in our example, ZW1) and assign it to a transport request.
4. Once the BSP application is created, a hierarchy will appear in the browser area of the Web Application Builder. The entry for the BSP application will be under Web Objects/BSP Applications in the Repository Browser menu.

Once the BSP application is created, you have to fill it with pages. To do that, right-click on the entry for the BSP application in the left-hand area and select the option Create/Page as shown in Figure 8-6.

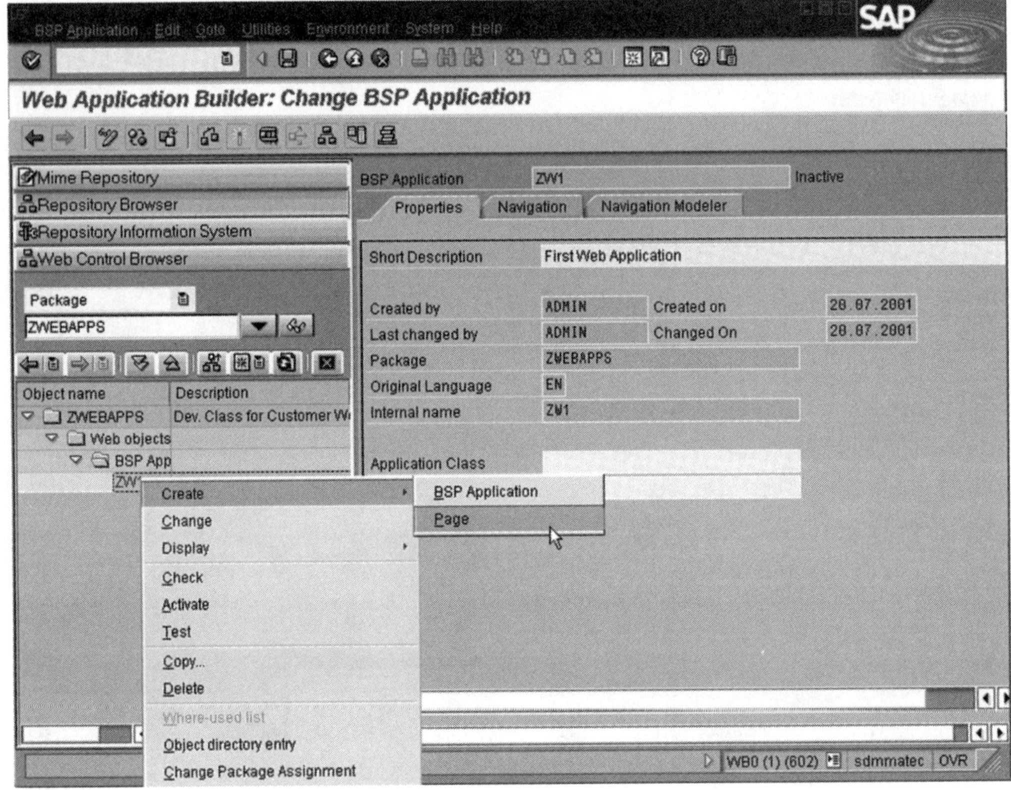

FIGURE 8-6 *Creating a page in a BSP application*

This leads to the Create Page dialog box shown in Figure 8-7. Here you can tick the small check box in the bottom left if you want this page to be a page fragment. The page whose name is default.htm will be considered by the BSP processor as the default page of the application; that is the page that will be sent to the browser when the user doesn't request any specific page.

After assigning the page to a transport request, the Development Workbench will open the text editor in the work area with a basic HTML template in it. You can now start typing your own code (see Figure 8-8).

Once the typing is finished, it is time to save the page. Then, it is possible to test it by pushing the Test button. An Internet browser window like the one shown in Figure 8-9 will open, showing the HTML generated.

When accessing the page with a browser, it will require the user to give a username and password. The SAP username and password used to create the application or any

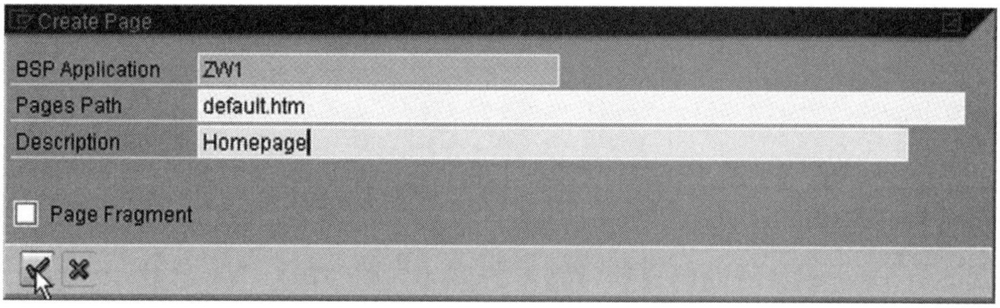

Create Page
BSP Application ZW1
Pages Path default.htm
Description Homepage
Page Fragment

FIGURE 8-7 *Dialog box to create a BSP page*

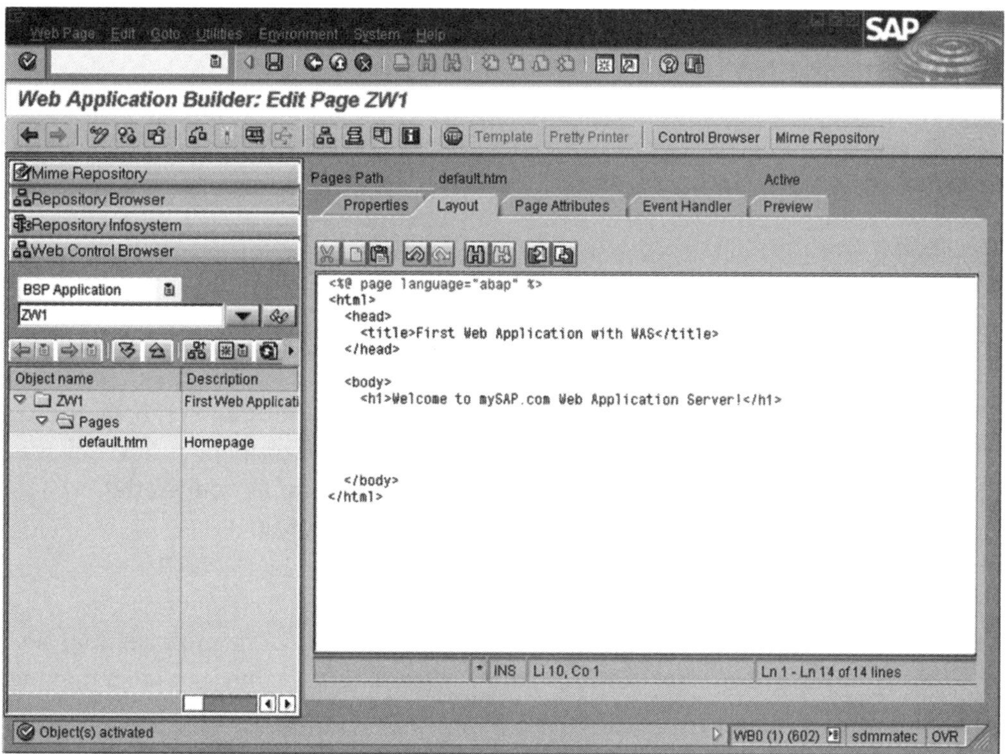

FIGURE 8-8 *HTML editor*

SAP user with administrative rights will be granted access. The URI in the server name space used to access the BSP application is normally /bc/bsp/sap/<BSP_application>/. In the example shown in Figure 8-9 it is /bc/bsp/sap/zw1/.

FIGURE 8-9 *Preview of the page in an Internet browser window*

The Web page shown in Figure 8-9 does nothing interesting; it is only a static HTML page and using a SAP WAS for serving it is probably overkill. The way to do more interesting things is by embedding programming code in the HTML code. In the BSP page shown in Figure 8-8 the first line is:

```
<%@ page language="abap" %>
```

A line like this is compulsory for BSP pages. It indicates the programming language that is going to be embedded in the page. There are only two programming languages available at the moment of this writing: ABAP and JavaScript (the server side implementation). In this case, I have chosen to embed programming code in the ABAP language. Note the <% and %> enclosing tags. These are the characters used to indicate to the BSP parser that the text enclosed between them is programming code and should be interpreted. The @ is a modifier to indicate that the text contained in the tags is a programming directive. This tags are borrowed from the Microsoft ASP syntax rules and are commonly used in various SAP WAS environments.

The application you are going to create is a simple application that will allow the user to list the contents of a table and to add new entries to the table. You are going to have the following three BSP pages in the application:

- **default.htm.** This will be the starting page of the application. It will show only links to access the other pages in the application.
- **list.htm.** This page reads the contents of table ZWEBUSERS and presents them in a table in HTML format.
- **add_entry.htm.** This page shows a form for the user to add a new entry to the table and will process the insertion of data when the user presses the submit button.

The source code for default.htm is shown in Figure 8-10.

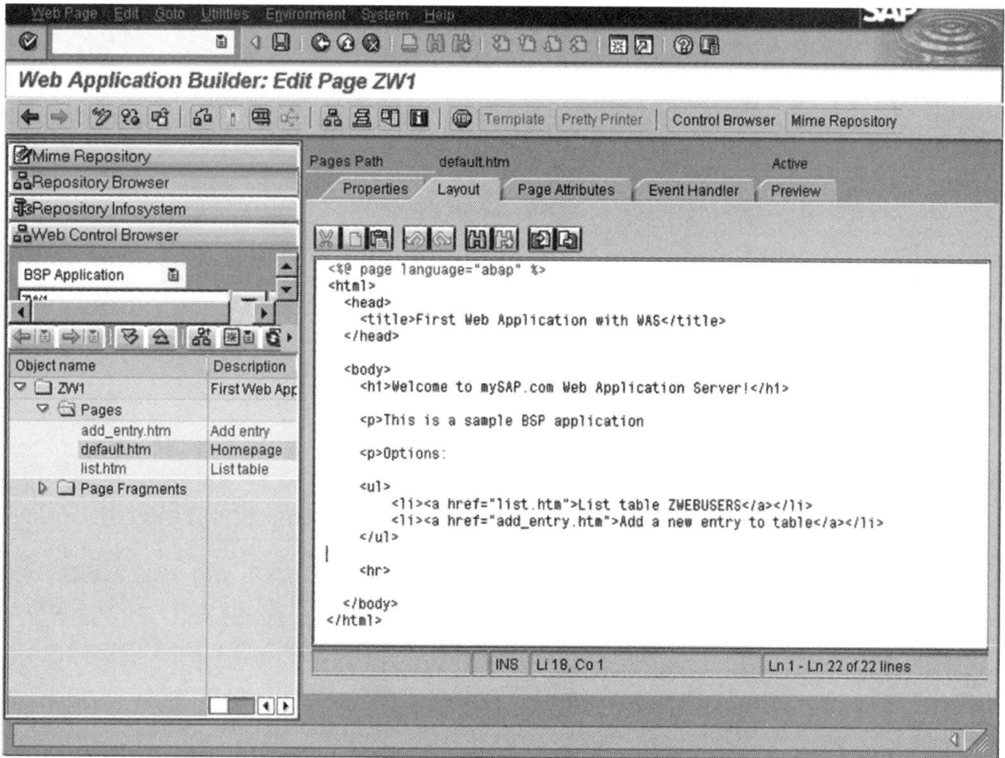

FIGURE 8-10 *Source code for default.htm*

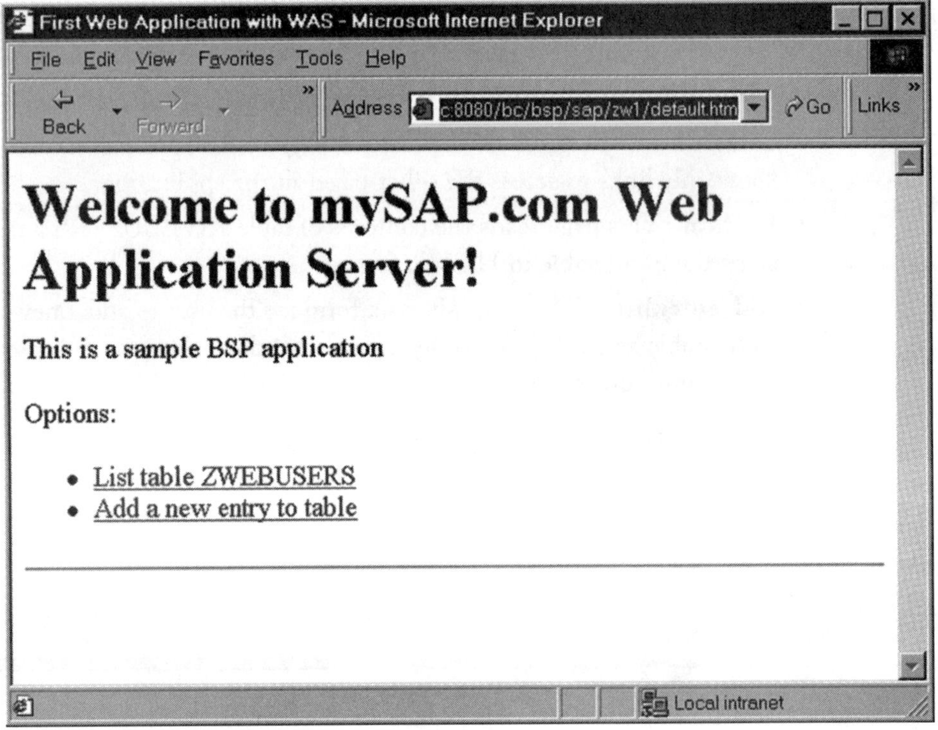

FIGURE 8-11 *Default.htm seen in a Web browser window*

To see the aspect of default.htm in a Web browser, click on the test button. A Web browser window like the one shown in Figure 8-11 will open.

Listing the Contents of a Table

The table you are going to use is a simple user list. Its definition in the ABAP dictionary is shown in Figure 8-12.

It is necessary to create an associated table data type for this table if you want to access it from BSP applications. The table type you have created is called ZWEBUSERS_TAB.

A BSP page needs to have a common point for defining data. Normally, variables defined in a BSP page are only visible on the scope where they are defined. This is a thing to always keep in mind, because it is possible to write code in two places: the page layout and the page event handler. That is, variables defined in the event

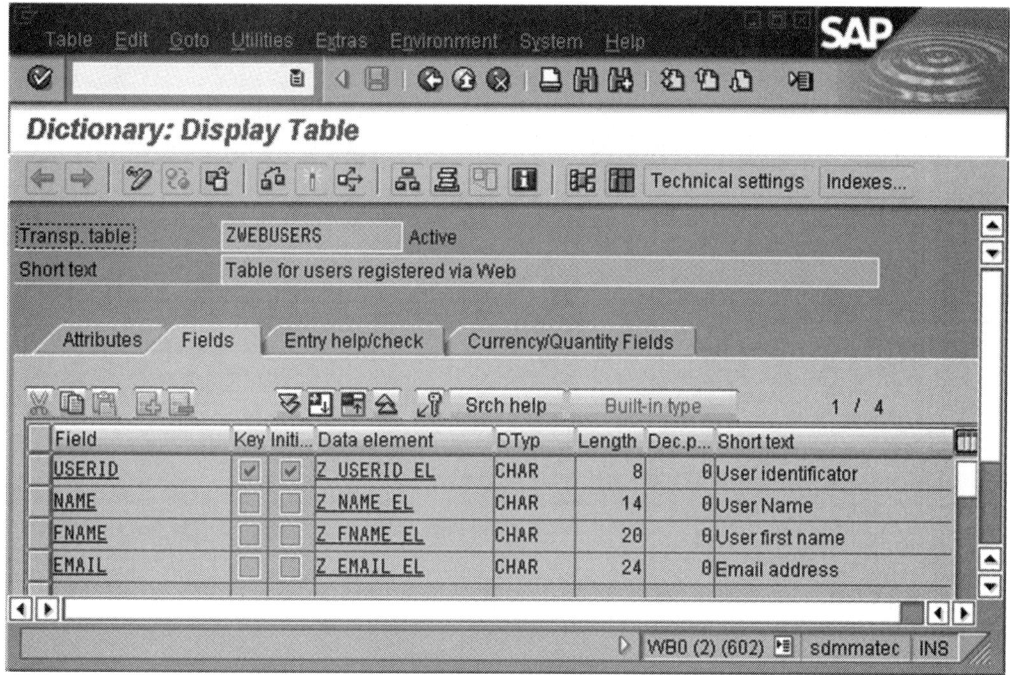

FIGURE 8-12 *Definition of the transparent table ZWEBUSERS*

handler are not necessarily visible in the page layout and vice versa. The right thing to do is to define global variables in the Page Attributes table and limit the definition of variables in code only if they should be visible exclusively in the scope of that piece of code. So, in order to be able to work with the data in the system table, you need to define one entry in the Page Attributes table: an entry defining an internal table of type ZWEBUSERS_TAB. I called this internal table WEBUSERS. Its definition can be seen in Figure 8-13.

Now, you have to prepare the code necessary to fill the internal table with data coming from the ZWEBUSERS table. For this, let's go to the Event Handler. Three events come predefined with the Event Handler:

- **OnInitialization.** This event will be raised any time the BSP page is started. As the Web models don't keep state, it is safe to assume that every time a page is loaded or refreshed, this handler will be raised, which is the same as saying that it will always be raised. So, any code that you want to be sure is always executed should be located here.

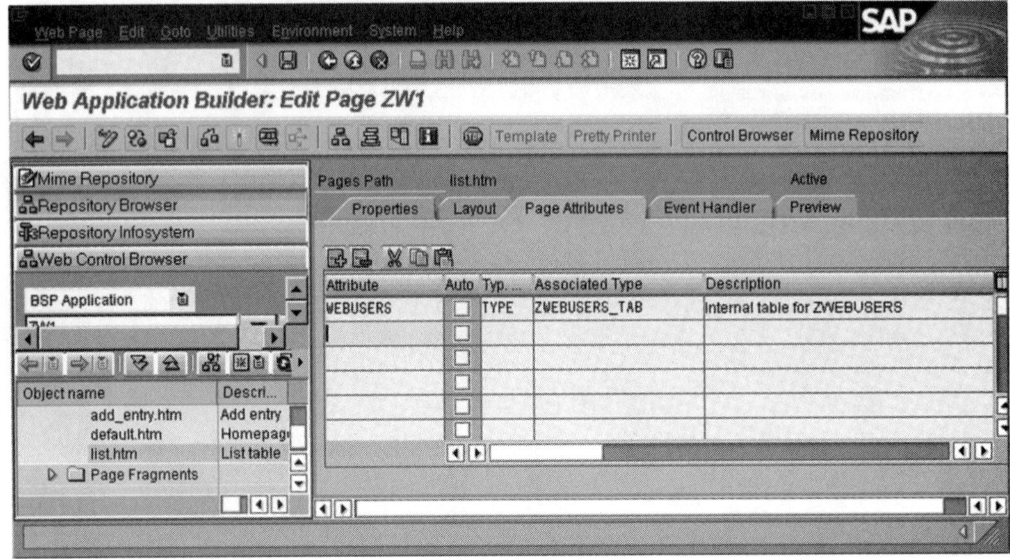

FIGURE 8-13 *Page Attributes table; defining the internal table WEBUSERS*

- **OnInputProcessing.** This event is raised when the page is called to process data sent from an input form. You will see more about that later.
- **OnManipulation.** This event is raised when some kind of manipulation is done through page elements defined with WCF. For the moment, you are not going to use that.

In the list.htm page, the code you have to prepare is code that does a select query to the database, and it is necessary that it is always run whenever the page is loaded. So, the code will be in the OnInitialization handler as listed in Figure 8-14. Here, you select all the contents of the ZWEBUSERS table in the internal table WEBUSERS defined earlier.

After defining attributes and OnInitialization code, the layout of the page that paints the table has to be written. The layout should be written in plain HTML, leaving detailed presentation to style sheets. In Figure 8-15 you can see the output of the BSP page list.htm. The code necessary to create it is shown in Figure 8-16.

As can be seen in Figure 8-16, the code to show the table is quite straightforward. It consists basically of a loop with all the rows that have been stored in the internal table WEBUSERS in the OnInitialization handler. Each loops paints a

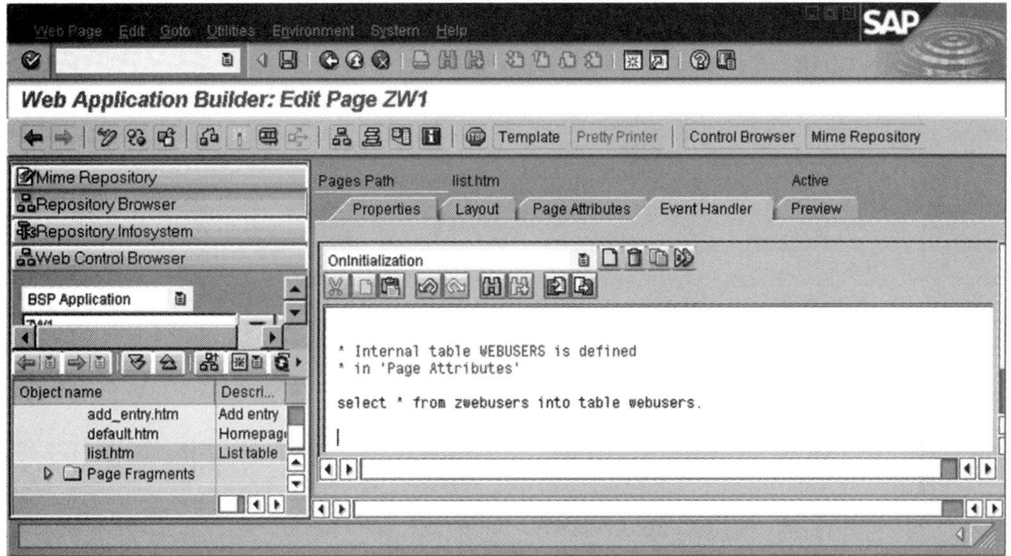

FIGURE 8-14 *OnInitialization code*

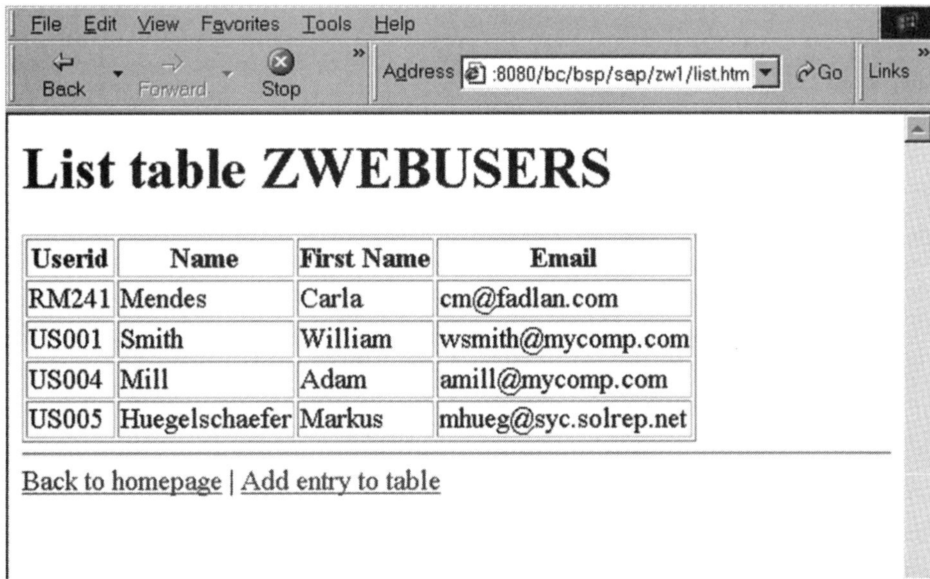

FIGURE 8-15 *Output of list.htm*

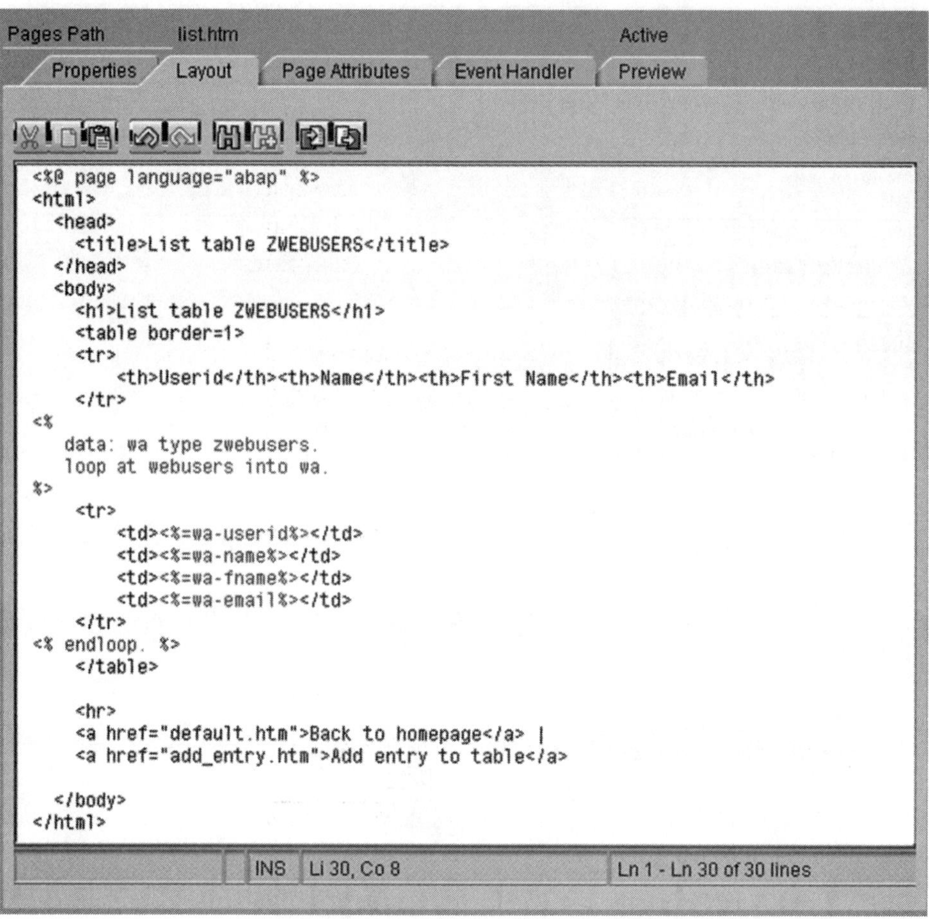


```
<%@ page language="abap" %>
<html>
  <head>
    <title>List table ZWEBUSERS</title>
  </head>
  <body>
    <h1>List table ZWEBUSERS</h1>
    <table border=1>
    <tr>
        <th>Userid</th><th>Name</th><th>First Name</th><th>Email</th>
    </tr>
<%
   data: wa type zwebusers.
   loop at webusers into wa.
%>
    <tr>
        <td><%=wa-userid%></td>
        <td><%=wa-name%></td>
        <td><%=wa-fname%></td>
        <td><%=wa-email%></td>
    </tr>
<% endloop. %>
    </table>

    <hr>
    <a href="default.htm">Back to homepage</a> |
    <a href="add_entry.htm">Add entry to table</a>

  </body>
</html>
```

FIGURE 8-16 *Layout code of list.htm*

HTML table row (all the code enclosed between the <tr> and </tr> tags). Each row has as many cells (<td> tags) as fields you want to show from the table. Inside each cell is printed the corresponding variable.

This code shows the tags to say to the BSP parser that some parts of programming code are really variables and which value should be printed literally. Those tags are the standard embedding tags with the = modifier. The modifier syntax is <%=variable_name%> and its result is to put the value in the HTML page.

Inserting Data in a Table

You have already seen what to do in order to show the contents of a table embedded in a HTML table. More precisely, what you have seen is how to put the results of an ABAP query into a HTML table. This part of the example shows how the BSP environment provides a very convenient method for receiving data from a Web form and processing it. Figures 8-17 and 8-18 show respectively the appearance of the inserting form (the add_entry.htm page) and the HTML layout used to generate it.

The HTML code in Figure 8-18 defines a form with four text fields. The HTML code used to generate the submit button has a special peculiarity: it has a name of OnInputProcessing(addentry). This is the method the BSP environment provides to ease the sending of form data from the Web browser to the SAP WAS. When the user clicks on the Add Entry button of the form, the Web browser creates a POST request with all the data encoded in a special format (called urlencoded). Traditional CGI programming required the programmer to be very aware of that and to do the decoding of the data. The BSP environment eases this task greatly

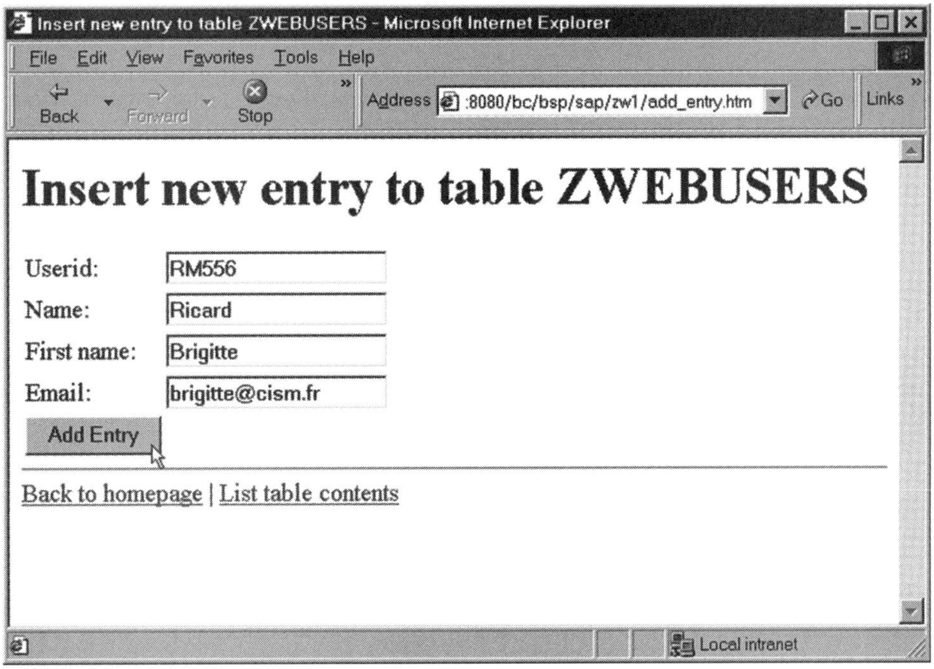

FIGURE 8-17 *The add_entry.htm Web form*

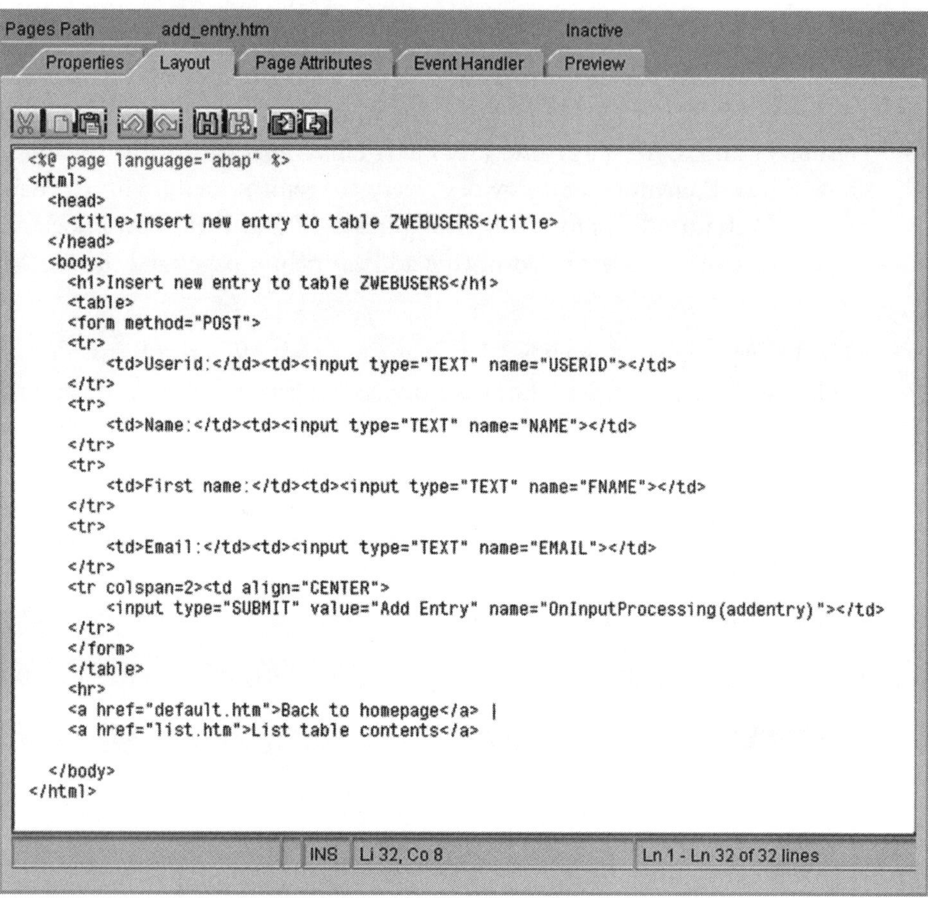


```
<%@ page language="abap" %>
<html>
  <head>
    <title>Insert new entry to table ZWEBUSERS</title>
  </head>
  <body>
    <h1>Insert new entry to table ZWEBUSERS</h1>
    <table>
    <form method="POST">
    <tr>
        <td>Userid:</td><td><input type="TEXT" name="USERID"></td>
    </tr>
    <tr>
        <td>Name:</td><td><input type="TEXT" name="NAME"></td>
    </tr>
    <tr>
        <td>First name:</td><td><input type="TEXT" name="FNAME"></td>
    </tr>
    <tr>
        <td>Email:</td><td><input type="TEXT" name="EMAIL"></td>
    </tr>
    <tr colspan=2><td align="CENTER">
        <input type="SUBMIT" value="Add Entry" name="OnInputProcessing(addentry)"></td>
    </tr>
    </form>
    </table>
    <hr>
    <a href="default.htm">Back to homepage</a> |
    <a href="list.htm">List table contents</a>

  </body>
</html>
```

FIGURE 8-18 *Layout code of add_entry.htm*

by doing all the "dirty" work itself and providing the data to the programmer in an easy-to-handle format. When a user submits this form, the BSP environment does two things:

- It decodes all the data sent and assigns the values to attribute variables defined with the same name they have in the HTML form.
- It generates an OnInputProcessing event identified with the string "addentry." It is possible then to program a handler for this event that could be used to differentiate whether this page has been requested from the submit button and process the query.

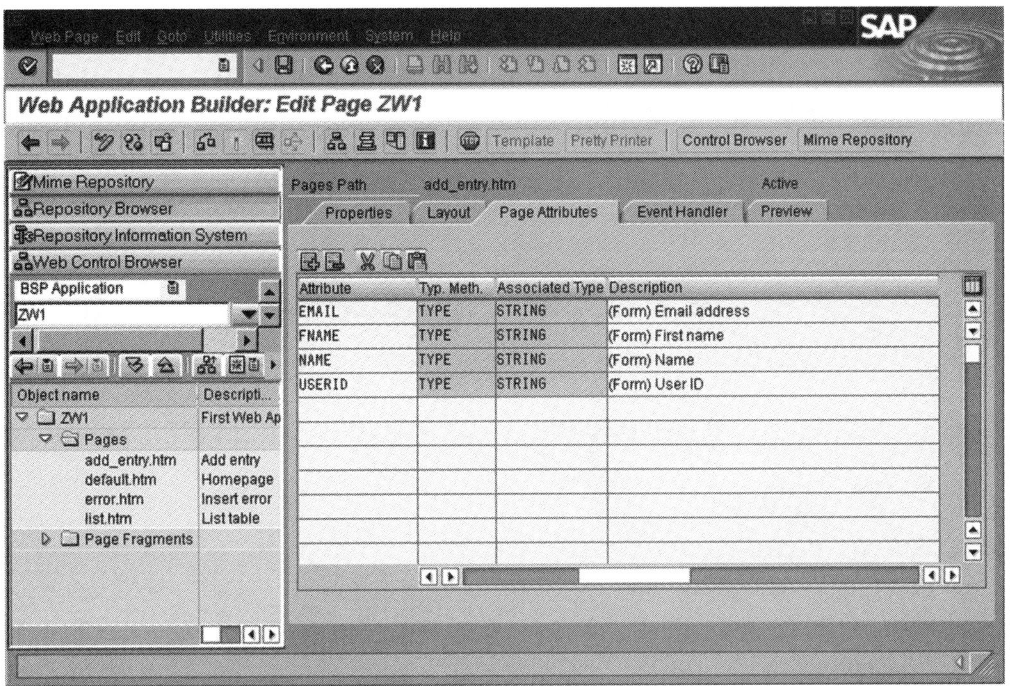

FIGURE 8-19 *Attributes variables for fetching data forms*

Figure 8-19 shows how the variables, whose values are going to be filled from the Web form, should be defined in the Page Attributes table.

The variables fetched from the Web form are marked as Auto. That means that the value is to be automatically fetched from the data the user has filled in the input fields in the form that have the same name. These variables are going to be processed by the handler defined in Figure 8-20.

This handler stores the values coming from the form and inserts them into the database. It does a check on whether the insert has been successfully done or whether an error has occurred (for example, trying to insert a duplicate USERID). In both cases, the program calls the navigation->next_page method. This method sends a redirect header to the Web browser. This header will go to the list.htm page if the insert has been successful, and to the error.htm page if the insert has not been completed. The values used to call the navigation->next_page method are defined in the Navigation table of the BSP application (see Figure 8-21).

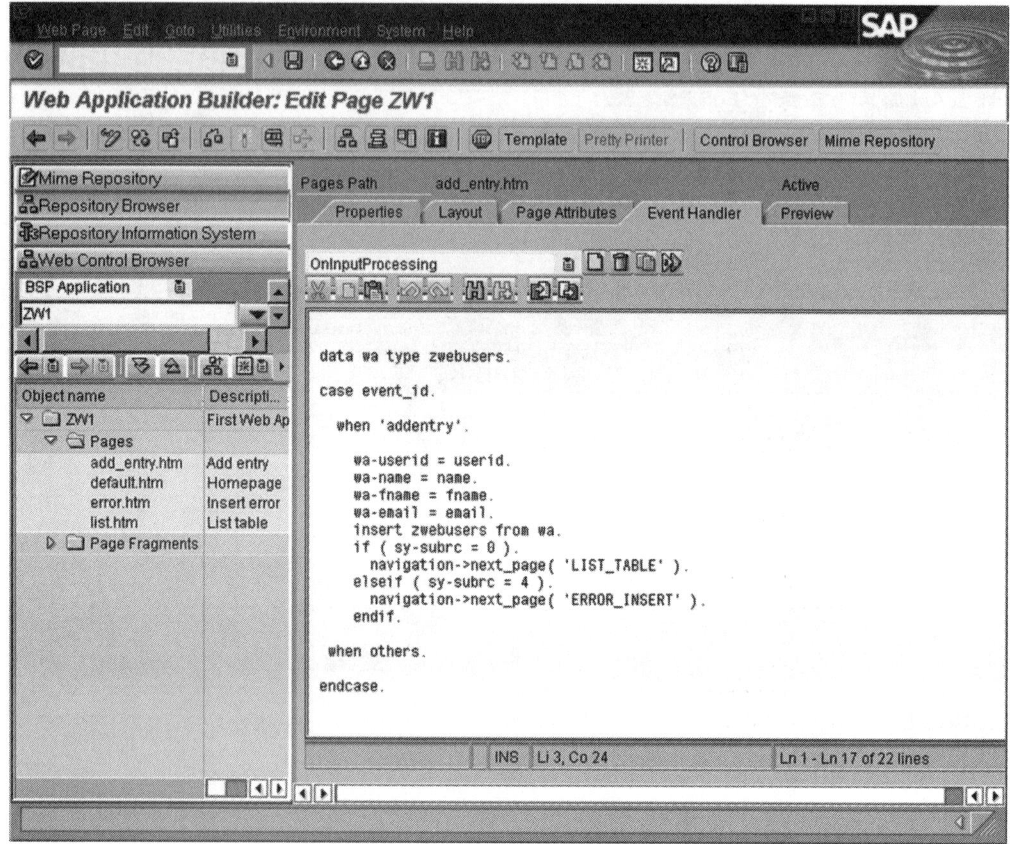

FIGURE 8-20 *The OnInputProcessing handler*

There you can define the navigation flow that sets how pages are related by navigation events. The Navigation Modeler is a graphical tool that eases this task.

The "trick" of passing the event_id value through the name of the submit button gives a lot of flexibility to this programming model. It is easy to imagine that a single Web page could be designed to do some different things, depending on which button the user has clicked on. For example, one button could go to an editing entry page, another could delete an entry, and so on.

To finish this example, Figure 8-22 shows the result of inserting the data that was filled in the form shown in Figure 8-17. As you have defined any successful insert

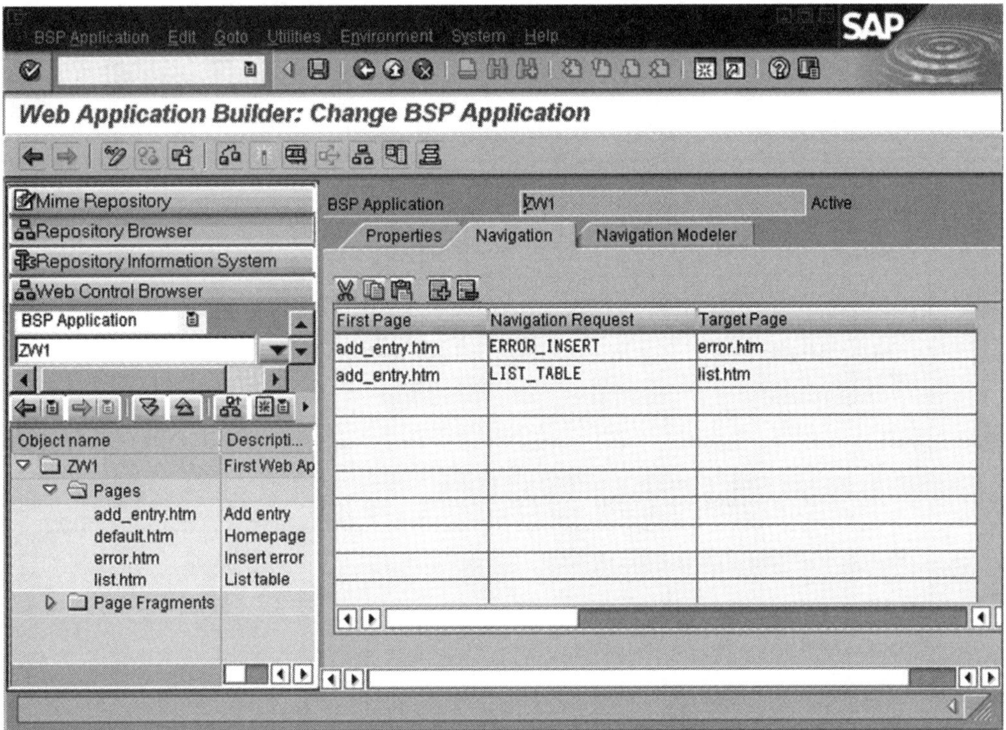

FIGURE 8-21 *Defining navigation requests*

to redirect the browser to the page that lists the table, the result is that the user can immediately see the entry inserted. This case is only an example. It is up to the application designer to model the navigation flow that the user is to follow when working with the Web application. For example, the result of the insert could be to go back to the add_entry.htm page in order to allow the user to add more entries.

More Examples

The example given above is a simple introduction that focuses on the ease of handling data coming from Web forms. This is one of the most powerful features of the BSP model, as it is the one that saves more work to the Web applications

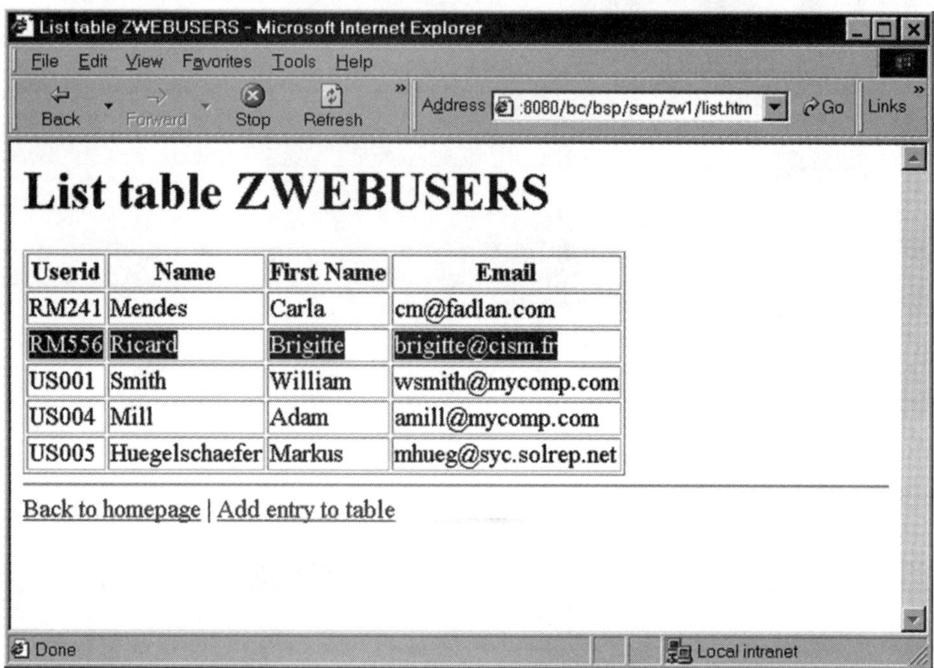

Userid	Name	First Name	Email
RM241	Mendes	Carla	cm@fadlan.com
RM556	Ricard	Brigitte	brigitte@cism.fr
US001	Smith	William	wsmith@mycomp.com
US004	Mill	Adam	amill@mycomp.com
US005	Huegelschaefer	Markus	mhueg@syc.solrep.net

FIGURE 8-22 *A new entry in the table!*

programmer. More complicated things are possible. With the default installation of the SAP WAS there come four examples that the programmer should read and understand in order to acquire a sound knowledge of the BSP model. These applications are called, in order of increasing difficulty, tutorial_1, tutorial_2, and tutorial_3. One nearly complete BSP application is also included: the Bookstore. The Bookstore is an Amazon-like Internet bookshop offering an implementation of a book catalog, a shopping basket, and a simple book search engine. This Bookstore Web application is shown in Figure 8-23. At the moment of this writing, it is only available in the German language.

The MIME Repository

The MIME Repository is the part of the BSP used to store all types of objects related to a given BSP application, especially images, style sheets, icons, page

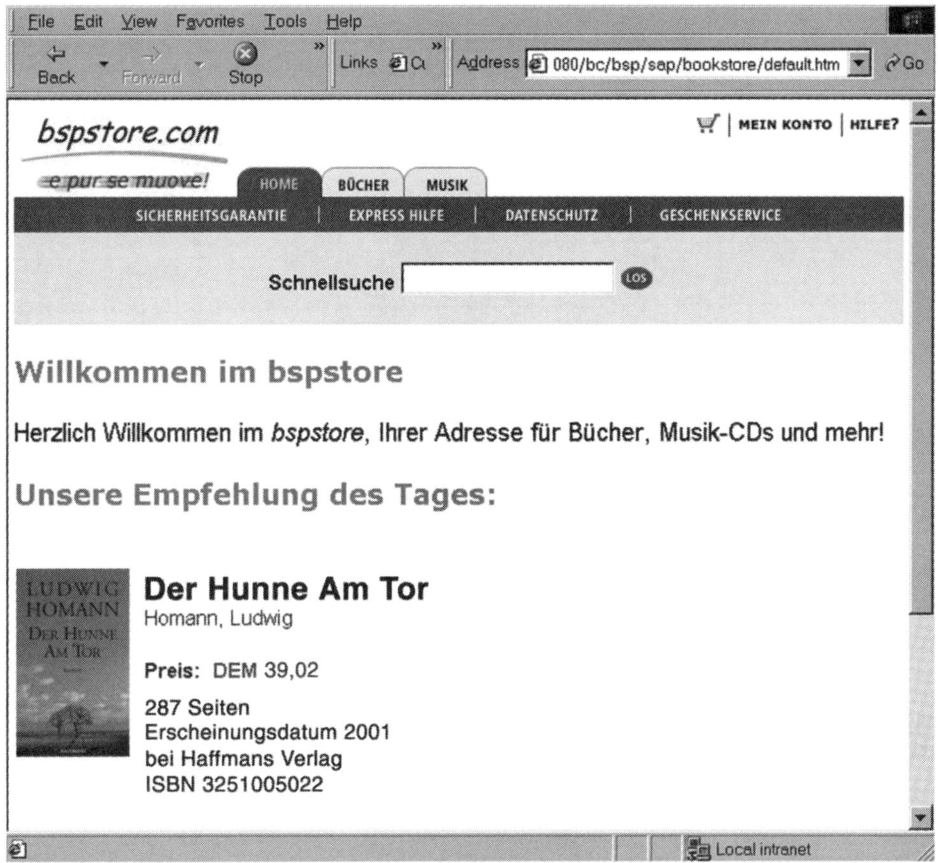

FIGURE 8-23 *The Bookstore demo BSP application*

drawing elements, multimedia files, and static documents. In fact, any type of binary or text file can be stored in the MIME Repository and therefore in the SAP database, so they became a part of a given project. The MIME Repository is part of the Web development infrastructure. All the changes made to the MIME Repository, like importing new objects, are written to a transport request. This allows full integration of the Web objects with the Web application that requires them.

The MIME Repository is arranged in a directory tree structure. It can be accessed with a repository browser, which appears in the navigation area (left-hand side) of the Object Navigator when toggling the MIME Repository button on the top left corner. The appearance of the MIME Repository browser is shown in Figure 8-24.

FIGURE 8-24 *The MIME Repository*

The left area of the browser window shows directory entries for each of the BSP applications existing in the system. (Note: If the directory for the application you want is not shown, click on the Display All Directories button). It is not allowed to create directory entries at the top-level directory; they are created automatically by the SAP system when a BSP application is activated the first time. Each BSP application has an identically named repository entry (in our example, ZW1). Objects located in this directory are directly accessible by the application (objects' relative hyperlinks are searched in the corresponding repository). These are application-specific MIME objects.

Besides objects specific to a given application, there are also cross-application MIME objects. They are located in the PUBLIC entry of the Repository and can be used by any Web application. The most important objects available for public access are the objects belonging to the WCF.

The following procedure illustrates how you can import an image object from the file system in the MIME Repository. First, right-click on the Web application entry desired (in this case, ZW1). In the pop-up menu that appears, choose the Create/Directory option. A dialog box asking for a directory name and description will appear. When it is submitted, you are given the chance of assigning this directory to a transport request. The result of creating a directory is shown in Figure 8-25.

Now you can import an image file and put it under the directory you have just created. The procedure is similar: right-click on the images entry and choose Import in the pop-up context menu. A File Navigation dialog box will appear to allow you to choose the file you want to import. Next, a Properties dialog box will appear (see Figure 8-26), where you can modify some of the object's attributes. In this box, you see how the system automatically detects the MIME type of the file.

FIGURE 8-25 *Creating a directory under a repository entry*

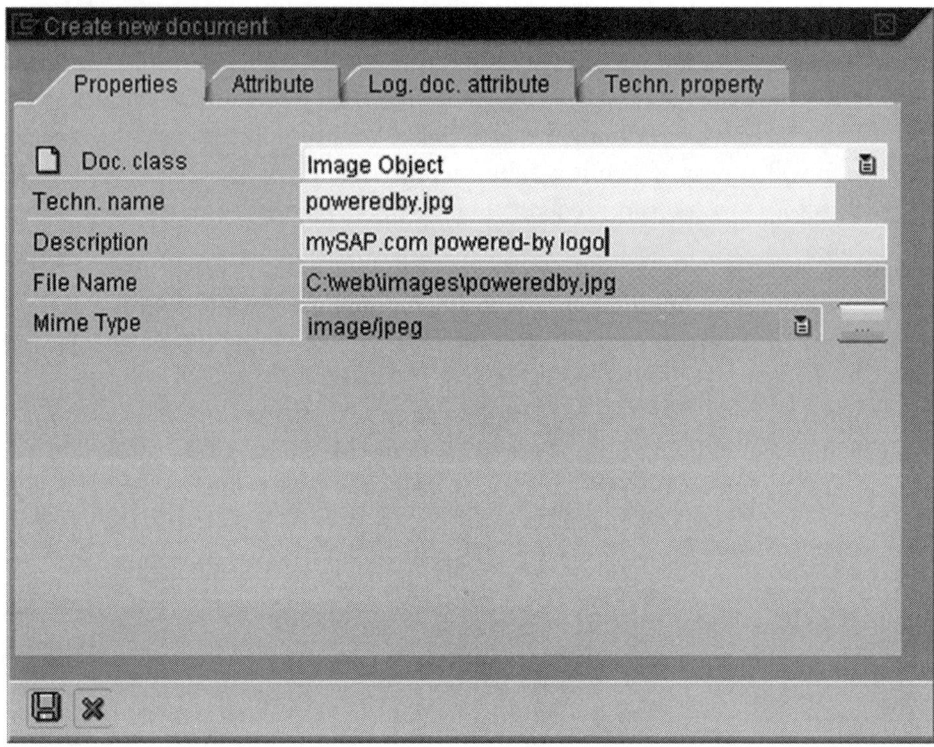

FIGURE 8-26 *Object properties*

After you click on the Save button and assign the object to a transport request, it is imported in the MIME Repository. If you double-click on the object, you can see a preview on the bottom-left corner of the object navigator (see Figure 8-27).

The objects in the MIME Repository would be of little use if they were not referenced by any of the Web pages of the BSP application. If you want to show this image in a Web page, you should insert an HTML *img* tag like this in one of the BSP pages:

```
<img src="images/poweredby.jpg">
```

The easiest way of doing this is with the drag-and-drop support of the Development Workbench. To do this, go back to the application Repository Browser and open the Web page in which the image is to be inserted. The page HTML layout should be in the right-hand work area. Then, go back to the MIME Reposi-

FIGURE 8-27 *Object navigator*

tory, select the image object, and drag it to the place in the HTML layout where you want it to be. The result is shown in Figure 8-28.

The drag-and-drop operation only inserts the textual relative reference to the Web object. The corresponding HTML code will have to be wrapped around to show it as an image reference or a hypertext link. If you put the code shown above around this text and activate the result, you obtain the Web page shown in Figure 8-29.

The MIME Repository also offers the following features and limitations:

- It is possible to convert a MIME object of text type (HTML, CSS, plain, and so on) to a BSP page and back, from a BSP page to a static text object.
- The browser allows nearly every possible operation with subdirectories and MIME objects in the same way as if they were real files. This allows

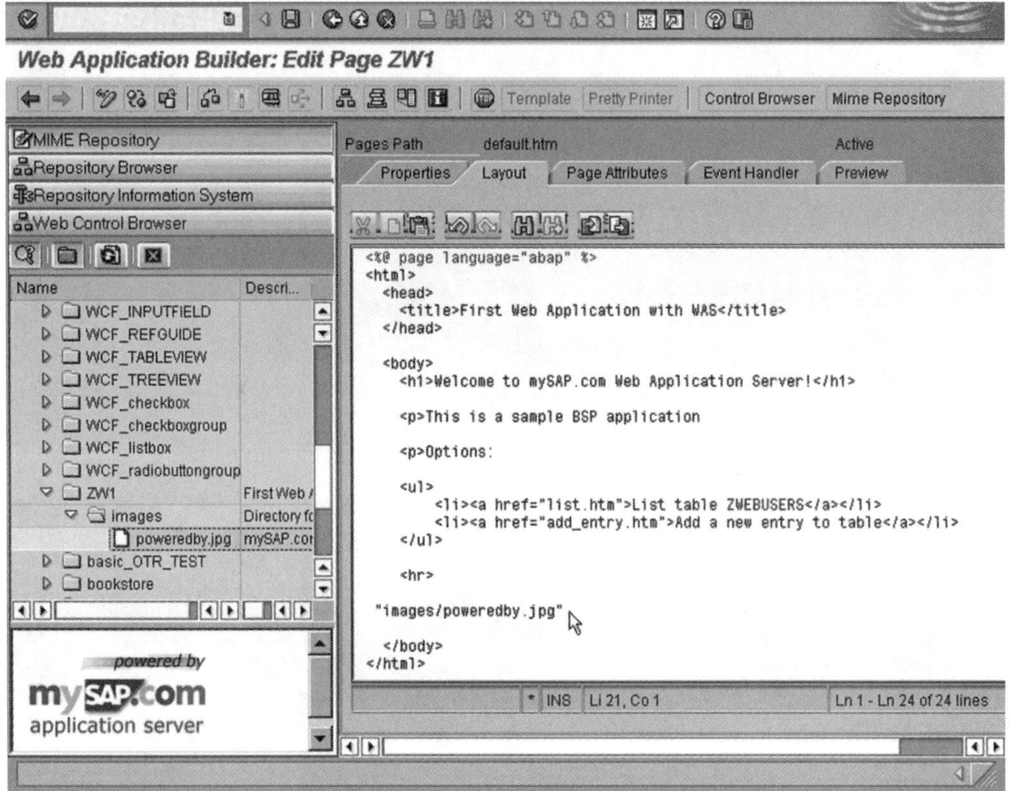

FIGURE 8-28 *Drag-and-drop to insert a MIME object*

reorganizing the files in the repository and copying them to the PUBLIC entry, if necessary. As stated earlier, the only actions that are not possible are to create and delete top-level entries, as these are handled directly by the development environment. When moving directories inside a repository entry, care should be taken to avoid lost references to them in the BSP pages.

- An object can be exported to the file system.
- External Web development tools can be used to manage the MIME Repository as long as they support the WebDAV protocol.
- Only one object can be imported at the same time. To work around this, it is possible to do a massive import from an external tool with the WebDAV protocol.

FIGURE 8-29 *An image from the MIME Repository*

One side effect of the MIME Repository—amply compensated by its advantage of relating static objects to the BSP application and handling them with transport requests—is the high overhead of serving them to Web clients. This is because the SAP system has to access the database to get a large object and then send it to the Web client. In order to avoid this, the SAP system automatically caches each static file in the cache directories set in the configuration the first time it is accessed and serves consequent requests from that directory.

As a consequence of that, it is recommended that very large pools of static data should be offered directly as static files from the file system or from another dedicated Web server. Actually, if the main purpose of our Web application is to serve static files, then using any Web application server is probably not a good idea, as traditional Web servers are specially optimized for that function. As a general rule, the MIME Repository should be dedicated to store only those static elements that are a fundamental part of a Web application, like page drawing elements, image logos, style sheets, and so on.

The Web Control Framework

The WCF consists of a set of predefined controls oriented to ease the generation of Web layouts. The WCF provides controls for page containers, tables, form elements like list boxes, check boxes, input fields, buttons, and so on.

Each Web control is actually a wrapper that automatically generates HTML when parsed by the BSP processor. The main reason for using Web controls instead of plain HTML is the ease that they provide for associating programming events with controls. For example, instead of dealing directly with all the rows of a table and inserting in all of them a form if you want to make a user action on one of them to create an event, WCF controls allow you to think in terms of a full table to which events can be related.

The other advantage of Web controls resides in the uniformity of aspect and appearance of all the elements in the Web page. WCF makes extensive use of style sheets, thus making sure that all the elements of a Web page have a consistent appearance.

For an example of the use of WCF in BSP applications, let's consider the HTML code for the list.htm page shown in Figure 8-10. An equivalent page that is mostly defined using WCF controls is shown in Figure 8-30.

The rest of the BSP page (Page Attributes and Event Handlers) are the same as those of list.htm, so the page aim is to make a listing of the contents of a table. The control prepared for that is called TableView. Controls are inserted in the HTML layout by using a special tag with the following syntax:

```
<bsp:ControlName var1="value1" var2="value2" ... />
```

The TableView knows which table should list with the parameter dataSrc. The origin of data should be a variable defined in the Page Attributes of one data table type. Like HTML tags, there are WCF tags that also can be enclosing tags around other Web page elements, with the DocumentBody control. Figure 8-31 shows the result of listing the table using WCF controls.

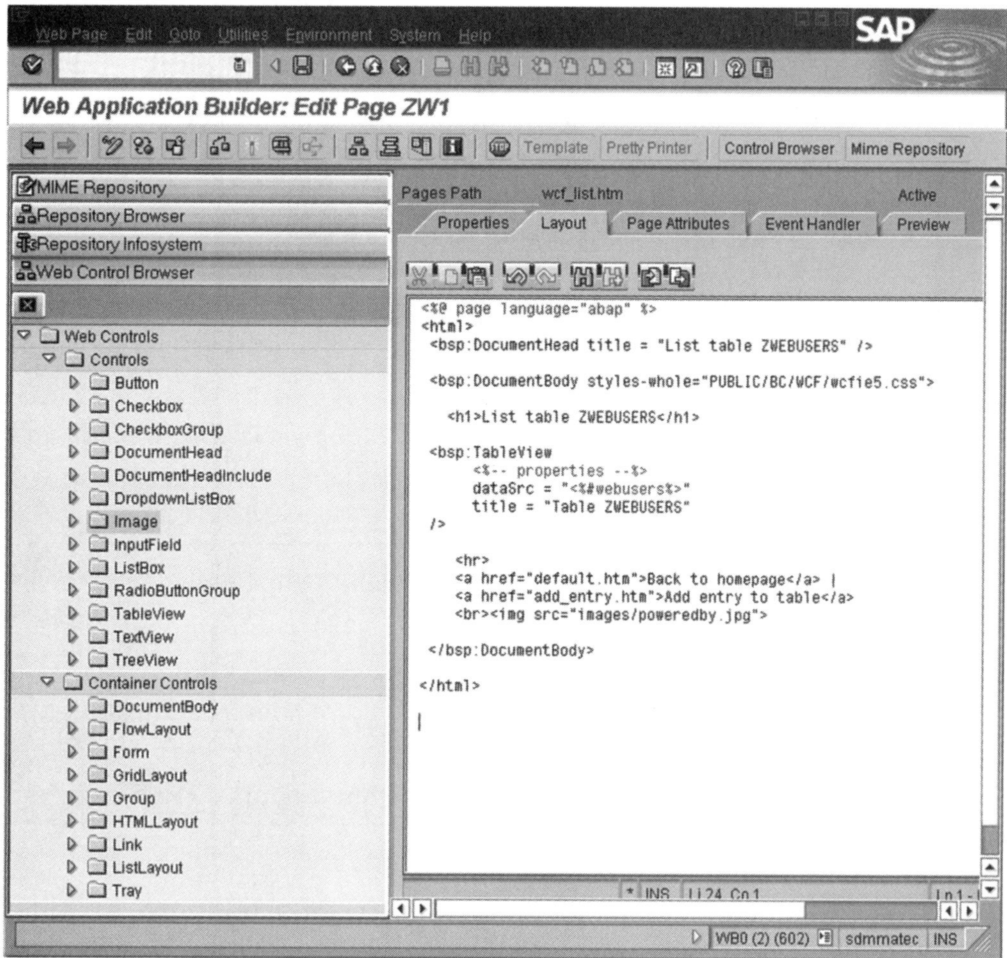

FIGURE 8-30 *Source code of wcf_list.htm*

If you compare the HTML code in Figure 8-10 with the WCF code in Figure 8-30, it is easy to see that the WCF code prevents the programmer from the need to handle the loop on the rows of the table. The default appearance of the table is also a lot better than the default appearance of a simple HTML table (see Figure 8-31).

WCF controls can be directly drag-and-dropped from the control browser in the left side of the Development Workbench to the page layout. That makes all the possible options that a given control can have immediately available. Some

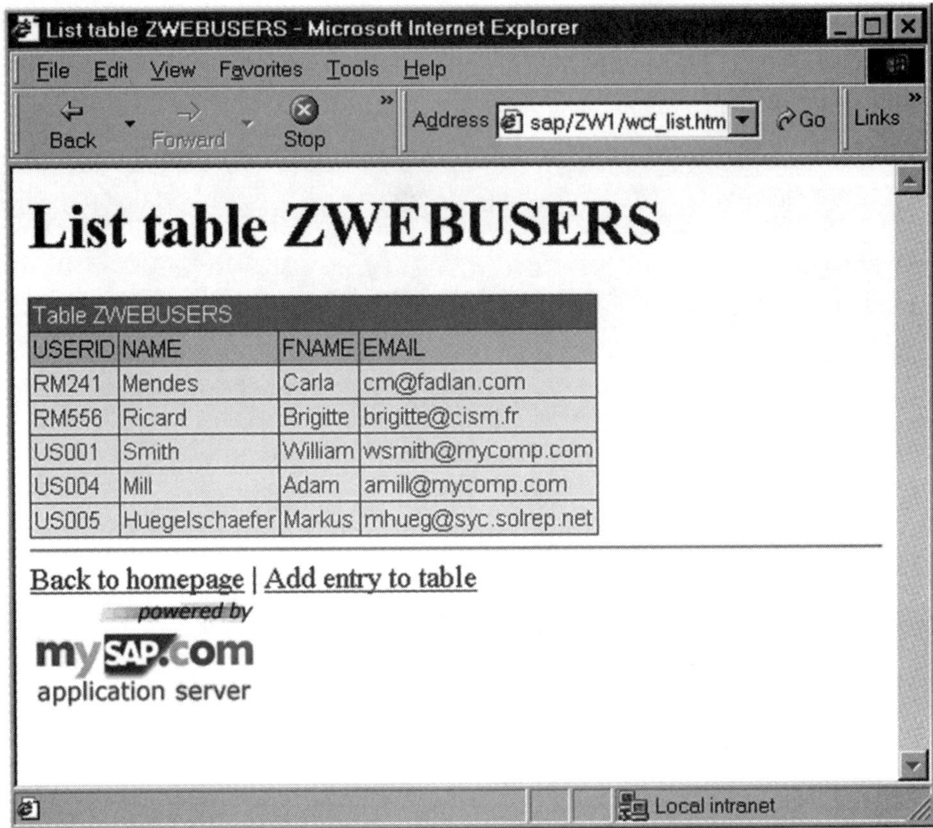

FIGURE 8-31 *Appearance of a WCF control in a Web browser*

options are directly converted to HTML tags modifiers, and some others are quite complex and will generate programming code intended to ease the development of advanced applications.

Extensive documentation is included with the WCF. It can be accessed by double-clicking the control for which you need information. The documentation comes in HTML format and is directly served by the SAP WAS.

WCF documentation is very comprehensive and has working examples for all the controls (see Figure 8-32). The Web application developer should always keep it handy.

In conclusion, the WCF provides a control-based orientation that makes development easier and converts the SAP WAS in a rapid application development tool. The advantages it offers of consistency of programming and layout design should

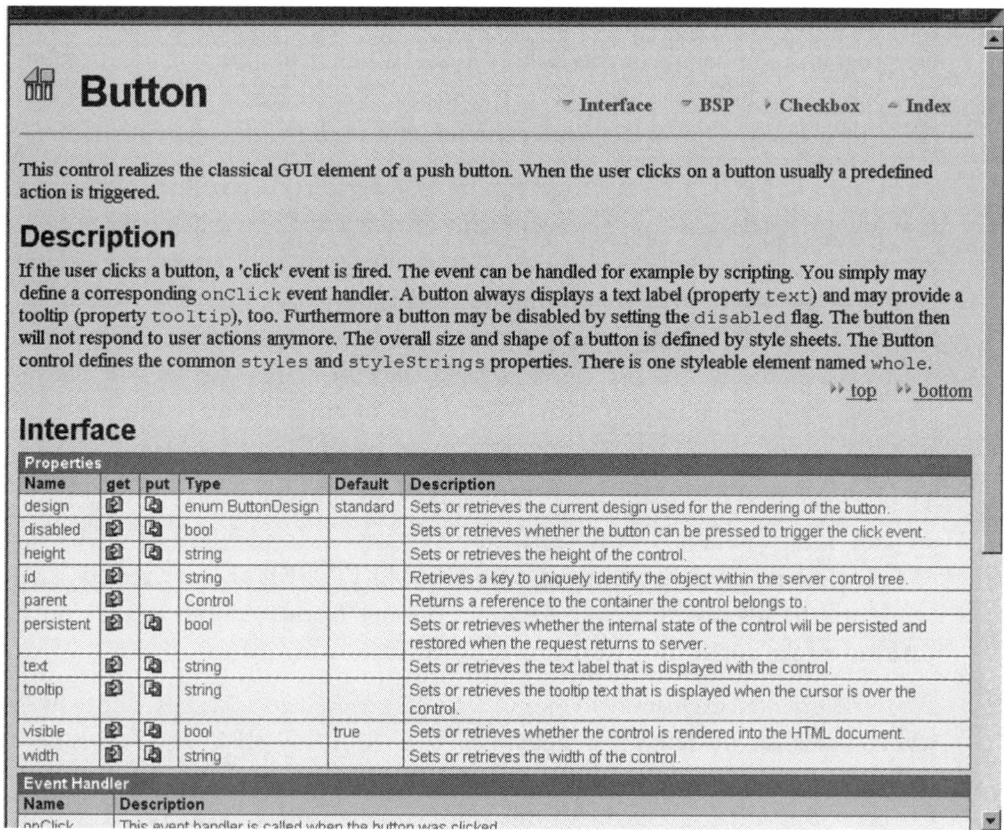

Button

Interface BSP Checkbox Index

This control realizes the classical GUI element of a push button. When the user clicks on a button usually a predefined action is triggered.

Description

If the user clicks a button, a 'click' event is fired. The event can be handled for example by scripting. You simply may define a corresponding `onClick` event handler. A button always displays a text label (property `text`) and may provide a tooltip (property `tooltip`), too. Furthermore a button may be disabled by setting the `disabled` flag. The button then will not respond to user actions anymore. The overall size and shape of a button is defined by style sheets. The Button control defines the common `styles` and `styleStrings` properties. There is one styleable element named `whole`.

top bottom

Interface

Properties

Name	get	put	Type	Default	Description
design	✓	✓	enum ButtonDesign	standard	Sets or retrieves the current design used for the rendering of the button.
disabled	✓	✓	bool		Sets or retrieves whether the button can be pressed to trigger the click event.
height	✓	✓	string		Sets or retrieves the height of the control.
id	✓		string		Retrieves a key to uniquely identify the object within the server control tree.
parent	✓		Control		Returns a reference to the container the control belongs to.
persistent	✓	✓	bool		Sets or retrieves whether the internal state of the control will be persisted and restored when the request returns to server.
text	✓	✓	string		Sets or retrieves the text label that is displayed with the control.
tooltip	✓	✓	string		Sets or retrieves the tooltip text that is displayed when the cursor is over the control.
visible	✓	✓	bool	true	Sets or retrieves whether the control is rendered into the HTML document.
width	✓	✓	string		Sets or retrieves the width of the control.

Event Handler

Name	Description
onClick	This event handler is called when the button was clicked

FIGURE 8-32 *WCF button control documentation*

clearly compensate for the time invested in learning how all the controls can be fully exploited.

The ICF

The ICF is the environment that provides the application programming interface necessary for handling HTTP requests and responses at the HTTP protocol level. This is actually an object-oriented extension to the ABAP programming environment specifically created to provide the basis for enhancing the SAP system to be fully integrated with the Internet. The ICF is accessed by means of an ABAP class that provides an interface to the HTTP handling functionality defined in the C SAP kernel. This book is not the right place to go deeply into the programming details of the ICF, so I only attempt to give a short introduction of how the ICF deals with HTTP requests. The readers interested in broadening their knowledge on the matter should refer to the SAP documentation.

The classes of the ICF allow programming of generic Web-oriented applications running inside the SAP system. Two points of view can be considered when talking about Web-oriented applications: Web clients and Web servers. Web client programming deals with generating HTTP requests and reading responses, whereas Web server programming is aimed at interpreting requests and generating responses. Both tasks are closely related, and there are programming classes allowing the programmer to create both types of applications inside the SAP WAS.

The interaction model between HTTP servers and clients has been introduced in section, "How the Web Works," earlier in this chapter. Inside the SAP WAS, for each request received, an object of type CL_HTTP_SERVER is created. This object will be filled with all the data that belongs to the request, and it can be accessed by the application through the object interfaces.

Programs oriented exclusively to receive requests are defined as classes. The request will be processed by defining a method called HANDLE_REQUEST. It is necessary to associate this class with a given URL so that the method will be run whenever this URL is called. All this work is done from transaction SICF. For example, SAP suggests that after a first installation of the SAP WAS it should be tested by calling the URL **http://some.newserver.com:8080/public/ping**, which simply sends back text stating that the server has been reached. Figure 8-33 shows the main screen of the ICF. Double-clicking on the PUBLIC/PING entry will lead to the URL definition. From the Handler List tab, it is possible to associate a class. The code of the method that will handle the request is shown in Figure 8-34.

Figure 8-34 clearly shows how this program is directly creating a HTTP response with the set_header_field method and a body content with the set_cdata method. This last method will also be in charge of calculating the content length and setting the corresponding header. The ICF thus provides the necessary methods that are needed for doing advanced Web server programming at the HTTP protocol level, as was explained earlier in this chapter . Corresponding get_* methods also exist for reading data coming from client requests.

If you have a detailed look at the window of transaction SICF, you also see that the BSP processor is there, as is the WCF entry and other handlers for requests

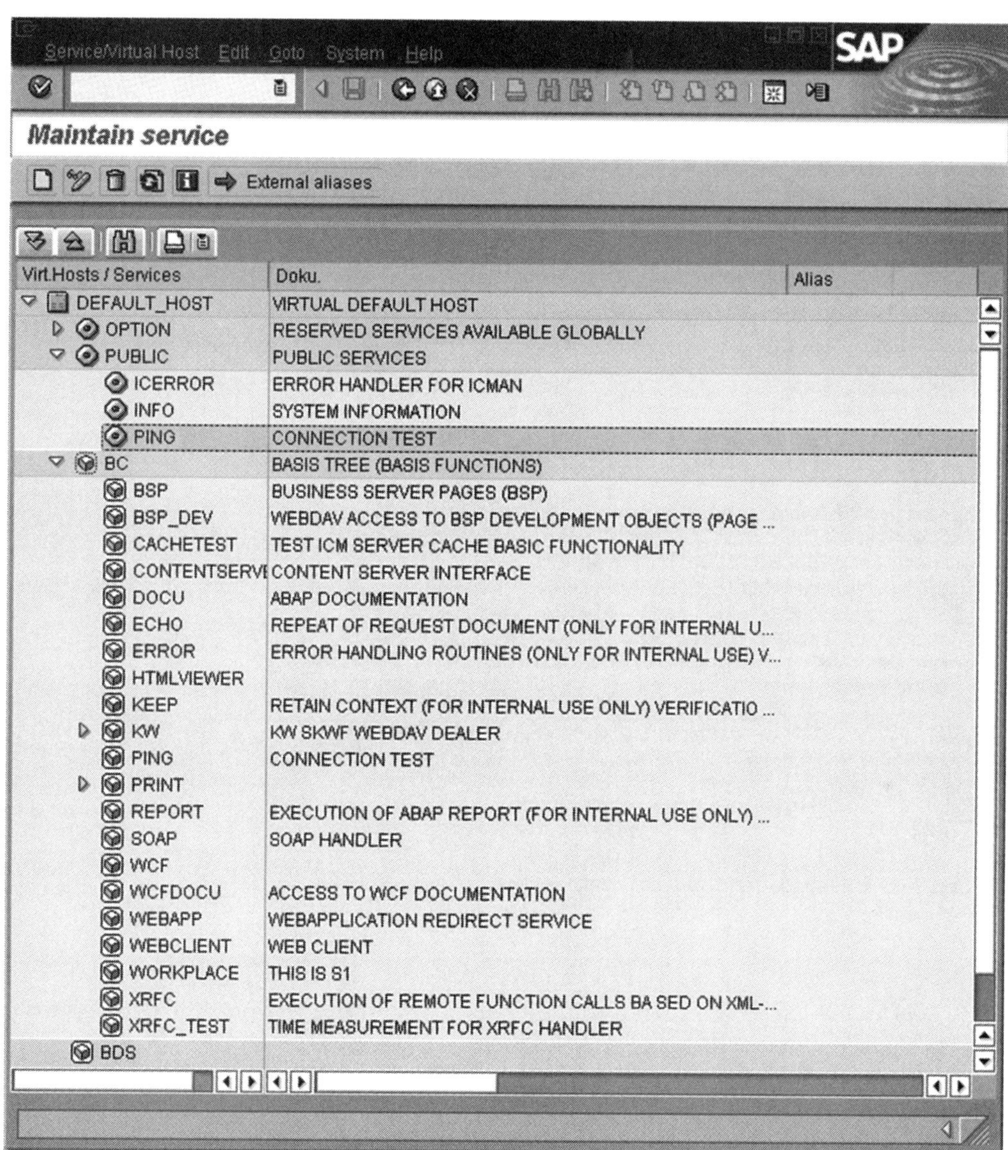

FIGURE 8-33 *The SICF transaction*

of type SOAP (*Simple Object Access Protocol*) and WEBDAV. All these programs are made in ABAP with the Web functionality given by the ICF. The ICF is thus the choice when there is a need for a more complex application or to extend the features and possibilities of the SAP WAS.

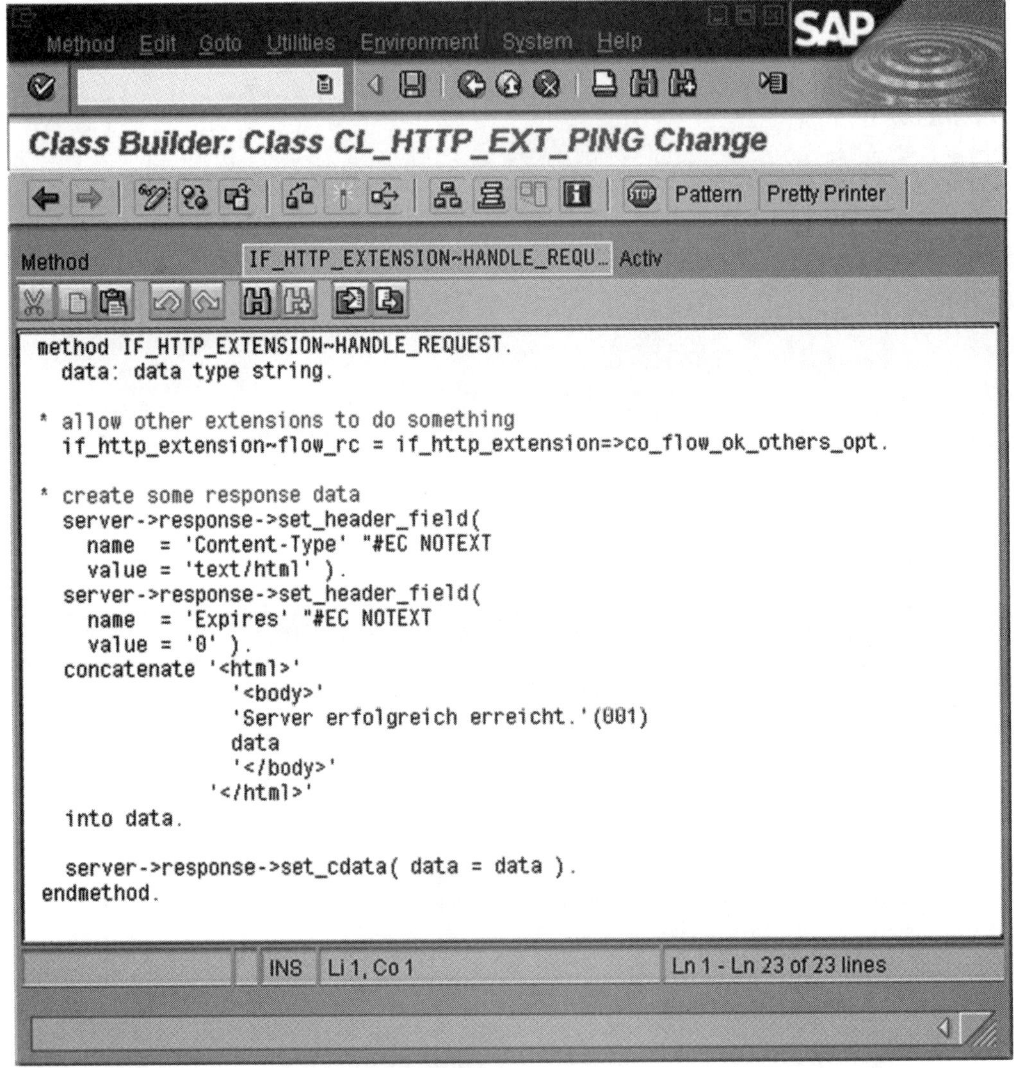

FIGURE 8-34 *Handler code for the /bc/ping service*

Configuration Options

The configuration options related to the SAP WAS are maintained as part of the instance profile, so it is possible to change its value with SAP transaction RZ10. The first parameter that you should take into account is the parameter that starts the ICM process. The other parameters that affect the behaviour of the dispatcher and the configuration of the ICM can also be modified there.

The table of configuration options given below is not comprehensive and is likely to have been modified or enhanced in the production release of the SAP WAS. In the release I have been working with in this chapter (see last section), some of these parameters are not recognized by the syntax checker of transaction RZ10. Nonetheless, most of them will work as described. It is also possible that some of these parameters will find their way into being considered parameters that can be changed dynamically (dynamic switching) as they deal mostly with Web server (ICM) tasks. Thus, there should be no reason for them to require a full SAP system restart in order to be activated.

Table 8-2 Configuration Options and Parameters for the SAP WAS

Profile directives:

exe/icman
Name of the executable file of the ICM.

Default values:

Unix: exe/icman=/usr/sap/<SID>/SYS/exe/run /icman

Windows NT: exe/icman=\\<SAPGLOBALHOST>\sapmnt\<SID>/SYS/exe/run/icman.exe

rdisp/start_icman
Indicates whether the ICM should be started in this SAP instance.

Possible values:

rdisp/start_icman=true ICM is to be started

rdisp/start_icman=false Do not start ICM

icm/plugin_<xx>
The plug-ins that should be started in order to allow the ICM to serve different protocols.

Possible values:

icm/plugin_0=PROT=HTTP, PLG=$(DIR_EXECUTABLE)/httpplugin.so

icm/plugin_1=PROT=HTTPS, PLG=$(DIR_EXECUTABLE)/httpsplugin.so

cm/plugin_2=PROT=SMTP, PLG=$(DIR_EXECUTABLE)/smtpplugin.so

icm/server_ port_<xx>
The TCP ports each plug-in should bind to. This field also specifies the timeout for existing connections. It is possible to set more than one port for the same service. Because of the TCP/IP design, it is not possible to use one port for more than one service, so no other programs in the operating system should be using that port.

Possible values:

icm/server_ port_0=PROT=HTTP, PORT=8080, TIMEOUT=15

icm/server_ port_1=PROT=SMTP, PORT=25, TIMEOUT=45

icm/min_threads
Minimum number of ICM threads that should be available. This is also the number of threads that are created at system startup. Values are integer numbers in the range from 1 to 3,200.

Possible value:

icm/min_threads=10

(continued)

Table 8-2 *(continued)*

Profile directives:

icm/max_threads
The maximum number threads of the ICMAN. This is the maximum number of connections that can be simultaneously served by the ICMAN. Values should be integer number in the range from 5 to 3,200.

Possible value:

icm/min_threads=30

The min_threads and max_threads are values set during system startup. The minimum number of threads is the minimum number of threads that should be running in a given moment. In the case server load increases, new threads will be automatically created to handle the new requests until the number of running threads reaches the value specified in icm/max_threads. When server load decreases, unused threads are silently destroyed until the number of threads equals the value in icm/min_threads.

icm/req_queue_len
The maximum number of requests that can be waiting to be serviced in the request queue. This value should be in the range 50–32,000 and should always be greater than icm/min_threads.

Default value:

icm/req_queue_len=100

icm/listen_queue_len
The maximum number of operating system listen queues. If this system queue is full, the operating system rejects connections. This value should be in the range 5–1,024 and is operating system dependent.

Default value:

icm/listen_queue_len=512

icm/max_conn
The maximum number of simultaneously open connections in the ICM. It can be greater than icm/max_threads because there can be inactive connections for which no thread is required. The limit is operating system dependent and is set by the maximum number of open file handles.

Default value:

icm/max_conn=100

icm/accept_remote_trace_level
This parameter determines whether a remote user is allowed to change the trace level of the SAP system.

Default value:

icm/accept_remote_trace_level=0

For security reasons, no remote user is allowed to change trace level. For debugging purposes, this value could be set to 1.

icm/HTTP/file_access_<xx>
This directive sets a URL in the Web server space that serves static files from a file system directory.

Example:

icm/HTTP/file_access_0=PREFIX=/doc, DOC-ROOT=e:\info\documents

The URL **http://Web.server.com/doc/intro.doc** will refer to the file intro.doc located in the e:\info\documents folder.

icm/HTTP/redirect_<xx>
This directive allows to set a URI in the Web server space that will redirect (HTTP status 301) the Web browser to some other destination.

(continued)

Table 8-2 *(continued)*

Profile directives:

Example:

icm/HTTP/redirect_0=PREFIX=/other_place, TO=http://some.other_place.com/

icm/HTTP/server_cache_<xx>
Cache directory to store objects served from the MIME Repository. Every object served from the MIME Repository is saved in the cache dir the first time a user requests it. The next requests are directly served from the cache to avoid database access and thus reduce system overhead.

Example:

icm/HTTP/server_cache_0=PREFIX=/bc/bsp /sap, CACHEDIR=f:\sapWeb\cache0

Sets a cache dir for storing all the static files requested with the URI /bc/bsp/sap. It is possible to create cache dir for different parts of the Web server.

icm/HTTP/server_cache_<xx>/max_entries
Maximum number of file entries that are to be stored in the given cache dir.

Example:

icm/HTTP/server_cache_0/max_entries=10000

icm/HTTP/server_cache_<xx>/clear
Whether to clear all the files in the given cache dir every time the server is restarted. Possible values are TRUE or FALSE.

Default value:

icm/HTTP/server_cache_0/clear=TRUE

icm/HTTP/server_cache_<xx>/expiration
Expiration time. An entry in the cache will expire when it is older than the time in seconds specified here.

Example:

icm/HTTP/server_cache_0/expiration=86400

When a file in the cache dir is older than one day (86,400 seconds) it will expire and will be erased.

icm/HTTP/server_cache_<xx>/size_MB
Maximum size that can use a cache dir specified in megabytes.

Example:

icm/HTTP/server_cache_0/size_MB=100

Roadmap to SAP WAS

At the time of this writing, an "official version" of the SAP WAS has not yet been released by SAP. It was planned to be released in the third quarter of year 2001. The examples shown in this chapter are taken from the preview version that was released in November 2000. The differences between the two versions are explained in the following sections.

SAP WAS 5.0 FCS (First Customer Ship)

This version was released in November 2000 as a test preview version to help SAP customers familiarize themselves with the new Web-oriented development model. It was built on a SAP basis release 5.0A. The focus was to integrate the main components for the development model: the ICF, the BSP engine, the MIME Repository, and the WCF. The HTTP and the HTTPS plug-ins were functional, but they still lacked some Web server advanced features.

This release was only for the Linux and the Windows NT operating systems and only for the SAPDB relational database system.

SAP WAS 6.10

This will be the official first release of the SAP WAS. This version is expected sometime at the third quarter of 2001. It will address some of the advanced features that were lacking or not fully functional in the preview version. Those new features are:

- An XML/XSLT engine
- Functional SMTP plug-in
- Support for the SOAP
- A graphical development tool
- Enhanced event model
- Controls for developing WML applications for the Wireless Access Protocol (WAP)

As this is an official version, it will be released for all the operating systems and database platforms SAP usually has supported. This version is the first in which the former SAP Basis component will be known as SAP Web Application Server.

Future Orientation

The SAP ITS has been the most used Web-enabling component in the mySAP.com system. It is expected that all ITS functions will be gradually integrated in SAP WAS, thus considerably simplifying the deployment of Web-based SAP applications. The ITS flow logic approach for creating Web applications is no longer necessary, as the BSP-based development model already covers this functionality. Although existing flow logic applications will be maintained, it is strongly encouraged to use the BSP model for new projects.

The most feasible enhancement to expect in future versions is full support for Java applications programmed with Java 2 Enterprise Edition (J2EE) standard. Java support, not only for development of Web applications, will be integrated into the SAP system. Two development languages, Java and ABAP, will coexist, and Java could be used for all SAP developments, including interfaces, administration, software logistics, and so on. The SAP WAS is strategically defined as the key piece for future application components.

Chapter 9

mySAP.com Projects

This chapter is intended to provide an overview of mySAP.com projects and how to approach them. It also includes the reasons to migrate to the mySAP.com e-business platform and the difference between this type of projects and traditional R/3 ones.

The chapter also introduces the SAP tools and resources to facilitate the design and implementation of this type of projects and the methodologies for the different approaches of implementing mySAP solutions. It also includes useful references for easily finding some of the best SAP resources for efficient implementation of mySAP projects.

Just as with the rest of the book, because of the number, magnitude, and ever-changing improvements on new releases and new tools, some SAP implementation tools and solutions described in this chapter were not available at the time of this writing.

Whereas an SAP R/3 project had the purpose of implementing an ERP (*Enterprise Resource Planner*) back-end system covering critical business areas of the company, a mySAP.com project has the purpose of designing and implementing an e-business platform, which provides all the advantages of the new economy and uses the potential for a vast marketplace enabled by the Internet and Web technology.

mySAP Projects

A mySAP.com project might involve the design and implementation of one or more mySAP solutions, as we have seen in previous chapters. A SAP R/3 implementation within mySAP makes sense if customers do not have an integrated ERP system and want to pursue the best possible integration among applications; however, in most cases a mySAP.com project is the natural evolution for existing and productive SAP R/3 customers.

Like traditional R/3 implementation projects, implementing mySAP solutions is fundamentally a business project (e-business), and so business managers should normally lead it. But there is a fundamental difference in terms of implementation costs and efforts that companies should be aware of. In the case of mySAP projects, technology issues have a much more important role and should be carefully considered. The reasons for this are discussed later in this chapter in the section "Challenges of mySAP Projects: Technology Issues."

Even if the mySAP solutions are focused on strategic business processes, the mySAP implementation projects should be seen as part of the overall vision of the company. mySAP solutions still provide a horizontal view of the business processes, just as the ERP system used to do, even if now the integration can be both intra- and intercompany, cross-system, and not just at the database and data model levels.

SAP is applying the same success factors that led R/3 to be the business operating system of many companies around the globe to mySAP global implementations: the fundamental role of the business process, the integration of the different components and solutions, the prototyping and implementation methods, the openness, and a solid technological foundation. And just as R/3 did, mySAP solutions are also aimed at including implicit e-business intelligence, in terms of providing functionality for the best e-business practices.

Customizing is still the basic process for configuring the mySAP solutions, but with additional possibilities, reuse of settings, and new facilities for making these tasks even easier. Ultimately, and by means of the mySAP Best Practices, customizing effort is completely unneeded. Again, programming requirements are extremely reduced and left for those specific company processes not completely covered on standard systems.

It is equally important in mySAP projects that upper management is committed, understands the environment, and thinks that this type of project is not just an IT project. The range of solutions within the mySAP.com initiative incorporates not only new Web technology, but also efficient and collaborative e-business processes, which might lead to organizational or structural changes for dealing with new markets and new business partners.

Implementing mySAP means to set up and configure one or more of the mySAP solutions to handle the company's new information needs and collaboration models enabled by the Web and to support efficiently the current and future e-business processes.

According to the nature of the mySAP projects, a company might implement one or more of the mySAP solutions or the *migration* of the classical R/3 systems to a mySAP environment. However, implementing mySAP solutions does not mean migration from R/3, but integration with it. An SAP R/3 upgrade might be needed, depending on the current R/3 release and the degree of integration required with the rest of the mySAP solutions. R/3 actually should be considered the ERP solution within the mySAP.com platform.

The activities to be performed by the project team must be supported by a corresponding solid implementation methodology. It was with R/3 that SAP developed the ASAP (*AcceleratedSAP*) implementation solution set as the set of tools, processes, and services to guarantee successful projects. In the more complex mySAP world, the set of implementation tools have evolved and improved for covering a full solution cycle and are supported by Web tools and interfaces to make it not only easier, but also more user-friendly.

mySAP Implementation Tools

With the mySAP platform, SAP has evolved and included new implementation tools and aid for facilitation of the implementation of the mySAP solutions, including a new comprehensive umbrella covering the full solution life cycle management to preconfigured systems.

Following is an introduction of these SAP initiatives to streamline the implementation process and help customers in this type of projects. Some of these topics are covered with greater detail in the next sections of this chapter.

- **Solution life cycle management.** SAP calls solution life cycle management the full life cycle approach for the implementation and continuous improvement of enterprise software. Under this umbrella lies the collection of tools and methodologies to be used by SAP customers and consultants from the process of evaluation to the implementation and to continuous feedback and improvement. These tools are the ASAP methodology, the C-Business Maps (*Collaborative Business Maps*), the Solution Composer, and the Solution Architect.
- **ValueSAP.** This was the first initiative in the form of a set of tools for supporting the entire customer cycle for the evaluation and implementation of a collaborative e-business platform, and so to help customers to transition to mySAP.com solutions. ValueSAP consisted of supporting five phases in the solution cycle: identify, define, implementation, manage, and improve. Figure 9-1 shows this cycle. Edition 2 of ValueSAP included ASAP, GlobalASAP, and the full solution life cycle for R/3, APO, CRM, BW, mySAP Workplace, and mySAP BBP (e-procurement).

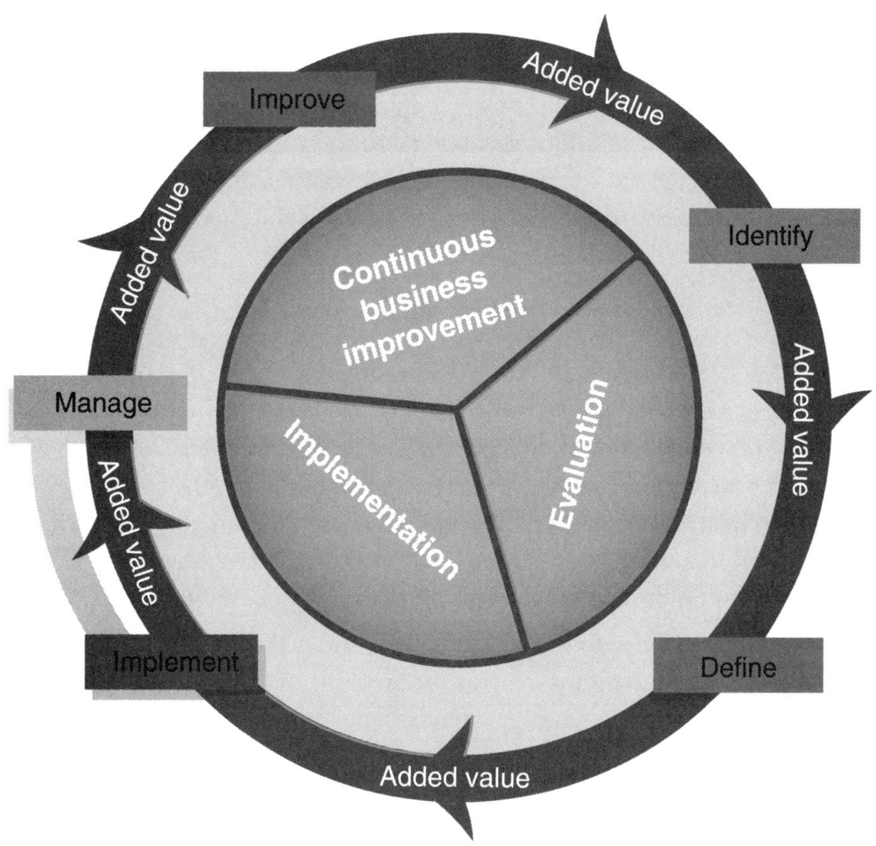

FIGURE 9-1 *ValueSAP solution life cycle* Copyright by SAP AG

- **ASAP.** This is the well-known methodology for classical R/3 implementation projects, now available for several of the mySAP solutions. For most projects, ASAP, which encompasses the methodology, the project plan and several of the basic tools for implementation, will be the basic framework for the definition of the activities and tasks involved in mySAP projects. ASAP is explained in detail in the following sections of this chapter. A variation of ASAP known as *GlobalASAP* is meant for supporting multisite and multiproduct implementations. These tools are shipped in specific CD Kits within the mySAP solutions.

- **Best Practices for mySAP.com.** In short, the Best Practices for mySAP.com are preconfigured mySAP solutions available for different industries and cross-industry implementations. With this type of prepackaged solutions, customers can quickly build prototypes and get systems up and running. It is obviously also a good solution for hosting or for ASP (*Application Service Provider*) solutions provided by SAP partners.
- **C-Business Maps.** These are SAP´s approach for graphically describing and specifying integrated and collaborative business scenarios supported by mySAP solutions. They are particularly oriented to interenterprise collaboration, and they can better show how the mySAP solutions fit into this particular type of processes in search for efficiency among collaborating companies. There are nearly 200 different C-Business Maps in many business areas. Figure 9-2 shows an example of a C-Business Map for the process CRM for Consumer Distributor. More C-Business Maps can be found on **http://service.sap.com/c-business**.
- **Solution Composer.** This is another tool that can be used by SAP customers to have a better view of the scope of the mySAP.com solutions. The Solution Composer includes access to the Solution Maps, the C-Business Maps, and the Role Maps. With this view, companies can make a better definition of the functionality and their business processes, which are needed for the implementation of SAP and SAP partners' solutions. To download the Solution Composer and all the content, go to **www.sap.com/solutionmaps**. Customers and partners can access it at **http://service.sap.com/s-composer**.
- **SOLAR (*SAP Solution Architect*).** This is best described as the mySAP.com implementation portal, and it is the latest implementation tool offered by SAP (available in the first quarter of 2002). The aim is to provide an online platform as a central point of access to all the other implementation tools, content, and methodology for supporting the full solution life cycle on mySAP solutions: evaluation, implementation, quick adaptation, and continuous improvement. Besides customers, partners can also use this tool to create content for their own implementation products. More information on SOLAR can be found on **http://service.sap.com/solutionarchitect**.
- **Implementation tools.** In addition to all the SAP initiatives to streamline implementation projects, all the mySAP solutions include improved

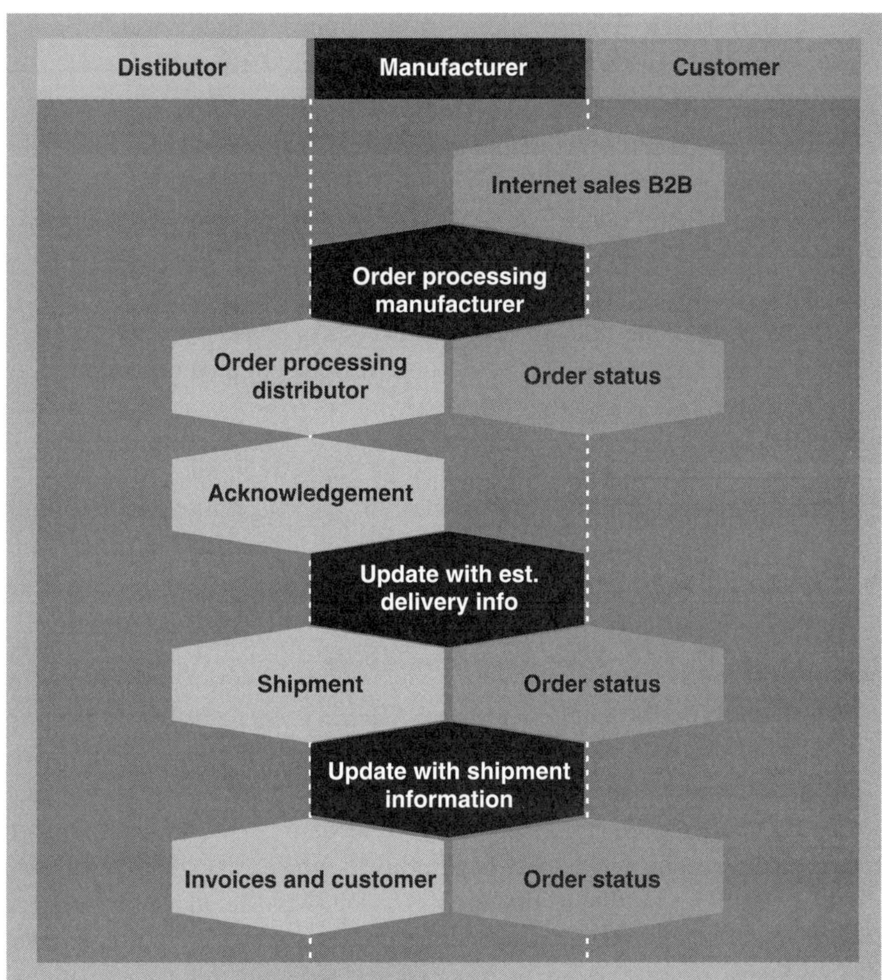

FIGURE 9-2 *CRM for consumer distributor* Copyright by SAP AG

customizing and implementation tools coming from traditional SAP R/3 systems. These tools allow for easier and better-controlled adaptation of business processes within mySAP environments. Among these are:

- IMG (Implementation Guide) as the electronic guide for doing a step-by-step configuration of the mySAP systems

    - Business Configuration Sets, which can be used for defining reusable copies of configuration and customizing settings
    - Test Workbench, which allows for setting test scenarios and performing integrated system and process checks
- **E-Business Case Builder.** This is a tool used within the SAP organization to help customers and prospects with a view of which would be the best mySAP solutions in e-business scenarios. It allows for building business cases based on the C-Business Maps and then evaluating which mySAP solution better fits into the scenario. This is a tool that provides a better understanding of the mySAP.com solutions and current market trends in collaborative e-business.

The following sections explain in detail the ASAP methodology and the mySAP Best Practices. Solution Architect is also introduced because it is meant to be the widely common framework for configuration of mySAP solutions.

Migrating to mySAP.com

As introduced earlier, migrating to mySAP.com is not actually a technical process of running a certain upgrade program. It is largely a concept of evolving ERP business processes into collaborative e-business processes and taking advantage of the potential markets created in the Net economy. Therefore, a migration to mySAP.com is more of a conceptual process, where ERP is still the back-office and critical business application, and new solutions are added and integrated to get better business value in a more global economy. There is, however, the concept of migrating to mySAP.com in terms of licensing, but this process can be better addressed by the SAP sales representatives.

The first question that arises is where SAP R/3 stands in this picture. Looking at the evolution of SAP software solutions, it was already 1998 when the New Dimension products were launched as predecessors to the more comprehensive platform represented by mySAP.com solutions. SAP evolved from a single product company (producing R/3) to a global solution one, but it was still R/3 at the heart and center of the picture.

According to SAP, R/3 is now one very important piece of the mySAP solutions and is being further enhanced and developed. The result is *SAP R/3 Enterprise*, as the new version of SAP R/3. An introduction to SAP R/3 Enterprise is explained in the last sections of this chapter.

There are many reasons for "migrating" to a mySAP.com platform. Some of these reasons are:

- Create value in the new economy in which electronic commerce has an essential role
- Efficiency and cost reduction in the relationships with business partners (customers, providers, other agents)
- Creating new business lines
- Universal access, without installation to enterprise portals
- Implementing real and collaborative e-business
- Easy contracts, all available software can be used if needed

The next question is, What does it take technically to migrate and take advantage of the new e-business platform? There is not a single answer but many, and it all depends on the nature of the business and the degree of integration and collaboration required, as well as the overall strategy of the company on technology trends. But an example of a migration process coming from R/3 would be the following one.

- If it's not already there, migrate SAP R/3 to at least release 3.1I or better, to latest releases such as 4.6C.
- Build a concept for an Enterprise Portal (using, for instance, mySAP Workplace solutions).
- Build a concept and implement one or more of the Customer Relationship Management solutions, for instance, Internet Sales, Mobile Sales, Customer Interaction Center, or all of them.
- Implement a Data Warehouse solution (Business Warehouse), which will be needed to analyze information and feedback the rest of e-business solutions and therefore incorporate Business Intelligence.
- Build a concept and implement one or more of the Supply Chain Management solutions, for instance, the APO (*Advanced Planner and Optimizer*).
- Build a concept and implement an e-procurement solution to streamline the purchasing and procurement processes. Consider also the implementation or integration within an e-marketplace.
- Integrate the components implemented with the back-end (ERP) systems.
- Build the role concept for users and business partners.

- Implement the Enterprise Portal and integrate all implemented components.
- Provide users and business partners with the information needed for performing their jobs or their relationships.

This is easy to say, but not easy to achieve to its full potential. So the approach should be step by step, phase to phase, getting results and benefits from each of the applications of the components being implemented.

Introduction to ASAP

ASAP is the traditional framework for SAP's implementation of R/3 projects and has been extended to cover not only R/3, but other mySAP solutions, such as CRM (*Customer Relationship Management*), APO, or e-procurement (BBP). Within the context of the solution life cycle management, ASAP is the basic and more important methodology for the implementation of complex projects. However, ASAP goes beyond just a methodology and provides a large number of its own tools and utilities for simplifying the implementation process. ASAP can traditionally be complemented with SAP and SAP partners' implementation services, such as training, support, consulting, and so on.

Although there are different ASAPs for the mySAP solutions, the general phases are quite common to all of them, the main difference being the activities and tasks for building the business process maps and the configuration options. So in the following sections, the generic ASAP is largely introduced, with R/3 implementations as the core for the work packages and activities explained.

The path proposed by SAP to reach the goal of getting a fast return on investment—that is, accomplishing a fast and cost-effective implementation—is based on the idea of facilitating a quick implementation of mySAP applications and guaranteeing the quality. To achieve a both fast and quality implementation, ASAP is based on the following issues:

- Clear definition of the mission, objectives, and the scope of the project. A clearly defined project scope is key to adjust time planning and to approach project cost plans to real costs.
- Increase the feasibility of realizing a detailed planning at the beginning of the project.

- Standardizing and establishing a single project or implementation methodology, as defined by ASAP itself.
- Creating a homogeneous project environment.

To realize those objectives, ASAP provides the project team with a methodology, tools, training, and services, as well as a process-oriented project plan known as the ASAP Roadmap.

The main tools provided by ASAP are:

- Implementation Assistant
- Global Question and Answer Database
- Business Engineer
- Knowledge Corner

The ASAP solution set is delivered in a CD-ROM that is installed independently of SAP systems, although it can be connected with them and will be readily available from the Solution Architect Portal. ASAP is release-dependent and is constantly updated. SAP provides periodic updates in the SAP Service Marketplace, and in the latest releases, it is included within ValueSAP. For more information about kits and updates, visit the **http://service.sap.com/valuesap** page.

In line with SAP strategy, the ASAP method of implementation is positioned according to the following objectives and strategies:

- ASAP is the mySAP implementation solution directly developed and supported by SAP and partners.
- ASAP offers a preliminary planning of the resource needs—time, costs, people—based on the initial customer information and requirements.
- ASAP provides an optimal environment for many different mySAP projects, even upgrade projects.
- ASAP is aimed at and especially suited for those implementation projects where the number of changes to standard SAP applications is reduced to a minimum.

The ASAP Roadmap is the project plan of the methodology. It's a well-defined and clear process-oriented project plan, providing a step-by-step guide during the life of the implementation project. The Roadmap is made up of five major phases, each one describing the main work packages, activities, and tasks to achieve the expected results. Together with the activities and tasks, ASAP provides all the process descriptions, tools, training, services, and documentation that will be useful for carrying out these activities. The next sections briefly introduce the common Roadmap phases.

Project Preparation

At this first phase, project preparation, the project mission and scope are defined. Some key issues of this phase are:

- Define clear project objectives.
- Reach total agreement on project issues among involved parties.
- Establish an efficient process for making decisions and resolving conflicts.
- Prepare the company for accepting cultural and process changes.

In this phase, ASAP provides tools, such as the Project Estimator, which helps and guides the project team using predefined questionnaires aimed at company upper management. Using the results of those questions, consultants can evaluate the answers and provide a high-level evaluation of the project scope, as well as an initial estimation of required resources and planning. This is the project starting point.

The outcome of this phase includes two essential documents in the implementation, the project charter and the detailed project plan. The management team or steering committee is responsible for evaluating such a plan and approving it if no objections are found. This will trigger the start for the next phase.

ASAP pays particular attention to ensure the quality in the whole project process and decisions taken throughout the execution of this phase. Any error or wrong decisions can negatively affect the subsequent flow of the project and might produce delays, which means longer project time and higher costs.

Business Blueprint

In the second phase of the Roadmap, the project team undertakes a complete and comprehensive analysis of requirements and business process, while documenting and defining the mySAP solution implementation in the company. To achieve these results, ASAP provides a group of predefined questionnaires, group sessions, individual interviews, and so on. Information gathered is critical and extremely useful for the project team, which can analyze and help to document the business processes and the future business requirements for the company.

Classical SAP R/3 projects used the SAP Business Engineer, including the SAP Reference Model and the Question and Answer Database, which are used for generating the Business Blueprint documents and the Business Process Master List. ASAP includes a business application repository with the tools that allow users to interact with and test the business processes of some of the mySAP applications. This is particularly useful within the context of mySAP Best Practices.

In this phase of the project, ASAP provides a specific methodology for analyzing and documenting the business processes. The result is a complete blueprint of the business. Within an overall implementation project, this is probably the most challenging phase. In a typical nine-month implementation project, this phase could last five or six weeks.

This phase combines the analysis and documentation of the business processes with the first level of training of project teams in the different mySAP applications. Within this phase is typically the work package for starting the design of the systems environment, which includes the design of the system landscape, the technical infrastructure, and defining and testing the system administration procedures. At this point, the development and test clients are set up, and the IMG is initialized for the starting of the customizing activities. Finally, an extremely important addition to this major phase is the inclusion of the Change Management program, in charge of dealing with all human and organizational factors that influence the implementation project.

Realization

With the Business Blueprint documentation generated as a result of the previous phase, the project team should be in good shape for starting the realization phase, which includes a collection of work packages where actual implementation of business processes takes place.

From the Business Blueprint documentation generated as deliverable from the previous phase, consultants and project team members have enough information to make a valid proposal covering most business processes, reports, and daily business transactions, trying to match those of the SAP standard. If other processes are found that do not seem to cover perfectly the company's business procedures, reports, or transactions, requirements will be a matter of a fine configuration and tuning.

Most important work package activities within the realization phase include:

- Review project management activities such as planning, reviews, schedule, and scope.
- Provide advance training to project team.
- Establish the system management strategy and configure the technical infrastructure and system landscape.
- Sustain the change management program.
- Configure and test an initial prototype (baseline) for main functions and processes.
- Develop conversion, interface, and data transfer programs.
- Develop enhancements for scenarios not fully covered by standard mySAP applications.
- Configure and verify final systems. This can be based on an iterative approach based on the prototypes.
- Create forms and reports.
- Establish the authorization concept and strategy.
- Plan and design the archiving strategy.
- Perform a final integration test.
- Prepare the end user documentation and training material.

As in every major phase, the last step will be a quality assurance realization process, where every element on the project phase is checked and verified. This phase will be the longest one in terms of time, efforts, and resources needed.

Final Preparation

This phase, where all implementation elements and configurations are tested to finish the preparation for going live, requires a close collaboration between the full project team and the end users. Main objectives from this phase can be summarized as follows:

- **Verification of implementation.** The team and the users should test that all requirements defined in previous phases, as well as the correct behavior of the implemented business processes, are met. This phase is the appropriate time for doing stress tests, which are very important not only for verifying the sizing, but also for optimizing the system's performance. It is also very convenient to undertake simulations of real operation as the most important point of integration tests. This phase might be the convenient time to request for SAP help by means of the available services, such as a GoingLive Check, which analyzes configuration and makes recommendations that can be evaluated and implemented.

- **End-user acceptance.** This is the main requirement for any project that is going to be deployed by a number of end users. Without a wide final user acceptance, the project's success is far from being guaranteed.
- **End-user training.** This is another key factor because the end users must receive the appropriate training according to their job profile and the needed application use. Training helps users to find themselves familiar and conformable with the new environment as soon as possible, which can provide an optimal user operation in less time.
- **Initial Data Loads and cutover.** At the moment that application and systems are ready for going live, all necessary data that is still resident in legacy or other systems must be transferred to mySAP systems. All those load and interface programs should be prepared, tested, evaluated, and optimized, as should the quality of data that is going to be transferred and the time it takes for loading.
- **Help desk strategy.** When starting a productive operation, from the very first moment, every system user should know where to call and how to get help when there are problems or simply doubts. A support group, usually known as a help desk, should be created to answer end user questions efficiently and to solve or escalate both technical and application problems. Problems and doubts that might arise can be classified according to their nature.

Go Live and Support

This phase starts the productive operation. The initial period after going live is the real evaluation period for everything done and designed in previous project phases. In most cases, it is recommended to have a progressive productive start, so that there is time to react to typical problems during this initial period, like:

- Not enough physical resources such as network, printers, and others
- Problems when printing reports, spool saturation, repetitive sending of the same output by the same users, and so on
- Wrongly configured end users' desktops, wrong server, deleted files, help files not reached, and so on

- Reports and transactions not completely meeting the full user needs
- Bugs in the standard systems requiring patches or repairs
- Database or run-time problems when running reports or transactions with real data
- Adding new users to the system
- Lack of end user training
- Help desk strategy not well defined or not defined at all

The degree of success or failure (unfavorable user reaction) in this initial period of productive operation will be a factor of the completeness and accuracy of the previous phases and how the possible problems were issued.

In this phase, a good procedure for communicating with SAP or partners to request their services might be important, for example, the realization of EarlyWatch (preventive maintenance) services. It is also the phase for testing the quality of operation and system administration procedures. Soon after, there will be a culture where the most frequent types of problems (around 80 to 90 percent) will already be classified and can be quickly solved.

From the technical and administration point of view, after the initial adaptation to the productive operation, there is a time for managing different activities of the productive mySAP system, such as:

- Managing the transports and change requests
- Applying and installing patches (collections of corrected programs and transactions)
- Planning EarlyWatch sessions
- Making changes and configurations as recommended by EarlyWatch reports
- Watching the systems performance and tuning most critical reports and transactions

Implementing an Enterprise Portal with mySAP Workplace

The following sections include an overview of the main aspects to consider for the technical and related activities when planning an implementation of an Enterprise

Portal using the mySAP Workplace solution. This is based on mySAP Workplace as of release 2.1.

Overview Task List for mySAP Workplace Projects

This overview should help mySAP Workplace customers to plan Workplace projects. It can be useful for project managers and is based on the practical experience of a group of experienced consultants in mySAP Workplace projects.

The mySAP Workplace provides users with centralized, easy-to-use access to all the information, applications, and services they need to participate in collaborative business processes. In an Enterprise Portal project, which includes different information, applications, and services, a number of different departments are involved. Which departments these are depends on the company structure. This section provides a quick overview about the most important questions that have to be solved during your project. With this overview, you are able to plan your workgroups; the required knowledge and this overview give you an idea about the time schedule.

For instance, the following departments can or should be involved:

- Network administration
- Security department
- SAP R/3 basic administration
- Application or business management
- Design or intranet/Internet department
- Web content management

You will see that many departments have to work together in one workgroup.

Architecture and Technical Infrastructure

An Enterprise Portal is a mission-critical system to succeed in e-business. If it is not available, most users—which could be your customers—can no longer work. Thus, high availability and reliability is key to Enterprise Portal deployment. The mySAP Workplace is built on reliable technology that supports 24/7 operations. The underlying technology of the mySAP Workplace server is platform-independent and provides all high-availability features supported by mySAP technology. Based on state-of-the-art SAP technology, the mySAP Workplace provides a highly scalable architecture that can serve thousands and thousands of users around the world.

Based on an ITS (*Internet Transaction Server*) architecture, the questions to be answered are:

- Is high-availability required? High-availability can be realized on the Web server, the ITS server and on the R/3 system.
- Should the ITS server be installed as single- or dual-host installation? Is a single-host installation sufficient?
- Where should I place mySAP Workplace server in the network?
- Where should I place the ITS server in the network?
- Is there enough bandwidth? How much do I need?
- Where does the Workplace user connect to the network?
- Where are the application servers located?

Some recommendations and tips are:

- It is recommended to install the ITS W-Gate and A-Gate on separate hosts (dual-host installation) because of security and scalability reasons.
- A single host installation is sufficient for a test installation.
- Spreading the Workplace landscape over different machines increases the scalability of the whole system.
- More ITS servers can be added during productive operation.
- For performance reasons, it is a good idea to bring the Web browser as near as possible to the Web server (the W-Gate).
- A good response time is very important for user acceptance.
- The change from the SAPGUI for Windows to the SAPGUI for HTML always increases the response time.
- The Workplace server is never the bottleneck. The network in your WAN will be the limiting factor.
- For ITS servers, a two-processor machine with at least 512 MB RAM and not necessarily more than 10 GB hard disk is recommended.

As a summary of the importance of this topic, the following points must be observed:

- This part takes place at the beginning of the project. The architecture should be as flexible as possible. Take your time for planning.
- Important part of the project.

- Hardware has to be ordered in time.
- To increase your bandwidth is time-consuming.

Role Concept

Through its role concept, mySAP Workplace Enterprise Portal ensures that only relevant content is provided to the user. Users find access to all information, applications, and services according to their daily tasks or fields of interest.

The mySAP Workplace role concept is designed to work for all customers you want to serve with an Enterprise Portal regardless of whether they are internal—that is, employees or sales representatives—or external: for example, a bank that wants to serve its customers might create roles for prospects, customer private banking, and customer corporate banking.

To jump-start mySAP Workplace implementation, SAP delivers role templates. These can be adjusted to the needs of the company and the audience to be served.

The questions to be answered regarding the role concept are:

- Which roles or activity groups exist? Can they be reused on the Workplace?
- Can I use SAP standard roles or do I have to create my own individual roles?
- Which MiniApps and Internet links are required in the roles?
- How many transactions should be in one role as a maximum?
- How many roles should be defined?

Recommendations and tips include:

- It is recommended to create small simple roles instead of big and complex roles to avoid unneeded entries in the LaunchPad of the user.
- In the first phase, it is useful to create general roles that can be used by all employees. For example:
    - ESS scenarios (vacation application, change of address and bank data, time sheets)
    - B2B scenarios (create shopping basket, check shopping status of shopping basket)
    - Very popular intranet links (menu, company news)

- Existing roles can be transferred from the component systems to the Workplace server by RFC (*Remote Function Calls*), transport or file copy. Downloading by RFC is the most convenient way.
- If possible, go to each Workplace user and check his or her daily work. Find out which transactions are really used, which information is needed, and which servers (applications) are involved.

As a summary of the importance of this topic, the following points must be observed:

- Main part in the project
- Very time-consuming
- Ongoing work to continue an operation

MiniApps Programming and Installation (MiniApps Community)

MiniApps form the push portion of the mySAP Workplace that delivers all kinds of content to the user. They are the windows to underlying applications and productivity tools and deliver information and services to the user in a simple way. In the SAP MiniApps Community (**www.sap.com/miniapps/**), you can find lots of MiniApps for different application areas (for example, Mail Inbox, Employee Self Service, and so on). But MiniApps are not solely provided by SAP; everybody can write and distribute MiniApps in order to provide any kind of content, including non-SAP and Internet services and information to the users through mySAP Workplace.

The questions about MiniApps programming and installation to be answered are:

- Which MiniApps are required?
- Which users need which MiniApps? (See role concept.)
- Can I use existing MiniApps from the MiniApps Community, or do I have to develop own MiniApps?

Recommendations and tips include:

- In the SAP MiniApps Community, you can find design guides and development libraries to reduce the development effort for MiniApps.

- MiniApps have different contents. You find general and role-specific ones. To reduce the administration in the first phase, it is useful to integrate only general ones.
- If you write your own MiniApps that present individual information that depends on the user logging in, and you want to use SSO (*Single Sign-On*) functionality for MiniApps that are not based on SAP's ITS technology, SSO tickets or digital certificates (X.509) are required.

As a summary of the importance of this topic, the following points must be observed:

- Another main part in the project if you do not use MiniApps from the community
- To program your own MiniApps can take a couple of days, depending on the application and complexity

Integration of Third-Party Applications and mySAP Components

Information is one of the most important types of content in an Enterprise Portal. The Enterprise Portal has to offer the possibility to integrate applications and external services, such as shipping services, for example. Only such a user-centered combination of information, applications, and services will guarantee the success and acceptance of an Enterprise Portal. The mySAP Workplace offers this possibility.

The questions to be answered about integrating third-party applications and mySAP components are:

- How can I call an application from the LaunchPad or MiniApps?
- How can I integrate a certain function or transaction from a third-party application?
- My mainframe application should look like a Web application, if possible. How do I integrate this?
- How can I integrate an application without changing the back-end application?
- Users should not have to type in data from one function into another function. Is there a way to automatically transfer data, for example, using Drag&Relate or XML?

- My users employ different computers. What do I have to do so that they can take their Workplace with them wherever they go?
- How can I design it so that each user only has to log on once a day, while at the same time being secure?
- Can I synchronize user master data from all systems so that I do not have to maintain the data in multiple systems? Can I use our LDAP directory?
- Will SSO work with third-party applications integrated into the mySAP Workplace?

Recommendations and tips include:

- From the outset, the mySAP Workplace has been designed in such a way that solutions to the above questions can be found using a minimum of resources.
- The goal is that users can access all the applications that they require for their work with a minimum of restrictions and without having to leave the mySAP Workplace. Apart from SAP components, it is possible to integrate any other applications in the mySAP Workplace. These include Web-enabled applications, that is, applications that are based on HTML or Java. Obviously, integrating this type of applications is a relatively easy task.
- In addition, non-SAP applications may include applications that are not Web-enabled. The multitude of existing PC applications must also be taken into account. Windows Terminal Services (WTS) are available to deal with these applications.
- Existing non-SAP intranet applications can only use the SSO functionality if the SSO is based on SSO tickets or X.509 certificates. SAP offers a library for using SSO logon tickets with non-SAP applications.

Security

mySAP Workplace Enterprise Portal ensures high security for e-business by supporting Internet security standards, as well as by offering state-of-the-art authentication and authorization mechanisms.

Authentication and authorization are not the same.

- Authentication identifies a user as to who he or she is.
- Authorization provides access rights to certain content.

Authorization resides in the component systems. No mirroring to mySAP Workplace is necessary.

Digital certificates (X.509) are supported by mySAP Workplace. To help your company to set up a Public Key Infrastructure (PKI), SAP supports the setup of a PKI through its mySAP Trust Center Service. Tickets are a solution provided by SAP. The benefit of this approach is that no additional infrastructure is needed for SSO to work on external systems.

The questions to be answered regarding security when implementing an Enterprise Portal are:

- Which level of security is required? Is it sufficient to encrypt the data, or should the user be identified with a digital certificate (X.509, for example, on a smart card)?
- How do I integrate external applications securely over the Internet?
- Do I need a new firewall concept?
- How do I monitor all network connections, especially from and to the ITS in a worldwide network?
- Is it necessary to set up a new PKI, or can I use an existing PKI like the mySAP Trust Center Service or VeriSign?

Recommendations and tips include:

- If you want to use a cookie-based SSO mechanism, you should consider using SSO logon tickets instead of standard SSO cookies, because tickets are signed with a public key mechanism by the Workplace server, and no private data, like the user's password, is stored. In standard SSO cookies, the username and password are stored.
- For a productive system, it is highly recommended not to use cookies, as SSO cookies only work with the same user ID and password in all component systems. Logon tickets only require the same user ID.
- Logon tickets can be certified by the Workplace server itself or by the SAP Trust Center. The first option is very easily installed.
- It is always a good choice to use SSL encryption (HTTPS) instead of normal HTTP for the communication from Web browser to Web server because HTTP transports all data as plain text (also logon information like username and password).

- mySAP Passports (X.509 certificates authorized by the SAP Trust Center) offer a high security and are free of charge. This solution requires an Internet connection to SAP.
- If you want to keep the overview over the digital certificates used, you can set up your own PKI to sign the certificates with your own certificate authority.
- For security reasons, users and roles should be administrated by one person only.
- Always work according to the "two heads are better than one principle": have a second set of eyes look over your work.

As a summary of the importance of this topic, the following points must be observed:

- Important part of the project
- Planning of this tasks takes most of the time
- Many different departments are involved in these tasks

Drag&Relate Function

The Drag&Relate function allows you to link data from one application with another application. You can navigate between the various objects in the transactions and the LaunchPad using Drag&Relate. By simply selecting an object (for example, a purchase order) and dragging it onto another object in the LaunchPad (for example, a Web page), an activity is carried out (for example, the delivery status of the purchase order is displayed). There is no need to remember order numbers or the proper underlying systems; users just do it in the most natural way. The Drag&Relate function works between SAP applications; for example, you can drag an object from the SAPGUI for HTML to another SAP application in the LaunchPad. But it is also possible to use the Drag&Relate function with "normal" Internet applications. For example, the user can drag a material number into the online shop of the supplier or other applications that support Drag&Relate technology (TopTier technology).

The questions to be answered about Drag&Relate functionality are:

- Which business relations can be used for Drag&Relate?
- Which external applications can be used for Drag&Relate?

Recommendations and tips include:

- Check www.toptier.com or www.sapportals.com.
- Check your business applications.
- It is not easy to integrate, especially for non-SAP products.

As a summary of the importance of this topic, the following points must be observed:

- These tasks should take place at the end of your project
- Depends of the number of applications to be integrated over Drag&Relate

Design (Look and Feel)

The Style Sheet Designer for the mySAP Workplace can be used to change the design of the mySAP Workplace and all the MiniApps and IAC (*Internet Application Components*). SAP provides the Style Sheet Designer as a tool that makes it easy for the user to perform these design changes in all applications. You can change all the common design elements provided in the HTML Business Function Library, such as push buttons, fields, tables, and the mySAP Workplace LaunchPad. The Style Sheet Designer can be used to adapt the images used (such as screens and graphics) as well as the colors and fonts of the elements. You cannot use the Style Sheet Designer to change the structural design of the mySAP Workplace. Such far-reaching modifications can be made with the Portal Builder.

The design questions to be answered are:

- Who is responsible for the design of Internet and intranet applications?
- What are the customers' corporate guidelines for the design of Internet and intranet applications?
- Is it possible to keep a standard design, or is it necessary to modify the Workplace appearance?
- What kind of design changes are required?

Recommendations and tips include:

- System administrators can use the Portal Builder to change style sheets to create a new layout and design for their Workplace.

The following areas in the layout can be modified:

- ◆ LaunchPad
- ◆ Workspace
- ◆ Web pages
- ◆ MiniApps that can be accessed using a URL

Challenges of mySAP Projects: Technology Issues

Technical issues on classical SAP R/3 projects played a secondary role in favor of optimizing business processes and companies' efficiency. Technology was the enabler. Technical implementation within a full R/3 project usually did not cost more than 10 percent of the total budget, excluding hardware costs.

In the mySAP.com world, the design, definition, and implementation of collaborative e-business processes are also the key. However, now technology plays an ever-increasing and more important role than it used to, in terms of its complexity, number of servers, and the integration into the Web world. The lack of seeing the increasing needs for technology experts and the right tools can severely affect the success of these complex e-business projects. In some of the mySAP solutions, such as mySAP CRM, the percentage of technical implementation compared to the global project can range into the 40 or 50 percent range, depending on the specific application.

As a reminder, the following is a list of technical issues that must be seriously taken into consideration when planning a mySAP project.

Systems Landscape

Designing a system landscape for mySAP means defining the strategy and layout of a group of servers where the mySAP solutions will be installed, configured, and, finally, used productively. Normally for each of the solutions, a group of three types of systems is recommended:

- ◆ A development system, for configuration (customizing) and development
- ◆ A quality assurance system, where the previous work can be tested

- A productive system, where actual end users work with real transactions and operations

Additionally, in the mySAP.com environment, we will find Web servers, ITS systems, and in some cases, other additional systems, such as index servers, mobile devices, and others.

The issue of planning, defining, and configuring a systems landscape is very important, because it is not an isolated issue and will have a direct impact on other technical issues, mainly on systems sizing, how the customizing settings and developments are transported to other systems, and how the testing will be performed.

The design of the systems landscape will have a direct impact on the tasks involved for installing and configuring the mySAP systems, as well as for their management and monitoring.

Some considerations for this activity are:

- A systems landscape configuration requires careful planning and systems sizing. Experienced technical consultants should perform this in the context of how it will affect other technical issues.
- The systems landscape design has to be clearly communicated and explained to the project team, even if the project team is not technical, and must be reflected in the project procedures. It is very common to associate project problems with just “machine” problems.
- Medium-term and long-term plans should be considered so there is a step-by-step approach to a full e-business systems scenario.

Sizing

Sizing is the process of analyzing and estimating the computing needs for the systems infrastructure, installation, and operation, in terms of computing power (CPU, memory), server’s distribution, disk volume, and network bandwidth. This is a very complex and never-accurate process, which requires more involvement than it is commonly given, requiring the help of not only SAP and the hardware vendors, but also the IT department and end users so that a better estimation of real work can be performed. In terms of the difference from classical R/3 systems, for mySAP solutions, the sizing is a matter of both the specific solutions being implemented and the awareness of the possibility of thousands of connections through the Internet. A failure to provide a good service level to users or business partners could be a disaster.

For these reasons, sizing on an overall mySAP system landscape includes the following elements that must be considered:

- Several types of and possibilities for installations, which will be a factor of how many servers and the applications to be installed in each of them
- The hardware and network configuration, including Internet access
- Disk volume and the layout and size of the file systems for each solution
- The installation of the different databases
- Expected systems availability
- Distribution of servers and services

Finally, the objective of the sizing process is to calculate some important figures, such as how much CPU power will be needed (type of processors, memory, number of servers) for each system within the landscape, how big the databases will be (disk space necessary), and the minimum recommended network infrastructure. The quality of the sizing will be just as good as the quality of the data supplied by the customer.

To ease the process, SAP provides the *QuickSizer* tool, which can be accessed through the SAP Service Marketplace (**http://service.sap.com/quicksizer**) With the QuickSizer service, mySAP customers can make an initial estimations of CPU, memory, and disk resources. The results in terms of SAP Application Benchmark Performance Standard (SAPS) and average disk volume requirements are immediately available, and customers can decide to pass on this information to the hardware partner directly from the QuickSizer form.

Security

The importance of security in the context of mySAP projects has been largely dealt with in this book, specifically in Chapter 7, "Dealing with Security within mySAP Environments." In the Web age, security, or the lack thereof, is the main concern of and the main barrier to e-business through the Web. Therefore, addressing security is key within mySAP projects, with the objective of providing confidence to business partners as well as protecting valuable business data and ensuring continuous and stable systems operations. For more information, refer to Chapter 7.

Systems Monitoring and System Management

With the increasing complexity in the number, installation, and integration of several different systems within mySAP landscapes, the issue of managing and monitoring these systems will be quite important and critical, both before and after the going live phases of the project. The need for performing systems management starts from the moment the first development systems are installed.

Administering the systems is the continuous process of monitoring, managing, supporting, optimizing, and securing the systems, with the objective of having a stable platform for smooth execution of business processes. The best practice for systems management is the one that is proactive, anticipating tasks and problems, rather than a reactive one. A proactive approach to system management can be achieved by having operating procedures and a daily and periodic checklist, either automated or by using third-party specialized tools, which takes into consideration the many different components within mySAP solutions and systems landscapes.

In the mySAP world, the skills and roles around systems management and monitoring are more demanding than were the classical tasks of SAP Basis system management, database administration, network monitoring, and configuration. Now there are new tasks, such as Web administration, increased security experts, and so on, in addition to the increased number of tasks regarding the integration among several systems.

This implies that there is an increased need for planning requirements on systems management, from the very beginning of the project. Some of the activities to be performed and taken into consideration are:

- Adapted and advanced training for the technical team
- Plan technical infrastructure, sizing, and scalability
- Test systems infrastructure and systems management procedures
- Get acquainted with the SAP support lines and services
- Design, write, and maintain technical documentation
- Design a clear help desk and support strategy and communicate it efficiently
- Focus on proactive systems management
- Search for the most convenient tools

Systems management will be the lengthiest activity throughout the SAP life cycle. As experience is gained through daily administration operations, new projects, and continuous change, a few challenges ensure and guarantee the smooth operation and stability of the R/3 systems.

Installations and Upgrades

Another challenge that has special impact, especially during the first phases of the project, is the increased number of installations, which often are different processes with different requirements and many notes and installation manuals. There is additional work in mySAP landscapes because postinstallation steps or technical customization requires the integration of several systems. Thus, depending on the solution being installed, the installations of plug-ins, the definition of RFC destinations, and so on are required. For these tasks, a high level of technical expertise with operating systems, management of database systems, and Web servers will ease the way into fast and successful installations. Other possible challenges occur when deploying highly available or clustered systems, which normally require some additional technical efforts.

In the case of upgrade projects, mySAP landscapes should not offer more difficulty than traditional SAP R/3 systems. However, some attention should be paid to what happens with the connected systems during the periods when some systems are down for taking them to the next release, especially in those cases where there is a transfer of data and information back and forth.

Change Management

As has been mentioned earlier, R/3 includes several tools with the purpose of controlling and managing in an orderly form the development and transport of customizing and development objects between systems in a consistent way.

Backup and Recovery

In classical SAP R/3 projects, the backup and recovery strategy has been a critical issue for both the technical implementation and operation of the SAP systems and because it was the only way to protect business-critical information and to guarantee the system's operation in the event of failure. Again, in mySAP landscapes, it can be a bit more complicated. For instance, consider the scenarios of Mobile Sales within mySAP CRM implementation, which is also connected to a backend ERP (SAP R/3) system. The failure of any of the components must be taken into consideration to be able to recover a synchronization status among systems.

For the analysis and definition of options in mySAP backup and recovery strategies to fit the landscape and business requirements, the following factors must be considered:

- **System availability.** Whether any downtime is possible for backups.
- **What to back up.** Databases, kernel files, archive files, interface files, local drives, and so on.
- **Size of files to back up and backup performance.** These determine the devices and the time.
- **Synchronization of backups.** Analyze interdependencies of mySAP components.
- **Type of backup.** Options are full, incremental, online, offline, and so on. This will be a function of the other factors.
- **From where to back up/restore.** Client/server backup and restore systems, the same operating systems, network, or others.
- **When to back up.** The specific time for launching backups will also be the result of a function derived from other factors.
- **Backup devices.** There are many options for backup devices, from simple tape drives to automated robots, which can perform backups using several tapes in parallel. There are also other alternative media to tapes, such as magnetic disks, optical devices, CD-ROMS, and, most recently, virtual disks on the network.
- **Backup management tools.** It will be very important to find the most suitable and reliable tools for managing backup and recovery processes. Here, specific interfaces with mySAP systems and underlying databases must be considered.
- **Backup tapes management.** The labeling, storing, and management of tapes or other media should not be forgotten.
- **Recovery procedures.** Often you find a quite clear backup strategy, but when there is a need to restore and recover what was previously backed up, lots of problems can be found. Defining a recovery procedure is not easy because there are so many possible situations: from simple copy procedure (backup and restore) to a single file missing. The point is to define the possible situations where a restore might be needed and *test it*.

When checking your requirements against the previous factors, you might come up with the solution that might best fit your company needs. The main message must be to test and monitor your backup and recovery strategy before going into productive operation.

SAP R/3 Enterprise

SAP R/3 Enterprise is the next version of SAP R/3 after 4.6C, which was code-named Mercury as the internal project name. Although mySAP.com provides the collaborative e-business platform for intracompany and intercompany processes, it is equally important that SAP R/3 evolves and integrates tightly into the whole strategy. For this reason, SAP R/3 Enterprise, the new release of SAP R/3, is designed and intended as the platform for providing the optimal integration into the complete mySAP.com picture.

SAP R/3 Enterprise is a part of the mySAP.com solutions and, as such, should be considered as an extension of mySAP.com. For instance, if an SAP customer is using the SAP R/3 logistics applications and would like to take advantage of the advanced functions provided by mySAP SCM, the customer can still use those back-end functions while integrating them with the Business Warehouse, APO, or the Enterprise Portal.

One of the main changes with SAP R/3 Enterprise is the delivery strategy for new functionality by implementing new methods of application upgrades. Therefore, besides the enhancement to business functions and applications, SAP R/3 Enterprise provides a new core technology for supporting these new delivery methods.

SAP R/3 Enterprise consists of two main components: the *SAP R/3 Enterprise Core* and *SAP R/3 Enterprise Extensions* (or Add-Ons). Both components interface with each other in the so-called nonmodifying fashion.

The SAP R/3 Enterprise Core contains new enhancements in the areas of legal requirements, performance, infrastructure, and continuous improvement. The SAP R/3 Enterprise Add-Ons contain primarily all new functional enhancements. These components are built in the SAP R/3 Enterprise system around the concept of separating developments in technology and in functionality. Therefore, for instance, new developments in application functionality will no longer be mandatory, so the customer can choose which ones to use and install.

The SAP R/3 Enterprise Core is necessary to operate the SAP R/3 Enterprise Extensions (Add-Ons). The functionality of the SAP R/3 Enterprise Core is very similar to that found in release 4.6C of R/3, but customers can upgrade to Enterprise from releases 3.1I and above.

SAP R/3 Enterprise Core

The Core component of SAP R/3 Enterprise focuses on enhancing areas such as performance, quality, legal changes, and requirements, as well as specific infrastructure. This is particularly possible and improved with the new Basis release, now called SAP Web Application Server (refer to Chapter 8, "SAP Web Application Server"). The SAP R/3 Enterprise Core has integrated the Internet and Web technologies into all areas of the system, which previously required additional systems or components, such as ITS. The SAP R/3 Enterprise Core will be maintained separately from the Add-Ons, and the upgrades will be performed with specific service packages.

Regarding the benefits and improvements of the SAP R/3 Enterprise compared to release 4.6 of SAP R/3, the fundamental change in the Basis system must be noted. This change provides Web enablement to all the areas of the system and makes it easier for integration with other mySAP components, as well as for universal access through an Enterprise Portal. Additionally, the separation of the functionality represented by the SAP R/3 Enterprise Extensions benefits the system especially when considering upgrade strategies, and thus will influence systems availability, stability, and performance. This is particularly important because it was one of the main concerns voiced by many SAP customers in the past.

SAP R/3 Enterprise Extensions

The Enterprise Extensions or Add-Ons are the components that will provide functionality, normally in a nonmodifying fashion. In case of the same functionality in more than one Add-On, SAP will possibly incorporate such functionality within the Core. According to SAP, normally an Add-On does not depend in any way on other Add-Ons, which allows for an easier and more flexible upgrade strategy.

In the case that two or more Add-Ons would interface with each other, they would do so in such a way that they do not become dependent on each other, rather they are really dependent on the release of the SAP R/3 Enterprise Core. The SAP R/3 Enterprise Extensions application packages will have their own release schedules. Functional changes will be made in the Add-On components.

Integration Technology

The SAP R/3 Enterprise is based on a new technical architecture, which will enable developments specific to an application area to be encapsulated. There is a clear goal in Application Integration Technology for improving heterogeneous applications and landscapes, and specifically in collaborative Web-based processes.

The SAP R/3 Enterprise Core incorporates an Application Integration Technology, based on what SAP calls a Collaborative Service Architecture, with the goal of supporting new types of interfaces and integration with other systems or applications. The Core will have a special component, known as the Interface Layer, which will be responsible for the management of interfaces that might be required for the connection between application components or with other systems. These can be, for example, the case of BAPIs, BADIS, RFC, or others. More information about the SAP R/3 Enterprise can be found at **http://service.sap.com /enterprise**.

Index

A

B

T

U

V

W

X